D1737286

Global Conflict and Security since 1945

Editors: Professor Saki R. Dockrill, King's College London and Dr. William Rosenau, RAND

Palgrave Macmillan's new book series *Global Conflict and Security since 1945* seeks fresh historical perspectives to promote the empirical understanding of global conflict and security issues arising from international law, leadership, politics, multilateral operations, weapons systems and technology, intelligence, civil-military relations and societies. The series welcomes original and innovative approaches to the subject by new and established scholars. Possible topics include terrorism, nationalism, civil wars, the Cold War, military and humanitarian interventions, nation-building, pre-emptive attacks, the role of the United Nations and other non-governmental organisations (NGOs), and the national security and defence policies of major states. Events in the world since September 11th 2001 remind us that differences of ideology, religion and values and beliefs held by a group of societies or people affect the security of ordinary peoples and different societies often without warning. The series is designed to deepen our understanding of the recent past and seeks to make a significant contribution to the debates on conflict and security in the major world capitals.

Advisory Board Members:

Professor Mats Berdal, Chair of Security and Development, King's College London

Ambassador James Dobbins, Director International Security and Defence Policy Center, RAND

Professor Sir Lawrence Freedman, Vice Principal (Research), King's College London

Professor Bruce Hoffman, Georgetown University and former Director of RAND's Washington Office

Titles in the series include:

Christopher Baxter
THE GREAT POWER STRUGGLE IN EAST ASIA, 1944–1950
Britain, America and Post-War Rivalry

Vesselin Dimitrov
STALIN'S COLD WAR: SOVIET FOREIGN POLICY, DEMOCRACY AND COMMUNISM
IN BULGARIA 1941–1948

James Ellison
UNITED STATES, BRITAIN AND THE TRANSATLANTIC CRISIS
Rising to the Gaullist Challenge, 1963–1968

Peter Lowe
CONTENDING WITH NATIONALISM AND COMMUNISM
British Policy Towards Southeast Asia, 1945–1965

Jon Roper
THE UNITED STATES AND THE LEGACY OF THE VIETNAM WAR

Lowell H. Schwartz
POLITICAL WARFARE AGAINST THE KREMLIN
US and British Propaganda Policy and the Beginning of the Cold War

T.O. Smith
BRITAIN AND THE ORIGINS OF THE VIETNAM WAR
UK Policy in Indo-China, 1943–1950

Forthcoming title:

Ken Young
WEAPONS SYSTEMS AND THE POLITICS OF INTERDEPENDENCE

Global Conflict and Security since 1945
Series Standing Order ISBN 978–0–230–52123–0 hardcover
(*outside North America only*)

You can receive future titles in this series as they are published by placing a standing order. Please contact your bookseller or, in case of difficulty, write to us at the address below with your name and address, the title of the series and one of the ISBNs quoted above.

Customer Services Department, Macmillan Distribution Ltd, Houndmills, Basingstoke, Hampshire RG21 6XS, England

The Great Power Struggle in East Asia, 1944–50

Britain, America and Post-War Rivalry

Christopher Baxter

Research Fellow in Intelligence History, Queen's University Belfast

palgrave
macmillan

First published 2009 by
PALGRAVE MACMILLAN

Palgrave Macmillan in the UK is an imprint of Macmillan Publishers Limited,
registered in England, company number 785998, of Houndmills, Basingstoke,
Hampshire RG21 6XS.

Palgrave Macmillan in the US is a division of St Martin's Press LLC,
175 Fifth Avenue, New York, NY 10010.

Palgrave Macmillan is the global academic imprint of the above companies
and has companies and representatives throughout the world.

Palgrave® and Macmillan® are registered trademarks in the United States,
the United Kingdom, Europe and other countries.

ISBN-13: 978–0–230–20297–9 hardback

This book is printed on paper suitable for recycling and made from fully
managed and sustained forest sources. Logging, pulping and manufacturing
processes are expected to conform to the environmental regulations of the
country of origin.

A catalogue record for this book is available from the British Library.

A catalog record for this book is available from the Library of Congress.

10   9   8   7   6   5   4   3   2   1
18 17 16 15 14 13 12 11 10 09

Printed and bound in Great Britain by
CPI Antony Rowe, Chippenham and Eastbourne

For my wife and mother
In memory of my grandmother

Contents

Acknowledgements

This book began its life as a PhD thesis at King's College London and its completion would not have been possible without the support of Professor Saki Ruth Dockrill, who has provided me with inspiration, encouragement and invaluable advice ever since I first met her as a raw undergraduate at the Department of War Studies in 1991. Special thanks must also go to Professor Keith Jeffery of Queen's University Belfast, and two former colleagues at the Foreign & Commonwealth Office, Dr Keith Hamilton, and Gill Bennett OBE, formerly the chief historian. They have read and re-read drafts of the text, giving up their time and providing me with guidance, personal support and constructive suggestions. I also owe a debt of gratitude to Tony Blishen and Dr Stephen Ashton for reading some of the earlier drafts of the text and making helpful comments.

A full list of archives may be found in the bibliography but I would like to thank the staff at The National Archives (TNA) in Kew, London; the National Archives in College Park, Maryland; and the Imperial War Museum in London, for their friendly guidance. I am also particularly grateful for the help I received from James Zobel, the archivist at the MacArthur Memorial Archives in Norfolk, Virginia; Sue Donnelly, the archivist at the British Library of Political and Economic Science, the London School of Economics, for allowing me to quote extracts from the Hugh Dalton diaries; Beth Brook, information policy adviser at the Office of Public Sector Information, TNA; Bob Clark, supervisory archivist at the Franklin D. Roosevelt Presidential Library in Hyde Park, New York; Caroline Herbert, archives assistant at the Churchill Archives Centre in Churchill College, Cambridge; Jane Hogan, assistant keeper, Archives and Special Collections, Durham University; Winifred Assan, archives assistant, Special Collections and Archives, School of Oriental and African Studies, London University; and Yvonne Oliver at the Imperial War Museum. I would also like to thank the *Trustees of the Liddell Hart Centre for Military History, King's College London*, for allowing me to quote from various private papers; and Ruth Ireland and Michael Strang at Palgrave Macmillan for their advice and support. Financially, this project would not have been possible without the John D. and Catherine T. MacArthur Foundation and the Department of War Studies at King's College London, who awarded me a fully funded three-year fellowship, enabling me to write my thesis and to fund a visit to the archives at Durham University. I must also add that some parts of Chapters 1 and 2 have appeared in two Taylor & Francis journals: 'In pursuit of a Pacific strategy: British planning for the defeat of Japan, 1943–1945', *Diplomacy & Statecraft*, Vol. 25 (2004) and 'The Foreign Office and post-war planning for East Asia, 1944–5' in

Contemporary British History, Vol. 21 (2007), both of which can be found at www.informaworld.com and I acknowledge their inclusion here. The maps, which are Crown copyright, are reproduced courtesy of the Controller of Her Majesty's Stationary Office (HMSO) and the Queen's Printer for Scotland.

Finally, I want to thank the many people who have influenced and sustained me in my academic life, providing unbending support and advice. Here, I would like to pay a special tribute to Professor Sir Lawrence Freedman, Professor Andrew Lambert, Professor Brian Holden-Reid and Professor Michael Dockrill of the Department of War Studies. Above all, friends and family have always provided encouragement, particularly Dr Andrew Stewart and Ian Dorrell, but I would especially like to thank my mother and my wife, Lynsey, who have had to accommodate an absent son and husband, sacrificing much in order to allow me to finish this book. I also apologise to my newborn son, James, who has not seen as much of his father as he should have done. Above all, I owe a great deal to my grandmother, who played a pivotal role in my life, and it is to her memory that this book is dedicated.

Every effort has been made to trace rights holders, but if any have been inadvertently overlooked, the publishers would be pleased to make the necessary arrangements at the first opportunity.

Maps

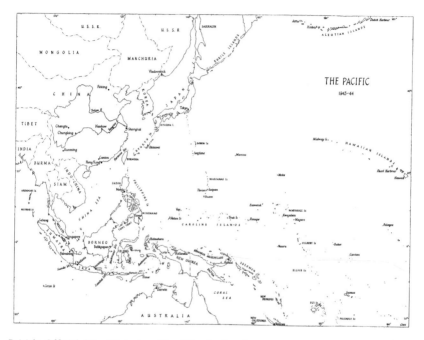

THE PACIFIC
1943-44

British Official War Histories. *The War Against Japan*, Vol. III: *The Decisive Battles* S. Woodburn Kirby, HMSO 1961. © Crown copyright material is reproduced with the permission of the Controller of HMSO and Queen's Printer for Scotland

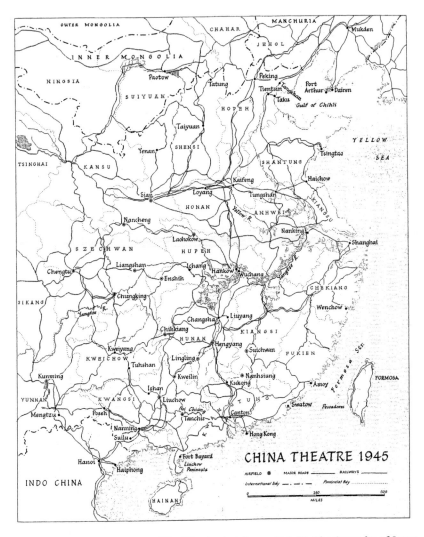

CHINA THEATRE 1945

AIRFIELD ⊕   MAJOR ROADS ———   RAILWAYS ———
International Bdy — · — ·   Provincial Bdy ················
0 .... 250 500
MILES

British Official War Histories. *The War Against Japan*, Vol. V: *The Surrender of Japan* S. Woodburn Kirby. HMSO 1969. © Crown copyright material is reproduced with the permission of the Controller of HMSO and Queen's Printer for Scotland

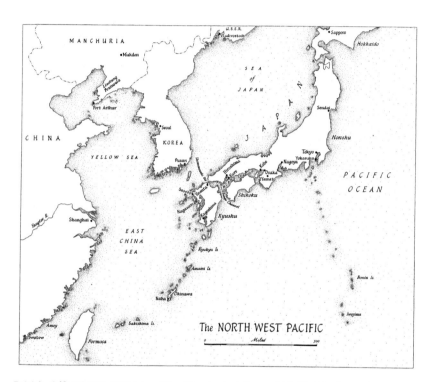

The NORTH WEST PACIFIC

British Official War Histories. *The War Against Japan,* Vol. V: *The Surrender of Japan* S. Woodburn Kirby. HMSO 1969. © Crown copyright material is reproduced with the permission of the Controller of HMSO and Queen's Printer for Scotland

Abbreviations

BBC	British Broadcasting Corporation
BCOF	British Commonwealth Occupation Force
BDCC (Far East)	British Defence Co-ordination Committee, Far East
CIA	Central Intelligence Agency
HSBC	Hong Kong and Shanghai Banking Corporation
JIC	Joint Intelligence Subcommittee/Committee
NATO	North Atlantic Treaty Organisation
NSC	National Security Council
NSRB	National Security Resources Board
OSS	Office of Strategic Services
PUSC	Permanent Under-Secretary's Committee
RAF	Royal Air Force
SANACC	The State-Army-Navy-Air Force Co-ordinating Committee
SCAP	Supreme Commander Allied Powers
SEAC	South East Asia Command
SIS	Secret Intelligence Service (MI6)
SOE	Special Operations Executive
SSU	Strategic Services Unit
SWNCC	State-War-Navy Co-ordinating Committee
UKLM	United Kingdom Liaison Mission, Japan
UN	United Nations
UNCOK	United Nations Commission on Korea
UNTCOK	United Nations Temporary Commission on Korea

Introduction

Much has been written about relations between Britain and the United States in the Far East and their mutual rivalry there, particularly during the Second World War. That literature has tended to concentrate on how the relationship developed in Southeast Asia and China.[1] There have been relatively few studies on Britain's early post-war interaction with the United States in East Asia,[2] and none looking at British policy towards China, Japan and Korea in the context of Anglo-American relations from planning for the defeat of Japan in 1944 to the outbreak of the Korean War in June 1950. The period is significant. During it Britain twice sent armed forces to a region by then perceived as having a relatively low position in Britain's foreign and strategic priorities. This book seeks to assess the reasoning behind Britain's decision to take part in operations that led up to the main assaults against the Japanese homeland and to explain why, five years after the end of the war against Japan, British forces were sent to fight in Korea.

This book focuses on the British response to American policies towards China, Japan and Korea. Although British officials rarely used the term 'East Asia' at the time, they often treated developments in the countries forming part of that region as a distinct entity within the Far East. This was largely the result of a division of labour formalised with the Americans in spring 1942 for the conduct of the war against Japan. Britain took responsibility for the area of British India and Southeast Asia, and the United States oversaw operations in the Pacific, under which the China theatre also fell.[3] It reflected the gradual shifting of power in East Asia from Britain to the United States.

During the 1930s, the Far East had remained a key element in British strategy until, with the outbreak of war in Europe in 1939, it dropped below the Mediterranean and the Middle East in the order of priorities. Before the Japanese attack on Pearl Harbor in December 1941, the United States therefore drove the Western response to Japanese overseas military expansion. By 1940, the British share in China's import trade was also third behind that of Japan and the United States, taking up just under 4 per cent of the market; while China's export trade showed Britain ranking second after the United States, with just under 10 per cent of the market.[4] Despite Japanese aggression and increasing Chinese nationalism, the British nevertheless maintained sizeable business interests inside China: total investment was estimated at £300m and the British community there numbered some 10,000. By 1942, however, the British were dependent upon US loans to maintain the war effort, while Japan had dispossessed Britain of large parts of its Far Eastern empire and also acquired control of the major Chinese coastal areas. Faced with economic difficulties at home and huge wartime commitments, the British were content for the United States to take the lead in East Asia and operations in the Pacific.[5]

The key issue for British ministers and officials during 1944–50 was whether Britain's exclusion from East Asian decision-making would affect its great power status, a term that had lost its distinctly European connotations and now signified the ability of a nation to exert its political, economic, military and cultural strength worldwide.[6] British moves to take part in the invasion of Japan is evidence that Britain felt its power could be affected. Although Britain's role in the war against Japan in Southeast Asia has commanded much interest,[7] its role in the projected assault on the Japanese Islands has received less attention.[8] The historiography on the end of the war against Japan remains vast and the interpretation of those events still stirs controversy among historians. It has taken on an increasing international dimension, but the British story remains under-examined.[9] This is understandable considering the reduced influence Britain could exert in the region, but those responsible for Far Eastern policy in the Foreign Office, for example, could not understand why the British voice should not continue to be heard in East Asia, as it had been in the past. There were also arguments that Britain could act as a restraining influence on an inexperienced United States as it began to assume greater international responsibilities and as the prospect of Soviet-American rivalry materialised.[10] The emerging consensus within Whitehall, however, was that Britain was in no position to play the prominent role it had done before 1941, whatever the repercussions for Britain's international standing. Britain had more than enough to contend with in South and Southeast Asia, where maintaining and dismantling its formal empire required the immediate attention of the British in the Far East.[11] Why, then, did the British not leave the United States to direct Western policy for post-war East Asia?

One argument was that Britain's status in the post-war world was dependent on its having a say in *all* global affairs. Another was that Britain had to fulfil its international obligations: it was committed to the unconditional surrender of Japan, it had signed the 1943 Cairo Declaration ensuring Korea's freedom and independence, and had professed to help China become united and democratic, relinquishing in January 1943 (along with the United States) extraterritorial rights. This put an end to unilateral privileges previously enjoyed by the British through 'unequal treaties' – such as concessions, settlements and rights to station foreign warships in Chinese waters – and removed the exemption of US and British nationals from Chinese law.

During the early post-war period the argument that Britain had to carry out its international pledges in East Asia came under close scrutiny, especially as the British were increasingly squeezed out of deliberating the region's affairs by the two emerging superpowers, the United States and the Soviet Union. They were both unwilling to listen to what Britain had to say about East Asia while British power became progressively more reliant on US financial help. Britain's economic difficulties forced it to look at ways of reducing overseas commitments and expenditure. A possible solution was to allow Australia to assume some of the burdens in East Asia, particularly Japan and Korea. This formed part of the continuing evolution of the British Commonwealth where the old dominions of Canada, Australia, New Zealand and South Africa had begun to pursue their own foreign policies.[12] Canberra had been campaigning vociferously for a greater say in Far Eastern affairs and British ministers accepted Australian leadership for the Commonwealth in the military occupation of Japan and involvement in a trusteeship for Korea if it materialised. The experiment was not successful and noisy Australian complaints of US unilateralism only served to strain Anglo-American relations. The Australians also seemed initially reluctant to assume the initiative for Commonwealth defence planning in the Far East. The British, meanwhile, recognised that the handing over of responsibilities to other powers, albeit in the Commonwealth, merely reaffirmed Britain's weakness while illustrating its inability to make its presence felt across the globe.

Such concern was one reason why the British were reluctant to disengage completely from East Asia. The principal reasons, however, were the failure of the United States to devise a comprehensive post-war plan for the region, other than the containment of Japan, as well as the emergence of Communist threats in China and Korea. With valuable colonial, economic and Commonwealth interests in South and South-East Asia, the British did not want to see the Asian mainland turn 'red' or witness the revival of the Japanese menace. Britain also sought to maintain its long-standing commercial and political influence in the region but understood it would need US support to help stabilise those countries in the Far East that had not succumbed to Communism. The results were mixed but the British would never let Anglo-American rivalry or rows over East Asia – which (unlike Australia) they tried to keep behind closed doors – endanger the US commitment to European recovery or US support for Britain's policy in the Middle East.

In East Asia, as in Europe and the Middle East, the British were coming to terms with a new world order in which the very notion of what it was to be a great power was thrown into question. They had to reckon with an emerging Cold War in which a bipolar system linked to an ideological conflict challenged older diplomatic precepts. Scholars have pointed out that Britain desired to remain a world power by maintaining its traditional imperial interests, particularly in the Eastern Mediterranean and the Middle East, while acting as an independent 'third force', but Cold War tensions and Soviet 'behaviour' gradually pushed the British to turn to the United States for help.[13] Although a gradual Anglo-American consensus grew on how to conduct the Cold War in Europe and the Middle East, the same could not be said for the Far East.

This came at a crucial time for the development and emergence of modern and contemporary East Asia. Our understanding of the Chinese Civil War, the emergence of a Chinese Communist state and the origins of the Korean War has been greatly enhanced since the 1990s, as historians have gained access to Chinese and Russian archives. These studies have stressed the ideological dimension to Sino-Soviet and Sino-American relations although it is not intended to relate those events in detail here.[14] The aim of this monograph is rather to throw fresh light on an important transitional period in British foreign policy, highlighting the changing and developing asymmetrical power relationship between Britain and the United States and explaining why the British got drawn into East Asia at a time when any objective observer would conclude their focus should have been on disengagement and not engagement.

1
Defeating Japan

In 1942 the outlook for a continued British presence in the Far East looked grim: Japanese victories in East and Southeast Asia had pushed the British Empire's multi-national forces back to the Burmese-Indian frontier. In the absence of British help, the dominions of Australia and New Zealand had to rely on their own limited defence capabilities and the retreating forces of the United States, who had also been reeling from a series of defeats in the Pacific at the hands of the Japanese.[1] Before Britain could re-build its empire in the Far East, which remained, despite the disasters of 1941–2, a clear aim of Prime Minister Winston Churchill and Foreign Secretary Anthony Eden, it first had to defeat Germany and Italy. In a global conflict where Britain was fighting for survival in Europe, while conducting campaigns in the Middle East and the Mediterranean (its second strategic priority), constructing a strategy for beating Japan was unlikely to be a foremost concern.

Franklin D. Roosevelt, the American president, agreed to the British strategic concept of 'Europe-first' while Churchill showed no objection to the United States, after its humiliation at Pearl Harbor, securing complete control over Pacific operations. Pearl Harbor had become a symbol of revenge for the American people, just as Dunkirk had acted as a 'watchword' and 'tocsin' for British society. Both setbacks captured the popular imagination and imbued a determination to defeat their enemies. Yet the reverses in the Far East and defeat at Singapore were 'a reminder of shame and ineptitude' to the British. Dunkirk and the war against Germany and Italy 'was fought on behalf of *being*', Singapore and the war against Japan 'on behalf of *having*, and the difference marked the entire war'.[2] The principal task for Anglo-American war leaders, nevertheless, was to win the war in Europe first and then work out how to beat Japan.

Searching for a strategy

The bulk of British interests in the Far East lay in Southeast Asia. Britain could not rebuild its position there without the active co-operation of its powerful ally, the United States, which had moved from a position of pre-war isolation towards what amounted to rabid 'anti-imperialism'. Welding the United States to a Europe-first strategy required the British to promise that they would help beat Japan, despite the lack of a clear plan to achieve this, once Germany had been defeated. At the Casablanca Conference in January 1943, Churchill was prepared to give such an assurance by supporting Roosevelt in his call for the unconditional surrender of both Germany *and* Japan. This pledge reinforced the US commitment to the European front but it tied an economically devastated Britain to undefined potential long-term military operations in the Far East.[3]

In devising plans for the deployment of forces against the Japanese, British strategists had to take into account a variety of issues: the Europe-first strategy, an increasing dearth of resources, relations with the United States, the remoteness of Far Eastern territories and a general apathy both in Parliament and amongst the public towards the war in the East. The dilemma for Britain was how best to use its meagre resources in a fight that lacked popular support and barely merited attention in the American psyche.[4] The dilemma proved difficult to solve and reminded Sir Alexander Cadogan, the Foreign Office's acid-tongued permanent under-secretary, of 'a blind man searching for a black cat in a dark room'.[5] General Hastings Ismay, Churchill's resilient and shrewd chief of staff known as 'Pug', also thought that when history came to be written the 'waffling' over the question of British strategy for the defeat of Japan would be 'one of the black spots' in the record of the conduct of the war.[6]

The exasperation of Britain's most senior diplomat and one of its top soldiers sprang from an inability to decide upon whether the concentration of British forces should be deployed in Southeast Asia or the Pacific. With unlimited resources, British planners would have no doubt sent substantial forces to both theatres to contribute to Japan's defeat. This option was not available and what emerged were rather elaborate plans from proponents of opposing strategies (the Pacific or Southeast Asian drive) to pursue each course vigorously without necessarily taking into account the resource implications and military realities on the ground. One reason was the intense British dislike of fighting the Japanese in the dense jungles of Burma, which conflicted with the American desire to re-open the Burma Road and supply China by land rather than hazardously and inefficiently by air. But plans to short circuit this strategy by carrying out amphibious operations towards Rangoon such as *Buccaneer* (a projected attack on the Andaman Islands in the Bay of Bengal south of Burma) were clearly beyond allied resources, while China's importance began to decrease after late 1943 when the Soviet Union declared its intention to join the conflict against Japan.[7]

Operation *Buccaneer* had been the brainchild of the charismatic and energetic Admiral Lord Louis Mountbatten, appointed Supreme Allied Commander of South East Asia Command (SEAC) at the first Quebec Conference in August 1943. The appointment, which Mountbatten took up in October, had been designed to demonstrate Britain's commitment to the war against Japan but he was a controversial choice and had many critics.[8] SEAC's aims were to clear the Japanese from British territory in the region and re-open the Burma Road but the Americans who joined Mountbatten's command felt uncomfortable being associated with re-conquering British colonial territory. As planning for *Buccaneer* fell apart, Mountbatten looked at re-working a previous plan, operation *Culverin*, a proposed amphibious attack against north Sumatra, which would eventually allow for a push towards Malaya and Singapore. Lacking the requisite large-scale amphibious and naval forces or American support, Britain's ability to carry out *Culverin* before Germany's defeat was highly questionable. The idea, nevertheless, attracted Churchill, a firm advocate of restoring Britain's imperial position in Southeast Asia, who hoped that if the inhabitants of these territories saw the British as liberators, the disasters of 1941–2 could be erased and British power reinvigorated. Churchill's maxim throughout the war was 'Hands off the British Empire', but his rigid conservatism on colonial issues antagonised many Americans.[9]

The Chiefs of Staff, and in particular Field Marshal Sir Alan Brooke, the Chief of the Imperial General Staff, were wholly unconvinced by *Culverin* and pushed instead for a role in the main Pacific operations against Japan. In his private diary, the uncompromising Brooke was damning of Churchill who, suffering from ill health, consistently tried to get *Culverin* accepted.[10] Operation *Culverin*, which depended on American resources, added little to the poor impression the United States had of the British effort in the Far East. From Washington, Lord Halifax, the former foreign secretary and now Britain's ambassador, told the Foreign Office that US criticism of Britain's war effort against the Japanese was intense. American opinion was convinced that British operations in Burma were 'a minor contribution' to the strategy of General Joseph Stilwell, the commander of American forces in the China–Burma–India Theatre, and 'not very effectively conducted at that'.[11] Stilwell's Anglophobia and misanthropy are well known. He was highly critical of Mountbatten and considered his planning sessions 'cock-eyed' and 'sad'.[12] Mountbatten's push for *Culverin* (like *Buccaneer*) tended to reinforce the US belief that the British had little concern for China's fate, and that they were more interested in regaining Malaya and Singapore.[13] The American assumption was largely accurate. From a British point of view, a determination to secure their interests first, especially prized colonial possessions that could help re-establish Britain's power in the Far East, was understandable.

Brooke, nevertheless, accused Mountbatten of egging on Churchill, 'determined to do something to justify his supreme existence' by backing an unworkable plan (*Culverin*), both encouraging each other with periodic personal telegrams.[14] Brooke's opposition was sound enough in terms of military realities but his solution, which revolved around a British effort in the Pacific, did not face up to some potential difficulties either. Halifax reminded

London that 'some' US naval and military circles were reluctant to facilitate a major British role in the war against Japan, seeing it as playing nothing more than 'the most subordinate of roles in the campaigns in the Pacific'.[15] Halifax's reference to opposition within naval circles was an allusion to Admiral Ernest King, the US chief of naval operations, who was adamantly opposed to the Royal Navy's participation in the Pacific. The British had long been aware of his sentiments and were sure that King was 'determined to keep the North and Central Pacific an American Ocean'.[16] In March 1944, however, even Roosevelt told Churchill that a British presence in the Pacific was unnecessary for the foreseeable future unless the Americans suffered 'unexpected bad luck'.[17] So, what was the reasoning behind Brooke's insistence on the British playing a larger part in the Pacific rather than Southeast Asia, which at one point in 1944 led the Chiefs of Staff to contemplate their resignation if they did not get their way?[18]

The Chiefs of Staff, like their US military counterparts, were animated by a desire to shorten the war, recognising the Pacific as the decisive theatre. They told Churchill that Roosevelt, in expressing the view that the addition of British units in the Pacific would be superfluous, had not 'fully seized' the scope of the task that lay ahead in beating Japan. The Chiefs of Staff knew full well Roosevelt would have sought military advice on this issue. Trying to claim this was the president's personal view seems rather disingenuous on the part of the Chiefs of Staff. The latter were certainly not to be deterred however. They felt a Pacific strategy, where several scenarios had been debated, would help solidify Britain's relations with Australia and New Zealand (damaged since the Singapore debacle) and see the continuation of the Combined Chiefs of Staff into the post-war period. The Chiefs of Staff ultimately saw a need to work closely with the US military, and were prepared to argue that Britain's colonial possessions could be recovered after the war. The ability of Australia to support a large British presence in the Pacific was not altogether clear and began to face opposition from General Douglas MacArthur, the Supreme Allied Commander in the Southwest Pacific Area, who was fearful of a threat to his position. The American general was not necessarily 'anti-British, just pro-MacArthur', but Brooke soon became convinced that MacArthur had John Curtin, the Australian prime minister, in his pocket, even though there appeared to be 'a great desire on the part of the Australians generally for British co-operation'.[19] The evidence for Brooke's last statement is very unclear especially as many Australians had embraced the Americans after Britain's failure to protect them in 1942, while the dominion was also suffering from what can only be described as industrial anarchy.[20]

Curtin's cautious attitude was displayed in May 1944, when he arrived in London for the Commonwealth Prime Ministers' meeting. Upon hearing Ernest Bevin, the minister for Labour and National Service, explain Britain would reallocate manpower resources after the defeat of Germany, Curtin pointed out Australia was afforded no such luxury as its effort was directed solely in the Pacific, where the end was not in sight.[21] Curtin told Churchill after the conference that he 'warmly' welcomed the idea of basing British forces on Australia (he could hardly have said otherwise) but went on at some considerable length to explain the difficulties of such an enterprise. A shortage of manpower was the main problem, the supply of which he noted had 'long since been exhausted' due to the commitments involved in supporting MacArthur's Southwest Pacific area, the Empire Air Training Scheme and the manning of certain ships for the Royal Navy. Further-more, Curtin wanted to reduce the strength of the army and the numbers in munitions and aircraft production. Resources (especially foodstuffs) from the allied nations would therefore be required to support additional British forces in the Pacific. Finally, he pointed out the Australians were under MacArthur's command and a decision by the Combined Chiefs of Staff would be needed to alter this situation.[22] In short, Australia was not an untapped reservoir of material resources ready to support full-scale British operations in the Pacific.

Behind the scenes, Admiral King stepped into the ring deliberately to stoke MacArthur's anxieties about the possible presence of the British in his theatre. A divided US command in the Pacific and competition for resources between MacArthur and Admiral Chester Nimitz, the commander-in-chief of the US Pacific Fleet, had long since placed a strain on US decision-making, and now it appeared the British might complicate matters further. After his visit to London in June 1944, King informed MacArthur that the Chiefs of Staff were considering operations that would take over a large part of the Southwest Pacific (including the Dutch East Indies and Borneo) after the projected fall of the Philippines.[23] This unwelcome news brought out the worst in MacArthur, a prima donna not known for sharing the fruits of victory or the role of others in his campaigns. Assuming from King's letter the British wanted an independent command, MacArthur replied violently that he was 'completely opposed' to the proposition. 'The British have contributed nothing to this campaign', he argued, but 'now propose to enter this theatre at the moment when victory lies clearly before us in order to reap the benefits of our successes'. MacArthur worried the British would draw Australian and New Zealand troops away from his command, while the Americans would be forced to provide logistic support through lend-lease over existing supply lines in the Pacific. He was suspicious of British motives, as were he claimed, the Dutch and the Australians – the assumption being (without any evidence) that Britain aimed to secure more colonial territory in the Far East. MacArthur then rather dramatically claimed that the whole idea would be 'destructive of American prestige' and damage their commercial prospects in the Far East.[24]

General George Marshall, the US army chief of staff, set out to reassure MacArthur, quoting a recent paper from the Chiefs of Staff suggesting that if a British fleet could not operate in the central Pacific – 'our distinct preference' – they would be willing to operate a Commonwealth task force under his command.[25] MacArthur remained suspicious fired up by Curtin who asserted he was under intense pressure in London to put his forces in an independent British command and had repeatedly to bat the proposition away. MacArthur presumed Curtin's refusal to give into British bullying no doubt accounted for the alleged change of heart reported by Marshall. MacArthur nevertheless set out his objections again to Washington in case the Chiefs of Staff tried to implement the idea of a British command later. Any form of 'appeasement' on this matter, he argued, would result in a 'deterioration' of 'British–American' relationships.[26] MacArthur's colourful and dramatic tone has to be treated with caution. Its use was down to a desire to protect his position at any cost. As one commentator has remarked, the general 'did not understand the British or their interests'. He was 'profoundly confused and often contradictory about international politics' and 'personalized everything'.[27] It was clear, however, that King, MacArthur and Curtin all for differing reasons were less than enthusiastic about the deployment of British forces in the Pacific.

Some British officials also saw few long-term benefits accruing from a Pacific strategy. Mountbatten's caustic political adviser, Esler (later Sir Esler) Dening, argued that despite US efforts to defeat the Japanese single-handedly, no American could state the extent to which the United States was willing and able to shoulder the burden of post-war Far Eastern security. Mountbatten considered Dening the Foreign Office's 'greatest expert on Japan and the Far East'. Born and raised in Japan, Dening had worked across a range of posts in the East Asia during the inter-war years, before being posted to Washington in 1941 and then joining SEAC. Broad, and stocky, the slow-speaking Dening was a stolid 'imperialist' in outlook and convinced that the British Empire would be an 'essential factor' in the maintenance of Far Eastern peace. 'A purely Pacific strategy', he told London, 'can have no political repercussions in vital areas commensurate with the attainment of its military objectives'. Dening argued that the Asian people, including the Japanese, were 'little interested' in the fate of Pacific Islands. Of more concern to the British, he asserted, a strategy that left the Japanese 'unassailed' in Southeast Asia would 'cast a considerable strain upon the already stretched endurance of the occupied territories' and could 'materially retard their rehabilitation upon recovery'. At the very minimum, Dening concluded, a strategy for Southeast Asia had to complement a Pacific strategy.[28]

These views resonated with political and diplomatic figures such as Churchill, Eden, Cadogan, John Sterndale Bennett, the head of the Foreign Office's Far Eastern Department, and later Bevin, as Labour foreign secretary.[29] Their position stemmed from a fear that the United States, to use Dening's words, sought to 'eliminate' Britain from the post-war Far Eastern order.[30] There is evidence to suggest that Roosevelt was thinking of creating a post-war Sino-Soviet-American 'entente' in Asia to the exclusion of

Britain, and the immediate policy discrepancies were at their worst in areas like British India and China, where Anglo-American forces together with a variety of intelligence agencies were operating to achieve what seemed to be entirely different objectives: for the British, the restoration of colonial rule and, for the Americans, the liberation of the Asian peoples from oppression.[31] Sir Horace Seymour, who worked as Britain's ambassador to China where economic and political rivalry was intense, informed Cadogan that for some Americans it was almost 'an article of faith' that British and American policy in the Far East was so different as to be 'irreconcilable'.[32]

Dening, Seymour and Sterndale Bennett had all worked in the Far Eastern Department at the beginning of the war and knew each other well, with the latter relying on the advice of his former colleagues when returning to the department as its head in 1944 after two years in Turkey as minister. Caution, however, needs to be ascribed to the language used by officials (and particularly Dening) responsible for British policy in the Far East, an environment that senior Foreign Office figures and the Chiefs of Staff felt sometimes got the better of them.[33] Indeed, although British ministers and diplomats worried about diverting limited resources away from Southeast Asia, some began to assess the political importance of being seen to be fighting alongside the Americans in the main assaults against Japan. Could not such a policy strengthen Anglo-American relations, raise Britain's fighting profile, and cement the British role in Far Eastern peacemaking? Clement Attlee, the deputy prime minister, and Eden, who never quite trusted the Americans, recognised these arguments.[34] The difficulty was to assess whether the forces Britain might contribute would actually make a difference militarily and whether the effort would have the hoped-for beneficial and influential effect on the post-war Anglo-American relationship.

Americans such as Cordell Hull, the US secretary of state, John Winant, the US ambassador to Britain, and Harry Hopkins, Roosevelt's presidential adviser, realised that notwithstanding the military difficulties, if they refused the British offer of providing forces to operate in the Pacific, which could save American lives, it might create long-standing resentment between the two powers.[35] Even at the height of his furious objections to British 'independent' participation in the Pacific, MacArthur left the door open, telling King 'the addition of British means to the Southwest Pacific Area would be most welcome', as long as they were under American 'leadership'. In competition with Nimitz for resources, MacArthur was aware a British fleet that would include escort carriers could prove useful to him as he might be starved of carrier protection once the US Pacific fleet headed north after the Philippine campaign.[36] In September 1944, a message from Churchill to MacArthur also eased the tension when the prime minister stated, 'I never had the slightest idea of diminishing your command' and he hoped the British would work 'hand in hand' with him.[37] Flattered, MacArthur's response was more than cordial, referring to 'informal sources' and 'wrong inferences' disseminating incorrect information with 'harmful results'. 'Beyond anything else', the general stressed, 'friction between the two Governments should not arise to imperil the future'.[38] On 8 September, faced with British proposals for the deployment of forces in the Pacific, the Joint Chiefs of Staff provisionally accepted the formation of an Empire task force headed by a British commander under MacArthur's control.[39] Where all the troops, aircraft and ships to create such a force were to come from was not discussed in any detail.

Could not the Americans have refused the proposal as unworkable or unnecessary? As Marshall explained to MacArthur, 'for our government to put itself on record as having refused agreement to the use of additional British and Dominion resources in the Pacific or Southwest Pacific area was unthinkable'.[40] Marshall's words suggest that the United States could adopt no other response to the British request. What began to emerge were political gestures to cement the Anglo-American relationship that both sides were in no position to refuse or backtrack from, which had little grounding in military necessity. At the second Quebec Conference in September 1944, Churchill could not fail to appreciate the impact of offering the services of the Royal Navy and the Royal Air Force (RAF) to take part in the main operations against Japan under American command. Roosevelt now accepted the concept of a British fleet in the Pacific on 13 September. He could hardly have said no yet King did his best to repudiate the decision. The admiral's position has been put down to a mixture of Anglophobia and also genuine concern over the Royal Navy's potential lack of experience of Pacific operations and the serious logistical difficulties required in supporting such a fleet. These latter points were not unreasonable but were arguments deliberately glossed over by Churchill.

King found little backing from Marshall, Admiral William Leahy, Roosevelt's chief of staff, or General Henry 'Hap' Arnold, the commanding general of the US army air forces. All three men recognised the political fall out if they rejected the British advance outright and, as one War Department official noted, King suffered 'a major reverse'. On the question of RAF participation in the Pacific, Arnold, nevertheless, was equivocal and felt a definite answer could 'not be given now', but Marshall asked the British for a paper on possible estimates and availability. The idea of an Empire task force operating under MacArthur was quietly dropped, the British Chiefs of Staff realising that such a force was way beyond British capabilities at this stage of the war.[41] The Australians, meanwhile, were becoming increasingly miffed at the fact that Pacific strategy was being discussed at all in their absence.[42] The British also still had a campaign to fight in north and central Burma (operation *Capital*) that was far from being won despite recent victories at Imphal and Kohima. In searching for speedy ways to liberate Burma, the British proposed a landing at Rangoon (operation *Dracula*) for March 1945, although Churchill would press Mountbatten to make the bill as low as possible. As it stood *Dracula* would require seven divisions, six of which would have to be found outside SEAC, their release dependent on the course of the war in Europe.[43]

The possibilities and timings of all Britain's future operations in the Far East still depended on events in Europe and the release of resources. At Quebec, the Combined Chiefs of Staff estimated it would take at least 18 months after Germany's defeat to secure Japan's 'unconditional' surrender. The overall strategy to achieve this aim was first to lower 'Japan's ability and will to resist by establishing sea and air blockades, conducting air bombardment, and destroying Japanese air and naval strength'; and secondly to invade and seize objectives in the 'industrial heart of Japan'. Marshall knew this formula was designed to allow for an invasion of the Japanese home islands. It also committed both powers to a long and costly struggle against Japan that would strain British resources to the maximum. But what these calculations had not accounted for was a currently neutral Soviet Union entering the conflict in the Far East.[44]

Securing Moscow's co-operation

The United States, adopting a notably mixed response to British gestures to take part in the main assaults against Japan, initially acted very differently when it came to trying to secure Soviet help. The Soviet Union possessed the potential to transfer substantial forces to the Far East but would not consider such a course until it was sure Germany would be beaten. In this respect, the German army's defeat at Kursk in the summer of 1943, which forced the Germans onto the defensive on the Eastern Front, allowed the Soviets to contemplate an involvement in the war against Japan. Although the Soviet Union had signed a non-aggression pact with Japan in April 1941, Joseph Stalin, the Soviet leader, and Vyacheslav Molotov, his foreign minister, began to intimate to US officials at the Moscow Conference in September 1943 their intention to join the conflict in the Far East.[45] Anticipating the prospect of Soviet participation being raised at Moscow, Ashley Clarke, then head of the Foreign Office's Far Eastern Department, told Eden that the principal inducement for the Soviet Union to enter the war against Japan was 'to stake out claims' to territory.[46]

In late November 1943, outside the plenary sessions of the Tehran Conference, Stalin informally pledged to join the war against Japan – after successfully securing Anglo-American agreement for a second front to be opened in Europe in May 1944 – and raised the price for Soviet intervention. No official record exists of Stalin's demands, but Averell Harriman, the recently appointed US ambassador in Moscow, recalled Stalin made it clear he wanted to tear up the Treaty of Portsmouth imposed upon Russia in 1905 by Japan. The use of Manchurian ports and railroads would also need to be discussed and Churchill, according to Harriman, thought the Soviet Union's legitimate needs should certainly be satisfied.[47] For the prime minister, such concessions represented no threat to British interests and they were to be encouraged because, if China accepted them, they would have little basis upon which to oppose Britain's recovery of Hong Kong.[48] Churchill also realised the opening of a Soviet front in Manchuria against the Japanese could accelerate the defeat of Japan. If this subsequently led to a collapse of Japan's Far Eastern empire, then Britain's colonial possessions in Southeast Asia and its position in China could be re-established earlier than anticipated, reducing already over-stretched financial and manpower burdens.[49]

It was not until late September 1944 that the Soviets raised the subject again, when Sir Archibald Clerk Kerr, Britain's ambassador in Moscow, together with Harriman, met Stalin to report on the second Quebec Conference. Concerned that the Quebec timetable had not included Soviet participation, Stalin enquired if Churchill and Roosevelt still desired Soviet entry in the war against Japan. Both ambassadors replied in the affirmative but required Stalin to initiate discussions and clarify his intentions. He appeared to begin this process that October when Churchill visited Moscow. It was a trip dominated by European questions but on 14 October, five days into Churchill's visit, the war against Japan was raised with Stalin in the presence of the prime minister by Major-General John Deane, the head of the US military mission in Moscow. On that occasion Stalin replied in rather vague terms as to when the Soviets might enter the conflict. The following evening at the Kremlin, a more in-depth discussion took place about Japan. In place of an ill Churchill, Eden attended the meeting along with Brooke, Harriman, the respective heads of the British and US military missions and General Alexi Antonov, the Soviet army chief of staff.[50] Antonov estimated some 60 divisions would take part in a Manchurian offensive to deal with the 45 Japanese divisions they expected. Brooke considered the meeting a success and had never doubted the Soviet desire to enter the war as soon as they could, although he recorded that Stalin wanted to know what his country would get for its help.[51]

It was agreed that the Americans and the Soviets should continue to meet for more detailed discussions but Stalin's demands, based loosely on what had transpired at Tehran, would not be formalised until the Yalta Conference of February 1945. Demonstrating Britain's waning power, it was excluded from these political consultations, but the prime minister was prepared to accept this state of affairs as he considered the Northeast Asian region an area of secondary importance to British interests.[52] In their view, the Chiefs of Staff, the Foreign Office and the Joint Intelligence Subcommittee (JIC) all agreed that the Soviet Union did not pose a direct threat to Britain's strategic sea routes and colonial possessions in Southeast Asia. One Foreign Office memorandum argued that if Britain adopted an understanding attitude towards Soviet desires in Northeast Asia, 'she seems unlikely to make trouble for us in the southern regions where our interests lie'.[53] Stalin, for his part, was concerned that the United States might attempt to negotiate a peace with Tokyo that would leave Japan strong enough to challenge the Soviet Union. Security rather than historical claims dictated Soviet involvement in the war, which could also help them lay a claim to the formulation of the terms of peace and provide insurance against Japan's revival.[54]

The JIC, in a report commended by Eden, anticipated that the Soviet Union would at least try to 'experiment' in a policy of collaboration with Britain and the United States. Within this framework and not a broader world security organisation, the JIC argued that the Soviets would hope to build a system of security outside their frontiers and settle any differences.[55] The assessment was sound: Stalin had little time for a United Nations (UN) organisation, and wanted to achieve his security goals – the dismemberment of Germany, Japan's defeat, and the securing of territory around his frontiers, particularly in Poland – through great power negotiation. The Soviet Union needed to rebuild its shattered war economy and could not afford to fall out with its wartime allies or enter another conflict. Roosevelt and Churchill also felt it was possible to build a lasting partnership with Stalin. The president was prepared to go to considerable lengths to achieve this as long as it did not antagonise US opinion.[56] Some sounded notes of warning, however. General Deane, for example, told Marshall on 2 December that although everyone agreed on collaboration with Soviet Russia, it would not 'be worth a hoot' unless based on mutual respect and made to 'work both ways'. Deane vividly described the Soviet suspicion of foreigners and felt the Americans were making too many concessions for little in return, arguing 'we should stop pushing ourselves on them and make the Soviet authorities come to us' but 'be friendly and co-operative when they do so'. Marshall sent Deane's observations to Roosevelt.[57]

As the war dragged on in Europe the timetable for defeating Japan was once again disrupted, highlighting the allied need for Soviet help. The Western allies had hoped to start moving resources to the Far East and the Pacific by the end of 1944 but with the failure of operation *Market Garden* at Arnhem in September, stiff resistance on the Italian front and the Ardennes offensive in December, it was accepted that Germany would not be beaten before the spring of 1945.[58] The setback at Arnhem immediately removed resources from *Dracula* forcing its postponement. Mountbatten complained of the damage to British prestige in the Far East but Churchill reminded him his priority was Europe.[59] Even the Joint Chiefs of Staff found it necessary to divert to Europe two infantry divisions, which had been originally intended for the Pacific in May 1945.[60] The potential of the atomic bomb was also still unknown. All these facts left Marshall firm in the belief of the need for Soviet assistance.[61] Roosevelt was therefore prepared to accept, in part, Stalin's demands in Northeast Asia to secure his goodwill and Soviet entry into the war against Japan. These concessions were thrashed out at the Yalta Conference in February 1945, when Stalin and Roosevelt agreed

to Soviet control over southern Sakhalin and the Kuriles, the internation-
alisation of the commercial port of Dairen (Dalian), a Soviet lease over Port
Arthur (Lüshun), the joint Sino-Soviet management of Manchurian railroads
and the maintenance of the *status quo* in Outer Mongolia. Roosevelt insisted,
however, that these concessions would have to be approved by Nationalist
China through some form of treaty of alliance with the Soviet Union.[62]

Britain was barred from these discussions and Churchill was not consulted,
but he put his signature to the terms, arguing (as he had before) that the
problem was 'remote and secondary'. Eden, together with Cadogan, who had
served in China during the 1930s, urged Churchill not to sign, concerned
about British exclusion from the negotiations. At Malta, the foreign secretary
had told Edward Stettinius, the new US secretary of state, that a deal should
not be done, as the Soviets would enter the conflict regardless. At the very
least 'a good return' should be obtained for any offer made. Churchill argued
that Britain was in no position to bargain: Soviet entry could 'save us many
thousands of millions of pounds' by shortening the war while 'the *quid pro
quo* far out values anything we are likely to get out of China'. Both arguments
had their merits but it is unrealistic to assume, in the spirit of co-operation
the two leaders were trying to achieve, that they would not have put some
sort of deal before Stalin. There is also much to be said for Roosevelt's
assertion that it was better to have an agreement limiting potential Soviet
gains than not.[63] One can nevertheless detect uneasiness on Churchill's part
regarding his role in this episode when he told Eden that he was 'shocked' to
see the Foreign Office had produced eight copies of the secret Yalta protocol.
'They ought not to be circulated except in a locked box', Churchill fumed,
and there was also 'no need whatever to inform the Dominions or to show
the document to anyone who was not cognizant of it'.[64]

The dilemma for both Churchill and Roosevelt was to restrain Soviet
ambitions in Northeast Asia and at the same time maintain a co-operative
relationship consistent with the interests of the Western allies that would
help defeat Japan and ensure post-war regional stability. During the bitter battle for Okinawa between March and June 1945, which indicated
that an invasion of Japan would be extremely costly,[65] Henry Stimson, the
United States secretary of war, and Marshall were convinced that Soviet
entry would have a profound military impact and save US lives. At this
stage, these persuasive arguments, which overestimated the strength of the
Japanese army in Manchuria, were a reason why Harry Truman, who succeeded Roosevelt in April 1945, and Stimson rejected attempts by Joseph
Grew, the under-secretary of state at the State Department, to revise the Yalta
accords. Truman, who felt it important to honour agreements already made
with the Soviets, was not experienced in international diplomacy and relied
heavily on advisers such as Stimson, Harriman and Grew. Their views had
certainly hardened towards the Soviet Union and its projected penetration
of Northeast Asia, but often fluctuated, and US armed service ministers, for

example, still remained unsure of the potential Soviet danger and wondered if Japan or Germany might pose the greater post-war threat.[66]

British forces for an invasion of Japan

As a result of the second Quebec Conference, the British now had to spread their resources across two theatres (Southeast Asia and the Pacific). On a tactical level, the British Secret Intelligence Service (SIS) and agents in its south China coast-watching organisation had already helped the Americans launch successful strikes on Japanese naval forces during the battle of the Philippines, which had started in October 1944. The intelligence was well received despite rivalries on the ground in China between the various British and American intelligence agencies.[67] The question of moving larger resources to the Pacific theatre, however, left Britain confronting a number of problems. First, the impact of deploying a Pacific fleet to operate from Australia (which had now become a reality) worried the Australian government, who felt that the British did not realise (or worse did not care) about the seriousness of their manpower problems. In November 1944, Curtin instructed Stanley Bruce, the Australian high commissioner in London, to tell A. V. Alexander, Britain's First Lord of the Admiralty, that as of 30 June 1945 Australia would have a shortfall of 50,000 manpower units.[68] Alexander expressed sympathy and told Bruce that the Admiralty fully realised Australia's difficulties but he was sure a solution could be easily reached. Sir Frederick Shedden, secretary of the Australian Department of Defence (who travelled with Curtin to London in May and was responsible for re-shaping Australia's war effort), thought Alexander's reply either 'stupid' or 'cunning', convinced that the British were attempting to offload their own manpower problems on the Australians.

As the British pressed ahead, the result was serious friction between the Australian government and Admiral Sir Bruce Fraser, the commander of the British Pacific Fleet. When the Royal Navy was informed that there was no prospect of Australia making any labour contribution towards the request of 5,000 men for the repair of British warships and as labour strikes continued, Fraser became exasperated. He thought the Australians were slow in tackling these problems and made a very public statement in April 1945 about the delays in docking British shipping. Jack Beasley, the acting minister of defence, enquired vigorously of Fraser what authority he had to undermine a self-governing dominion in such a manner. Unmoved, Fraser thought the Australian attitude 'deplorable', and argued incorrectly that as they had asked for a British Pacific Fleet they should have been striving at all costs to meet its needs. The Australians felt Fraser had 'no conception' of their domestic problems and Shedden saw remarks by both Churchill and Fraser about the 'prestige of the British Commonwealth being at stake' as 'rather unrealistic Imperialist rhetoric'.[69]

Despite these difficulties, the British Pacific Fleet managed to take part with varying degrees of success in battles off Okinawa in March 1945, enjoying good tactical and operational relations with the United States Navy.[70] Whether the British presence really made a substantial difference to the outcome of the campaign is rather more questionable.[71] Nevertheless, as the war against Germany came to an end and US preparations were made for an invasion of Japan, the Chiefs of Staff set out to reinforce the British Pacific Fleet and build up a strategic bombing force for operations against the Japanese mainland.[72] The Chiefs of Staff had secured US agreement to the deployment of a very long-range bombing force in the summer of 1945 when the Joint Chiefs of Staff, after lengthy discussions, approved plans to offer the RAF a base at Okinawa for ten largely self-supporting heavy bomber squadrons to be under US command. The original British proposal had been for 40 squadrons (20 as bombers and 20 as tankers) and the Cagayan Valley on northern Luzon in the Philippines was allocated as a potential base but MacArthur deemed the area impracticable due to the huge logistical effort required. Throughout these discussions, where the Americans privately questioned the utility of British bomber forces, the Chiefs of Staff maintained that a British role in the bombing of Japan could help secure an influential voice at the Far Eastern peace table while reassuring the United States that Britain was prepared to share in the heavy cost of an invasion of Japan.[73]

Yet would the Americans have listened to the British any less at the peace table just because they failed to commit what, in comparison to the US effort, were very small resources to the Pacific? The Americans were not depending on British resources to make a decisive impact on the Pacific campaign. In one paper before the offer of air bases at Okinawa, the Joint Staff Planners wrote that the United States had 'more than sufficient air strength available for employment in the Pacific' and 'all needs for strategical or tactical air forces in the Pacific can be filled entirely from U.S. resources'. The planners did recognise that RAF units could permit a reduction in American air force units to be deployed to the Pacific but the situation was hardly critical. It took the Americans eight months to reach a definite decision (indicating their indifference) much to the concern of Sir Charles Portal, the British Chief of Air Staff and Marshal of the RAF, who was 'anxious' to make preparations for the deployment of engineers to Okinawa. Meanwhile, it was proving more than a headache for the Americans to try and squeeze the British onto Okinawa when space was at a premium.[74]

As the British tried to make an impact on Pacific operations they remained heavily committed to operations in Southeast Asia. Even when they reached Rangoon in early May 1945, successfully executing a scaled-down version of *Dracula*, SEAC's planning was set for the long term. An amphibious assault on the west coast of Malaya (operation *Zipper*) was scheduled for September while the follow-up assault on Singapore (operation *Mailfist*) would not be launched until December or January 1946. Planning was not helped by the dissolution of the British coalition government on 23 May 1945 in prepara-tion for a general election in July. The fight for political advantage led the intervening caretaker government to announce the release of long-service combat personnel while the War Office reduced the length of its overseas tour by four months to three and a quarter years. These measures removed two divisions from SEAC and damaged the morale of British personnel in the Far East who feared that by the time they returned home there would be a shortage of jobs.[75]

To offset these problems, the Chiefs of Staff argued in May that once Singapore had been captured priority should be given to the creation of a Commonwealth invasion force, because the occupation of Japan itself would lead to the speedy collapse of resistance in the outer areas. The Chiefs of Staff did not want to divert resources for morale-sapping mopping-up oper-ations in Southeast Asia.[76] These arguments took on greater force when US plans for an invasion of Japan were set in motion on 18 June, with Truman approving Marshall's plan for a two-phase assault on the southern mainland, attacking Kyushu in November 1945 (operation *Olympic*) and Honshu four months later (operation *Coronet*). Marshall was convinced that an invasion combined with Soviet entry into the war 'may well be the decisive action levering them [the Japanese] into capitulation'. In the same breath, Marshall noted that the British might raise the question of combined command and thought this would immediately increase difficulties with the Soviets and the Nationalist Chinese. More critically, he argued, 'the obvious inefficiencies of combined command may directly result in increased costs in resources and American lives'. Later in the discussion Marshall returned to British partici-pation, warning the president he would find Churchill 'very articulate'. 'He is interested', Marshall argued, 'in showing that the British Government has played a full part in the defeat of Japan'. Marshall was 'glad to have any real help or any assistance that would result in striking a real blow' but thought in reality 'British participation in some ways would constitute an embarrassment'.[77]

Had the British known Marshall's views, one wonders whether their atti-tude towards participating in the Pacific would have been different? His criticism was damning but not without foundation. Unaware of this yet informed of general plans for the invasion by the Joint Chiefs of Staff before Truman's announcement,[78] the British military soon proposed the building of a Commonwealth force of three to five divisions to take part in *Coronet*. Rather tenuously but as Marshall predicted, the British suggested the set-ting up of a Combined Chiefs of Staff system in the East once the Straits of Malacca had been opened. The Joint Planning Staff also argued that Britain should stake a claim to a share in the final occupation of Japan. British partic-ipation in *Coronet*, however, was completely dependent upon the punctual capture of Singapore and any delay would prevent the release of forces for operations in Japan. Once deployed for *Coronet*, the need to support the invasion force would also inevitably curtail operations in SEAC (Britain's primary area of interest) through a lack of troopships and administrative personnel.[79]

In the Foreign Office's Far Eastern Department, Sterndale Bennett studied these proposals. While recognising that there might be political dividends, he wondered if involvement in *Coronet* was the most rapid way of bringing the war to an end for Britain. He feared that 'after the main excitement was over' the British would be left with a difficult and prolonged mopping-up process in Southeast Asia where Britain's material interests were 'greatest'. There was unlikely to be any US support for such mopping-up while delays could have an unfavourable impact on British prestige. He was also deeply concerned over the evolution of American ideas for the occupation of Japan, which he thought were 'likely to end in failure'. This being the case, was it therefore wise for Britain to lobby for anything more than a token partici-pation? Influenced by recent arguments from Dening, who still had major doubts about Pacific operations, Sterndale Bennett concluded, 'ocular evi-dence of the defeat of the Japanese in the areas which directly affect them will have more effect than hearsay evidence that British troops have taken part in the attack on Japan proper'. Indeed, by 1945, world grain was already in short supply and with Burma, French Indo-China and Thailand (Siam) forming the main rice-producing areas of the world, averaging a pre-war exportable surplus of some six million tons, the control of rice supplies would be a fundamental stabilising influence throughout the Far East. A con-tinued disruptive Japanese presence in Southeast Asia would be disastrous if the return of the British was associated with post-war famine.[80]

Despite Sterndale Bennett's fears about British participation, he took a step back from suggesting that Britain should play no part in the enterprise, even though his arguments were damning of the whole concept. When Sterndale Bennett's thoughts were sent to Halifax, the ambassador rounded on the conclusions, and particularly on a further suggestion that it would make little real difference to US public opinion if Britain did not take part on the assault of Japan. Non-participation, the ambassador argued, would damage future Anglo-American relations and convince the detractors that Britain was only interested in recovering its colonial possessions. He continued:

> Over and above this there would be a general feeling common to our friends as well as to our critics that the British had quit when the boar was at bay whereas the United States had seen it through in Europe. Even if British participation were of necessity small or comparatively so, there would be an overwhelming difference between this and total absence.... [I]f British troops are to be absent from the final assault on Japan, it would be much better for us that this should be the result of a refusal by the United States of a British offer of participation than of failure to make an offer. If we offered and the United States persisted in refusing I should

be strongly in favour of our letting this be known at once whether by newspaper or failing that by a suitable leakage.[81]

This broadside disturbed Sterndale Bennett, who told the Chiefs of Staff that Halifax had 'misinterpreted' current Foreign Office thought. The latter was not suggesting non-participation in the final assaults, but merely pointing out 'it was probably illusory to expect that participation... would earn much positive credit' in the United States or alter the American belief that their arms had won the war against Japan. The solution to this problem already suggested by Halifax and endorsed by Eden was to attach as many US correspondents as possible to British forces to maximise publicity.[82] Faced with arguments deployed by such a powerful figure in Halifax it was never likely that Sterndale Bennett would dare move to override the ambassador's advice.

On 4 July, both Churchill and Truman signed up independently to further Anglo-American co-operation in the Pacific. Truman, after a discussion with close aides, advisers and friends, agreed to the full participation of Britain in the Pacific,[83] while Churchill was prepared to accept the Chiefs of Staff's plan for a British Commonwealth invasion force for Japan.[84] Now committed to a Pacific strategy, Churchill told Curtin the day before the Australian prime minister died that such a force would 'form a striking demonstration of Commonwealth solidarity' and that it was 'important' to share with the United States the burden of the assault on Japan.[85] That burden looked increasingly more onerous after Sir John Anderson, the Chancellor of the Exchequer, had told the cabinet in June that it would be 'impossible' both to maintain the scale of effort in the Far East 'as at present planned' and to meet minimum civilian needs at home. Lord Cherwell, the paymaster general and close friend of the prime minister, expanded these arguments in July, informing Churchill that Britain now needed extra manpower to begin the revival of British exports, otherwise the outlook for the civilian during the coming winter would become 'most serious'. It therefore seemed 'quite out of the question' to consider any expansion of Far Eastern commitments without a genuine guarantee from the armed services that this would not inflate still further their manpower demands. Cherwell concluded, 'It is utterly impossible, I am sure, to expect the civilian to put up with heavier burdens now that the German war is won.'[86] Churchill's argument for Commonwealth solidarity also looked slightly less convincing when the British learnt the Canadians had already independently offered a division for use in the invasion and that the Americans had accepted this.[87]

Churchill's decision to embrace a Pacific strategy remained influenced by the continuing need to show solidarity and secure American post-war friendship, especially in the face of an increasingly unpredictable Soviet Russia. There is little evidence, however, to suggest that the United States viewed a British land contribution as critical or that they would have issued a rebuke if Britain had not stumped up forces for the invasion. In fact, Marshall told

MacArthur (who sought his views on the matter) that British divisions would merely replace American divisions like for like. But he hoped this would meet with 'public approval' by lessening the requirements for US soldiers and quieten Britain's detractors and those who attacked the Truman administration over the non-participation of allies in the conquest of Japan.[88] In the realm of military realities these considerations made little impact upon MacArthur, who again objected, this time in his new capacity as the commander-in-chief of United States Army Forces in the Pacific. As with the British Pacific Fleet and the long-range bombing force, American doubts carried the day. When the three great powers of the Grand Alliance met at Potsdam in July and August 1945, in bilateral discussions, the US military forwarded MacArthur's reservations to the British, ruling out the Commonwealth force's employment in a separate sector along national lines. He also wanted it re-equipped with US matériel, dismissed the use of a British Indian division due to language complications, worried about the availability of assault lift, and felt it was 'not practicable' to plan for the use of forces whose availability was contingent upon the conclusion of other major operations (*Zipper* and *Mailfist*).[89]

In MacArthur's defence, the outcome of *Zipper* and *Mailfist* was quite uncertain,[90] and considering the wide discrepancies in the forces to be deployed, Britain's rather ambitious claims for a quarter-share in the control of Pacific operations not surprisingly hit a brick wall at Potsdam. The United States was prepared to discuss strategy but the final decisions would rest with them. Marshall, however, agreed in principle to a Commonwealth land force for *Coronet* and promised to 'make room' for British troops.[91] The balance of power in the Pacific, as in 'Tube Alloys' (the codename for the British nuclear programme), lay with the United States and it was for them to make the main strategic decisions.[92] The discrepancies in forces available to the United States and Britain were clear for all to see. The Joint Staff Planners estimated that the Americans would have 36 divisions available for the main assaults on Japan; the British Commonwealth force would initially comprise three divisions for *Coronet* (a division each from Britain, Australia and Canada). The British Pacific Fleet was only equivalent in strength to a task force within the US Fifth Fleet and estimates suggested that Britain's strength in first-line aircraft would be about 8 per cent of the American total.[93]

Despite the imposed limitations on British forces, at Potsdam, Truman made it 'perfectly plain' to both Churchill and Stalin that 'my first interest is the USA, then I want the Jap War won and I want 'em both in it'.[94] Truman's main concern was to save American lives, even with the atomic weapons card in his hand (now a reality), which had so excited both Churchill and the US Secretary of State James Byrnes in the realm of bargaining power with the Soviets. Byrnes, a democrat from South Carolina of Irish-American extraction, had been a firm friend of Roosevelt, the latter taking him to Yalta to negotiate with the Soviets. Byrnes had also been a mentor to Truman during his days in the Senate. Truman relied heavily on his counsel and Byrnes, a firm advocate of using the atomic bomb, felt Soviet intervention could now be dispensed with. Churchill picked up on Byrnes's stance towards Soviet participation, reporting it to Eden. But Byrnes did not reflect the complex and wide-ranging US views on the subject. There was no certainty that the dropping of the atomic bomb would guarantee Japan's surrender, which was a view Marshall tended to lean towards. Truman therefore accepted the need to secure Soviet, and to a lesser extent British, military help. Soviet entry and the use of the atomic bomb were not either/or strategies: both were necessary to help shorten the war against Japan. It was also impracticable to prevent the Soviets from joining the war. The allies had courted them since 1943 and it was almost certain they would enter the conflict regardless of any actions the United States might attempt to initiate.[95]

Truman's form of words – 'I want 'em both in it' – was, however, unfortunate, as it tended to suggest that Britain was not in the war against Japan in the first place, an unintentional slip of the pen one hopes but unsurprising considering the continual downplaying of the British war effort by the US press and the poor exposure the British Pacific Fleet had received.[96] MacArthur had also shown he was prepared to disregard allies, witnessed by his refusal to use Australian troops in the battle for the Philippines.[97] Despite these disquieting trends, Attlee, who returned to Potsdam on 27 July after becoming prime minister in the new Labour government, maintained the policy of sending British forces to fight in *Coronet*. On 31 July, he told Ben Chifley, the new Australian prime minister, that the necessity for taking part in Pacific operations was 'premised on the belief that the defeat of the enemy's armed forces in the Japanese homeland is a pre-requisite to unconditional surrender, and that such a defeat will establish the optimum prospect of capitulation by Japanese forces outside the main Japanese islands'.[98] The Chiefs of Staff would therefore accept MacArthur's proposals as they stood.[99]

On 8 August, the day that the Soviet Union entered the war against Japan and its forces advanced into northern parts of China and Korea, the British Defence Committee met to discuss planning for the Japanese war. During the previous month, Dening had continually bombarded the Foreign Office about how a Commonwealth invasion force would halt all SEAC operations after *Mailfist* and delay the liberation of Southeast Asian territories by up to two years, which would be nothing short of a political disaster for British power in the region.[100] These views found the receptive ear of Bevin, the new foreign secretary. At the Defence Committee, he stated his concerns about mopping-up operations in Southeast Asia while maintaining the identity of the small-sized Commonwealth Corps, especially as it was being equipped with US resources. Bevin also reiterated that 'the magnitude of our effort in South-East Asia has never been realised in the United States'. Attlee was equally unsure as to whether Japanese garrisons in the outer areas would surrender if Japan was invaded or its central government collapsed, but he thought the Chiefs of Staff's proposals remained 'the best that could be done under the circumstances' (hardly a ringing endorsement), confirming the enterprise remained an important political gesture.[101]

For a prime minister who would challenge many of Britain's strategic commitments in the post-war period, his reluctance to reverse Britain's pledges in the Pacific at a time of economic hardship can only be put down to a fear of the bad impression it would make upon the Americans. But one wonders whether Attlee would have or should have changed his government's mind if he had read a memorandum by the Joint Chiefs of Staff on 9 August. This paper began 'to question very seriously the feasibility of utilizing any British forces requiring both U.S. equipment and amphibious training in an assault role'. The Joint Chiefs were unconvinced by the information furnished so far by the British regarding the amount of time it would take to train men for amphibious assault operations for an invasion. The Joint Chiefs also wanted to be able to reassure MacArthur, which they presently felt unable to do, that any troops deployed would be ready for battle and adequately maintained and what the impact would be on SEAC with regard to assault shipping, 'a critical item in this problem'.[102] The Australians, too, were worried that the British would not be ready to take part. The dominion did not want to be left on the sidelines (as in the Philippines) during an event of 'paramount' importance that could affect Australia's standing in the region after the war.[103]

On 15 August 1945 Japan surrendered, a result of the psychological blows of two atomic bombs dropped on Hiroshima (6 August) and Nagasaki (9 August), combined with the Soviet declaration of war. At the Far Eastern Department, where there had been no knowledge of the atomic bomb, the terrible effects inflicted by the weapon on the Japanese population led the department to believe that untold damage would be done to the allied cause. There were also still complaints that the United States did not recognise the extent of the British effort in the Far East or the Pacific. One Foreign Office official sought an authoritative ministerial statement about what

> the Far Eastern War has meant to this country – of how we have mortgaged our future and piled up an immense external debt to see it through, of what it has meant in economic, and social and human terms as well as what has been accomplished in terms of campaigns and armies and ships.[104]

It is, of course, open to speculation whether the British decision to send combined land, sea and air forces to the Pacific might have made a difference to the popular US perception of Britain's role in the East, but the initial signs were not encouraging while questions have also been raised about the ability of the British Pacific Fleet to maintain itself into 1946, which lends some justification to King's opposition towards the whole idea.[105] On 16 August, Mountbatten told MacArthur that he was 'most grateful' for the way he had handled the British Commonwealth participation in *Coronet*, convinced that the general's doubts were justified while stressing how the invasion force would have wrecked his (Mountbatten's) ability to carry out SEAC's continuing operations.[106]

This chapter has shown that it was the British who pressed for their own role in the Pacific rather than the Americans wanting them there. In approaching the Americans, the British hoped to derive 'political' benefits, such as strengthening the Anglo-American relationship, having a greater say in the region and dampening criticism about their 'imperialist' motives in the war against Japan. For the sake of unity, the Americans could not realistically decline British offers but the following chapters will show the perceived benefits on the part of Britain never really materialised. That the British decision to send forces to the Pacific for noble reasons and kinship were genuine is not in doubt but it was never very realistic to assume the dividends would amount to much, as Sterndale Bennett intimated. Only substantial forces, like those possessed by the Soviet Union, would have made such an impact. What occurred instead was a dilution of British resources, which should have been more profitably concentrated on securing Britain's key interests in Southeast Asia, such as Malaya and Singapore. This may have alienated Congress and popular US opinion but their suspicion of British imperialism was deep-rooted and the sending of land, sea and air forces to the Pacific to be merely dwarfed by American and subsequently Soviet arms was unlikely to change this view nor did it do much to impress the nascent superpowers or the peoples of Asia.

2
Post-War Planning in Wartime

Churchill's exclusion from the deliberations of Roosevelt and Stalin at Yalta was a fair measure of how Britain's two major allies perceived its interest in East Asia. The future of China, Japan and Korea, nevertheless, featured on Britain's diplomatic agenda. Officials in Whitehall, particularly those in the Foreign Office's Far Eastern Department who were responsible for this area, were determined to have a say in planning for peace in the region. This formed part of a wider desire to help preserve worldwide security and stability in order to derive commercial and financial benefits, and maintain equality with the United States *and* the Soviet Union ensuring Britain's continuing place in the top international pecking order. In short, a belief prevailed that Britain had a rightful role to play in the region's destiny. Influencing others to apply these criteria to East Asia was a different matter. Focused on the future of Europe, the Mediterranean, Middle East and Southeast Asia, the military and the Treasury, for example, baulked at the diversion of any resources to East Asia. Victor Cavendish-Bentinck, the ever-perceptive chairman of the JIC, argued that there was 'a general tendency' in the Foreign Office 'to urge that we should undertake military commitments far beyond our manpower or our future financial and material resources'.[1]

By 1945, senior Foreign Office officials conceded Britain would not be able to play more than a token role in post-war East Asia. Ministers therefore had to assess whether Britain's exclusion would affect its global security or damage its future relations with the United States and the Soviet Union. The costs of planning for an active British involvement in East Asia were clearly far too high and unnecessary, particularly as a friendly power, the United States, took the lead in the region, a state of affairs Churchill happily conceded. Yet why did Britain not decide to withdraw completely from its international responsibilities in an area that was such a low priority? One theme that consistently emerged was the opinion that Britain, a world power and force for good, must live up to *all* its international responsibilities however small and its expertise or say on East Asian affairs was necessary for the region's development. The British voice in East Asia, nevertheless, was rarely consulted and sometimes deliberately excluded by the emerging superpowers, which called into question Britain's continuing need to play an international role in the region.

The post-war planning apparatus

The Burma, Colonial and War Offices had carried out post-war planning for the future of British possessions in Southeast Asia in great detail soon after Japanese victories in 1941–2, but in 1944 there was no apparatus in place for a more systematic co-ordination of policies within Whitehall. Wider issues, such as US attitudes and policy, the views of Australia and New Zealand, the future of British India, and the position of other European colonial powers in the Far East (France and the Netherlands), suggested the desirability of a co-ordinating body,[2] a point made by Sterndale Bennett in August 1944. His accepted recommendation was the reconstitution of the cabinet's Far Eastern Committee, in abeyance since the Japanese attacks, hitherto turned down by Sir Edward Bridges, the cabinet secretary, on the rather spurious grounds that its absence had not led to any inconvenience.[3]

Progress was slow. Sterndale Bennett worried that everyone was going to wind down after Germany's defeat, also telling Dening that the number of people who understood or took an interest in the Far East was limited. The Far Eastern Committee would not convene its first meeting until November. It aimed above all to 'bring about the greatest possible degree of co-operation with the United States'.[4] Sterndale Bennett was forced to admit, however, in December and again in June 1945 that his department was barely 'scratching the surface' on post-war Far Eastern problems, dealing with questions 'from hand to mouth' and forced to react to US policy, foreclosing detailed consultation with the dominions and creating the danger that 'we may blunder into trouble'.[5] Detailed post-war thinking about China, Japan or Korea was non-existent.

In contrast, research sections within the State Department in Washington had been examining East Asian problems since 1942 and systemised them in October 1943 with the creation of the inter-divisional area committee for the Far East under the chairmanship of the Far Eastern specialist and academic, Dr George Blakeslee. In January 1944, a Post-War Programs Committee was set up to assist the secretary of state in formulating post-war policy but there was no guarantee that any of their recommendations would become accepted policy, especially as Roosevelt tended to make decisions without consulting Hull. There was also scant co-ordination with other departments, such as the Navy and War Departments. This was rectified by the creation of the State-War-Navy Co-ordinating Committee (SWNCC) in December and its sub-committee for the Far East established in January 1945, with the latter told to prepare policy papers for Japan and Korea.[6] Stimson hoped SWNCC might bring order to the 'chaotic situation' in Washington as Roosevelt's health declined but the president still ignored the body as he proceeded to Yalta.[7] It was unsurprising then that Joseph Grew, the assistant secretary of state, turned down a Foreign Office approach in January to discuss Far Eastern questions at the departmental level.[8]

The approach by Nevile Butler, the superintending under-secretary for the Far Eastern Department, had been instigated by a desire to deny rumours the British and Dutch were secretly reaching understandings on political, economic and security questions in Southeast Asia.[9] There is truth in the assertion that the United States was reluctant to enter into post-war talks on the Far East with an 'imperialist' power such as Britain, but one wonders what the Americans would have made of Sterndale Bennett's remark that Britain should simply aim to recover its territories, beat the Japanese and build a better world: 'I do not see that we need hesitate to proclaim the programme to the Americans or despair of co-operating with them on the basis of it.'[10] It was not a sound foundation for conversing seriously with State Department and they were justified in telling the Foreign Office that it was 'hardly worth talking' as British post-war planning was so far behind their own. British diplomats only became suspicious when in the same breath the State Department claimed they were 'not ready to talk'.[11] Throughout 1945, British approaches were continuously rebuffed and, in July, Byrnes made it clear he wanted to 'defer' any conversation with the British on the Far East until he was 'more familiar' with the issues.[12]

Post-war planning on both sides of the Atlantic suffered from the fact that Anglo-American leaders were engrossed in trying to win the war, which made it difficult to elicit any clear views on the future. Cadogan's diary demonstrates his exasperation with Churchill and the cabinet on such matters as a world organisation, none of whom, he noted, knew what was wanted from such a body.[13] After reading a paper by the ineffective Post-Hostilities Planning Committee, even Cadogan thought it was 'a waste of time and manpower' to make assumptions about Britain's post-war rights and obligations in the Far East.[14] Ismay similarly presumed that committees analysing how to win the peace, and thereafter organising the British Commonwealth, Europe and the world, were dealing with problems 'so nebulous and complicated as to be almost insoluble'. As far as the armed services were concerned, he wrote, 'all the better brains are required to deal with our immediate affairs, and the post-war problems have perforce to be left to lesser lights, who are long past their best'.[15] The situation was slightly different at the Foreign Office where the intellectually self-assured Gladwyn Jebb, the head of the Economic and Reconstruction Department, was put in charge of overall post-war planning, although even here the Far East took a back seat until the necessary staff could be assembled after the end of war in Europe.

It was therefore left to semi-official bodies such as Royal Institute of International Affairs (Chatham House) and Britain's leading academics to articulate

British thought on post-war East Asia. Chatham House did consider Japan's future during the war but its focus was mainly on Southeast Asia. The Foreign Office kept its distance when a Chatham House publication was leaked in 1945, calling for the retention of the Japanese emperor. Although sympathetic, the Foreign Office could not be seen publicly backing such a recommendation when prevailing US opinion called for a harsh peace. Inside the Foreign Office, nevertheless, academics gathered in the Research Department, headed by the historian Arnold Toynbee, and included Charles Webster, the Stevenson professor of international history at the London School of Economics, and the Far Eastern specialist Geoffrey Hudson, a fellow of All Souls' College, Oxford. In Washington, Sir George Sansom, the respected Japanese scholar and diplomatist, who acted as Halifax's principal adviser on the Far East, also led discussions on post-war Japan. These individuals attempted to move the agenda forward on Japan and Korea and, to a lesser extent, China, hoping to encourage senior British figures into considering Britain's future in East Asia.[16]

Planning for post-war China

Wartime relations between Chiang Kai-shek (Jiang Jieshi), the Chinese Nationalist leader and supreme commander of the China theatre, and Churchill were poor. Chiang's visit to British India in 1942 set the tone. He made clear his preference for nationalist leaders rather than his colonial hosts and deplored the debacle that had befallen British forces at the hands of the Japanese, informing Churchill personally of his shock at the military and political situation in India.[17] The British view of Chiang was equally disparaging. They saw his régime as corrupt and were dismayed by the performance of the Nationalist army against the Japanese. Chiang's grip on the whole of China was partial at best, forced by Japanese invasion to relocate his capital from Nanking (Nanjing) to Chungking (Chongqing), deep in the interior. Catastrophic economic policies, bickering warlords and a rival Communist movement led by Mao Tse-tung (Mao Zedong), based at Yenan (Yan'an) in the northern province of Shensi (Shaanxi), all plagued Chiang's regime and served continually to undermine the stability of China.[18] Chiang reminded Brooke of a 'ferret', who he thought had 'uncommonly little' to contribute to the defeat of Japan. Churchill dismissed out of hand Roosevelt's assertion that China was a 'world power' calling the idea 'an absolute farce'. Stalin was equally unconvinced that China could act as one of the 'four policemen' in the post-war world.[19]

Roosevelt's vision, however, was set for the long term, a point Churchill and Stalin failed to grasp. The president recognised Chiang's foibles and the limited military role he could play, especially after the successful Japanese *Ichigo* offensive launched in April 1944, which nearly cut China in half. The offensive threatened Chungking and by the end of the year saw the removal of Nationalist Chinese divisions and US transport aircraft from SEAC, just at a time when the British were on the offensive in Burma. The decision dealt a further blow to both Anglo-Chinese and Anglo-American relations, the British furious at the diversion of resources at such a critical time, and confirming in Dening's mind the indifference of the United States towards SEAC, which he argued they considered the 'unnecessary front'. Whatever Dening's accusations about the US infatuation with China, the Americans still aimed to minimise their commitments there, keep China in the war and tie down Japanese forces. The Americans even flirted with aiding Mao in late 1944 and early 1945 in order to fulfil such objectives. The Nationalist Chinese were certainly not the recipients of 'lavish' US aid as Churchill rather erroneously suggested in the House of Commons.[20]

Churchill's attitude towards China, which reminded his physician Lord Moran that he was 'a Victorian', left officials in no doubt that Britain should reclaim Hong Kong and try to replay its pre-war commercial role in China.[21] In 1944, old China hands like Alwyne Ogden, the consul-general at Kunming, were even convinced that the 'surrender' of extraterritoriality in 1943 meant little, as before the war concessions, for all practical purposes, existed only at Shanghai and Tientsin (Tianjin). Called back to London for consultations with the government and merchants, Ogden, though, did not pretend that post-war political and financial chaos might make conditions initially unfavourable for trade. In addition, Japanese-held British internees (over 6,000 were interned or imprisoned in Shanghai) were likely to be in poor health, unable to immediately undertake active work. Ogden thought it unfortunate that China had been earmarked a US sphere for war purposes, as the Chinese only saw US forces, while Britain's former concessions would fall under US and Nationalist Chinese control. Ogden nevertheless tried to remain upbeat. He wrote a widely circulated paper arguing that Britain could re-build its former position in China by virtue of ownership of land and buildings at all important trading centres; the British community with its expert knowledge and relations with the local Chinese traders; and goodwill and cultural factors built up over a century of trading.[22] Seymour embraced these conclusions and he felt that in whatever state China emerged from the war, British trade 'on a valuable scale' was still possible. This was not to say Seymour did not hold his own doubts, especially over the impact of extraterritorial rights and how merchants might face a body of nationalistic legislation that could make international trade very difficult. Yet, his despatches back to London remained positive about the commercial role Britain could play in post-war China.[23]

Chinese xenophobia had certainly increased during the war and Sino-British diplomatic relations were strained by differences over Hong Kong, Tibet, the China–Burma border, overseas Chinese and the terms of a British loan to China.[24] Eden nonetheless was prepared to push for the return of British influence and trade in China as a counterbalance to the American influence over the Chinese Nationalists and wanted merchants competing on equal terms with US businessmen, so long as it avoided a 'selfish rivalry' with the United States.[25] The inevitable restriction on the grant of credits and other difficulties facing Britain's immediate post-war export trade would dictate whether such a policy was possible. That Britain and the United States were rivals as well as allies in China has also been well documented.[26] Apart from Roosevelt's desire to hand Hong Kong back to China, a consistent American rumour, particularly within their embassy at Chungking, was the belief Britain desired a weak and divided China in order to carry out 'imperial' designs. This was the reverse of US policy, which sought to work for a united, democratic China that would help maintain peace in East Asia. Although some Americans hoped this was not the official view of the British government, the US ambassador to China, Major-General Patrick Hurley, a right-wing Irish-American former secretary of war, continually expressed it.[27]

In January 1945, the Foreign Office did succeed in inserting into a statement made by Lord Cranborne, the Dominions Secretary, that the British desired a strong and reunited China. On the same day the announcement was made, one member of the British business community, who worked for the Special Operations Executive (SOE), the clandestine sabotage organisation, undermined it almost immediately. Working under the cover of the British embassy, John Keswick, a director of the trading company Jardine, Matheson & Co., spoke openly to an official at the US embassy about the emergence of a loosely federated China after the war and said that the US policy of trying to bring Mao and Chiang together to unite the country was 'unrealistic' if not 'unwise'. He corrected himself by declaring that the British did not want a weak and divided China, but the damage was done.[28] As one intelligence historian has remarked, SOE resembled 'empire trade in khaki': its head in the Far East, for example, was Colin Mackenzie, a director of J. & P. Coats Ltd., which had large regional textile interests. Throughout the war, the Foreign Office remained wary of SOE but the Colonial Office thought its sister department worried too much about the American anti-colonialist stance and encouraged the organisation, especially in its activities directed towards re-establishing the British position in Hong Kong. In China, SOE with its strong commercial make-up exploited banking and business contacts, indulging in black market currency, which provided foreign exchange for private and public organisations.[29]

The big companies that formed the core of the British business system in China had been well established during the era of 'high imperialism' before the First World War. They included Jardine, Matheson & Co., Butterfield & Swire, Sassoon (E.D.) & Co., the Hong Kong and Shanghai Banking Corporation (HSBC), the Chartered Bank of India, Australia and China, the Chinese Engineering and Mining Co. (the British partner in the Kailan Mining Administration), the Peking Syndicate and Unilever's China Soap Co., to name but a few. Evidence suggests, however, that from the 1920s these firms along with British multinationals such as the British-American Tobacco Corporation and Imperial Chemical Industries had begun to invest heavily in China, becoming more deeply entangled in indigenous commerce and politics. This meant that many firms were re-investing and distributing a large proportion of their profits back to China, instead of remitting them to Britain. Protecting and promoting the interests of the big commercial firms was the China Association, based in the City of London and established in 1889, with functions similar to those of a chamber of commerce. The Association would constantly urge the British government to do more in the way of helping to re-build the business community and promoting trade, which had been disrupted by war and now faced increasing US competition and Nationalist Chinese interference.[30]

The China Association's demands, which failed to recognise some of the emerging realities on the ground together with Britain's waning international position, were not without their supporters inside British official circles. Geoffrey Wallinger, Britain's minister at Chungking, Lieutenant-Colonel Gerald Wilkinson, SIS's former liaison with MacArthur now based in New York's British Security Co-ordination headed by William Stephenson, and Sir George Sansom, all encouraged Eden to believe that the British could compete with the Americans in China, particularly in export services such as business management, shipping, banking and insurance. It would be possible to rationalise Anglo-American co-operation by blending the United States' greater immediate financial and industrial potential with Britain's experience and established interests in the old Treaty ports such as docks, warehouses and banks. A 'healthy commercial rivalry' could exist as long as the United States did not take advantage of its position and tie up China with post-war contracts on a big scale, which might then provoke an 'embittered rivalry'. The charismatic Wilkinson, who had his own business interests in the Far East, argued that favourable taxation abroad, Treasury investment and a joint Anglo-American approach to the Chinese over economic matters were natural requirements for the success of this strategy.[31]

The Board of Trade and the cabinet's Far Eastern Economic Subcommittee peddled similar arguments and also called for the granting of credits to Nationalist China. In March 1945, Sterndale Bennett assimilated many of these recommendations into his own memorandum that he wished to put before ministers. It pushed for an active post-war British involvement in China. With the financial aid agreement of May 1944, Britain had already provided the Nationalist Chinese with a credit of £50 million, and Sterndale Bennett lobbied for its continuation after the war. Britain could also offer technical assistance and military training. It was hoped these policies would debunk the myth that the British were working against the US goal of building 'a strong, stable and friendly' China. Idealism apart, officials in the Far Eastern Department were also seeking to check an American monopoly of Chinese markets and to exercise greater influence within China.[32]

The memorandum instantly fell flat. The Treasury made it clear that there was 'no hope at all' of continuing the financial aid agreement after the war. The only reason why the British had been able to send supplies to China was due to lend-lease imports. How could Britain seek orders for China in competition with the United States, the Treasury argued, when they 'would take the line that we would be doing so at the expense of lend-lease'?[33] Edmund Hall-Patch, the pragmatic assistant under-secretary at the Foreign Office responsible for economic issues (who had both pre-war and wartime experience as a financial adviser on Far Eastern affairs), was more brutal. The paper should not be discussed at cabinet level, as there was little to debate: Britain's financial resources were 'desperately small for our great responsibilities' and could not be spared for a bankrupt China. His answer was for the post-war reconstruction of China to be carried out on a UN basis, which would remove the prospect of competition with the United States, especially as the British were in the middle of negotiating an American loan. Cavendish-Bentinck agreed, as did Anderson, the Chancellor of the Exchequer. Cavendish-Bentinck even went so far as to say China was 'not vital' to the British Empire and 'we can do without our China trade'.[34] Pre-war figures indicating that exports to China, including goods passing through Hong Kong, had not exceeded the 2 per cent mark of overall British exports, illustrated Cavendish-Bentinck's point.[35]

The effect of this backlash on Sterndale Bennett was evident when the latter met China Association officials in May. He told its chairman, W. B. Kennett, that the government would not send a commercial mission to China as the Association had urged. China was a US sphere and the British had to take into account American reactions and the probability they would exploit this position to advance their commercial interests. Britain, Sterndale Bennett argued, could not pursue an active policy in China or give the impression of 'putting one over' the Americans. Warren Swire, the vice-chairman, pressed Sterndale Bennett to start organising advance parties, in uniform if necessary, to travel with allied forces once they began re-occupying parts of China from the Japanese in order to secure British properties. The head of the Far Eastern Department replied that it was impossible to know in what circumstances Britain would get back to places such as Shanghai or what troops would be employed. Members of the China Association were immediately disturbed but Sterndale Bennett continually reiterated it would be a mistake for commercial concerns to anticipate that representatives would be allowed into Shanghai in the first stages of liberation solely for the purposes of securing the possession of property.[36]

The requests made by Warren Swire who, with his older half-brother, Jack, had overseen the considerable expansion of shipping in the family company John Swire and Sons Ltd., no doubt reflected some of the reports received from his employees on the ground in China. They reported US industrial salesman 'in and out of uniform' talking about 'firm finance and early large-scale delivery'. The Nationalist Chinese, one employee observed, turn first to the United States 'with an intact economy, not to Britain with a smashed one to repair'.[37] The one card the British aimed to use to redress this imbalance was the recapture of Hong Kong.[38] It provided, however, the background to an explosive exchange between Churchill and Hurley, the US ambassador to China, when the latter visited London in April. Sterndale Bennett told Ambassador Winant that he hoped the visit would be of 'real value' and 'greatly contribute towards bringing our policies in line with each other'.[39] He also impressed upon Robert Smyth who accompanied Hurley on his trip that he did not think the Americans kept the British sufficiently informed of their plans for China. Close collaboration particularly in the field of commercial relations was necessary, members of the Far Eastern Department argued, because of the poor treatment British and American businessmen might receive at the hands of the Nationalist Chinese.[40]

Hurley's visit, unfortunately, did little to soothe Anglo-American relations concerning China. Churchill noted that the ambassador tried to confine their conversation to 'civil banalities' but that he (Churchill) 'took him up with violence about Hong Kong and said that never would we yield an inch of the territory that was under the British Flag'. Churchill considered Hurley an 'old-world American figure' and rather naively wrote, 'I do not think any harm could have been done by my talk with him.' Hurley transcribed his conversation slightly differently, recording that Churchill exclaimed Hong Kong, contrary to Roosevelt's wish, would be taken from the British Empire 'only over my dead body!' and the long-term US policy for China was 'the great American illusion'. The statement tended to nullify Churchill's separate assurances that he would support the US effort to build a strong, democratic China and unify its armed forces.[41]

Sterndale Bennett tried to undo the damage by calling on Winant to put to the State Department the need for 'a free and frank exchange of views' on China and the Far East generally, particularly with regard to the civil re-occupation of Shanghai and a commercial treaty with China in the wake of extraterritoriality. The Americans stonewalled using the forthcoming San Francisco Conference (April–June 1945) on the UN as the reason for being unable to conduct the talks the British desired. Grew, however, was not entirely negative and argued that the State Department had discussed with British embassy officials problems relating to Shanghai and the U.S. draft of a commercial treaty, which had been presented to the Nationalist Chinese in April. With regard to the draft commercial treaty, Sterndale Bennett told Winant that he was 'frankly disappointed' as the discussions were 'very general'. He had been led to understand that there would be ample time to discuss the treaty properly before it was to be submitted, but he hoped the British could have more detailed talks before the treaty was signed.[42]

Winant and the State Department's Division of Commercial Policy did not foreclose the possibility of talks at the operating level especially as the latter recognised 'the economic and political situation in China will be chaotic and dangerous in the months to come', so that Britain and the United States must 'avoid working at cross purposes'. Despite this they recognised that the United States should not give Nationalist China or the Soviet Union the impression that the Anglo-American powers were working in concert against them and they would defer to higher advice.[43] Talks never took place, and in June, Truman afforded the British no prior consultation with Harry Hopkins on his presidential mission to Moscow, which aimed to discuss China, the Far East and European issues. Stalin accepted US leadership in China and indicated that the United States was the 'only power' with resources to aid Chiang who, regardless of his faults, he proposed to back. The visit deeply disturbed Churchill, unhappy at British exclusion.[44]

By July, Sterndale Bennett had reworked his earlier memorandum on China to reflect recent developments both at home and abroad. There were no recommendations that Britain should play any role in China's post-war reconstruction, compete with the United States or involve itself in China's civil war. He merely concluded that Britain's post-war policy should aim for the recovery of Hong Kong, the restoration of British property and equipment and the negotiation of a new commercial treaty with China's Nationalist government. Bevin signed off the paper without putting it to the cabinet.[45] On the ground, Major-General L. C. Hayes, in charge of Britain's military mission in Chungking, considered Britain was being 'pushed around' by the Americans, losing prestige daily. Quite simply, Hayes argued, as the US controlled supplies to China they also controlled Chinese policy, whether military, foreign or domestic.[46] Hurley, meanwhile, had been doing his best to tell Truman to adopt a firm policy towards Hong Kong, arguing the British would 'yield' if various items of lend-lease were withheld from them.[47] More realistically and fortunately for the British, SWNCC was adopting a slightly calmer attitude towards the British colony, suggesting that the United States should 'avoid involving itself' over Hong Kong.[48] Before the Japanese surrendered, however, an active British policy for China, and one in concert with the Americans, seemed an unlikely prospect.

Planning for Korea

Except for the period prior to and during the Russo-Japanese war of 1904–05, the British had not devoted much time to Korea. During the years 1935–39 the average annual exports from Britain to Korea had amounted to just £156,000 while imports from Korea to Britain peaked at £9,000.[49] Korea occupied a pre-eminent strategic position in relation to China and Japan. Once Japan had been defeated and its rule in Korea ended, it was likely that the latter would remain weak, dependent upon the protection of other powers for a considerable period. In March 1943, when Eden visited Washington,

Roosevelt raised Korea, intimating that it might be put under an international trusteeship. Eden did not disagree but privately held grave doubts about what the overall concept of trusteeship might mean for Britain's empire in the Far East. That October, Sansom suggested that the immediate post-war solution might be to allow the Koreans to take over the country at once, provided that 'allied' advisers could temporarily oversee and direct the administration. In conversation with Stanley Hornbeck, the Director of the Office of Far Eastern Affairs at the State Department, the latter did not disagree with Sansom's ideas but showed no eagerness for the United States to act as the mandatory power. Hornbeck thought the first difficulty would be to find amongst the Koreans now playing a political part in the United States and China, persons adequately qualified to carry out any sort of government.[50] British and American officials were also hamstrung by the fact that their knowledge of Korea was limited and all business connected to that country had been conducted through Japan.[51]

Beyond shared opposition to Japanese rule, popular Korean figures such as Dr Syngman Rhee, Kim Kyu-sik and Kim Ku had little in common with their leading Communist counterparts, Kim Il-sung and Pak Hon-yong. Disunity was also prevalent in both these opposing political blocs. Rhee had been a firm opponent of the Japanese and participated in the Korean government-in-exile at Shanghai, but later severed his ties with this organisation, spending a large proportion of his life in the United States where he gained a doctorate from Princeton University.[52] The Foreign Office, meanwhile, refused to recognise exile Korean bodies, such as Kim Ku's provisional government based in Chungking, doubting how genuinely representative it was, especially as it did not speak for the Koreans living in the Soviet Union, a number of whom had served in the Red Army.[53] Geoffrey Hudson argued that whereas the Korean groups in Chungking and the United States were 'merely exiles', the Soviet Union had a substantial resident Korean population (mainly in the Vladivostok area) numbered around 180,000. He felt that the question seemed to be not whether the Soviets would demand a large share in the administrative regulation of Korea, 'but whether they will be disposed to permit any other nation to have any say at all'.[54]

Recognising the potential for conflict, the United States aimed to seize the initiative. At the Cairo Conference in November 1943, Harriman drafted a memorandum for Roosevelt stating it would be prudent to agree to the independence of Korea under some type of trusteeship in which the great powers would participate. This proposal had the dual purpose of attempting to prevent any one power dominating Korea while allowing the politically divided Koreans time to create an independent state. The allied war aim of securing the unconditional surrender of Japan and its expulsion from territory acquired since 1895 led Churchill to subscribe to the Cairo Declaration of December 1943, pledging that the United States, Britain and China, 'mindful of the enslavement of the people of Korea', were 'determined that in due course Korea shall become free and independent'. This declaration would tie the British to the affairs of Korea for the next ten years. At the Tehran Conference, Stalin informed Churchill that he thoroughly approved of the Cairo Communiqué. It was right, Stalin cautiously stated, Korea should be independent but he said little else on the subject.[55]

Although Britain was a signatory to the Cairo Declaration, it was six months before the Foreign Office set up a committee to prepare a paper on the future of Korea. The committee, composed of experienced East Asian diplomats and research department officials, took another six months to draw up the paper.[56] In the State Department, Blakeslee's area committee had already arranged for an international controlling body including Britain, China, the United States and the Soviet Union to oversee Korean independence. It was a clear attempt to prevent Korea from becoming a major US responsibility.[57] At this point, however, there was no indication Britain would wish to provide personnel for such an enterprise. The area committee's paper was also far from being accepted as policy and throughout 1944 the subject remained in abeyance. In October, Harriman informed Stalin that the Joint Chiefs of Staff were not contemplating major land operations in Korea, encouraging Stalin to believe that his forces would play a major part in Korea's 'liberation'.[58]

The British were not privy to these discussions, which could have had an impact upon the course an occupation of Korea might take.[59] The Foreign Office committee tasked with analysing what form a post-war Korea might take finally issued its report in December 1944. Charles Webster explained to the Foreign Office they had no indication of US thinking on Korea but confidently, if not rather arrogantly, predicted they 'would very likely be influenced by anything we might be able to send them'.[60] The paper, which was entitled 'The Future of Korea', favoured some form of international tutelage to oversee Korea's independence as it would be initially beyond the Koreans to set up their own government due to the control Japan had imposed over the running of the country. The paper was sure that Nationalist China would be too weak to play a major role but recognised the potential for a conflict of interests as Korea flanked the approaches to Tientsin, Dairen and Vladivostok and was the closest point on the Asian mainland to Japan. Should Britain take part though? The memorandum argued:

This question will depend mainly on whether the United Kingdom is prepared to endeavour to maintain its former position as a Great Power with a major interest in the Far East. The settlement would be more likely to work and there would be less danger to the peace of the world if she took part in a régime in which the United States and the Soviet Union participated... It seems unlikely that the United States would not welcome British help in a situation in which difficulties with the Soviet Union are likely to occur.

The paper was adamant that Britain could not remain aloof.[61]

Korea, however, was not in the region of British responsibility as agreed with the Americans in spring 1942, and it was an area where Britain expected the United States to take the lead. As with China, Sterndale Bennett, agreeing with the paper's recommendations, still pushed for a British role in Korea. He minuted on 8 January that, 'if the post-war set-up is going to succeed this time, we shall not be able to adopt an "isolationist" policy towards any problem which may contain the seeds of international dispute'. This meant preventing Soviet 'annexation' if they entered the war and 'as we have committed ourselves to the independence of Korea' Britain had to see to it that independence was achieved. First, however, Sterndale Bennett wanted a decision from ministers.[62] As with China, his endorsement of the committee's paper was quickly rounded on, with the Economic and Reconstruction Department the most vociferous in its objections to a British role in Korea. Britain should 'keep out', let the Americans make the running and was in any case in no position to provide manpower for an administration (or occupation) of Korea. Gladwyn Jebb asserted that 'we should stop fussing' about post-war Korea. 'I don't really know,' he minuted, 'what particular British interest is served by getting ourselves involved in such a hornet's nest'.[63] Nevile Butler agreed but refused to draw back from taking no interest in Korea and wanted to wait to see if anything emerged at the forthcoming Yalta Conference.[64]

Webster was crestfallen that his paper was savaged,[65] but the errors in his assumptions about Britain's place in the world were made clear at Yalta. Here Roosevelt spoke in private with Stalin about Korea and deliberately excluded Churchill. On 8 February, Roosevelt put the idea of a trusteeship for Korea to the Soviet leader, arguing it might last up to 30 years. The trusteeship would comprise the United States, the Soviet Union and China, not Britain. The exclusion of the British, Roosevelt stated, might cause resentment and he sought Stalin's advice. Stalin replied that the British would most certainly be offended and argued that they should be invited, otherwise Churchill might 'kill us'.[66] Nothing was entered in the official record at Yalta and British ministers remained unaware of these discussions until after the war. Roosevelt knew that Churchill and Eden did not feel comfortable with the idea of trusteeship, as they feared it could be applied in turn to British colonial possessions. Stalin was also unenthusiastic about the idea of trusteeship and consented to it in an uncommitted way, aware that the Red Army might be in a position to fully occupy Korea but there is no evidence to suggest this was a clear Soviet aim.[67]

The British were again excluded from discussions about Korea when Hopkins travelled to Moscow in June where Stalin agreed that there should be a trusteeship for Korea. This time their discussions included Britain in the trusteeship.[68] At Potsdam, buoyed by news of the successful testing of the atomic bomb, Truman and Byrnes were reluctant to enter into details about the future of Korea in an attempt to limit the Soviet control of territory in Northeast Asia. Stalin did not force the issue as the Soviets had yet to enter the war against Japan, unwilling to jeopardise more important matters in Eastern Europe, US aid for Soviet post-war reconstruction or a possible place in the occupation of Japan.[69] Marshall also reiterated that the Americans did not contemplate mounting an offensive against Korea until well after the invasion of Japan, again indicating to Stalin that the Soviets might by then be in a favourable position on the Korean peninsula once they entered the conflict (estimated for August). British opposition to the concept of trusteeship was also growing when Churchill impatiently brushed aside proposals for such a scheme in the former Italian colonies of North Africa. An attempt by Stalin to turn the discussion to Korea was equally unsuccessful.[70] Before Japan surrendered, then, there was no British commitment to play a role in Korea nor had ministers expressed a desire to take part. Given the division of labour in the Far East this was understandable (it was an American area of responsibility) and despite British exclusion from the Soviet–American discussions about Korea, no core British interests had been affected.

Planning for an occupation of Japan

Preparations for the occupation of Japan were marked by confusion whereby both the British and the Americans did not understand each other's position but assumed they did. For the British, the 'Europe-first' strategy in terms of both wartime and post-war planning combined with the prolonged British debates over whether or not to take part in the invasion of Japan delayed serious planning for the post-war control of Japan until 1945. Some early thoughts on the future of Japan had appeared in a 1943 cabinet paper, when Eden outlined a security system for the Far East in a memorandum on organising the peace, the majority of it drafted by Webster. The paper presumed Japan would be deprived of its empire and the Japanese people would only be able to feed themselves if they were allowed to develop their imports and exports. In order to stop Japan building aggressive armaments again, its import of the necessary raw materials could be rationed by an international authority commanding wide control. To enforce this control, the allied nations could construct a defence system using air and naval bases in the Pacific and East Asia, rendering the need for a military occupation of Japan unnecessary.[71]

These thoughts on Japan, which had long been espoused by Sansom in unofficial bodies such as the Institute of Pacific Relations,[72] became the framework for Foreign Office thought but they remained rudimentary and when stated publicly reinforced the US conviction that Britain wanted a 'soft' peace for Japan. During 1944, in London, British views on the future of Japan were only recorded in minutes in reaction to US academic publications or provoked by 'poorly constructed' Post-Hostilities Planning Committee papers.[73] State Department thinking during 1944, meanwhile, remained fluid. Dr Hugh Borton, the Japan specialist in the Far East research group, drew up papers that included the retention of the Emperor. In this argument, Borton was encouraged by both Blakeslee and Sansom, his mentor. At the Post-War Programs Committee, senior officials would then either support or criticise the area committee's papers. For example, Hornbeck, distrustful of the Japanese, tended to favour harsh measures for Japan, whereas Grew, as a former ambassador in Tokyo, adopted a more accommodating outlook.[74] The question of the Emperor apart, State Department papers agreed that there was to be an occupation of Japan, its character predominantly American with little foreign participation and certainly no zonal divisions. When Japan had been disarmed, democratised and economically reformed, it could then rejoin the community of Far Eastern nations.[75]

That the Americans drew up detailed papers for the occupation of Japan was natural considering that the Pacific area was their, and not a British, responsibility. Unsurprisingly, Britain did not turn its attention to the future of Japan until 1945, when Sterndale Bennett produced a draft memorandum for the Official Committee on Armistice Terms and Civil Administration. The paper recognised a decision to help occupy Japan would be dictated by limitations of manpower, the remoteness of Japan, the nature of the Japanese people and the scarcity of allied personnel with knowledge of the country and language. The paper recommended, however, that the British Commonwealth should play its part to reflect its 'great war effort' and Britain's long-term political interests in the Far East.[76] The paper was sent to Major-General A. V. Anderson, the director of civil affairs at the War Office, who replied positively, noting that 'a purely American conquest of Japan would destroy the whole conception of the "United Nations" arrayed against the Japanese', which was an important factor 'likely to penetrate their Oriental minds'.[77] As with China and Korea, others immediately sought to question the whole idea.

Where were the British troops to come from? No direct provision had so far been made in the Chief of Staff's future manpower estimates for occupying Japan and SEAC might therefore have to be stripped of forces needed for mopping-up operations in Southeast Asia. The British also had commitments to post-war Germany, British India and the Middle East (their other direct responsibilities), while the United States, with its larger population, had no 'comparable' commitments.[78] Cavendish-Bentinck doubted whether very large forces would be required at all and he did not believe there would be available British manpower to 'permit us to take an appreciable part'. His apocalyptic vision for a defeated Japan was that:

> We shall find ourselves in possession of the Japanese islands in which all the cities will be rubble, ashes or charred skeletons of buildings, the shipping sunk, the railway transport completely out of action, with a

population that will be starving and with incipient epidemics. Whether this population will be cowed or whether they will give trouble to the occupying forces and attempt to avoid control only a Japanese expert could foretell. Personally I suspect that being tough, deceitful and vicious many of them will give trouble, though this trouble could probably be dealt with by comparatively small forces if stern measures are adopted.[79]

Once again the British stepped back from disengaging completely although a revised version of Sterndale Bennett's paper stressed it might be necessary to limit physical occupation to a minimum. The revised paper argued that the occupation and control of Japan was 'bound to be a difficult and thankless task' and US public opinion might not tolerate large numbers of US troops being stationed in Japan indefinitely. There was therefore no reason to suppose that the United States would wish to oppose British participation. Yet the paper was forced to concede that Britain had no clear idea of American intentions regarding the treatment of a conquered Japan.[80]

Some of these British assertions resonated with the Americans. That same month (April), the State Department saw little point in shutting the allies completely out of any control of Japan, otherwise the Americans alone would be forced 'to bear whatever cost, effort and responsibility were necessary for such control – a condition which the American people might support only grudgingly'. The Japanese also had to realise that 'the greater part of the world, both Occidental and Oriental, is against them'. As a result SWNCC had recommended the need for a Far Eastern Advisory Commission, which would ensure the coordination of policies after Japan's surrender. Initially this body would include only the United States, Britain, China, and (if it entered the war) the Soviet Union, with other interested powers (such as Australia) being invited on request.[81] Admiral King and the Navy Department, however, disapproved of the whole concept suggesting it 'inadvisable' to bring China or Britain into the planning for the occupation, 'since this will result in demands to take part in operational planning', which King violently opposed. He wanted Navy Secretary James Forrestal to recommend SWNCC to develop plans for the control of Japan 'on the basis that the United States will play the sole or leading role in the matter'. 'When the situation is clearer' other powers could be invited to take part in the surrender.[82]

Before Roosevelt's death, there was no firm decision on the policy to be pursued for post-surrender Japan. Many were in the dark over what had passed at Yalta while rumours were also floating around that Treasury Secretary Henry Morgenthau, the president's friend, who took charge of post-war planning for Germany through his Informal Policy Committee on Germany, was about to turn his hand to Japan. Morgenthau's committee had recommended for Germany the elimination of its central government, the dismantling of heavy industry and zonal divisions.

Roosevelt approved a directive for post-war Germany based on this policy, which moved SWNCC's subcommittee on the Far East to quickly lay down a paper for the control of Japan that recommended an American supreme commander, no zonal divisions, Japan's complete disarmament, democratisation, economic reform, which did not include the dismantling of heavy industry, and the utilisation of a Japanese government.[83] On 12 April, Roosevelt died and Morgenthau's influence evaporated but a policy for Japan still lacked any presidential authority, a fact one member of SWNCC was apt to point out.[84]

Roosevelt's death immediately spurred the Chiefs of Staff to ask their US counterparts for their views on the occupation of Japan,[85] and Sterndale Bennett now sought to 'get to grips' with problems arising out of the defeat of Japan and put papers before cabinet planning committees.[86] Cadogan's deputy, Sir Orme 'Moley' Sargent, still, nevertheless, questioned the desirability of using any British soldiers for an occupation of Japan and first sought the advice of ministers. Sterndale Bennett disagreed with his master, arguing that non-participation would affect Britain's whole position in the Far East and the world if it stood aloof from the arrangements for 'keeping Japan down'. Although he recognised that the United States 'may be keeping us at arm's length at present in regard to the Pacific war and the ultimate settlement of it', he was sure that they would welcome British participation in the control of Japan.[87] The bad news for Sterndale Bennett was that the State Department were unwilling to discuss detailed planning until Britain had gone through the same process. This attitude led Churchill to approve the study of problems for the occupation of Japan before American views crystallised.[88]

The day before Churchill's agreement, the crystallisation of US policy was indeed taking place and moving towards a harsh peace for Japan. The State Department told Halifax on 29 May that they were not aware of any intention on the part of the United States to invite other powers to participate in the control of Japan, an argument that now resembled Navy Department thinking. Even if a Far Eastern Advisory Commission was created, the State Department contended that it would only serve as a guide for the supreme allied commander in occupied Japan. The argument that the United States should control Japan was unsurprising given its effort in the Pacific war and by the fact Japan remained a US responsibility. What worried the British more was when Grew showed Sansom a draft paper setting forth US policy for the control of Japan. It argued that a supreme allied commander (American) should exercise complete authority over all Japanese affairs, including the break-up of the monopolies of the great corporations, known as the *Zaibatsu*; and the suspension of the constitutional powers of the Emperor and all organs of policymaking, which would be assumed by a military government.[89]

The British reaction was hostile, unwilling to believe that the Americans had counted the cost of a protracted total occupation of Japan combined with all the assumptions of government. The Japanese were a 'proud, stubborn race' that had not known any foreign control since the beginning of their history, and the British therefore considered the Americans would need to deploy substantial forces to make the enterprise a success.[90] The somewhat harsh tone of the draft American paper is interesting given the visit of Grew, in charge of the State Department due to Stettinius's absence at San Francisco, to Truman on 28 May urging the president to moderate the terms with regard to protecting the position of the Emperor in order to trump Soviet gains in Northeast Asia and speed up Japan's surrender. In fact, Grew, in the strictest confidence, did tell Sansom about his desire to retain the Emperor but his attempts to persuade Truman to revise the Yalta accords failed, even though Washington was looking at ways to limit the impact of Soviet entry into the conflict. The latter consideration also goes someway to explaining the US desire to stake firm control over Japan after its defeat.[91]

The arrival of the draft American document forced the Foreign Office to prepare hurriedly a British paper on policy towards Japan. Sansom with the help of Dening (both in London) formulated the paper, which diverged little from Eden's 1943 cabinet memorandum. It dismissed the need for a protracted occupation and argued against the dismantling of industries, as a large proportion of the entire urban population of Japan, up to half of the total of 76 million, would be unemployed and inadequately fed if not starving. Such conditions were not likely to favour the evolution of a democratic type of government in Japan. Sansom favoured instead the institution of economic controls and the necessity of working through the constitutional powers of the Emperor. Japan could not survive without the ability to trade and economic controls could therefore induce the Japanese to introduce their own reforms, ensuring future good behaviour.[92] Dening informally passed these preliminary views but not those about the Emperor (a politically charged subject) to the US embassy in London, and also told the latter that planning for the Far East was in full swing both at the inter-departmental and at the ministerial level, an attempt no doubt to convince them that the British could now confidently converse with them.[93]

Sansom's ideas produced what turned out to be the only dedicated British wartime paper on the occupation of Japan. The Foreign Office was particularly dependent on his expertise and Sterndale Bennett was clear that Sansom had 'unrivalled knowledge and prestige' both in Britain and in the United States. The problem was that Sansom's experience of Japan and his criticisms of US policies permeated throughout the Foreign Office, leading them to adopt an overly negative outlook. As one commentator notes, Sansom was an 'old Tory' yet 'New Deal conceptions of active government and social engineering' dominated US plans for the occupation. Sansom remained opposed to ideas of radical reform.[94] With the absence of any formal consultation with the United States on Far Eastern matters, Anglo-American policies deviated. The State Department, with little evidence, confidently assumed that the British government would 'probably go along' with their policies as British sentiment was 'neither unanimous nor so strong as American opinion'.[95] The Chinese Nationalists also wanted severe economic measures against Japan while hoping to rebuild a Sino-Japanese relationship on terms favourable to the Chinese. A majority in Australia and New Zealand too wanted Japan dealt with ruthlessly. Whatever the views of others, however, the United States still appeared reluctant to divulge its detailed plans to allies.[96] And, despite the need to pay attention to allied consultation or their possible participation in an occupied Japan, SWNCC was sure the United States 'should insist on the control of the implementation' of those policies.[97]

On 4 July, the day that Churchill authorised British participation in *Coronet* (the attack on Honshu), Sterndale Bennett wrote to Major-General Leslie Hollis, secretary to the Chiefs of Staff Committee, suggesting that it now rested with the Chiefs of Staff and the Foreign Office to agree on the best way to proceed. First he proposed that Halifax put Sansom's views formally to the State Department and second that papers should be prepared for the Far Eastern Committee. The Chiefs of Staff agreed to these proposals on 12 July and for Eden to inform cabinet.[98] The passing of Sansom's views to the State Department, however, was held up, as the foreign secretary (at Potsdam) was not familiar with the subject owing to recent illness and absence.[99] Eden was particularly worried about the British position on the Emperor: 'I do not want us to recommend to the Americans that the Emperor should be preserved. They would no doubt like to get such advice, then say they had reluctantly concurred with us.' Reports in the American press had already alleged that there was British agitation to modify the surrender terms.[100] In June, Stalin also told Hopkins that he had heard rumours (completely false) of talks between the British and Japanese regarding conditional surrender. A prolongation of the war suited the Soviet leader's agenda in order to secure his gains at Yalta.[101]

The British, including Churchill who raised the matter at Yalta, had begun to question the desirability of demanding the unconditional surrender of Japan.[102] They felt the suspension of the Emperor's powers – 'the most abject humiliation' – implicit in the term unconditional surrender, would delay the war unnecessarily.[103] Senior Japanese ministers and officials who sought ways to end the war were indeed concerned about the price of surrender and in particular the future of the Imperial system.[104] US officials such as Stimson and Grew also believed that the preservation of the Emperor could save thousands of American lives. Yet Byrnes, a long-time leader in Congress, was convinced that a public retreat from unconditional surrender could have devastating consequences for Truman, since the vast majority of American opinion was still opposed to the retention of the Emperor.[105] At Potsdam, although Churchill, at the behest of Ismay and the Joint Chiefs of Staff, suggested that unconditional surrender might be expressed 'in some other way', he did not go into details.[106] On both sides the consensus was to say nothing publicly about the future of the Emperor despite a recognition that the latter could better command troops to lay down their arms in outlying areas. The British therefore did not push for the imperial system to be preserved in the text of the joint declaration to be issued to the Japanese and Sansom's paper was modified to suggest that the allies, instead of assuming functions of government, should 'work through a Japanese administration'.[107] In early August, Sansom's ideas, which did not contain dominion views, were finally handed to the State Department,[108] but Britain's views remained rudimentary and there was trouble looming with Australia who advocated a stern occupation and expected to play a full part in it.[109] Six days before the end of the war, Bevin was forced to tell the cabinet that Britain did not have a substantial policy for post-surrender Japan.[110]

By the time of Japan's defeat in August 1945, British involvement in the affairs of China, Japan and Korea looked uncertain and even unnecessary. The area was a US responsibility and the Americans dictated the tempo of considering whether the British should play a role in the region. Ministers approved investigating ways of maintaining a regional British presence, reflecting their long-held views of Britain's place among world powers of the first rank, but their input into post-war planning for East Asia was minimal. It was left to the Far Eastern Department to take up the charge. Essentially, it fought a losing battle to maintain a strong British voice in the post-war affairs of China, Korea and Japan, where the United States and the Soviet Union consulted each other, excluding Britain. Britain's poor manpower situation and economic troubles clearly precluded the adoption of a proactive role in East Asia. The difficulty for some old China hands and Far Eastern Department personnel, in particular, was an inability to recognise that events on the ground had changed irretrievably and that the United States would not necessarily be particularly interested in what the British had to say. Britain's previous experience and position in East Asia held little sway and it was time to assess the continuing need for the British to play an active international role in the region.

3
Japan Surrenders

The two weeks from Japan's acceptance of surrender terms on 15 August to their formal signing in Tokyo Bay on 2 September saw each great power set out to secure its key interests in the Far East and the Pacific. The division of labour between Britain and the United States left the latter responsible for the Pacific and Northeast Asia and the former for Southeast Asia, while Chiang Kai-shek remained in charge of the China Theatre. The arrival of the Soviet Union into parts of Northeast Asia, however, redrew these lines of responsibilities as Stalin sought to consolidate his gains agreed at Yalta, play a part in Korea's future and even attempt to lobby for a role in the occupation of Japan. Considering the Pacific its prime responsibility, the United States set out first to control Japan unilaterally, second, to fulfil its pledges made towards Korea and, third, to help Chiang disarm and repatriate Japanese soldiers from China but avoid involvement in fratricidal civil war. Britain's principal aim was to recover former colonial territory in Southeast Asia. The British also wanted to re-establish their rule over Hong Kong and help their communities in China's former treaty ports, play a role in the occupation of Japan and pave the way for the French and Dutch to return to their former colonial territories in the Far East.[1]

Within Britain's global policy, the Far East, nevertheless, remained a low priority, below that of Europe, the Middle East and the Mediterranean. The Attlee government also recognised that the Empire in the East would look very different to 1941, with British India and Burma clamouring for independence. First it was necessary to stabilise Southeast Asia, and for the immediate surrender period that meant the return of the British. The latter hoped peaceful rehabilitation would win the support of the local inhabitants and secure goods such as tin and rubber, which were an important source of dollars in the Empire. Mountbatten was charged with ensuring this smooth transition but apart from Burma he was denied a spectacular return as liberator. MacArthur's insistence on accepting the instrument of surrender in Tokyo first, further held up British forces and allowed nationalist fervour to build. The job of maintaining control was also made harder by SEAC's boundaries extending to the Dutch East Indies, Thailand, Borneo and French Indo-China south of the 16th parallel. The area covered 1.2 million square miles, had a population of 128 million and contained 750,000 Japanese soldiers waiting to be repatriated. These new commitments burdened Britain with restarting rice production in the principal exporting countries of Burma, Thailand and French Indo-China. This task was essential in order to avoid major outbreaks of famine and procure regional stability but SEAC had meagre resources with which to achieve its aim, especially when the Americans terminated their involvement in that command in October 1945.[2]

Inadequate shipping, food and numbers of personnel, combined with the problems of prisoners of war and Japanese repatriation, provided major logistical difficulties for SEAC at the start of its short post-war life. It was no surprise therefore that Britain was happy for the United States to take the lead in setting the policy agenda for China, Japan and Korea. A pertinent question was whether the British needed to play any role at all in these countries and, if they did, what benefits were expected. A reliance on US 'leadership' in the region was sensible given Britain's global commitments but it soon became apparent that the United States interpreted leadership as meaning exclusive control. It was an attitude that grated with the British but they were never prepared to force an open row with the Americans over East Asian issues, as they needed US help for reconstruction at home and support for their policies in Europe and the Middle East. Britain's acceptance of this position tended to infuriate its increasingly vociferous dominion, Australia. The latter, together with New Zealand, had signed an agreement in January 1944 demanding representation in any post-war settlement. Australia saw the Far East as essential to its security and, as a participant in the war against Japan, felt it had a right to a say in the region's future.[3] It was a stance that complicated not only Anglo-Australian dialogue but also Britain's relationship with the United States.

Staking claims

From the moment Japan indicated a willingness to surrender on 10 August, the United States moved to stamp its authority on controlling the surrender. Although Byrnes accepted a British suggestion the Emperor should not personally sign the surrender terms, he did not show them the final draft. This change in procedure displeased Chungking and Canberra, especially when the United States claimed that all the powers had agreed to the modification.[4] The Soviet Union, meanwhile, continued its offensive into Manchuria and Korea, and Molotov told Harriman that the Soviets should accept Japan's surrender jointly with the Americans. If Harriman did not like the suggestion, 'he knew what [text indecipherable] with it', Molotov exclaimed. Considering the late entry of Soviet forces into the war against Japan, Stalin was never likely to push the issue, and along with the British and Nationalist Chinese, he accepted MacArthur as the Supreme Commander Allied Powers (SCAP) on 12 August.[5] The following day the State Department apologised to the Foreign Office over the lack of formal consultation, using as an excuse their desire to prevent Soviet and Chinese comment on the surrender terms.[6] Pierson Dixon, Bevin's private secretary, saw the American handling of the affair as 'ill-judged' and 'hysterical' but 'characteristic of their healthy aggressive mood to wish to take the lead and be the spokesman'.[7] Cadogan realised that Britain 'must accept this, and if the Dominions complain we can say that we, too, were not consulted'.[8]

The British were more concerned with the early release of prisoners of war and the speedy reoccupation of colonial territory in Southeast Asia to prevent chaos. The Chiefs of Staff also wanted Mountbatten to secure Hong Kong, a key symbol of British power in the region. It was, in their opinion, 'highly important' for Britain to accept the surrender of Hong Kong and 'show the British flag in the main Chinese ports'.[9] The American General Order Number 1 issued upon the Japanese surrender refused to specify whether Hong Kong was 'within China' and Attlee immediately told Truman that the British were intending to re-establish their rule over the colony to which the president assented as long as the request was made through Chiang as the supreme commander for the China Theatre.[10] Chiang agreed to delegate his authority to a British commander but it cut little ice with Seymour who, relaying instructions from Bevin, told him categorically he had no powers to delegate: Britain would enter Hong Kong as a crown colony and receive the surrender on behalf of His Majesty The King. This attitude invoked protests from the Americans. General Albert Wedemeyer, the commander of US forces in China, told Seymour that Britain was 'setting a bad example to the Russians' while MacArthur claimed that the Chiefs of Staff had 'gone behind the backs of the Americans' and, with Mountbatten's pressure, were 'undermining his trust'.[11]

MacArthur's outburst was the result of British anger at his order to halt all plans to accept local Japanese surrenders until the main instrument of surrender had been signed in Tokyo on 2 September. MacArthur argued that local commanders would not surrender until they received instructions from the centre. Mountbatten's plans had been to land in Malaya on 24 August and Singapore from 28 to 31 August. Now, relieving the suffering of prisoners of war would be delayed, Mountbatten told the Chiefs of Staff and, he observed, in China, Wedemeyer was transporting Chiang's troops to North China while Soviet forces continued their operations in Manchuria, which was hardly in accordance with MacArthur's request.[12] Despite the latter telling Mountbatten 'to keep his pants on or he'll get us all into trouble', Dening was in a conspiratorial mood, convinced that the move was anti-British and that the order was to ensure MacArthur remained at the 'forefront of the stage'. Dening declared that the British should not wait but the Chiefs of Staff, wanting to avoid a blow up with the Americans, overruled him. The evasive and unhelpful attitude of the Japanese in Korea towards a group of US officers from the clandestine Office of Strategic Services (OSS), who flew to Seoul to ascertain the safety of prisoners of war, highlighted the potential for difficulties, forcing the mission to return. The British nevertheless ignored MacArthur's order with regard to Hong Kong and, on 30 August, a detachment of the British Pacific Fleet under Rear-Admiral Cecil Harcourt entered Victoria Harbour, three days before the formal surrender in Tokyo. The British were determined to avoid the humiliation of either Nationalist Chinese or American forces handing back the colony to them.[13]

The British had less room for manoeuvre within China itself. On 13 August, Bevin instructed Seymour to effect the immediate re-opening of the British consulate at Shanghai by approaching Chiang, seeing no reason 'to wait for the Americans to give us the lead in the matter'. Seymour was not so sure, especially as the US authorities at Chungking refused to accept any representatives, except key men for the rehabilitation of utilities and the evacuation of internees and prisoners. He suggested instead sending Alwyne Ogden to accompany an American representative being sent to Shanghai. The Foreign Office agreed but reminded Seymour that the British had over 7,000 civilian internees in China as against 800 Americans and 'our property and other interests in Shanghai and elsewhere are far more important than theirs'. Bevin therefore implored Seymour to secure authority for British civilian officials to proceed to Shanghai as 'essential personnel', along with commercial representatives who, it could be stated, would reinforce inadequate consular staff and not look after their own individual interests.[14] Ogden recalled the frosty reception he received from US embassy officials at Chungking in trying to secure their co-operation for landing facilities to reach Shanghai. Hurley refused to see Seymour and it was left to Lieutenant-General Sir Adrian Carton de Wiart, the prime minister's personal representative to Chiang (a hangover from Churchill's premiership), to call in a favour from the Generalissimo to allow the British to proceed.[15]

London's telegrams demonstrated a severe misunderstanding of conditions on the ground in China. Chungking was a very long distance away from the important centres; internal communications were scanty and primitive; and relief from the sea would not come rapidly. The possibilities of disease, starvation, looting, rioting and general chaos were, in the words of one British official, 'terrifying'.[16] Carton de Wiart also told Ismay that he did not see how civil war could be avoided.[17] The British were completely dependent upon American and Nationalist Chinese acquiescence over the moves they wished to make. On 24 August, Seymour informed London word had already leaked out that Britain intended to appoint businessmen as vice-consuls at Shanghai, and that the proposed scheme to send commercial representatives would backfire. London backed down on this issue but remained defiant, instructing Seymour to tell the

Nationalist Chinese (extraterritoriality notwithstanding) that they expected British properties and rights in all the former treaty ports to be respected. Bevin also remained convinced that the Americans would have 'no hesitation' in introducing their own businessmen under military cover. Yet the Americans, under-resourced themselves, had no such plans for the re-entry of consuls or businessmen into Shanghai and other ports until after Japan's formal surrender.[18]

One reason for the prickly British attitude towards Hong Kong and other former treaty ports was sparked by events in northern China, where the Soviets began to secure their objectives, moving into Dairen and Port Arthur, on 22–23 August. It had been agreed in the 30-year Sino-Soviet Treaty of 14 August that Port Arthur would be 'jointly' administered and half of the port of Dairen leased to the Soviet Union free of charge. These concessions, along with the joint control of the Manchurian railroads and the recognition of Outer Mongolia after a plebiscite, were reluctantly traded in return for Stalin's assurances that he would only recognise the Nationalists as the government of China and respect their 'full sovereignty' over Manchuria. For Stalin, the treaty legitimised the secret Yalta protocols, while for Chiang, faced with Stalin's threat that the Chinese Communists would 'get into Manchuria', the deal could prevent outright collaboration between Mao and the Soviet leader.[19] Unsure of Stalin's intentions, the United States decided to despatch two Marine divisions to northern China to help Chiang's troops disarm and repatriate the Japanese. A strong US presence could also detect any development of a closed Communist *bloc* forming in the area, preclude a Chiang-Stalin understanding at the expense of the United States and prevent the 'loss of advantages' the latter now enjoyed in the Far East.[20]

Complementing this approach, Hurley urged Chiang to invite Mao to Chungking to 'discuss state affairs'. The British had long ruled out any desire to involve themselves in internal Chinese politics, but Stalin forced a reluctant Mao to accept Chiang's offer in the belief that he had little chance of achieving power. Stalin's first priority was always to secure Manchuria as part of his Far Eastern security belt, whether through talks with the Chinese Nationalists on 'economic co-operation', the encouragement of looting, curtailing Mao's room for manoeuvre or by using the latter to screen the advance of Soviet forces into the region.[21] Although Wedemeyer spoke in dark terms about the turn of events in China, his requests for General Order Number 1 to be amended to allow Chiang and not the Soviet Union, whom he was convinced would collaborate with Mao, to take Japanese surrenders in Manchuria and for his theatre to receive the first priority on American divisions, both received refusals. 'The prompt occupation of Japan', MacArthur told Washington, 'is paramount', with the occupation of Korea receiving second priority and China third.[22] In fact, the Americans were careful not to clash with the Soviets in areas they did not deem vital and pulled back from sending forces to Dairen once the Soviets arrived there while also allowing them to occupy all the Kurile Islands. Truman was not, however, prepared to entertain Stalin's demand for a zone of occupation in northern Hokkaido, part of Japan proper.[23]

During the three-week period of Japan's surrender, the United States made it clear they were less than willing to contemplate the arrival of other powers in the control of Japan. The Americans immediately tried to lessen the impact that proposed bodies such as a Far Eastern Advisory Commission or a five-power control council (a British suggestion to accommodate Australia) would have on the direction of MacArthur's ability to carry out his directives. The Americans even alleged Britain agreed at Potsdam to no control commission for Japan, a claim Churchill flatly denied.[24] The Americans, unwilling to bend, argued that a control council must be discussed through the advisory commission. Their aim was to maintain control under one commander throughout the occupation in what was deemed a primary US interest.[25] Britain had no interest in openly challenging these American desires and was also prepared to accept the US suggestion that only the four powers – Nationalist China, Britain, the United States and the Soviet Union – should sign the instrument of surrender at Tokyo Bay. The Americans presumed Admiral Fraser could accept the surrender on behalf of the dominions.[26]

The last proposal was totally unacceptable to the Australians, especially the irascible Dr Herbert Evatt, their minister for external affairs, and they insisted on taking full part in the signing of the surrender terms. The period of the Japanese surrender was a fraught time for Anglo-Australian relations, as Australia demanded independent participation in international councils and a separate voice on Far Eastern affairs, with the frequent accusation that Britain was not doing enough to support them in their aspirations. Yet, as Attlee tried to explain to Chifley, this was not 'a matter which we ourselves can decide alone. All we can do is to support and press Australia's claims.'[27] Australian pressure did meet with some success and Truman reversed the initial decision to restrict the signing of the terms to surrender to the four powers by also inviting Australia, New Zealand, Canada, France and the Netherlands to be present.[28] There was no consultation, however, over the actual terms of the surrender and the British had fared little better on this score either. The Australian determination to have a significant say on the proposed control bodies for Japan also made no progress and again the British were likewise not achieving much. As Australian complaints began to mount, some of them in public, resentment among British ministers increased, forcing Attlee to reject out of hand the assertion that Britain was not doing enough to secure Australia's right to be consulted in all Far Eastern matters.[29]

A major Anglo-Australian spat occurred over the formation of an occupation force for Japan. Britain aimed to take part in the occupation of Japan with a Commonwealth force including contingents from Australia, New Zealand, British India and Canada, which the Joint Chiefs of Staff accepted in principle on 17 August. A lack of shipping meant that the estimated arrival of the force of five brigades (one from each country) would be 'substantially' delayed.[30] Trouble brewed when the British proposed that the Commonwealth force should be under their command. The Australians, however, wanted to send a separate force under their control responsible only to MacArthur.[31] The Chiefs of Staff were furious, strongly favouring a unified force, willing only to accept that the inter-service commander-in-chief could be an Australian responsible to the British and Australian governments. Sir John Stephenson, assistant under-secretary at the Dominions Office, doubted if the Australians in their present 'somewhat truculent mood' would accept such an offer.[32] Stephenson was right and one day before Japan's formal surrender, Attlee was urging Chifley to sign up to a joint Commonwealth force under Australian command, convinced that this would 'carry much more weight' with the United States. Yet Attlee was forced to confess that he did not know what the Americans expected from such a force or the role they had in mind for them. As MacArthur was planning on the arrival of up to 16 American divisions, a Commonwealth force amounting to a handful of brigades suggested that the British (and Australian) role would be limited, and if anything, unnecessary.[33]

The British were much less equivocal about their ability to provide forces for an occupation of Korea. General Order Number 1 specified Korea would be split along the 38th parallel, with US responsibility south of that line and Soviet responsibility north of it. The Joint Chiefs of Staff argued that this secured Seoul, and 'a sufficient portion' of Korea, so that parts of it might be reserved for Britain and Nationalist China if a quadripartite administration 'eventuates'.[34] When the Joint Chiefs then asked the Chiefs of Staff to 'furnish their views' concerning forces for Korea in line with the agreements reached at Yalta for quadripartite trusteeship for that area, the British had no idea what they were talking about. Churchill even told Attlee that there was 'no foundation' for these statements, unwilling to believe that Roosevelt had never mentioned them to him. Whatever the truth, the British made it clear they had 'no military interests' and that such a provision would be 'an embarrassment'.[35] Stalin, meanwhile, was prepared to accept the 38th parallel: he could have possibly faced Japanese resistance and Korea was low on his list of priorities anyhow. MacArthur allocated two divisions for the peninsula to arrive after the formal surrender of Japan.[36] SWNCC therefore laid down (in the absence also of Nationalist Chinese forces) that the initial occupation would be by American–Soviet forces but it worried MacArthur was likely to face trouble from the latter and by the fact that the 38th parallel was not a natural geographical, economic or political subdivision of Korea.[37]

Priorities in the post-war world

Britain emerged from the war bankrupt, yet a victorious ally with its military intact and in possession of one of the largest empires in the world. Despite a dependency on US financial help, which abruptly came to a halt with the termination of lend-lease on 21 August, slowing economic growth rates and an awareness of the rise in Asian nationalism that threatened much of the Empire, it was difficult for many to accept that Britain's place in the world had changed. Britain's commercial and financial reach remained truly global and half the world's transactions were in sterling. As one scholar argues, the British people, known for their 'pragmatism and gradual political evolution', would find it difficult to kick the habit of 'Great Powerhood'.[38] Jock Balfour, Britain's minister in Washington, remarked that although a 'concept' had developed in the United States, which saw Britain occupying a position on the world stage 'inferior' to both them and the Soviet Union, he was confident that the Americans had not written off their ally.[39] The United States, 'without necessarily knowing it', was also 'bound to see the world in large measure through the British window', the Foreign Office argued, while US strategic power depended on the resources and the geographical distribution of the British Commonwealth. Britain could utilise its world influence as a 'third force', through a British-led Western European bloc that would maintain equality with both the United States and the Soviet Union.[40] They were conclusions that the politically skilful Bevin embraced and he would strike up a strong bond with his Foreign Office officials.[41]

This view of Britain's place in the world had to contend with the imposing Hugh Dalton who, as Chancellor of the Exchequer, sought rapidly to demobilise the armed forces and reduce overseas expenditure. Dalton recruited the economist Lord Keynes to explain the potential 'financial Dunkirk' that faced Britain with deficits rising to £1700m between 1946 and 1949.[42] Yet, it was difficult for many to accept hardship and the Chiefs of Staff, for example, in the 'afterglow of victory', were not ready to back policies that liquidated British commitments across the globe.[43] The United States, too, fully expected Britain to play a prominent global role but the State Department and the Joint Chiefs of Staff initially overestimated British capabilities.[44] Lingering isolationism among US public opinion and in Congress, leading to calls for rapid demobilisation, limited the Truman administration's ability to meet its newly inherited worldwide commitments. In 1945, it was also far from clear whether the United States would support Britain or resist the Soviet Union.[45] Direct Soviet–American co-operation worried the British, particularly if they reached agreements on the Middle East and North Africa. The Chiefs of Staff saw the defence of the Middle East as a matter of life and death: they argued that if Britain disengaged as Attlee had proposed, the Empire would be cut in half and British power dissolved. Bevin agreed. This was not the time to make concessions, especially to the Soviets, and the UN was not able to handle all international problems.[46] Only when a post-war settlement had been agreed amongst the great powers, Bevin told his cabinet colleagues (many of whom held an internationalist outlook), could the UN then police it, which meant Britain had to fulfil its international obligations.[47]

Did those obligations, however, involve a British commitment to far-flung areas of East Asia and the Pacific? As we have seen, Mountbatten was fully engaged in Southeast Asia, an area of direct interest to Britain, but his command was last on the list of British global priorities. The region would never recover the former primacy in British policy that it had enjoyed before the Second World War. There was an argument, then, for cutting back on any unnecessary commitments particularly since the United States was prepared to take a lead in East Asia. Sterndale Bennett disagreed, deploying Bevin's argument about international obligations. Britain had signed the Cairo Declaration of 1943, which guaranteed the return of Manchuria to China and Korea to become free and independent. Britain would therefore 'not be able to keep out' of the region's affairs.[48] There was also the question of influence. If the British had no voice in Japanese affairs, policies drawn up solely by the United States could affect Britain's Southeast Asian colonies and British India with regard to their defence and trade, and also the British domestic economy, such as the shipbuilding and textile industries. Ultimately, exclusion from the occupation of Japan would hurt Britain's general prestige in the Far East, and be criticised at home in view of the sacrifices made in the war and the need to be involved in ensuring the removal of the Japanese menace.[49] Yet there was no way to verify these sweeping statements or dispute an alternative argument that if Britain did not take an interest in China, Japan or Korea, the outcome would be any different.

Returning to China

The initial signs for a British return to China were not encouraging. Neither the Americans nor the Nationalist Chinese seemed enthusiastic to work with the British to re-establish their commercial concerns. A British relief and rehabilitation effort required the help of the Royal Navy but plans to send detachments of the British Pacific Fleet into former treaty ports with the US Navy met with strong disapproval from Chiang and Admiral Thomas Kinkaid, the commander of the US Seventh Fleet. Kinkaid quickly detached the British Pacific Fleet from his command as Chiang argued that there was no justification for the Royal Navy in Chinese waters. The Nationalist Chinese and the Americans were both carrying out post-surrender tasks in the theatre and Chiang claimed that the presence of the Royal Navy would arouse national feeling and provoke incidents. In contrast, the US Navy was allowed the free use of Shanghai and other harbours. It also turned up unannounced at Hong Kong so it could help move Chiang's armies into northern China, although Rear-Admiral Harcourt, the head of the provisional military government in the colony, described relations with his US opposite numbers as 'co-operative' and 'happy'.[50]

The State Department, meanwhile, confident that they would be able to maintain their concessions in some form despite extraterritoriality, showed no inclination to make a joint protest with the Foreign Office to Chiang over the protection of claims for their nationals.[51] At the London Council of Foreign Ministers, Bevin was therefore forced independently to approach T. V. Soong (Song Ziwen), the Nationalist Chinese foreign minister and Chiang's brother-in-law, asking him what safeguards he had in mind for the British business community. He received a rather non-committal reply.[52] Although Ogden, now as consul-general, made a good start in Shanghai, preparing the way for the re-entry of British businessmen, while Seymour secured visas for the representatives of six firms, by October 1945, the ambassador told the Foreign Office that Britain would have to rely entirely on its own efforts to re-establish its interests in China. Seymour therefore saw Hong Kong as 'the best centre for the exertion of that effort', and urged London to ensure that the crown colony received the early provision of shipping, fuel and other commodities as a priority.[53]

Part of the British Pacific Fleet was now at Hong Kong as the rest deployed to Singapore, which could bring urgent relief to prisoners of war and internees, and restart trade to China, since, as Seymour recognised, the colony was a valuable commercial centre. In November, however, Hong Kong had no more than a surplus of 14 days' rice, possessed minimal facilities to resume trade, and was short of civilian staff, hundreds of whom were detained in British India owing to a lack of transport, a major problem that confronted SEAC across the region.[54] The British were nevertheless determined to hang on to their colony. Extraterritoriality and the loss of influence in the affairs of the International Settlement at Shanghai gave Hong Kong added significance. Yet, the Americans argued that Britain should return Hong Kong to China in the interests of peace and stability, particularly in view of the new status of China as one of the world powers. The colony was indefensible, the State Department argued, and they were sure the emotional content of the issue – the loss of Hong Kong might imply the possible sacrifice of other parts of the Empire – 'is probably more important than either the economic or strategic interests in determining British attitudes'.[55]

In public, when Seymour visited Shanghai in October, he declined to answer questions from journalists about Hong Kong. He simply said British policy was 'to buy Chinese goods, to sell British goods, to work for the day when the internal situation quietens down, [and] to hope for long years of friendly relations'. In reply to a question from a correspondent that British businessmen were much concerned that US long-term loans gave their businessmen advantages, the ambassador stated Britain was simply not in a financial position to assist China in that way: 'her whole position has changed, and she was now the world's greatest debtor nation'.[56] The ambassador's downbeat mood, not lifted by the fact that Britain's Shanghai community was still living in six makeshift camps, proved justified. The

Nationalist Chinese refused to return British properties and the British-owned public utilities were now under Chungking's control and finding it impossible to carry on. The China Association noted that US telephone and power companies were free of such control after Wedemeyer and Hurley had made strong representations. The Americans, meanwhile, halted aid to British internment camps and also ignored British requests to transport consular officers across China, leaving them short-handed. Ogden was 'overcome' with work and Hong Kong remained 'dead commercially', still dependent on the need for shipping. Lacking people with Chinese experience, the British could not open many of their Chinese posts, apart from those at Shanghai, Nanking, Tientsin and Canton (Guangzhou), while the Nationalist Chinese did their best to stall their opening at all. In contrast, the United States quickly re-established their diplomatic outposts throughout China.[57]

A British JIC report compiled in November argued that the US press, and the actions of some its political and military officials in Nationalist China, had given the Chinese reason to believe they would have US support in any anti-British activities. Nationalist China was forced to keep on good terms with the Soviet Union, the JIC argued, owing to its proximity, and with the United States, in the hope of financial and material aid; which meant Britain was 'liable to bear the brunt of China's xenophobia'.[58] Just as the JIC issued their report, the Americans were questioning their commitment to China. In late October, Wedemeyer sent signals to Washington declaring that his mission would soon be complete: American personnel had been recovered and the two US Marine divisions assigned to Tientsin, Tsingtao (Qingdao) and Chefoo (Yantai), were ready to hand over responsibility to the Chinese Nationalists. To retain the Marines now would 'inextricably' involve them in the Nationalist-Communist civil conflict and this could not be justified under the terms of his present mission, he argued. Wedemeyer recommended that the Marines should withdraw on 15 November and that he refuse to transport another of Chiang's armies to northern China. The Joint Chiefs of Staff, however, began to prevaricate and John McCloy, the assistant secretary of war, told Byrnes that Chiang would need US support to absorb the Manchurian area. Yet, McCloy had no evidence of Soviet support for Mao and there was a danger that if Stalin declared openly for him (Mao) the Americans might get into 'a real mess'.[59]

The matter remained unresolved throughout November. When the Joint Chiefs of Staff proposed setting up a military advisory group of over 3,000 personnel in China, John Carter Vincent, the Director of the Office of Far Eastern Affairs at the State Department, felt the United States would move towards the establishment of a relationship with Nationalist China, which 'has some of the characteristics of a *de facto* protectorate with a semi-colonial Chinese Army under our direction'. Vincent, no admirer of Chiang, had spent a large part of his career in China and warned Byrnes that such a scheme would encourage the Generalissimo to solve his internal difficulties by military means only, and drag the United States increasingly into the internal affairs of China, which would 'not pay dividends'. The State Department had agreed with Wedemeyer's recommendations but now, to Vincent's dismay, the War Department was advocating a reversal of his orders until northern China had been stabilised. Vincent was immediately sceptical over what the phrase 'reasonable stability' meant.[60] The counter-argument put forward by Everett Drumright, the efficient and conservative chief of the Division of Chinese Affairs at the State Department, was that the United States had invested much into securing a friendly, united China, which would bring stability to the region. This was now under threat and evidence was mounting that Mao was making 'a supreme effort' to establish control over northern China and Manchuria 'aided and abetted' by the Soviet Union. Drumright's advice was clear: assist Chiang in order to avoid the substitution of a Japanese-dominated puppet regime in northern China for a Soviet one, which would only promote insecurity and possibly lead to a Soviet–American clash.[61]

Sterndale Bennett told Winant that the British were similarly disturbed by events in northern China. His information was 'fragmentary and confused' but it seemed the Sino-Soviet treaty was not having a beneficial effect (reports of widespread Soviet looting and rape were rife) while information that Mao's troops had marched into Mukden (Shenyang) with Soviet permission was 'disturbing'. The Foreign Office believed Soviet policy was to build up Communist strength in Manchuria as a check on Chungking and for use 'as a lever' in any difficulties that may arise over the Sino-Soviet treaty.[62] The evidence suggests that this assessment was correct. Stalin had also become annoyed over the exclusive US occupation of Japan, which had led to a hardening of his policy in China and greater co-operation with Mao. Yet, as tensions increased and Chiang complained to Truman that Stalin was breaking the Sino-Soviet treaty, the Soviet leader modified his policy. Stalin acceded to Chiang's request to delay the Red Army's withdrawal in order to give the Nationalists time to enter Manchuria in force. The move still foreclosed the possibility of the arrival of US troops into the region and allowed Stalin to consolidate his Yalta gains. Mao, meanwhile, although similarly desirous of a prolonged Soviet presence, was finding it difficult to associate his forces with the violent actions of the Red Army. The British intelligence community, via SIS reports and Colonel Eric Jacobs-Larkcom who had travelled to Mukden to inspect the consulate, was aware of the strained relationship between Mao and Stalin, and some debate ensued about whether the Soviet leader would attempt to 'Communise' Manchuria through Mao or not.[63]

Yet, it was only the Americans who were in a position to substantially alter events on the ground in Manchuria, not the British. Although Wedemeyer stuck to his guns about withdrawing the US Marines, he too realised that Chiang was 'incapable' of repatriating millions of enemy troops and civilians and simultaneously being able to solve China's political and economic problems. Truman needed to make a decision and the general reported that the British were either unwilling or unable to help Chiang. Seymour told Wedemeyer that they would not provide extra shipping to move some of Chiang's forces north, recounting many grievances, such as discriminatory acts and restrictions against Britons with heavy investments and commercial interests in China. Seymour asked him to prevail upon Chiang to take remedial action. Uncomfortable, Wedemeyer exclaimed, 'I am asked to scratch the back of the British Lion to insure that the British Ambassador will do some scratching along the tortuous spine of the Chinese Dragon.'[64]

As Nationalist–Communist negotiations looked increasingly unlikely to reach a successful outcome, Hurley suddenly, and publicly, tendered his resignation on 27 November, much to Truman's astonishment. Hurley had accused his subordinates of being Communist sympathisers and claimed that the 'imperialist' nations (an allusion to Britain) aimed to keep China divided.[65] The British were not unnaturally pleased to see him go while they also noted a marked improvement in Nationalist attitudes towards them as the uncertainty over US policy continued. Bevin, nevertheless, fired off a warning to the Chungking embassy about cosying up to Chiang, which could be construed as a crude attempt to profit from the Hurley affair. It was in the British interest to stay out of China's internal affairs, a point he made in the House of Commons and, he stated, there was no evidence to suggest Britain's trading concerns were affected.[66] In an attempt to stop a full-scale civil war and the continual Soviet looting of Manchuria, while also lessening the impact of Hurley's resignation, Truman despatched General Marshall to China. Truman wanted to take a strong stand and told Marshall to resolve the Nationalist–Communist conflict, ensure Chiang's domination over Manchuria and remove Soviet troops from there. Marshall immediately advocated support for Chiang employing many of Drumright's earlier arguments, and the formation of the military advisory group. As a result, Wedemeyer's orders were rewritten so he could assist in the movement of Nationalist troops northward.[67] Britain remained a mere spectator to these events and the Americans made no requests for British help or sought their advice on the matter. The British were instead barely managing to recover a position equivalent to that they had held in China prior to 1941.

The control of Japan

Truman finally initialled American policy for Japan on 6 September. The objectives were to ensure that Japan did not become a menace to the peace and security of the world; to disarm and demilitarise the country; to establish a peaceful and responsible democratic Japanese government (as long it was not imposed on the people); to encourage civil liberties; and to develop an economy which would permit the peacetime requirements of the population to be met but to work for the dissolution of the *zaibatsu*. SCAP would also exercise his authority through a Japanese government and the Emperor. The United States would make every effort to accommodate the views of other allied nations. If there were any differences, US policy would prevail.[68] In reality, the United States was prepared to pay little attention to the views of others and the first Sterndale Bennett heard of the approved policy was through the British Broadcasting Corporation (BBC) and the press. The Americans were confident the British would be content to leave them to control Japan.[69]

The devastation heaped upon Japan by the ravages of war left the British in no doubt that the United States was in the best position to take the lead and bear the financial brunt of rehabilitation.[70] George Atcheson, the head of the Office of Political Advisor in SCAP's Diplomatic Section, described Tokyo as 'a gloomy place', perhaps 70 per cent destroyed as compared to Yokohama's 90 per cent, while the people looked 'drab' and 'not very well fed'.[71] Nine million Japanese were homeless, factories lay idle and over one and half million soldiers had died.[72] Although the Foreign Office wanted to make it clear that the British acceptance of MacArthur did not imply acquiescence in US policy,[73] the general had different ideas and sought to harness total control over the occupation. In Washington, Sansom remarked he could glean little information from the State Department on Japanese affairs, as they also knew 'very little'.[74] According to Atcheson, this was due to the fact that on all matters of substance: 'General MacArthur or his Chief of Staff [General Charles Willoughby] and other members of the Bataan Club who act as his Privy Council or *genro* wish if possible to keep the State Department out'.[75] MacArthur, seeking the 1948 Republican presidential nomination, attempted to use Japan as a political stage. Setting up his headquarters at the *Dai Ichi* insurance building in central Tokyo, he issued some 550 directives during September 1945–January 1946. Washington sent MacArthur a lengthy set of directives on how to conduct the occupation, yet the intent was more to clarify his powers than to recommend specific policies. MacArthur was determined to stamp out militarism, secure a full democracy with a constitutional monarchy, break up the *zaibatsu* and encourage trade unionism to a degree, and also emancipate women and reform education. Truman, who appointed MacArthur with no particular enthusiasm, considered the general an excessive egotist but while both agreed there should be minimal outside interference in the occupation, MacArthur attempted to exclude Washington as well.[76]

MacArthur was particularly anxious that there should be no question of a Commonwealth occupation force being allotted a zone of its own, since such an arrangement would make it very difficult for him to resist a similar request by the Nationalist Chinese and the Soviets.[77] The composition of a British Commonwealth Occupation Force (BCOF) for Japan was finally resolved in September, when Australia, after strong British representations

to Evatt in London, accepted Britain's offer for an Australian commander to take charge of the multinational force numbering approximately
37,000 that included British, Indian, Australian and New Zealand personnel. The outcome undoubtedly dealt a blow to British power in the region.
The BCOF, under the command of the Australian, Lieutenant-General John
Northcott, would not arrive until 1946 but its allotted role in western
Honshu and the island of Shikoku together with overall control by SCAP
compromised its standing and independence. Australians reported general
American 'touchiness' about the occupation being termed 'allied', while
the Australian–American negotiations over BCOF's role and status took so
long that by late 1945, Bruce Fraser, the New Zealand prime minister, wondered whether the force was actually needed, reporting that the enthusiasm
for it in his country had 'flagged very considerably'. The British were not
unprepared for such a disappointing outcome and focused on other ways of
safeguarding their interests.[78]

The answer, according to Lieutenant-General Sir Charles Gairdner, Attlee's
personal representative to MacArthur, was to establish a British liaison mission in Tokyo.[79] Gairdner, the popular raconteur, had had an excellent
relationship with MacArthur since acting as the prime minister's liaison officer to the general from the summer of 1945. MacArthur had no objection to
the proposals and Britain approved the formation of a United Kingdom Liaison Mission (UKLM) to add political, financial and other technical experts
to Gairdner's existing staff.[80] It was a move that took on greater importance as the fracas over the control mechanisms for Japan continued. As
matters stood, Britain would participate in the Far Eastern Advisory Commission on the same footing as the Philippines and that body could only make
recommendations.[81] When the British returned to the need for a five-power
control council, Byrnes batted Bevin away. At Chequers, he told the foreign
secretary that the American aim was to prevent a Soviet call for separate
zones in Japan.[82] The British therefore accepted Byrnes's words to 'trust him'
on implementing a control council later and for the moment satisfy themselves with an eleven-power Far Eastern Advisory Commission to sit in either
Washington or Tokyo.[83] Byrnes was quick to brush the Soviets aside as well,
stating it was not within his brief to discuss a control council at the London
Council of Foreign Ministers held during 11 September–2 October. Sterndale
Bennett was unhappy with the way Britain's role had been marginalised,
especially as policies for Japan could impact upon British trade in British
India and Southeast Asia, but he knew an open row with the United States
was not feasible, an outcome that could damage Anglo-American relations
in general and jeopardise future economic help from its Atlantic partner.[84]
Evatt, less concerned about a row with the United States, argued that Britain
should simply refuse to discuss such matters without Australia present.[85]

The Soviets were equally unhappy, particularly as Byrnes protested at their
behaviour in the Balkans, arguing for a broadening of the commissions in

Roumania and Bulgaria. Harriman not unreasonably argued that Byrnes was in no position to castigate the Soviets in the Balkans and then block all such arrangements for Japan. Both Harriman and Frank Roberts, the minister at the British embassy in Moscow, noted in October that Stalin's attempt to raise the issue of the control of Japan was not just to use it as a bargaining chip in his dealings over Eastern Europe and the Balkans but also sprang from fears about the revival of Japanese militarism and the possible use of Japan by the United States against him. Truman, Byrnes, Leahy and MacArthur, however, all objected to a control body for Japan, fearing a reduction in SCAP's power and the introduction of zones similar to that in Germany. It was not a position they were willing to accept, as they considered the United States had done the bulk of the fighting in winning the war against Japan.[86]

The Americans, nevertheless, tried to come to some arrangement with the Soviets, but from the discussions that emerged Byrnes soon drew back from his earlier promises to Bevin. He now proposed a four-power control council (not five), the fourth power being a member of the Commonwealth. The council would consult with SCAP but the last word rested with him. As matters stood, Byrnes suggested that the Australian military commander should represent the fourth member only and the problem of what now amounted to total British exclusion was the latter's 'headache'. Sterndale Bennett was near to blowing up when he heard this considering it pure 'jungle' diplomacy.[87] In Washington, meanwhile, Byrnes told Robert Patterson, the US Secretary of War, he agreed with recent remarks made by Stalin that the provision of occupation troops should be left to the Americans, like Soviet troops in Romania, and that no one really wished to participate except the Australians. Byrnes emphasised the need to avoid 'ganging up' on Stalin and wanted the Joint Chiefs of Staff to know they were not 'doing him a favor' by suggesting that allied forces take part in the occupation. Even Patterson, who appeared slightly concerned at Byrnes's train of thought, noted, 'of course, MacArthur would be happy to have a purely American force' but the rate of demobilisation might mean allied troops could prove useful.[88] US thinking at the highest levels was indicating how little concerned they were about a British role in Japan.

Taking a pragmatic approach, Cadogan, realising that the United States was seeking to maintain ultimate control over the occupation, whatever the Soviet–American formulations for a Far Eastern advisory commission and control council, knew Britain had to 'fall into line'. Both mechanisms would be 'pretty ineffective', Cadogan observed, if SCAP retained the overriding say. He even persuaded Bevin not to lodge a protest with Byrnes for making him, as the foreign secretary described it, look 'foolish'. As long as Britain could share on an equal footing with the Soviet Union and Nationalist China in the formulation of policy and provided Britain had independent political representation in Japan (UKLM), Cadogan and even Sterndale Bennett felt it was worth avoiding a dispute with its former wartime partners. The issue was not vital to British interests, and Cadogan concluded it was sensible to abandon Britain's original five-power proposal and nominate Australia as a fourth member in any control body.[89]

Korea and trusteeship

All the great powers considered Korea as an area where vital interests were not at stake and a low priority in their post-war foreign policy. US troops did not arrive in Korea until 8 September and on that day the Foreign Office produced a short paper on its attitude towards the peninsula. Britain's economic interests there were 'negligible' and it was not an area of strategic or imperial interest. The British were therefore content for the United States to play the hand in what would no doubt prove to be 'an uneasy partnership' with the Soviet Union, while both powers had clearly been arranging the peninsula's future behind Britain's back. Here, then, the Foreign Office should have declared it had no further interest in the future of Korea but it did not, and left the door ajar, pointing out Britain had signed the 1943 Cairo Declaration guaranteeing Korea's independence, mitigating the possibility of adopting 'an entirely isolationist outlook'. It would prove to be a costly decision.[90]

Once Japan had formally surrendered, the Americans had little clue whether the British knew about any of the arrangements made for Korea at Yalta and later between Stalin and Hopkins that centred on a four-power trusteeship. When SWNCC's subcommittee on the Far East met to discuss Korea on 11 September the consensus was to get rid of the 38th parallel as a dividing line and set up a centralised administration. In response to a query from a member of the committee as to whether there would be any effect on American plans if the British did not agree to a trusteeship, Vincent replied 'none'.[91] He did, however, consider it necessary at least to tell the British about what was afoot for Korea and approached the embassy in Washington. Apologising to a member of Halifax's staff for this apparent 'oversight', Vincent explained he had already received Soviet and Nationalist Chinese agreement to a four-power trusteeship but that the British were in no way committed to accept it.[92] The British did not immediately answer but here was another chance for them to pull away from a commitment to Korea. Vincent was clearly indifferent to their involvement. Officials at the Far Eastern Department called Vincent's attempt at an apology 'lame'. Yet the Foreign Office drew back from refusing to commit to Korea at all and instead looked at the possibility of Australia representing the British Commonwealth who, 'judging by present form', would demand to play a role.[93]

Discussion at the Foreign Office departmental level spoke of Korea having 'hardly any direct interest' for them and 'a tiresome commitment', while Britain did not possess men or resources 'to throw about in every corner of the world'. There were not even 'enough good men for our zone in Germany'. During these exchanges (on 18 September) Truman released a statement, declaring that the rebuilding of Korea had begun with the assistance of the United States, the Soviet Union, Britain and China, 'who are agreed that Korea shall be free and independent'. The president had had no indication of British policy and his statement was rather presumptive but it may unwittingly have served to halt the British from contemplating a complete disengagement from Korea. In fact, the ploy to use Australia had an attraction for Foreign Office officials, serving to take the 'wind out of Dr Evatt's sails', while there was no need to be 'squeamish' about the American attitude to this solution, as they had gone to 'considerable lengths without bothering to consult us'. Cadogan seemed to write with some satisfaction that 'if they (the Americans) make difficulties, that will be a U.S.-Australia row'. Bevin showed no objection to the outcome of this discussion. The Dominions Office, however, quickly recognised that it would be difficult to ask Australia to assume a responsibility 'only because we do not wish to be bothered with it ourselves'. If there was 'a real British interest, or even a mere prestige interest', it could hardly be protected by delegating its representation to Australia. The Foreign Office view nevertheless prevailed and, on 25 October, ministers endorsed a decision for Australia to represent the British Commonwealth on any trusteeship for Korea, a concept the British doubted would work in practice.[94]

Britain still delayed formally communicating this decision to the United States – not prepared to commit itself fully for the present – and sought Commonwealth views on Korea, principally those of Australia, New Zealand and Canada. The Foreign Office hoped that the Australians might take the initiative in pressing for a five-power trusteeship for Korea and if this proposal were turned down, then the way would be open for the British to suggest that Australia take their place.[95] Oblivious to these discussions, SWNCC and the State Department wilfully assumed Britain would fall into line with the concept of a four-power trusteeship, arguing it was 'directly concerned' with Korea. The only evidence for this American argument of British interest was the Cairo Declaration. The slight change in the US attitude of securing British involvement sprung from a concern that 'rivalry for the control of Korea may again develop'.[96] Events on the ground indeed appeared out of control. Commanding US forces in Korea was Lieutenant-General John R. Hodge, who had no knowledge or regard for the country, little experience of politics and was bereft of direction from the State Department. He reported on fruitless efforts to establish some sort of agreement with the Soviets on the military level. Responding to dire local conditions, Hodge continued to employ Japanese and collaborationist Korean conservatives in administrative posts, causing outcry. The Soviets on the other hand immediately replaced Japanese officials with exiled Koreans. H. Merrell Benninghoff, Hodge's political adviser, spoke of intense Korean political agitation for independence; indiscriminate Soviet acts of rape, pillage and looting north of the 38th parallel; and evidence of Soviet agents spreading 'their political thought' south of the line. Coal was also short because communications, along with the electric power supply in the north, had been cut. The advice to Byrnes from Americans based in Seoul was the 38th parallel was killing any prospect of a united Korea and trusteeship was unworkable.[97]

Byrnes, however, wanted to negotiate with the Soviet Union first before introducing any new ideas.[98] He told Attlee in November that it was essential to reach an early decision about the future of Korea. Unless this was done the United States might be faced with a *fait accompli* of Soviet control. From Washington Halifax commented that the United States was 'evidently anxious' to get their troops out of Korea.[99] The British did not dispute the fact that a settlement was needed although Sterndale Bennett told Winant that Britain still had an open mind over Korea, seeing trusteeship as unworkable. Yet the ambassador reported back to Washington that 'if it can be shown that there is reasonable chance of a four-power trusteeship working out in practice', Britain might go along with it.[100] The British now pressed Australia for its views on Korea. On 6 December, the Australians agreed with the principle of trusteeship but thought a UN trusteeship would be far more preferable to a four-power arrangement, as the latter was 'undesirable and opposed to our general policy in Pacific affairs'.[101] In Washington, Evatt privately thought the four-power proposals most 'unsatisfactory' particularly as they were put to Britain and not Australia. He told Canberra that it was now time for the British government 'to state quite frankly' to the United States and the Soviet Union that in relation to all matters affecting the settlement of Japan 'they will participate only on the basis that Australia also participates as a party principal'. His hopes would crash at the second post-war Council of Foreign Ministers due to be held at Moscow in December.[102]

The Moscow Council of Foreign Ministers

In November, Byrnes was convinced that he could solve some of the major post-war problems by direct engagement with Molotov. Pressurising the British to attend a meeting of the three foreign ministers in Moscow, Attlee and Bevin questioned the wisdom of holding such a meeting. If Europe was discussed, France would not be present while 'other Governments' would be absent from talks about the Far East, a reference to Nationalist China and Australia. Had not Truman also announced that further meetings of heads of government were unnecessary? When Bevin enquired what the agenda might involve, Byrnes replied, Korea, Japan, China, Iran, the control of atomic energy and the recognition of Romania and Bulgaria. Bevin thought the list 'formidable' and expressed 'bewilderment' in reconciling Truman's recent statement and Byrnes's proposal for a meeting. It was inconceivable that Britain could refuse to attend but they agreed only on the proviso that the talks would be 'exploratory' as other countries needed to be consulted.[103] Upon hearing the British decision, Evatt was outraged and could not believe that Bevin had agreed to attend without consulting Australia first or even securing their representation. Evatt argued that Australia was 'entitled to that status', by its leadership of BCOF, the British proposal Australia share in the trusteeship of Korea, and the recent suggestion that (if pressed) the British and Australians should act jointly through one representative on a control council for Japan. At the very least he hoped the British would consult with the Australians before taking any decisions at Moscow.[104]

As the British feared, the Moscow Council of Foreign Ministers (16–26 December) proved to be a dreadful experience for them. Cadogan described the talks as tense, with Molotov 'sticky on every subject', Bevin frequently losing his temper, and Byrnes trying 'to sell us completely to the Russians'.[105] Major-General Sir Ian Jacob, the military assistant secretary to the cabinet, who attended the sessions, also confessed it was 'awful to think' that US foreign policy 'should be in the hands of a shanty Irishman from Carolina, advised by a rather vague visionary like Cohen'.[106] Benjamin Cohen, Byrnes's trusted aide, had been influential in drawing up a protocol for the end of the conference, which attempted to incorporate Molotov's demand for a statement on China that referred to 'the broad participation of democratic elements in the National Government *and its other central and local organs'*. The British were clearly uncomfortable with putting their name to these words without consulting the Nationalist Chinese government, as it constituted a direct interference in the latter's affairs. Cohen told the British delegation that they did not need to put their name to that part of the protocol if it disturbed them. Bevin saw the text just half an hour before meeting with Byrnes and Molotov on 26 December and objected to being pushed into 'amplifying' such a statement but he did succeed in removing the words 'and its other central and local organs', which meant Mao could only be represented if part of Chiang's government.[107]

Bevin subsequently told the cabinet that he had found it 'embarrassing' to talk about China at a meeting in which that country was not represented.[108] He had taken little part in the discussions over China in which the main issue of Soviet–American troop withdrawals went unresolved.[109] He was also a spectator during the Molotov–Byrnes exchanges on Korea where it was agreed that a Soviet–American Joint Commission should convene to work out the particulars of a four-power trusteeship to ensure independence in five years, while in the interim a unified administration should be developed to remove the divisive boundary of the 38th parallel. Vincent offered to show Sterndale Bennett (both at Moscow) these papers 'some time' but not to give him a copy, confident that it would meet any British concerns.[110] Britain's blackout from East Asian affairs was complete over the negotiations for the control mechanisms for Japan. Molotov was against including British India in a Far Eastern Advisory Commission (now renamed the Far Eastern

Commission), arguing it was not a sovereign state, while both he and Byrnes objected outright to separate Australian participation in a control body for Tokyo.[111] Although Molotov gave way over the inclusion of British India in the Far Eastern Commission, he, along with Byrnes, left Bevin with no option but to nominate Australia as the fourth member of an allied council for Japan to represent the British Commonwealth. Both bodies had embedded in them the four-power majority procedures, with SCAP always able to retain the overriding authority, effectively rendering them impotent.[112]

The proceedings of the Moscow Conference brought forth a wave of British and Australian disappointment on matters pertaining to East Asia. Bevin told the Australians that he was faced by a Molotov–Byrnes front that was attempting to reach common agreements at the expense of Britain. Yet Bevin stressed to the Australians that he could not jeopardise the chance of bringing the Soviets 'back into the circle' to deal with the settlement of Japan and other Far Eastern issues. Evatt could not believe that the British were making decisions without consulting him.[113] Unsurprisingly, Bevin began seriously to resent Byrnes's attempt to deal with Molotov unilaterally while Cadogan went so far as to say 'Ernie hates him', remarking the American was 'a little donkey' and 'a nasty, slippery little devil'.[114] What the Moscow meeting did was to highlight yet again that a British role in East Asia was either unwanted or unnecessary. From Japan's surrender, the Americans appeared to ignore Britain completely over the affairs of China, Japan and Korea, dismissing the need for their wartime ally's help. The British accepted the fact that the region was a US responsibility and were never prepared to force a row with them over an area that was such a low priority, but the nagging question remained why the British, faced with a plethora of other more pressing global commitments, persisted in their efforts to maintain an international role in East Asia at all?

4
Occupation and Civil War

The Moscow Council of Foreign Ministers proved a sobering experience for the British and it continued to confirm that the United States and the Soviet Union were prepared to exclude them from deliberations over East Asia. Lord Vansittart, the former permanent under-secretary and chief diplomatic adviser at the Foreign Office, told readers of the *Manchester Guardian* that the discussions over Korea were just one example of where 'the Big Three are tending to become the Big Two' and it was time 'to cry halt'.[1] Why Britain needed to have a say in the future of Korea was not entirely clear. The British remained preoccupied with the need to supply food and raise living standards in Southeast Asia, sending the experienced diplomat, Lord Killearn (formerly Sir Miles Lampson) to Singapore as a Special Commissioner for the region in March 1946.[2] Britain's desire, however, to obtain free rice from Thailand, which it saw as an enemy state and the United States did not,[3] caused untold friction between the Anglo-American powers. Dening spoke of the Americans remaining aloof from Britain's problems in Southeast Asia, seeking economic penetration instead while retaining the right 'to continue to suspect us and criticise us'. Sterndale Bennett recognised that Britain was essentially 'on trial' in its territories. Unless Britain rehabilitated them, he argued, it should either pull out or increase military expenditure in an attempt to maintain its position.[4]

In Southeast Asia the choices were stark, but Sterndale Bennett suggested rather tenuously that Britain's non-participation in the occupation of Japan would also 'shake our whole position in the Far East'. There was little evidence to support his sweeping assertion. British troops were only just due to arrive that spring; the Americans remained indifferent; and there was no evidence to suggest that the indigenous populations of the Far East cared whether the British were or were not sending forces to Japan. Yet, the older generation of British diplomats, like Sir Robert Craigie, Britain's former ambassador to Japan, still thought it 'unhealthy' to delegate some of Britain's Far Eastern responsibilities, as it only tended to confirm the nascent and, in his opinion, 'absurd belief that this country is no longer able to play its part as a great world Power'.[5] Such a view was looking increasingly unrealistic. To play the role of great power Britain needed help. First, financial assistance in the form of a US loan and, second, the need for political support by driving home the extent of British weakness in order to compel others, principally the Truman administration but also the dominions, to take a share in dealing with their overseas problems, most of which seemed to boil down to threatening Soviet behaviour.[6] Washington was aware of British aims and Truman was 'tired babying the Soviets', especially over their reluctance to withdraw troops from Iran, but he was a long way yet from convincing Congress or US public opinion of the need to prepare for a confrontation with the Soviet Union.[7] The view of the president from the British embassy in Washington was unflattering: he was seen as repetitive, a 'diligent mediocrity' or 'a bungling if well meaning amateur'.[8] And, what of US leadership in East Asia? If events there began to unravel, could the British count on them to stay the course in a region where civil strife was increasing and the lives of American soldiers were at risk?

Defence planning

During 1946, the big three wartime allies remained unsure what the term 'security' meant for their national defence, yet tension increased as Stalin sought to convince his people they were surrounded by enemies while the Anglo-American powers presumed Communism would immediately fill power vacuums.[9] The retention of large Soviet forces in the Far East did nothing to dispel such suspicions.[10] In Moscow, it was George Kennan and Frank Roberts who famously warned Washington and London that Stalin believed peaceful co-existence between the communist and capitalist 'centres' was impossible. In his 'long telegram', Kennan, the chargé d'affairs at the US embassy, argued in February that Stalin would seek to expand the limits of Soviet power 'wherever it was considered timely and promising'. Roberts, holding the rank of Minister in the British embassy, echoed these sentiments but both men agreed that the Soviet Union would seek to avoid war. An all-encompassing strategy was nevertheless needed to educate domestic and overseas opinion about Soviet intentions.[11] Kennan's remarks received wide attention within the Truman administration while Roberts' despatches were circulated to the cabinet. What they were saying was not new but along with public outbursts such as Churchill's 'iron curtain' speech in March at Fulton, Missouri, they reached a more receptive audience. British and American public opinion, however, remained unsure about embracing a new, hostile stance against their former wartime ally and in some cases a large minority of US pollsters believed Britain was out to dominate the world![12]

While the Foreign Office assessment of Soviet aims darkened in 1946, leading them to set up a Russia Committee in April, they also thought Moscow and Washington were 'in large measure bluffing'. The Soviets, the Foreign

Office argued, hid internal weaknesses, despite huge armed strength, while the Americans forgot their military impotence because of 'over-hasty' demobilisation. By March 1946, the United States had 400,000 men under arms compared to 3.5 million at the end of the war. A major British concern was that in East Asia such 'bluffing' could lead to conflict.[13] Yet, the Far Eastern Civil Planning Unit, a cabinet committee, knew that in East Asia the United States must play 'the principal part for the next few years'. The Unit had produced a major review of Britain's position in the Far East, which had undergone several bouts of redrafting since the end of the war and pulled together Whitehall-wide departmental views. There were no startling revelations: Britain should confine its effort to Southeast Asia and avoid entanglements north of the Tropic of Cancer. The paper argued that the principal threat to Britain's position in the Far East was likely to result from Soviet–American rivalry in East Asia and it was hoped Britain could adopt a 'restraining influence' as long as its attitude was 'realistic' and 'as it often could be, disinterested'. This statement begged the question why it was necessary to keep occupation forces in Japan, an area of US responsibility where there was no Soviet–American rivalry. Schemes put forward by the Joint Planning Staff for a system of interlocking US–British Commonwealth bases in the Far East were also wildly optimistic in 1946, and the Civil Planning Unit inserted these plans with caution stressing they had not received general approval.[14] It was unlikely that the Soviet Union would seriously threaten Britain's colonies in Southeast Asia and China was far too weak. War with the United States remained unthinkable.

In fact, Admiral Fraser in command of the British Pacific Fleet told London that the heavy ships under his control carrying large numbers of men were becoming 'a serious embarrassment' to him. 'With our shortage of manpower and shipping', he told the Alexander (still First Lord of the Admiralty), 'there must be some weighty reason for keeping them out here but the Admiralty will not tell me'. Fraser considered his job in the Pacific 'finished': the fleet was moving its base away from Australia to Singapore and Hong Kong and he could accomplish 'little' in China or Japan. He therefore wanted to be relieved.[15] Fraser's fears were not unfounded. When the RAF tried to slow down demobilisation in the Far East, a large number of airmen at Mauripur (near Karachi) refused to return to duty leaving the Air Ministry facing open revolt.[16] Throughout 1946, Attlee failed to see the need for a large fleet in the Pacific, and Britain could not afford to 'show the flag' as it once had in support of its commercial interests. There was no one to fight in the region and in view of US predominance in the Pacific the cabinet forced the Admiralty to make cuts.[17]

Challenging Britain's role in the world formed part of a wider debate in the Attlee administration. Dalton continually reminded the prime minister about Britain's overseas deficit and applauded Attlee's attack on the necessity of a strategy for the Middle East. If India went 'her own way', Dalton noted in his diary, there would be even 'less point in thinking of lines of Imperial communications through the Suez Canal'.[18] Bevin, along with the Chiefs of Staff, disagreed, with the latter placing the Middle East second on its strategic agenda after the defence of Britain. The US military accepted that the Middle Eastern area was vital to defence planning but unrest in Palestine, the threat of expulsion from Egypt, and the probable loss of Indian troops saw Washington gradually turn its attention to Turkey and Greece instead.[19] Throughout the Mediterranean and Middle East, Bevin and Byrnes sought to block Moscow's demands. Yet, how real was a Soviet threat to this and other areas? Instability in Europe, the Middle East and the Far East was often down to a complex array of factors, which included nationalism, corrupt governments, civil strife, economic hardship and also communist agitation. Moscow's hand was not behind every development that appeared to threaten Western interests. Soviet probing in the Middle East and the Mediterranean served to antagonise the West but the area held no vital interests for the Soviet Union. Attlee argued that a firm British stand in this area was unnecessarily provocative and also untenable because of the advent of air power.[20]

In the Far East, Frank Roberts felt Stalin's policy was 'cautious' due to the absolute US control of Japan but the Soviet leader would nevertheless exploit opportunities if they arose. The war had shifted Soviet industry and agriculture into the Urals and Siberia, so Stalin could not ignore the 'vast potential wealth' of Manchuria, a granary for its Far Eastern territories and outlet to warm water ports. Manchuria possessed nearly three quarters of Chinese heavy industry, with immense coal and iron resources still untapped and, under Soviet control, could form the basis of a 'power system in the Far East'. In Korea, the Soviets remained uncompromising and viewed the peninsula as strategically important, providing a shield for Vladivostok and the Soviet land frontier. Japan, a traditional enemy of the Soviets, meant Moscow also watched with alarm the US refusal to reduce Japanese industry to a minimum level and destroy their present social and economic system.[21] Roberts made no suggestion that Britain should play a role in this area and recognised that the future of East Asia would essentially depend on the strength and continuity of US interest, internal developments in China, Japan and Korea, and both the Soviet and American ability to devote resources simultaneously on several fronts or to free themselves from European or Middle Eastern commitments. The British could do no more than keep a watching brief, protect their dwindling interests in the area and consider what response they should take if the Americans asked for help in restraining Soviet influence.

The occupation of Japan

British observers provided London with mixed reviews about Japan's rehabilitation. Dermot MacDermot, the Foreign Office official on special service in Japan, and Sansom, representing Britain on the Far Eastern Commission, provided the two most influential reports, both reaching Bevin. Each man had served in Japan before the war but at 39, MacDermot was a generation apart from Sansom at 63, which shaped their outlook towards the Japanese. As a young man MacDermot served in the Far East during a period when Japan was no longer Britain's ally and embarking on aggressive expansion in China. Sansom, on the other hand, had intimate contacts with many Japanese and had known Japan not just as an aggressor but also as a firm ally, since the days of the Anglo-Japanese alliance from 1902 to 1923. MacDermot distrusted the Japanese and thought they had changed little, replacing totalitarian with democratic slogans to placate the Americans who they saw as 'tourists' collecting 'flashy souvenirs'. The 'easy-going sloppiness' of the US soldier, he noted, simply illustrated to him what the Japanese had read about 'our "spiritual inferiority" '. They were alert to dividing British and American policies and merely 'counting the hours until our withdrawal', which given the publicity to the American wish to return their troops home as quickly as possible did not appear long. Although militarism had been 'wiped out' there was, MacDermot observed, a danger in assuming all was well: Japan was 'playing on her home ground against a rather scratch team'. To establish a 'New Order', he argued that the allies had to commit publicly to an occupation of 20 years.[22]

Sansom disagreed with MacDermot. He doubted that an occupation longer than five years would produce anything other than an unstable coalition, which would 'fly apart' once SCAP left. Sansom was sceptical that by indoctrination it was possible to change the political habits of a whole nation and to destroy or at least greatly modify its intellectual tradition. He knew of no historical precedent. Sansom argued that the allies should strive for modest aims: an assurance Japan would not aggress again; the emergence of a democratic system; civil rights for the Japanese people; and an economic policy that would not 'run counter to our own'. 'If we get these things', he concluded, 'we shall have done pretty well'.[23] Sansom's views prevailed as he confidently told his wife that the majority of Far Eastern Department thinking on Japan was 'inspired' by himself.[24] On duty with the Far Eastern Commission in Tokyo and, with MacArthur's approval, Sansom had also met old Japanese friends, such as Dr Hitoshi Ashida, now the welfare minister, and Shigeru Yoshida, the foreign minister. He thought Yoshida 'lazy' and 'never really first class', and Prime Minister Kijūrō Shidehara 'a melancholy figure' unfit to lead his country in a crisis. Alive to the possibilities of the Japanese playing the British off against the Americans, Sansom nevertheless agreed with Ashida's view that Britain was more likely to have 'sound' long-term views than the United States.[25]

Although MacDermot was less prepared to give the Japanese the benefit of the doubt than Sansom, both men praised MacArthur's excellent start with disarmament, demobilisation and the rescue of prisoners of war. US unilateral control of Japan was also a welcome antidote to current European 'muddles' but the scope for direct involvement in SCAP seemed limited. MacDermot's hope for a British role in education looked tenuous after Sansom approached SCAP's Information and Education Section and they refused to 'integrate' British advisers into their own machine because it would also mean accommodating the Soviets. Gairdner snapped this was a convenient excuse. Sansom also attempted to warn members of SCAP that a harsh policy towards breaking up the *zaibatsu*, which differed 'only in degree and not in kind' from similar combinations in the United States, was 'not practical but merely vindictive'.[26] Yet, during the first years of the occupation, SCAP, contrary to Sansom's advice, aimed to reduce the power of the *zaibatsu*. In addition, MacArthur instituted land reform, remodelled education, fostered trade unions and drew up a new constitution along US lines, which disavowed the use of war. The Emperor renounced divinity and many prominent Japanese wartime figures were put on trial for war crimes at an International Military Tribunal.[27] MacArthur never toured Japan to see things himself, living in virtual pro-consular remoteness 'above the clouds', and the fact that SCAP was a military organisation must have reinforced a belief the soldier counted for more than the civilian.[28] When witnessing large crowds gathering daily at MacArthur's headquarters to watch his arrival and departure, one political adviser to UKLM remarked, 'he is admired, of course, as a great commander, not as a democratizing influence'.[29]

MacArthur had his British critics. The press attacked him with stories alleging the large-scale fraternisation of US soldiers with Japanese women, while *The Times* correspondent, the Japanologist Frank Hawley, made no secret of the fact that he felt the Americans were blundering around in Japan. British public opinion was also bitterly hostile to Japan as Fleet Street made charges that SCAP was being unduly lenient.[30] MacArthur's 'dictatorial methods' and 'overbearing temperament', Sterndale Bennett argued, invited criticism. The latter was aggrieved that MacArthur had 'jumped' everyone (including Washington) on the issue of a draft constitution, with no reference to the Far Eastern Commission.[31] A new young team responsible for Japanese policy in the Foreign Office, a result of the break up of the Far Eastern Department, also had reservations. The Japan and Pacific Department, staffed by three men in their thirties, but superintended by the experienced Dening (back from SEAC), was annoyed that MacArthur relegated the Far Eastern Commission and Allied Council to mere 'moral umbrellas' for the execution of his own policies. In addition, the department foresaw potential economic rivalry with the United States, such as their desire to bring Japanese trade permanently within the dollar area. In a brief for Bevin's forthcoming meeting with dominion prime ministers in London, the department nevertheless concluded that the foreign secretary's most important task was to convince the dominions (especially Australia) that the Americans were meeting the Commonwealth's broader requirements, such as rendering Japan incapable of aggression, and 'of the wisdom of leaving well alone'. The brief stated

Britain's 'vital interests' were in Southeast Asia, that it was 'not prepared to spend any money on Japan' beyond supporting BCOF and UKLM, and despite his faults, MacArthur was carrying out his tasks 'admirably'. It would therefore be 'foolish' to antagonise him.[32]

The weakness of the British position in Japan was demonstrated by what turned out to be a pointless cabinet discussion on allowing Japan to rebuild merchant ships once more. Ministers like Bevin and Sir Stafford Cripps, the President of the Board of Trade, argued that Japan must export to live and pay for shipping to carry its exports rather than making others pay, while those with military portfolios, such as Alexander and Alfred Barnes, the Minister of War Transport, worried that allowing Japan to build merchant ships might enable it to create a valuable war potential of skilled men and technical expertise. This caution was shared by Australia and New Zealand, whose views had been sought, only for Bevin to tell cabinet on 8 March that the United States had just announced that Japanese shipyards had (since Japan's surrender) rebuilt 524 vessels totalling over one million tons and had under construction 133 new merchant ships. Their whole debate, Bevin told his colleagues, was completely 'redundant' owing to US unilateral action. The cabinet merely agreed to conclude that Britain was not prepared to undertake any financial burden in meeting the economic consequences of restrictions imposed on Japan's industry.[33]

The Commonwealth, Japan and regional defence

In 1946, US intelligence assessments on the value of the British Commonwealth and Empire were mixed. The dominions, British India and the colonies, they noted, possessed a wealth of manpower, natural resources, strategic materials and a substantial contribution to Britain's industrial potential, without which the latter would be 'at best a second class power'. At the same time the Empire and the Commonwealth imposed heavy obligations on defence, covering 12.5 million square miles of territory and holding one-fifth of the world's population. The Americans calculated there were only nine white persons per square mile of temperate land and that the manpower of a dominion for its own defence was limited largely by the size of its white population while the Indian army was now unlikely to be relied upon. In addition, the war had exposed the 'falseness' of Britain's ability to protect Australia and New Zealand. The two Pacific dominions, the Americans argued, would now look to the United States for help while Britain would face difficulties persuading Australia and New Zealand to follow a British lead.[34]

According to the Dominions Office, Australia was the most Pacific-minded followed by New Zealand while Canada turned its attention towards Europe.[35] Indeed, at the dominion prime ministers' conference in London during April–May 1946, Chifley told his opposite numbers that Australia's

main military commitments were to BCOF and repatriating Japanese personnel from Australian territories. He also felt the difficult question of allocating
British bases in the Pacific to the United States, which the Americans were
pressing for, should form part of an overall regional security plan in the
Pacific.[36] Lieutenant-General V. A. H. Sturdee, the Australian chief of the
general staff, had told Chifley that Australia should now be the 'dominant
partner' in the Western Pacific. It was time, he argued, for Britain to 'trust'
Australia to be able to control and maintain Commonwealth forces 'in theatres where a particular Dominion has predominant Empire interest'.[37] The
Chiefs of Staff, however, preferred to model Commonwealth defence on
a combined chiefs of staff system, which would be 'sufficiently elastic' to
allow the central direction of any war effort to shift from Britain to one of
the dominions, potentially crucial in the age of atomic warfare. Defence co-
ordination would remain a hot topic but Chifley and Evatt, recognising the
need to make a larger contribution towards defence, felt it was in the Pacific
where the best Australian effort could be made. The extent would be down
to the available manpower and financial resources, a line of argument with
which Attlee readily sympathised.[38]

All agreed that any central set-up concerning defence must allow for
machinery of co-operation with the United States. For the moment, the Foreign Office and the Chiefs of Staff thought it would be prudent not to tie
the American request for bases in the Pacific to a formal regional security
arrangement.[39] Despite Bevin's urging in May at the Paris Council of Foreign
Ministers, the cabinet, and Australia and New Zealand were not prepared
to cede Pacific islands (such as Tarawa) to the Americans, especially when
Byrnes tried to wrap the issue around Congressional agreement for the US
loan.[40] At this stage, the United States was clearly uninterested in organising joint defence arrangements for the Pacific and continued to pay short
shrift to Britain's Pacific dominions.[41] In June, the US embassy handed the
Foreign Office a revision of the draft treaty for the disarmament and demilitarisation of Japan, which 'totally ignored' the necessity for the signatures
of the dominions principally concerned. The British hoped the Soviet Union
would reject the whole idea of a treaty to 'save us contesting this continued
exclusion of the Dominions' but if they did not, Sargent, now permanent
under-secretary at the Foreign Office, was prepared 'to dig in [his] toes' and
insist the dominions sign.[42] Fortunately, the treaty would be subsumed in
the wider discussions for a Japanese peace treaty that emerged in 1947.

A far more divisive issue raised its head in 1946 over the Australian representative to the Allied Council. The British had been unhappy with Evatt's
appointment of William Macmahon Ball to the Council, preferring Keith
Officer, the veteran diplomat. Ball, as head of the political science department at Melbourne University, had little experience of diplomacy but Attlee,
wary of current Australian sensitivities, did not press the matter. British fears
proved well founded: MacArthur despised Ball, calling him a communist

while the Australian referred to the general as 'God'. There was initial British sympathy for Ball after US tactics at the Council (usually in the form of long lectures) rendered the body impotent. Even Gairdner, an avid admirer of MacArthur, believed that the general was becoming too dictatorial and too impatient of criticism, seeing Communist influences at work 'in places where they exist only in his head'.[43] The Allied Council was not, however, the forum to have a row with the Americans, a point Ball failed to grasp when he sometimes lined up with General Kuzma Derevyanko, the Soviet delegate or tried to play the mediator between the Soviet and the American representatives. Evatt nevertheless refused to openly criticise Ball (his stance played well at home) while UKLM fretted that Ball's attitude would affect their 'excellent' relations with MacArthur, especially as the Soviets mischievously referred to him as the 'British representative'. Yet, for the sake of Anglo-Australian relations, Attlee was reluctant to demand Ball's resignation and put faith in Evatt's assurance he would impress upon Ball the importance of giving the United States support on all essential matters.[44]

British disillusionment with BCOF was also growing by mid-1946. Brooke had thought it essential for British troops to be seen alongside the Americans in Japan, to show a united front to the Japanese and the Soviets, but on a visit to London, Gairdner told Bevin that Australia's predominance in, and leadership of, BCOF, now under the command of Lieutenant-General Horace Robertson, was reducing Britain's prestige and position in the Far East to a 'very low ebb'.[45] The China Association considered the allotment of zones in Japan to Britain virtually useless with respect to trading interests.[46] The poor amenities and drab living conditions for BCOF troops were also being reported in both the Australian and the British press.[47] In September, the War Office moved to re-deploy badly needed manpower away from BCOF, proposing to withdraw the British 5th Infantry Brigade (3,500 men). The brigade had barely been in Japan for six months but Brooke's successor as the chief of the imperial general staff, Field Marshal Viscount Montgomery of Alamein, not one to mince his words, told the Chiefs of Staff it was best to tell the Australians point-blank that the British wished to withdraw the brigade.[48] The Defence Committee accepted this advice and Attlee sent a long cable to Chifley in November, underscoring Britain's global commitments. Britain, Attlee explained, was striving to reduce its forces in Hong Kong, Malaya, the Middle East and Europe (including Germany) but the only area where troops could be removed with minimum risk was from Japan.[49] Montgomery gambled correctly and the Australians and MacArthur raised no objections to the withdrawal of the brigade.[50]

The emerging British consensus was that the occupation should be short. The BCOF took no part in governing Japan, it was not aiding Commonwealth trade interests, and the strategic objective of preventing Japan from threatening world peace or falling under the domination of a hostile power was being met by the United States.[51] Although the War Office moved to pull out completely its army component from BCOF, the question remains whether the British should have sent any forces at all? Fraser, the New Zealand prime minister, thought the whole enterprise meaningless. One counter-argument expressed by the Joint Planning Staff was that BCOF acted as a platform to spur wider Commonwealth defence, but it was easy to forget that the Australians had initially wanted to send occupying forces independently of the British. Rather less convincing was the argument that if the BCOF pulled out, it would have a lasting affect on co-operation with the United States. MacArthur, for example, did not want BCOF's removal, yet the Americans had all along remained indifferent to the participation of other nations in the occupation, and one cannot help think that MacArthur's reluctance to let BCOF dissolve stemmed from a fear that his tag as an 'allied' commander would look less authoritative and not because of any sound military necessity.[52]

The British were left with little choice but to attempt to exert influence within SCAP through UKLM. In July, the first civilian head of UKLM, Alvary Gascoigne, arrived in Tokyo.[53] 'Joe' or 'Boomer' Gascoigne had served in China and Japan before the war and was a former head of the Far Eastern Department (1934–6) but he was initially unhappy at being posted back to Japan and felt awkward in front of Gairdner. Gascoigne, however, would see MacArthur and other members of SCAP with considerable frequency, enjoying an amicable relationship with him before 1950. 'Bluff and reasonably direct', Gascoigne was no intellectual but a man of 'shrewdness and common sense'. His military experience during the First World War no doubt played well with MacArthur, who also deemed the relationship worthwhile seeking support for his policies.[54] Like other British officials, Gascoigne shared a mixture of respect for MacArthur's achievements but concern over how truly 'democratic' and remorseful the Japanese really were. He was also unsure how effective their current government was in combating unemployment, inflation and the distribution of foodstuffs.[55] Gascoigne though did not dare contemplate an occupation without MacArthur and argued that the British should back him '100 per cent', despite the fact that he was 'a real power unto himself' and did not give a 'tinker's curse' for either the Far Eastern Commission or Allied Council.[56] SCAP was also continuing to block the return of British business representatives back into Japan, arguing they were not 'of direct operational assistance to the occupation'.[57]

Getting businessmen back into Japan was one issue that led the British to prompt MacArthur about when to expect the 'normalisation' of relations with the Japanese, especially as the new constitution was to come into effect in May 1947. Yet, in a private talk with Gascoigne, MacArthur did not envisage any change until after a peace treaty had been signed. The general also wanted to ensure some guarantees against Japan's re-occupation by a foreign power (a reference to the Soviet Union) and hoped the Japanese would ask to be protected by the allies for a period after the signature of a treaty.[58] Gascoigne was disheartened by this interview, telling Dening the non-resumption of normal relations was a 'dreary prospect';[59] while the Foreign Office was a little alarmed MacArthur dismissed the UN as the rightful body to police Japan after a peace treaty. Jebb rather dryly remarked that the issue was to make sure Japan did not aggress again, not protect it against aggression.[60] The added complication for MacArthur was that a military withdrawal from Japan would adversely affect the US occupation in Korea. If the Americans left Japan, they would have to leave Korea, a development that MacArthur observed meant the Soviet annexation of the peninsula. The general therefore wanted his guarantees and if he did not get them, he felt he had sufficient influence to ensure that there would be no peace treaty and the US occupation would last 'till hell freezes'.[61]

The occupation of Korea

In 1946, Korea remained a clear area of American responsibility and the necessity for any British involvement still seemed questionable, especially as they had little insight into US policy. Almost immediately after the Moscow Council of Foreign Ministers, American views hardened against trusteeship, while figures such as Harriman, MacArthur and Hodge warned Washington that in Korea, as in Eastern Europe, the Soviets aimed to establish 'political domination'. Control of Korea could help expand the Soviet strategic position in the Far East, facilitate the penetration of China and support the industrial development of Siberia. In February 1946, Hodge, MacArthur and Colonel M. Preston Goodfellow (a former OSS deputy director) moved to install Rhee as leader of the Representative Democratic Council, an anti-communist rightist party. North of the 38th parallel, Kim Il-sung became leader of the Interim People's Committee, gradually removing all opposition to his rule. In the middle, the Democratic National Front emerged as a bold effort to accommodate moderate leftists and communists.[62]

The British had little first-hand information on Korea, apart from that gathered by MacDermot after he had paid a flying visit to Seoul in December 1945 in order to inspect the British consulate premises there. He reported on the difficulties that Hodge faced, observing that the Koreans employed by the military government were 'hopelessly incompetent', which militated against 'thrusting independence on a people so ill-fitted for it'. In addition, MacDermot noted that the Americans found the people 'dishonest and stupid'. In short, the economic condition of Korea was governed by the 38th parallel, which, if maintained, 'would cripple it'. For the moment, MacDermot also ascertained that business would not be possible until some exchange rate could be fixed but the issue was essentially unimportant for the British as their economic interests on the peninsula were next to non-existent. The Americans nevertheless did not object to the return of some form of British representation to Korea, which MacDermot reported and the Foreign Office decided to follow up. A Royal Naval Volunteer Reserve officer, Lieutenant D. P. Lury, was sent from Japan to Seoul in the meantime to patch up the consulate and make preparations for the arrival of a British diplomat.[63] Despite being so cut off from developments in Korea, the Foreign Office also clung to its right to deliberate the final recommendations of the Joint Commission, which had now begun its work. The Dominions Office could not understand such reasoning and thought the Foreign Office 'extremely dilatory' over the whole subject. The Foreign Office, however, made it clear that it was for Britain, not Australia, to take a decision on any trusteeship proposal that emerged, even though they hoped Australia would assume the burden as the fourth power.[64]

Foreign Office reluctance to disassociate itself entirely from the Korean settlement seems ludicrous given that Britain was trying to relieve the burden of many of its global responsibilities. Korea possessed no strategic, economic or political significance for the British and why it was not possible to let Australia represent its interests immediately, as it had done for the Allied Council for Japan, is unclear. The Americans and the Soviets cared little for British views on Korea and the peninsula was far less important to Britain than Japan, providing London with another opportunity to give Australia (to use Evatt's words) a 'special status' in the Far East and the Pacific. One can only speculate why the Foreign Office took such a stance: was Australian representation in an international body for Japan deemed enough; or did they seriously believe Britain was tied to the 1943 Cairo Declaration, even though other powers had long seemed indifferent to whether the British adhered to it or not? The overriding suspicion is that the Foreign Office was holding on to Britain's pre-war position as a great power and its right to have a say in all global affairs. As Korea was so low on Britain's foreign policy agenda, Labour ministers rarely involved themselves in the issue, allowing the Foreign Office to direct policy.[65] It was not until April that the Foreign Office despatched Derwent Kermode, who held previous pre-war consular experience of Korea and Japan, as a liaison officer to Hodge's headquarters. Kermode reached Seoul in May but his position (or rather plight) was embarrassing. He was housed in a bleak residence where lack of glasses forced him to use jam jars to serve drinks. He had no safe, could not use ciphers (precluding a secure means of communication), and telegraphic material had to be sent via US channels to Tokyo for transmission, considerably delaying the delivery of despatches to London.[66]

In fact, the Foreign Office's most reliable insight into Korea came not from Seoul but Moscow when Frank Roberts, due to his excellent relations with the US embassy, now headed by the wartime general, Walter Bedell Smith,[67] was unofficially passed 'Top Secret' information unbeknown to Washington. In the strictest secrecy, Roberts told London that in a conference before the Joint Commission (16 January–5 February), the Soviet team, headed by

General Terentyi Shtikov, opposed schemes for unification, insisted upon 'utterly impracticable' quantities of rice, and refused to discuss capital goods, where evidence continued to indicate the removal of such equipment. In addition, no agreement was reached on making available to southern Korea electric power generated in the Soviet zone. When the Joint Commission convened on 20 March, the Americans, Roberts reported, aimed to form a 'Korean Consultative Union' that would represent all parties and offer advice to the Commission. The Soviets wanted to exclude parties hostile to the Moscow Declaration (effectively all democratic parties in the southern zone), insisted on separate consultation with each party, and blocked moves for inter-zonal meetings of Korean leaders. Roberts also passed back US intelligence on the 'abnormal quantities' of Soviet troops in the northern Korea. Agents reported more than one Red Army officer boasting it would take five days to overrun southern Korea. In short, the Americans were 'gloomy' about the long-term prospects for Korea but they intended to put up a fight as best they could.[68] Upon reading Roberts' report the Foreign Office was not so sure and thought the United States could well 'sell out' to the Soviets in order to consolidate their position in Japan.[69]

The Soviet delegation to the Joint Commission left Seoul on 9 May signalling its failure and the evidence suggests Stalin backed the strong line taken by the delegation.[70] The deadlock, which saw the Joint Commission adjourn for a year, brought forth a wave of nationalism in South Korea, along with mass demonstrations, rioting and the murder of leftist leaders.[71] The Foreign Office, meanwhile, received more secret reports from Roberts and also UKLM. This included Hodge's aversion to the concept of trusteeship; reports from officers of the Strategic Services Unit (SSU, the successor to OSS) attached to Edwin Pauley's reparations commission; and intelligence that the Red Army had a force of 250,000 men on the peninsula. It was a risky move on the part of Smith and MacArthur to sanction such a free exchange of information and the former made it clear the Americans could not be seen discussing Korea in advance with Britain until they had 'cleared their own minds'.[72] Yet it was a risk probably deemed worth taking in the sense of being seen to be co-operative, especially as they knew British involvement in Korea was at this stage nil, precluding any Anglo-American disagreement. Indeed, the first Foreign Office memorandum on Korea for 1946 was constructed completely from second-hand accounts.[73] When Kermode's despatches arrived in June, they added little to what was already known and reflected the gloom inside Hodge's headquarters where US officers were describing Korea as 'the first battleground in a new war'. This was not surprising as Kermode was completely reliant on the Americans for his information.[74]

It is difficult to understand what the Foreign Office hoped Kermode could achieve for them. They were being well informed about Korea from plenty of sources and even shifts in the US attitude over trusteeship, particularly

Byrnes's gradual shying away from the idea, were picked up first in the press.[75] Initially, Kermode's presence only served to potentially draw Britain into the Korean imbroglio. Hodge's political adviser, William F. Langdon, asked Kermode in June whether the British would be prepared to approach the Soviet Union to help bring about a resumption of the Joint Commission. It forced the Foreign Office to engage in a lengthy discussion about what to do, the consensus being that it was no place for Britain to get involved in attempts to save the Joint Commission. It begged the question whether there was a need to be involved at all but Dening, summing up the discussion, depressed at what he saw as the poor American handling of the Korean situation, did not see how Britain could remain 'permanently aloof', especially if the United States decided to stay the course in which a bitter struggle would ensue and they would look for moral support.[76] Why, though, did Britain need to provide even moral support when hitherto the Americans had paid scant attention to British views on the subject? Indeed, when Langdon suggested to Byrnes that the British approach the Soviets, his scheme was rejected outright.[77]

At this stage, the Americans did not want to approach the Soviets on a governmental level, which both Langdon and Hodge had pressed for, or call for the simultaneous withdrawal of Soviet–American forces. SWNCC thought such moves would indicate to both the Soviet Union and the Koreans signs of 'impatience' and that the United States wished to rid itself of the responsibility it had assumed in Korea. In a letter to Pauley, Truman had already stated that his administration needed to 'to see the job through' and 'have adequate personnel and sufficient funds to do a good job'. US officials now drew up an interim policy specifically suited to the development of the southern zone. The State Department, with War and Navy Department approval, wanted to encourage the employment of Koreans suitable for high administrative posts through electoral processes, which would work towards a unified administration for Korea. As the policy developed, SWNCC also considered revitalising the educational system and helping to develop the Korean economy. This time the British had no foreknowledge of American action even though the new policy had been wired to the Moscow embassy.[78] They learned of it instead through a short non-attributed piece in *The Scotsman* of 12 July, stating Truman had approved a 'far-reaching policy' for Korea, which intended to continue the occupation of Korea 'indefinitely', to establish a separate southern Korean government and to concentrate on revival in the U.S. sector only.[79]

Without checking the piece's authenticity, Arthur de la Mare of the Japan and Pacific Department launched into a private tirade over the lack of US 'frankness', and the 'cavalier treatment of their staunchest ally', which was symptomatic of their conviction across the Far East that Britain would fall into line with whatever they set down. He moaned that US tactics were simply to 'implore us' to show a united front against the Soviets if there were signs of disagreement, taking advantage of 'our anxiety not to increase their difficulties'. De la Mare had seen this tactic used far too often in block-ing British efforts to re-establish influence in Japan. He did not deny the right of the United States to play the leading role in East Asia but 'if we are to stop the abuse of our honest and sincere desire to be as helpful as possible we must sooner or later let them know that our subservience cannot always be taken for granted'. It was fighting talk from the junior official (the son of a Jersey farmer) but he was calmed somewhat after Kermode wired that *The Scotsman* had got hold of a 'garbled' version of the facts. The Americans, he observed, were 'too weak to risk so provocative a step' as establishing a separate government.[80] The episode highlighted once again how uninter-ested the Americans were in keeping the British abreast of their policy for Korea. When Sansom visited Vincent to discuss Korea in September, in what must have been a strained interview, the former clearly thought the director ignorant of Korea, scoffing at some of his assertions, particularly Vincent's claim that the Joint Commission would work and there would be no public disapproval of a long occupation, which Sansom argued was because the US people did not understand the dangers.[81]

As the Americans instituted a new policy, they invited the British along with the Nationalist Chinese and French to set up a consulate at Seoul. The British agreed to install Kermode as a consul-general, invoking the example of Germany where consular offices had also been established, despite the allied occupation. The move was nevertheless odd as there were no British subjects in Korea.[82] Kermode's role continued to be that of polit-ical reporting, most of it based exclusively on information from Hodge's headquarters. His assessment was largely negative, which in turn guided the Foreign Office reaction. Lack of experience, the continuous change of personnel caused by demobilisation, the venality of the Koreans on whom they relied, Communist sabotage in the south and the ostensible strength of the Soviets, all contributed to a feeling of frustration amongst Americans. Foreign Office officials declared that Kermode's despatches made 'grim reading' and they were sure the United States was 'not up to its job'.[83] These events remained largely shielded from the British public as the press and parliament unsurprisingly took little interest in Korea. Brigadier Fitzroy Maclean, the Conservative MP and former SAS officer, did visit Korea and raised the uneasy situation in the House of Com-mons but he was a poor speaker and the impact was minimal.[84] In late 1946, as Hodge sent back alarmist despatches, which UKLM obtained, that the Soviets were preparing for an invasion using a force of Kore-ans armed and trained by the Red Army, Washington looked for ways out.[85] Vincent hoped some kind of unified administration would emerge to allow the Americans to leave while General John Hilldring, assistant sec-retary of state for occupied areas at the War Department, argued that if the Soviets came forward with a proposition for both sides to pull its troops out, 'we would decide – and very properly in my opinion, to haul our freight'.[86]

Civil war in China

The situation in China was proving to be just as much as a headache for the Americans. The British, who took a greater interest in developments there, considered it was 'wholly in the balance' whether China would emerge as a unified country on the way to becoming a modern state. The Nationalist–Communist 'war', as Wallinger described it, was 'gathering momentum' and unless a truce was obtained, the British predicted Chiang would at best be in control of the large coastal and river ports while maintaining partial control of the railway zones. Britain, contrary to some US claims, did not want a de-stabilised China. A united China, albeit under Nationalist control, meant better conditions for trading, a safer environment for the British community and improved prospects for Far Eastern regional security on Western terms.[87] Seymour hoped that Marshall's arrival in China with his specific objective of brokering a settlement could deliver such an outcome. Chou En-lai (Zhou Enlai), the chief Communist representative in Chungking with whom SIS had had a link during the war, told Seymour there must be a cessation of hostilities, as long as 'political' matters – the formation of a coalition government, a national assembly and so on – had been settled and their armies could share in taking the Japanese surrender in the north. When the ambassador told Marshall of his conversation with Chou, the American warned Seymour that the Chinese found little difficulty in agreeing general and ill-defined principles but when it came to translating them into practice the discussions were vague and inconclusive. Despite a ceasefire in January reports of fighting in northern China continued and Seymour soon reported it was difficult 'to be sanguine about any solid settlement'.[88]

Negotiations continued, however, and Marshall secured assent from both sides to an all-party assembly (as a precursor to the formal drafting of a constitution) and the reduction of the Nationalist army to 60 divisions of which 10 were to be Communist. Yet Washington, concerned about Soviet aims in East Asia, continued to give Chiang a substantial aid package (just under $840m since V-J Day). The ceasefire soon broke down in Manchuria and the public release of the Yalta accords provided Chiang with a powerful weapon to stir up populist anti-Soviet propaganda. Chiang had remained reluctant to endorse Marshall's efforts, convinced that Stalin, under the umbrella of the Communists, would extend his influence over northern China. Seymour, while not condoning civil war, agreed that the Soviet aim was to lay a 'solid' Communist foundation in the north and northeast, creating 'a belt of satellite states' running from Sinkiang (Xinjiang) via Inner Mongolia to Korea. This could be done either through the holding of vital areas by the Chinese Communists or through Soviet treaty rights over the main railways, Dairen and general penetration efforts. Evidence suggests that Stalin maintained an equivocal relationship with Mao in the first months of 1946 and the latter received little help from him. Only when the Red Army began to withdraw from Manchuria in March did Stalin give Mao the opportunity to occupy Harbin and Changchun, which was promptly met by a strong Nationalist offensive. In all this, Seymour claimed that it was pointless for the British to pretend to exert any influence in the region 'beyond general support of United States policy', as the Soviets knew Britain was 'quite incapable' of helping to build up China (or, he added, for that matter Japan).[89]

Seymour's statement made a mockery of the claim by the Joint Chiefs of Staff that Britain was bidding to secure a military advisory group in China on the same lines as the United States, up to 4,600 personnel! Byrnes signalled his anxiety that the whole enterprise looked liked a 'projection' of US power onto the Asian continent, but the Joint Chiefs refused to back down arguing they were carrying out announced policy, though they agreed to limit the total to 915 personnel until the political and military organisation of China was clearer.[90] This debate came at a time when both American and British officials were considering their response to the Soviet refusal to withdraw their troops (scheduled for 1 February) from Manchuria until a satisfactory outcome over the disposal of Japanese industrial equipment had been achieved. The Soviets were prepared to drop their demands that the equipment was 'war booty' provided they received shares of stock in the enterprises, and demanded 51 per cent interest in heavy industries and 49 per cent in light industries. This effectively undermined the policy of the 'open door', which had elicited an American *démarche* to Moscow on 9 February after strong pressure from Harriman and Marshall but which fell short of a 'blast', after Vincent felt this was an issue for the Inter-Allied Reparations Commission, operating within the framework of the Far Eastern Commission.[91]

When Moscow failed to reply, Dr Wang Shih-chieh (Wang Shijie), the Nationalist Chinese foreign minister, approached the British for help, telling Wallinger the problem could not remain 'unsolved', upset that US policy was not 'very clearly defined'.[92] The Foreign Office reaction was initially mixed: Christopher Warner, the head of the Northern Department, thought the British should make searching enquiries of the Soviets and then give them publicity – *The Times* had, for example, followed events in Manchuria closely – in an effort to force the Americans to react and take lead. Sterndale Bennett and Paul Mason, the head of the North American Department disagreed. This was American business. It would do them 'good to stand up to the Russians for once' Mason quipped but Britain should support them. Even Chiang impressed upon Marshall that the outcome depended on the strength of the American, not British, stand and he hoped Truman's tough stance over Iran would be replicated in China. Unbeknown to the British the Americans did make further protests, which drew a rather prickly response from Sterndale Bennett in conversation with Waldemar Gallman, the chargé at the American embassy in London, that he hoped the United States would inform him of further actions. He did not wish to suggest a policy of 'ganging up' on the Soviets but told Gallman that the British were due to issue their own note to Moscow stressing that Japanese industrial equipment should form part of the total available for division between allied governments.[93] Bevin explained to cabinet that he was against taking up the issue of the 'open door', fearful of being dragged into the dispute about US troops in China but he felt it important to at least put on record the British view as a claimant nation, even though he recognised most of the equipment had probably gone.[94] The Soviets finally agreed to withdraw their troops that spring and replied to the British note, dismissing its contents stating that requisitioned Japanese equipment were 'trophies' of the Red Army. A US inquiry estimated the Soviets had made off with equipment worth $2 billion. There was little Britain or the United States could do.[95]

As the Soviets left and, with their approval, the Chinese Communists attempted to fill the vacuum, Chiang's armies, receiving US logistical help, launched an offensive in North China, capturing Changchun in May and occupying the central region of Manchuria. Taking a gamble that his alliance with the United States would hold as the international situation darkened, Chiang, however, miscalculated. Marshall warned the Nationalists that if they did not terminate the fighting, his mission would become untenable; arranged the appointment as ambassador of John Leighton Stuart, the president of the Yenching University in Peking (Beijing) who had called for Chiang's resignation; and imposed an arms embargo (effective in August 1946) on the Nationalists. It was clear that Marshall's mission had become unworkable set against an American policy that could never achieve impartiality. Marshall blamed 'die-hard' elements within the *Kuomintang* (the Nationalist ruling party) for pushing Chiang towards war but Vincent was unconvinced. He also thought the Nationalist leader was never likely to be able to eliminate the Communists from China. If he tried, newly conquered areas would entail the utilisation of force on a 'ruinously expensive scale'. Yet, the Generalissimo pressed on and when Nationalist troops took Kalgan in northern China in October, Marshall asked to be recalled.[96]

Britain tended to monitor the civil war in relation to the effects it had on Hong Kong, commercial prospects and the British community. As the civil war deepened, Nationalist attention towards Hong Kong waned and the colony began to emerge as the only 'safe depôt' on the Chinese coast for trade. Whitehall had debated returning Hong Kong to China in 1946 but Bevin and Sargent, who were not prepared to give away parts of the Empire when there was no pressure to do so, rejected the idea. On the advice of the Chiefs of Staff, however, the Defence Committee of the cabinet did accept that Hong Kong be declared an open port, as it could not be protected against attack by a major power in occupation of the Chinese mainland. Two battalions were maintained there simply to ensure order.[97]

In Shanghai, the situation was far worse: the cost of living there was 4,000 times that in 1936 but the number of Chinese dollars to the pound was only 500 times greater. All the public utility companies in Shanghai were operating at a loss due to inadequate control prices; strikes were a constant feature; interest rates were fantastically high; and the black market, fuelled by American soldiers and 'carpet baggers', was so large that healthy trading was impossible. Ogden complained that the Americans were also acting in an 'overbearing' manner, requisitioning buildings, seizing berths and wharves, and assuming virtual unilateral control of the port, only handing it to the Chinese authorities in July 1946 as the US Navy moved a large part of its fleet to Tsingtao (and this was more in theory than practice). When Seymour visited Tsingtao and Tientsin, where shots were heard in the streets at night and looting was frequent, he found the British community 'depressed'. In the south of China, Sir Ronald Hall, the British consul-general in Canton, told Seymour there was nothing cheap enough worth exporting and trade was dead. British merchants were not re-establishing their interests and letting their buildings, prompting Hall to declare 'we have changed locally from a nation of tradesmen to a nation of landlords'.[98]

During the rest of 1946, the newly created China Department of the Foreign Office, headed by the experienced China-hand, George Kitson, put together a series of memoranda, which reflected the dire conditions in China. They reiterated the main thrust of previous assessments: the need for a stable China, the inability of Britain to provide economic or financial aid, the restoration of British property rights; and the need to preserve some footing for a return to Chinese markets at a later stage – a forthcoming trade mission was one example, along with the appointment of shipping and labour attachés, and negotiating a commercial treaty. In reality, little had changed since the end of the war, and the British were refused access to the Yangtze on the grounds their ships would arouse nationalist feeling and provoke incidents; while the Foreign Office struggled to fill 11 of the 20 consular posts that had been open before the war due to political conditions in the north and the lack of new entrants.[99] The new British ambassador to China, Sir Ralph Stevenson, tried to press Britain's case when he arrived in August taking up his residence in Nanking but found nearly all members of the ruling *Kuomintang* 'obsessed' with the Soviet Union, which 'ran like a bright red thread through the rather drab woof' of all his conversations with them. Stevenson did, however, manage to establish cordial relations with his US opposite number (Stuart) at a time when the Foreign Office considered they were completely in the dark as to American intentions in China. It was unfortunate that the 70-year-old anglophile Stuart possessed little influence with Washington, knew 'nothing' about US foreign policy, and left embassy work to the career man, W. Walton Butterworth, who had no experience of China either.[100]

In August, alarmed at the turn of events and the prospect of chaos spreading throughout China, the Foreign Office wanted Halifax's successor, Lord Inverchapel, to elicit from the State Department what the Americans intended to do, especially as in Korea they had constructed an interim policy but in China now seemed to be taking a step backwards. In putting across these points, the embassy had to 'avoid giving the impression' that Britain had 'any desire to assume a share in the responsibility for the present United States policy which may well end in failure'.[101] When Hubert Graves of the Washington embassy confronted Vincent, the latter reassuringly responded that the United States had no intention of withdrawing its Marines – which was of concern to the British as their removal could affect the safety of British communities in Tientsin and Tsingtao – until the situation permitted them to do so, while Marshall was still trying to broker a peace. Yet, there was no desire, Vincent argued, to give 'all-out support' to Chiang to prosecute a war, a view emphasised by Marshall and Butterworth, which directed the United States to a policy of 'holding the ring' and persuading the Generalissimo and Mao that the fight was draining both sides. Vincent added that his official experience in China led him to believe that adopting a waiting policy was best in the circumstances. Relived, Kitson felt Vincent's response 'gave us, as well as the Americans, a breathing space' though, as Dening observed, British policy was completely dependent on American and Soviet moves and how they responded to the internal situation. Britain could only sit and watch and react accordingly as best it could.[102]

On the ground, when a British trade mission toured China in late 1946, it had no authority to enter into any commercial commitments or to hold out prospects of credits of any kind. The Foreign Office warned the Board of Trade, who along with the China Association had pushed for the mission, that the Americans remained suspicious of the British over post-war China trade and were still refusing to show London their draft commercial treaty on the pretext consultation would amount to 'ganging-up on the Chinese'.[103] That autumn, when Vincent asked Inverchapel for British views on their policy on China, the Foreign Office made a plea for closer consultation in order for them to 'keep in step' with the Americans. British policy had to be 'broad and flexible' but limited to moral support to the Nationalist government to encourage a strong, stable and democratic China; resisting ultra-nationalistic attempts to discriminate British commercial interests; and widening cultural relations with the Chinese. The British wanted to avoid a Communist take-over of China, which could affect their position in Southeast Asia, given the large Chinese communities, for example, in Malaya and Burma but for the moment (as Dening had stated), there was not much Britain could do.[104] Fundamentally, both the British and the Americans thought time was on their side, while Washington believed if assistance to Chiang was suspended, he would have to remove 'reactionary elements' and undertake reforms that could win the support of the people, and as a result lessen Soviet interference by drawing Mao away from Stalin. Truman, ignorant of Chinese affairs, relied implicitly on Marshall, and when the latter sought to reduce the Marine force to 5,000 men, the president replied, 'whatever General Marshall wanted done would be done'. By the end of the year Marshall's mission was effectively over.[105]

Throughout 1946 Britain had prodded at ways to maintain its influence in East Asia when the evidence suggested it was unnecessary (as in Korea), largely ineffective (as in Japan) and virtually impotent (as in China). In the region as a whole, the Americans and the Soviets still remained indifferent to British views. In attempting to maintain Britain's international profile (and here the Foreign Office was the department most inclined to try) instead of accepting a very low-key role, there was a likelihood that the Americans would turn to their Atlantic ally for support only when they ran into trouble. Had the Americans been more co-operative during periods without crisis, a willingness to support them would have been difficult to question, but why the British felt compelled to continually push for a greater say in East Asian affairs, when the United States at best grudgingly accommodated British desires, is difficult to understand. Since the war, the Americans had claimed that the area was their responsibility almost exclusively so and one cannot help wonder if the British had expressed a desire to show no interest in Korea, withdraw all its troops from Japan, run a smaller version of UKLM; and worry less about keeping in step with the Americans in China, whether Washington would have really cared? Parliament certainly took little interest: Maclean was the only MP to tour the region properly, and as we have seen he was rather ineffective (apart from allowing Gascoigne to send MacArthur his glowing articles of the occupation). According to Drumright, now the first secretary at the American embassy in London, the British public was also indifferent, as the future of Germany, Palestine and India began to dominate the press and the diplomatic agenda.[106]

5
Questioning Engagement

In 1947, the British failed to see a clear US strategy for East Asia. Marshall's failure in China, chaos in Korea and a faltering economy in Japan led Dening to refer to 'the absence of an American policy', which was 'endangering the whole position in the Far East'. Britain, however, was not able, as the *Manchester Guardian* suggested, to exert its influence in East Asia to 'prevent that fatal hardening of policies' between East and West which was developing in Europe. There had been nearly 250,000 British Commonwealth troops under arms in the Far East in October 1945. By July 1947, that figure dropped to 30,000. British influence in the region was no longer about 'a display' of armed strength and British forces could fulfil only a limited role in the Far East, their main task being the maintenance of internal order in Britain's colonial territories. The imminent British withdrawal from British India, Ceylon and Burma also required a fresh approach to the region. The greater use of cultural and information organisations was seen as one answer; liquidating Lord Killearn's special commissioner's post, another. The press and MPs attacked his large staff, built up during the food crisis in 1946, and London sought to fuse his role with the Governor-General of the Malaya States and Singapore, a post held by the small, wiry and engaging Malcolm MacDonald.[1]

As Britain headed for what Killearn called the 'worst economic and financial crisis in its history' – the suspension of the free convertibility of sterling occurred in August 1947 – a reduction in commitments to the Far East made sense.[2] The bitter winter of 1946–7 had paralysed Britain's economy creating large coal shortages and high unemployment while Europe was failing to recover from the war. Dalton was desperate to reduce overseas spending and cut military expenditure.[3] He pressed the Chiefs of Staff to make cuts, arguing that economic disaster was the 'greater danger', not the risk of being unprepared for war. Forced by the cabinet to set spending below £700 million by 1949, leaving total personnel at 713,000, A.V. Alexander, now the new Minister of Defence, warned his colleagues that Britain would soon be forced to abandon its position in the Pacific, while its strength in the Middle

East and Germany would be seriously weakened. The cuts would leave only 80,500 men for Britain's global responsibilities outside Europe.[4] With the loss of Indian manpower – the emergence of India and Pakistan as two separate dominions occurred on 15 August – a Far Eastern theatre reserve would disappear. The protection of British interests in the region would depend principally on the formation of eight Gurkha battalions based in Malaya. In Japan, Indian troops left BCOF on the heels of both British and New Zealand withdrawals, while the Chiefs of Staff considered removing all British personnel in September.[5] By the end of 1947, just 700 British specialists were left in BCOF and the latter stood at 17,000 personnel compared to 110,000 US troops still present.[6] As the British complained about the lack of US engagement in the Far East, Britain appeared to be carrying out its very own policy of disengagement.

The British accusations were also unfair. General Marshall, now the new US Secretary of State, was keen to maintain an American presence in East Asia. He had no desire to disengage from either China, Japan or Korea. Marshall, a welcome appointment to many in Britain, brought order to the State Department by establishing a Policy Planning Staff in April under George Kennan and by ensuring that all divisional recommendations went through Dean Acheson, the undersecretary of state, and his successor from July, Robert Lovett. That same month, Congress passed a National Security Act, leading to the creation of the National Security Council (NSC), the National Security Resources Board (NSRB) and the Central Intelligence Agency (CIA). The White House sat in the centre of this new apparatus but Truman rarely attended NSC meetings and as departments pushed for more initiatives, commitments exceeded capabilities. Divergences in thinking also emerged. The State Department wanted to lessen the US burden in China but engage in Korea; the Pentagon sought a greater commitment to China yet wished to withdraw from Korea. There was more harmony when it came to Japan, with no support in Washington for MacArthur's attempt to pull US troops out of Japan proper or conclude a peace treaty at speed.[7]

Assessing the dangers

In 1947, the future of Europe and the Middle East continued to dominate both the US and the British policy agenda. The Far East remained much lower on the list of priorities. As the international situation darkened, the British sparked a crisis when they informed the Americans in February they could no longer provide aid to Greece. Those within the Truman administration had little doubt the United States should provide help. If Greece and Turkey fell into the Soviet orbit, London and Washington could be faced with the general unravelling of the Western position in the Near East. Militarily, Anglo-American war planning demanded access to the Eastern Mediterranean to allow air strikes from the Middle East. On 12 March,

Truman told a Republican-dominated Congress and an uneasy public that nations had to 'choose between alternate ways of life' and for those who looked to Washington the latter had to provide leadership. In a dramatic speech, the president spoke of 'a fateful hour' and requested $400m in aid for Greece and Turkey. By the early summer the legislation had been passed and the 'Truman Doctrine' would pave the way for the Marshall Plan, European recovery and the rehabilitation of Germany and Japan. In July Kennan's 'long telegram' was published anonymously in *Foreign Affairs*.[8] In response, Andrei Zhandov spoke of 'two camps' at the founding conference of the Cominform in September, while Stalin saw the Marshall Plan as a US attempt to gain predominant influence in Europe, revive German industrial and military potential and then direct it at the Soviet Union.[9]

Whatever Stalin believed, American resources remained finite and US policymakers had to consider carefully which countries required engagement and which would receive Congressional support. Korea, for example, was not a vital American strategic interest and US war planning called for the evacuation of troops from the peninsula in a future global conflict.[10] US policymakers such as Forrestal therefore asked whether it made sense to keep troops in the southern half of Korea, particularly as instability prevailed and there seemed to be a lack of popular Korean support for the US occupation. Politically and ideologically, however, could the United States be seen backtracking from a commitment that was an American responsibility? If the Truman administration walked away from Korea, what did it mean for US leadership throughout the world – were they prepared to live up to their obligations and responsibilities? The difficulty for the administration was that if they tried to authorise aid for Korea, it would be hard for them to ignore Chiang Kai-shek's repeated requests for assistance. And, if Congress were faced with too many requests in the East Asia, it might affect appropriations for Europe.[11]

Britain was first in line in the European queue for such aid, while Inverchapel reported from Washington that British difficulties in Greece, Germany and Egypt, the 'retreat' from British India, and industrial stagnation all signified Britain's 'decay' to many Americans. Although Inverchapel reported that the US view of Britain improved as the year went on – the British did not, for example, withdraw from their zone in Germany, they stayed on in Greece, and Indian and Pakistani independence was portrayed as a progressive move – ministers were far too preoccupied to worry about East Asia.[12] When asked about Korea in the House of Commons, Bevin merely remarked that the Joint Commission was due to reconvene and he had 'not got time' to 'weary' the House with all the details. In the same session, although Bevin wanted to make it clear 'everything may not be as we want it in Japan', both sides of the House paid tribute to MacArthur and the foreign secretary was hopeful a Japanese peace treaty would be signed by the end of the year. After complaints from MPs that the British voice was not heard in Japan, Bevin retorted this was 'wrong', as the British exerted influence both in Washington and in Tokyo.[13] Meanwhile, in an earlier debate at the House of Lords, Lord Jowitt, the Lord Chancellor, told a handful of peers in a virtually empty chamber that Britain was in no position to strike out an independent line in China and had to follow a US lead. The press made no comment and Drumright, reporting back to Washington, observed there was 'little likelihood' that British policy would change in the foreseeable future.[14]

Bevin was not unaware of the potential for conflict in East Asia. He told the Labour Party conference in Margate in May 1947 that Korea was 'a grave danger spot'. Yet, he simply did not have the time to invest in Far Eastern issues, especially ones that were a US responsibility.[15] Furthermore, the British considered a direct threat to their Far Eastern territories remote. By the summer of 1947, British strategy hung on three main pillars: the defence of Britain, the control of essential sea communications and a firm hold in the Middle East, a pillar Attlee finally accepted after intense pressure from the Foreign Office and the Chiefs of Staff. A fourth pillar, involving the co-operation of India and Pakistan and the possible development of an offensive base in Western Pakistan, was also considered although this idea gradually fell away as hostilities broke out in Kashmir. The pillars, the Chiefs of Staff explained, were based on the 'possibility' of war with the Soviet Union. That threat was not deemed imminent: the likelihood of war in the next five years was small but it would increase as Soviet economic rehabilitation gathered pace. It was important therefore to show 'a preparedness' to use armed force if necessary. Increased Commonwealth defence co-operation and closer consultation with the United States would also bolster the West's resolve in dealing with Moscow.[16]

How the Far East fitted into this global strategy was unclear to many political and military officials who worked in the region. The British, nevertheless, while discussing the post of a commissioner-general for Southeast Asia (formally adopted in May 1948), began to centralise all their operational and intelligence bodies around Singapore. After SEAC was wound up in 1946, there eventually emerged a British Defence Co-ordination Committee (BDCC), a commanders-in-chief committee and a JIC for the Far East. Despite this reorganisation, when Montgomery visited the Far East in the summer, he remarked that the defence committee at Singapore had only 'a hazy idea' of the part it would play in British strategy. There was also no big naval headquarters at Singapore, as Admiral Sir Denis Boyd, commander of the British Pacific Fleet, remained at Hong Kong. When Far Eastern admirals got wind of Montgomery's preference for a centralised command of all three services at Singapore, they complained that the latter was totally unsuitable. Singapore dockyards were becoming unreliable and expensive, while the majority of the Navy's work was being conducted in Chinese and Japanese waters. If the Royal Navy had to move away from Hong Kong, Boyd considered it nothing less than a 'retreat' from the coast of China.

Montgomery's aides cattily remarked that Boyd only wished to stay at Hong Kong because he was 'Kin Pin' and his wife 'Queen Bee': if they moved to Singapore they would be well down the list of precedence. The issue proved divisive amongst the Chiefs of Staff until well into the following year but the Navy would eventually be forced to give way, as the situation in China worsened and Hong Kong looked vulnerable.[17]

The policy of non-interference

In 1947, the British were in no position to project any significant influence across China. Commercial traders and industrialists still faced hardships: British property continued to be held by the Nationalist Chinese, there was restrictive legislation imposed on shipping trying to navigate on the Yangtze; and the government, unlike the Americans, had failed to conclude a commercial treaty with Nanking. There were also complaints in the House of Lords, the press, and from the China Association, that there was not one first-class British consul-general in China, all of which summed up Britain's state of weakness.[18] When Chiang sought to make Carton de Wiart, Attlee's personal representative in China, his personal adviser, Stevenson declared that the appointment would cause unnecessary tension with the Americans. A senior British figure in Chiang's government would be proof that Britain was prepared to take a hand in Chinese internal affairs, which, Bevin made clear to Attlee, 'we are not prepared to do'.[19] Britain's adherence to a policy of non-interference was not absolute. In January 1946, after pressure from Chiang, the Attlee government made good an outstanding 1944 naval agreement, loaning several warships to the Nationalists on the pretext of cementing British maritime interests. The discrepancy in Anglo-American power in China was clear, however, when Washington leased 271 surplus warships.[20]

Such discrepancies in power often dictated the direction of British policy. Britain, for example, would follow the US lead in enforcing an arms embargo on the Nationalist Chinese from August 1946. When Carton de Wiart received several approaches from Nanking to provide ammunition and arms, the cabinet refused to accede to the requests and Bevin remarked that Britain should 'keep completely clear of the whole business'.[21] Yet, Brigadier L. F. Field, the British military attaché in Nanking with plenty of China experience, worried that if Chiang could not secure an early victory, the current embargo would mean the virtual disarmament of the Nationalist army once ammunition and all expendable stores ran out. Although the Generalissimo remained confident of beating the Communists within two years and was making great inroads on the map, Field noted that Chiang was not securing any popular sympathy, as the behaviour of even minor Nationalist officials was worse than that of the Communists. Field also thought the Communists were 'sitting fairly pretty' so far as equipment was concerned and were in a position to re-occupy much of what they had lost if Chiang faltered. Although during the period of the embargo (August 1946–May 1947), the Nationalists continued rearming their second-line troops – something they presumably could not have done had they not had the equipment for front-line troops – Field was not surprised to receive further approaches from Nanking for arms in January 1947. He estimated that the Nationalist army had enough resources for 6–7 months of operations, about the time it would take the British to deliver weapons from its shores to troops operating in Changchun.[22]

Nationalist requests for arms were nevertheless refused and Bevin was equally keen for the British to stay out of unfolding events in Manchuria. Drumright told the Foreign Office (also in January 1947) the State Department had issued instructions to its ambassadors at Nanking and Moscow to urge the restoration of Dairen to Nationalist Chinese control and reopen it to international shipping, as provided for by the Sino-Soviet treaty of 1945. The ambassadors had also been instructed to press for the resumption of traffic on the Chinese Changchun Railway. Bevin rebuffed a suggestion by George Kitson at the China Department that Britain make a similar representation. Bevin and Dening were struck by the US reluctance to take a firm grip of East Asian issues, the former worrying that if the United States got 'cold feet', Britain could be left in a position of having to sustain an attitude without their support.[23] On the ground, Field provided ammunition for Bevin's caution. Major-General John Lucas, the head of the US military advisory group in China, told Field that he had never been given a clear definition of what he was supposed to be driving at. There was little appreciation in Washington, he complained, of the difficulties in helping to build a modern army in a country that lacked a complete modern industrial organisation and Lucas doubted if Marshall even 'fully understood them'.[24]

As Field began to offer virtually no odds at all on Chiang achieving victory in Manchuria and T. V. Soong, the Generalissimo's brother-in-law, spoke of the Nationalist government suffering economic collapse in a few days if aid was not forthcoming (a contention readily dismissed by British and American officials), Bevin was anxious to talk to Marshall about China before the Council of Foreign Ministers due in March at Moscow. The request was denied: the Americans worried that a visit by Marshall to London beforehand could provide the Soviets with an opportunity to level an accusation that the Anglo-American powers were 'ganging up' on them. It was also unlikely that Marshall would have wanted to discuss China with Bevin, particularly after his failed efforts at mediation in the civil war. The issue was still a raw one and when Forrestal, Patterson and Marshall discussed China in February, the argument became heated. When Marshall argued that present developments had been completely 'foretold', Forrestal retorted 'as we go out the Russians come in'. Marshall quickly interrupted him, said he had come to no firm conclusions and pointed out he neither wished to hand China over to the Communists nor 'walk through the deep mud' of a stubborn, corrupt and inefficient government. During this exchange, Patterson was only able to offer vague ideas and the State Department was privately scathing that the War Department had given no thought to China. Marshall did make one point clear, however: there could be no joint international efforts as Chiang was 'exceedingly violent' regarding any suggestion of bringing either the British or the Soviets into discussions on China.[25]

The Marshall-Forrestal spat only served to illustrate the difficulties that the Americans would have in conversing with the British on China. When the subject did come up for discussion – usually through State Department-Foreign Office exchanges which could not offer a full picture of US thinking – the British were left feeling discouraged. Vincent told one member of the British embassy in Washington that he could not see in what way the United States could help. There was no prospect of balancing the Chinese budget so long as 60–80 per cent of expenditure was on armed forces. Asked if he agreed a financial collapse would entail the downfall of Chiang's régime, Vincent replied: 'you could not knock down a plank that was already lying on the ground, but it might rot'. There remained, Inverchapel noted, a firm belief the crisis was still not serious while Vincent claimed that the present situation scarcely affected the majority of Chinese people. At Moscow, when Bevin finally found an opportunity to talk with Marshall, the latter told him it was only 'a matter of time' before the Communists would be in control of all China north of the Yangtze. The conversation did not move on to what might happen next.[26] The British felt disheartened. Kitson thought Vincent's statements held good if one accepted that China's economy was content to remain in the medieval and agricultural condition it had enjoyed for the past thousand years. A collapse of the present government and a descent into regionalism, he concluded, 'must put back for a decade China's reconstruction and her emergence as a modern world power'.[27] In China, Stevenson wondered incredulously how exactly the scarcity of essential commodities, the disruption of communications, currency inflation and military activity by both sides did not affect the majority of the peasant population.[28]

That March, Stevenson wrote a long despatch to Dening on the future of China. He spoke of Mao's agrarian policy appealing to millions of Chinese peasants. The ambassador further contemplated a return to semi-autonomous areas if the Nationalist government collapsed, which in the past would 'not greatly disturb British and other foreign interests' but now, in the current context of ideological struggle, might benefit the Soviet Union. Although the Chinese Communists would take 'a considerable period of time' to extend their influence, if the Anglo-American powers had to deal with them as the government-in-being, it would 'radically' alter the whole situation in the Far East to the 'grave disadvantage' of London and Washington. Stevenson therefore hoped for an armed peace, with neither side in the ascendant. His language then gradually began to slip into how the British had traditionally viewed China, suggesting it would not be in Britain's interest for the Nationalists (i.e. one particular faction) to hold undisputed sway over the country. It was an argument which ran counter to years of recent official public pronouncements that the British wanted a strong, united China. Arthur Scott, the deputy head of the China Department, appreciated there was little Britain could do to alter the sad events that were unfolding in China 'except to stand aside and hope for the best' but he was slightly disturbed (reading between the lines) that Stevenson saw little difference between the Nationalists and the Communists. If a choice had to be made, the Nationalists allowed far greater latitude for foreign interests and participation in reconstruction and trade. Indeed, Mao stated clearly in 1947, in a report on domestic and international relations, that he saw Moscow as the leader of the anti-imperialist camp, of which China should become a member.[29]

There was British hope that US policy might stiffen as the international situation darkened. Drumright, talking to Dening, vigorously refuted the idea (expressed by some Chinese) that the United States might abandon China in favour of creating their main bastions in Japan and Korea. US disillusionment was still present though over the lack of political and economic reforms in China, which were seen as the key prerequisite to enduring peace. In contrast, Chiang thought the United States opportunist and racist and that it only wished to pursue a 'Europe first' strategy. There was, however, soon to appear some relief for the Chinese Nationalist leader. As the Generalissimo struggled to contain the Chinese Communists, under pressure from Congress and the War Department, the State Department advised Marshall to lift the arms embargo and give him aid, so long as it was recognised that the aim was to prevent a collapse in China. Marshall had already agreed in February to leave 4,000 tons of ammunition behind for the Nationalists as US Marines began to reduce their numbers in North China. The Americans would also ship 130 million rounds of rifle ammunition to the Nationalist army so as not to unnecessarily impair its defensive effectiveness. The transfer of 137 naval vessels to Nationalist China was similarly approved along with the rapid completion of an assistance programme for the Nationalist Air Force. London was informed of the change in US policy. Should Britain lift its embargo? The Foreign Office worried about criticism in Parliament because of Britain's policy of non-interference and being 'dragged on the coat-tails' of what it saw as an indecisive US policy that could lead to another Spanish Civil War, with the Soviet-American powers as background protagonists. The British therefore decided against lifting their arms embargo.[30]

From mid-1947 and into 1948 that position became less robust. The British were confused: did the Americans now intend to give the Nationalists 'all-out' aid? Was it not too late and, the Foreign Office argued, unless reinforced by large-scale financial and economic assistance 'it might merely serve to annoy the Russians and prolong the civil war'? What was clear, Bevin informed the cabinet, was that the prospects for an agreement between Nanking and Yenan were 'negligible', and events in Manchuria were causing him great concern. The difficulty, remarked Dening in October 1947, was that the Americans 'do not seem to be able to make up their minds whether to support the *Kuomintang* or not.'[31] As the military situation for the Nationalists in Manchuria deteriorated, the supply of arms took on greater significance. When the British found out that the Canadians had sold to the Nationalists 150 Mosquito aircraft, fitted with Merlin engines manufactured in the United States, London found it 'galling', as Rolls Royce had lost out on the order (worth £1 million) and the Nationalist government had now obtained British aircraft and engines. At the Ministry of Supply, it was felt 'we are likely to get very little kudos from our moral rectitude, since the rest of the world will simply see that China has obtained British armaments from the British Commonwealth'. The Foreign Office concluded that the only alternative to the Nationalists was a 'Soviet'-dominated government in China, which was certainly not in the British interest.[32]

In January 1948, Sargent laid these arguments before Attlee and persuaded him to reverse current British policy. On a case-by-case basis, the British now sold war materiel to China, such as 1000 Hispano-Suiza guns (worth about £30,000) for Mosquito aircraft supplied through an agent in Canada. Engine parts and Rolls Royce engineers were also sent to De Havilland, Canada, to help service the Mosquito aircraft. In order to protect the interests of oil companies in China, Shell Oil was allowed to supply 43,000 barrels of aviation fuel to the Nationalist Chinese. The Foreign Office comforted itself by arguing that in all these cases there was no direct export of arms and munitions of war to China, but the fact that Dening underlined there should be 'no publicity', rather indicated the bankruptcy of being able to cling to the moral high ground of a non-interference policy.[33]

The benefits derived from such a change of policy seemed limited. Reports from inside China (both American and British) spoke of the Nationalist army in a 'panicky state', with poor leadership, low morale, surrenders and desertions commonplace, which contrasted sharply with the better solidarity and fighting spirit of the Chinese Communist army. Angus Ward, the US consul-general at Mukden, reported that the troops of the Nationalist army were far away from 'home' in Communist territory, amongst an 'alien' and unfriendly populace. There now existed, Ward argued, the possibility of 'a sudden debacle' laying all of Manchuria open to the Communists 'whenever they choose to take it'. There was no sign of Chiang willing to make compromises, much as Stuart, the US ambassador in Nanking, tried to persuade him to make a public declaration for peace and reopen negotiations with the Communists. The lifting of the arms embargo only encouraged the Generalissimo to pursue military victory, while Mao was in a stronger position than hitherto and likely to demand peace on his terms if he thought Chiang was coming to the table from a position of weakness.[34] Vincent despondently concluded to Marshall that there was 'no action' the United States could take in the immediate future to rectify the situation except through direct involvement in the civil war. The limited military and financial aid to be administered now (on Marshall's instructions) was designed to have a 'moderating influence' only.[35]

This prognosis led Vincent to disagree violently with a contention put forward by the Joint Chiefs of Staff that increased military aid could turn the tide and offset the inherent ineptitude, logistics and food problems afflicting Nationalist forces or cause Mao to accept terms offered by Chiang. The Joint Chiefs' were guilty, Vincent claimed, of 'wishful thinking'. Military aid needed to be combined with massive economic assistance to ensure effectiveness, and also accompanied by close American supervision and valid guarantees of political reform on the part of Chiang. Such a course could mean the use of US troops and even a clash with the Soviet Union. The outlay would not justify the commitment. The Joint Chiefs view that the Chinese Communists were merely the tool of the Soviet Union was also too simplistic, he argued. Yes, the Soviet Union had played its part in helping the Chinese Communists establish themselves in Manchuria, but so had Mao's own military, organisational and propaganda efforts, which together with Chiang's incompetence were major factors. Given the 'awakened nationalism' of the Chinese people, Vincent argued, Mao was unlikely to be Stalin's puppet. The Chinese were not interested in Western concepts of democracy to help eradicate Communism, as the Joint Chiefs suggested, but more in economic security. Reform in China, Vincent concluded, 'must come from the Chinese themselves'. Marshall agreed with Vincent's assessment.[36]

Forrestal, however, was increasingly concerned about a premature withdrawal of forces from China (he had picked up rumours of such talk from the US embassy at Nanking), warning Marshall the Soviet Union might in that event attempt to facilitate a permanent occupation of North China, strengthening their position across East Asia. US Marines were also present to protect American lives and property, the Navy Secretary argued. Marshall took a month to reply: with the passing of extraterritoriality, the United States could no longer maintain forces ashore on a permanent basis. The US government would look increasingly to the Nationalists to assume this role but if greater danger threatened those Americans with interests in China they should be advised to withdraw. Marshall considered it was still too early to warrant final decisions on major issues and wanted to await a report by General Wedemeyer, who he had sent to China and Korea to assess the situation. For the moment, the advice that Vincent was sending to Marshall revolved around the need for the United States to strengthen its commercial and cultural activities, particularly in Shanghai and Tsingtao, in the hope that US business enterprise would spread to other areas, which would then allow for more extensive economic assistance. 'This will take time', Vincent realised, but 'the question is whether time is on our side; whether we have time. I am inclined to think we have because the Russians do not seem anxious to move aggressively and precipitately into the morass of China.'[37] He was correct in assessing a cautious Soviet approach,[38] but also seemed to be indulging in some 'wishful thinking' himself. Vincent would further underestimate the growing influence of military thinking in post-war US foreign policy. Neither the United States nor Nationalist China were ready for his liberal solutions, especially as many of his countrymen began to equate liberalism with Communism and therefore with disloyalty and subversion. He would later be attacked as one of the architects that brought Chiang down.[39]

Kitson thought (as Vincent had acknowledged above) the only real solution to Nationalist China's ills was large-scale US military *and* economic assistance, to enable it to 'resist effectively the tide of Communist infiltration'. Their current post-war policy had 'failed to pay dividends', Dening observed, which unfortunately for the British meant they were 'sensitive about the subject', precluding a frank exchange of views.[40] The absence of an American response to the emerging chaos in China had worried the British, especially when labour disorders and student riots broke out in Shanghai in the summer of 1947, endangering British lives and property. There were now 4,000 British subjects in Shanghai out of a total of 5,500–6,000 British residents in China, and the Foreign Office told the State Department that the Admiralty had concurred to a request for Stevenson and Ogden to appeal to the commander of the British Pacific Fleet for the use of a cruiser and two destroyers if needed. The State Department, however, saw no need for alarm and had not prepared any rescue or evacuation plans. When Arthur Scott raised the question with Drumright, the latter noted that it seemed clear if a wholesale evacuation was needed in the event of an emergency in China, the British would 'in all probability be disposed to call upon the U.S. Navy to assist in the evacuation of British subjects'. On this point, the Americans indicated a willingness to help but it was an embarrassing admission of British weakness in the region.[41]

Whether Scott's enquiry also sought to provoke a statement from Drumright on the future of US policy towards China is open to speculation but it seems likely considering what the British saw as confusion and division in Washington. Marshall, in consultation with Truman, had sent Wedemeyer to China to satisfy influential Congressional opinion that questioned why Washington was sending aid to Western Europe, Greece and Turkey to fight Communism but not China. Yet, the announcement in July had caught both the State Department (aware of the mission three days before its announcement) and its embassy in Nanking (which learnt of the mission through the Nationalist Chinese) by surprise, indicating it was Marshall himself who took all the major decisions on China. Kitson told Drumright that he saw little point to the mission: what new facts could Wedemeyer possibly learn? Rather unconvincingly, Drumright replied that Marshall was probably seeking a reliable assessment of the military position and whether Chiang could use any aid effectively. Only Wedemeyer with his experience and training could make that judgement, he said. Vincent rolled out the same view to the British embassy in Washington who, at the request of the Foreign Office, used the announcement of the mission to enquire what the Americans intended to do in China. Inverchapel's conclusion was short: he reported that Vincent almost admitted that the United States had no China policy worth the name but a course of action would be decided after Wedemeyer submitted his report.[42]

Before Wedemeyer submitted his report, Kitson tried to guess the outcome. The United States would 'shrink from trying to underwrite China's recovery of Manchuria', especially with such a doubtful horse to back and in an area of 'vital' Soviet strategic interest, and would 'seek instead to try and stop Soviet infiltration at the Great Wall' (i.e. south of Manchuria)'. The option of Nationalist–Communist reconciliation was dead but a 'decisive' Nationalist victory was the 'only hope of resisting Communist (and Soviet) infiltration into China'. The trouble was Congress did not reassemble until January and 'China's need is an urgent one', Kitson remarked. Dening agreed, but unless there was evidence of Soviet assistance to the Chinese Communists, he expected Congress to oppose the allocation of further vast sums, leaving the Truman administration in 'an unenviable position'. Sargent minuted, 'a gloomy outlook', and Bevin, 'very bad'.[43]

During July and August 1947, when Wedemeyer carried out his mission he was appalled by Nationalist incompetence, corruption and unpopularity. The Nationalists thought him rude and were shocked by his visit. Additional aid, Wedemeyer argued, had to be contingent on further reform. He did not find any evidence of Soviet involvement in north China but still hoped to remove Communist power from Manchuria. The State Department disagreed with this last point and believed Manchuria had to be abandoned. As the British predicted, the State Department now attempted to focus on saving central and south China, which they deemed more important to United States interests.[44] That August, Kitson did not think the Americans would 'be in the least interested or concerned should we stand aside & continue to refuse to give help if they themselves decide on a policy of all-out support to Chiang Kai-shek'. In fact, the only drawback that Kitson worried about, underlining the ever present Anglo-American rivalry in the region, was that this policy could witness Sino-American collusion to exclude British trade from China, undermining Britain's commercial activities in Hong Kong.[45]

Another three months would pass before the British once again considered approaching the Americans about what they intended to do in China, but the question of immediate importance was China's attitude towards a Japanese peace conference. Dening felt it was worth letting the matter of China rest until Marshall came to London for the forthcoming Council of Foreign Ministers. During that time, the British embassy in Nanking reported that Chinese foreign exchange reserves were no more than $230m; prices in

Shanghai were soaring; and labour unrest and strikes there continued. To highlight the chaos inside Shanghai, Brigadier Field reported how:

> [A] brisk row broke out in a cinema because a Military Police Officer claimed that an ordinary policeman had pinched his reserve seat. The row became general and both sides called up successive relays of rein- forcements until a hundred or so were engaged on either side – not, as one might imagine, for the purpose of restoring public safety; but simply to shoot up the other side. Score, as at present unknown, Police, dead, 7. MP [Military Police] allegedly no casualties, but this is hard to believe... The next day the Police came and broke up the cinema; then they went on strike.

Field mentioned this episode for the reason that there was 'not anything unusual about it. The same thing goes on', he noted, 'more or less, in every town and village in the country'. A Chinese Communist offensive in Septem- ber, meanwhile, had led to the capture of 13,000 Nationalist troops with their heavy equipment and, on 3 October, Angus Ward reported Manchuria had temporarily lost all land communications with China.[46]

As the relapse of China into anarchy looked a distinct possibility, which seemingly left the way open for the spread of Communism, Marshall summed up the dilemma for the United States when he declared that every- one inside the Truman administration was in agreement that they wished to prevent a Soviet domination of China but there was no unanimity on the way in which assistance could be rendered. The continuing confusion and lack of consultation led Dening to complain, 'Where does the US stand in relation to China? We do not know, and I do not know whether the Ameri- cans know themselves. Their present tendency to let Far Eastern affairs drift is likely to have the most deplorable consequences.' Like Vincent, many Anglo-American officials, however, thought time was on their side. When Soong told Stevenson that the situation in China was more critical than Western Europe – he foresaw a complete collapse of the Central govern- ment, followed by a period of chaos and the assumption of power by the Communists – both Stevenson and Stuart disagreed. The British ambassador was not convinced there would be an imminent, complete and dramatic collapse and Stuart did not believe the situation was more serious than West- ern Europe. As Field watched Chiang issue the customary sheaf of orders on every conceivable subject similar to Hitler in the latter days of the war, which bore little relation to the facts, even he remarked a crisis could 'last longer than in China than, possibly, anywhere else'.[47] When the US embassy in Nanking reported in December that Manchuria was 'gone' many in Britain remained blissfully unaware of the momentous events taking place in China, and Drumright reported back to Washington that the British public 'finds itself virtually cut off from information on China'. The *Economist* agreed and pointed out that China rarely entered the British consciousness.[48]

Japan and a peace treaty

During the first three months of 1947, MacArthur began to lobby for the occupation to be terminated. In part, he used Gascoigne to leak information by suggesting he had successfully demilitarised Japan and almost achieved its 'democratisation'. MacArthur told him that the occupation had been predicated on three stages: first, the demobilisation and demilitarisation phase; second, a political reconstruction phase ('clearing the stage for democracy'); and, third, an economic rehabilitation stage. SCAP claimed that although he had pretty much accomplished the first two stages, the allied powers were at fault for the delays in tackling the third stage. Despite this barbed criticism, which the British thought ironic as they had been calling for the opening of Japan to private trade, Dermot MacDermot was upbeat and thought the conclusion of a peace treaty would be 'a fairly simple one to achieve'.[49] Sansom also took exception to MacArthur's comments regarding the fulfilment of his third stage, as Britain had 'continuously emphasised the importance of economic rehabilitation'. Sansom told London: 'the Supreme Commander's vision has been clouded by his idealistic views as to the possibility of a complete democratisation of Japan at short order'. This attitude had led him to 'underestimate the importance of economic rehabilitation until the crisis was in sight'. A fundamental confusion in SCAP's statement was that he appeared to conceive his three stages as three distinct problems to be tackled in chronological order one after the other, when in fact, as Sansom concluded, 'the three aims could and should have been pursued side by side'.[50]

Without informing Washington, MacArthur gathered correspondents in the Foreign Press Club at Tokyo, repeating his claims to Gascoigne publicly. Japan, he said, was long overdue a peace treaty, and did not require an American military umbrella nor an expensive recovery programme, a subtle attack on Truman's attempt to rally the US public, Congress and European allies in favour of economic and military plans for Soviet containment. No one in the Truman administration shared MacArthur's upbeat assessment (or wished to support his political ambitions) and most feared Japan would collapse if the occupation ended abruptly. MacArthur's public speech also coincided with a crisis in Japan's economy. Faltering economic policy, such as SCAP's vacillation over dissolving the *zaibatsu*, had contributed to falling production, rising unemployment, high inflation and a huge trade deficit. To preclude an economic collapse the United States needed to provide annual assistance of $400 million. In a speech delivered that May, Acheson argued that the dollar gap and the chaotic economic situation overseas, stemmed from the fact that the 'greatest workshops of Europe and Asia, Germany and

Japan', remained idle. World stability required rebuilding the 'two work-shops' on which the 'ultimate recovery of the two continents so largely depends'. In short, the United States would remain in Germany and Japan until their economies revived.[51]

Dening warned Gascoigne to be careful about being sucked into providing moral support for MacArthur's measures in which the Truman administration, and in particular the State Department, might be opposed. Dening reminded Gascoigne that when it came to a Japanese peace settlement, 'we shall have to rely upon the goodwill of the State Department in the negotiations to achieve our main objectives in the common interest'.[52] Kennan, for example, thought it highly dangerous to enter into discussions on peace terms until the United States knew what it was trying to achieve. A draft treaty overseen by Dr Hugh Borton, now chief of the Division of Japanese Affairs at the State Department, emphasised the 'permanent' and complete' disarmament of Japan, a council of ambassadors and control commission to monitor Japanese behaviour, and no provision for US base rights. MacArthur at least wanted US military bases on the Japanese Mandated Islands and Okinawa but argued that Japan proper could remain ungarrisoned with a UN guarantee to ensure its security. These schemes sent pulses racing in the Pentagon, especially as the latter was now planning to utilise Japan as an air base for atomic strikes in any war with the Soviet Union. The Joint Chiefs of Staff did not think Japan was ready for a peace treaty or that international guarantees could deny the country to the Soviet Union. While the British Chiefs of Staff suggested that the Ryukyu and Bonin Islands should fall under an American trusteeship, they did not see the need to retain armed forces in Japan and recommended an 'inspectorate' backed by economic controls.[53]

Although Washington was unsure about the goals it desired for a peace treaty, in July 1947, the State Department, as a result of the unwelcome pressure exerted by MacArthur, sent out invitations to the powers of the Far Eastern Commission to attend a preliminary peace conference that would operate on a two-thirds majority basis. There followed a series of proposals and counter-proposals from the United States, Nationalist China and the Soviet Union. The Nationalist Chinese initially accepted the US offer then changed their minds in November, proposing an eleven-power gathering so long as the four powers retained the veto. The Soviets insisted the Council of Foreign Ministers discuss a peace treaty only, with veto powers. In the middle, the British had planned to hold a Commonwealth meeting at Canberra in August where Japan was to be a major issue of discussion. This meant delaying the start of a preliminary peace conference, which Washington had suggested for the same month, but all the Commonwealth powers were prepared to accept the US proposal. Evatt, for example, was keen to conclude a treaty in order to reduce the US monopoly in Japan. The Australians, according to Borton, were showing 'a highly exaggerated' fear of Japan's threat to their security, and their sharp (and at times uncomfortable) protests over Japanese whaling expeditions in the South Pacific, provided a source of embarrassment for the British.[54]

Before the Commonwealth conference at Canberra, Evatt paid a visit to Tokyo in July, during which British and Australian officials reported that he had come under MacArthur's 'spell'. After his conversations with the general, Evatt told Gascoigne of the need for closer Australian–American security relations – at the expense of British influence – and had remarked to journalists that 'as far as Britain is concerned, no need to worry about that bloody place; we are taking care of Japan ourselves'. Evatt also described Macmahon Ball as 'destructive', 'sulky' and 'argumentative' and began to disassociate himself from his fellow Australian. Ball eventually told Evatt 'to go to hell'. For the British, Ball's resignation was no loss but this did not stop Evatt criticising UKLM with charges that the latter continually let Australia down.[55] Evatt's desire for Australia to play a larger role in the region looked slightly less convincing after Field Marshal Montgomery paid a visit to Canberra to talk about regional defence. When he suggested that Australia might be made responsible for defence planning in China, Japan, the Japanese Mandated Islands, Indonesia, Malaya, Burma and Tibet, Australian ministers were 'rocked back on their heels'. While Montgomery accepted that any forces required would have to come from Britain, Chifley was adamant that Australia was not prepared to accept primary responsibility for any strategic area at present. General Sturdee was also forced to admit to Montgomery that the Australian army could barely maintain itself in Japan if the remaining British specialist troops were withdrawn from BCOF.[56] The ability of Australia to play the role of great power designate for Britain in Far East seemed open to serious doubt. British briefing papers for the Canberra conference also made it clear that Britain was not about to renounce taking the political lead for the Commonwealth in the region. The declared effects of such a relinquishment on British 'prestige' in Soviet and American eyes, not to mention Asiatic countries such as India, Pakistan, Burma and Ceylon, were obvious the briefs declared.[57]

Dening, who was part of the British delegation to Canberra, told Bevin on his return that the whole of the Far East seemed anxious to resume trade with Japan and that the initiative to make peace lay with the West, though principally the United States. 'Anti-Japanese sentiment in these countries', he concluded over-optimistically, 'has, curiously enough, faded to a marked degree'.[58] The emerging consensus was that no occupation forces should be retained in Japan after the treaty had come into force, as this would merely throw an additional strain on the Japanese economy, although it was agreed any monitoring (or 'striking') force should be principally American. Strict controls and reparations were, however, a theme the Australian and the New Zealanders pursued with vigour. The evolving economic conundrum for London was this: a resurgent Japan could witness increased competition in Southeast Asian markets, while a weak Japan and a costly occupation might see the diversion of American financial resources away from Western Europe.[59]

In Washington, senior military and political figures, many outraged by MacArthur's unilateral pronouncements, began to baulk at any post-treaty international supervision of Japan. Kennan's Policy Planning Staff led the way, suggesting that the US required a stable, friendly Japan, integrated into the Pacific economy. Kennan thought it 'highly dangerous' to enter into discussions on a peace treaty until 'we know precisely what it is that we are trying to achieve'. In consultation with the Army and Navy Departments, Kennan put forward a new paper in September for a peace settlement that now recommended the re-building of 'Hirohito's islands as a buffer state'. By the end of the year, Forrestal, in his new position as Secretary of Defense, pressed Truman and his cabinet to declare publicly that the survival of the non-Communist world depended on re-building the 'two nations [Germany and Japan] we have just destroyed'.[60]

The prospect of a peace conference also slowly diminished as the Nationalist Chinese moved to secure their right of veto. Frequent stories appeared in the Chinese government-controlled press that MacArthur was too lenient and that the US had 'abandoned' its ally in favour of building up that 'treasonable' enemy, Japan. The Nationalists were also annoyed at Wedemeyer's outspoken criticisms, and worried that a peace treaty could see the Soviet Union decree the Sino-Soviet treaty void. The Americans were now disinclined to head the Nationalist Chinese off and Marshall told Bevin in November that if all the other powers agreed with their idea (an eleven-power conference with a four-power veto), the Americans might do likewise. Evatt 'violently opposed' the proposal according to Marshall and if it were put forward his (Evatt's) intention was to 'blow it sky high'. Bevin found himself 'embarrassed' by Marshall's position as he presumed they had reached 'a common line' with the Americans on the two-thirds majority proposal. Lewis Douglas, the US ambassador in London, however, told the British that Evatt had been trying secretly to double-cross them by extracting a veto from the United States. The Soviets were meanwhile still insisting that the Council of Foreign Ministers was the right arena to conclude a treaty and tried to tempt Nanking by suggesting the conference be held in China. The Foreign Office thought it made no difference whether the Soviet Union was a party to the peace settlement or not. They were convinced that Stalin had 'no interest' in the restoration of settled conditions in East Asia. If the Soviets aimed to convert Japan into 'a Communist satellite state', the Foreign Office thought that course would be pursued in either case. Yet, on both sides of the Atlantic, policymakers were confident that Stalin had no intention of occupying Japan by force. Covert attempts to Communise Japan, the Foreign Office argued, could also be thwarted by the Japanese themselves: 'their recent history and upbringing renders them naturally antipathetic to both Russia and Communism'. Unsurprisingly, the Anglo-American powers rejected the Soviet suggestion for a peace conference and Washington considered the whole mess 'fortunate' as the United States could have ended up with a treaty it did not want.[61]

Korean solutions

In early 1947, Hodge and MacArthur pressed Washington for a solution to the Korean problem. Hodge argued that the situation on the ground was unravelling before his eyes while MacArthur could not leave the Korean problem unsolved if he wanted to successfully conclude a Japanese peace treaty. Both men spoke of the need for government-to-government level talks between the United States and the Soviet Union: Hodge wanted the Joint Commission to reconvene and MacArthur spoke of referral to the UN and four-power consultation. In February, Marshall told MacArthur that he and Patterson (who was far from convinced of the need to stay in Korea) had decided to convene a high-level State and War Department Committee to make recommendations on future policy in Korea and requested Hodge to return to Washington for consultation. Two weeks later the special interdepartmental committee presented its findings. It reported that the Korean people were growing antagonistic towards the US military occupation and if this trend continued the American position would soon 'become untenable'. On the other hand, if the Americans withdrew it would be seen as complete political defeat. It was also dangerous to impose a 'superficial' solution of granting 'South Korea' independence. Congress was unlikely to grant aid to a country it was not responsible for; it would not solve the economic issues; and it would represent a direct breach of wartime commitments to establish a united and independent Korea.[62]

The committee argued that no other powers could help the Americans in their predicament, while approaching the UN would only signify the United States had failed in Korea. Instead, the committee recommended Marshall discuss Korea at the forthcoming Council of Foreign Ministers at Moscow (10 March–24 April 1947) through 'a properly planned, aggressive approach' to minimise the appearance of weakness. At the same time the committee requested Truman put before Congress a three-year $600m aid package to help Korea; appoint a civilian high commissioner; seek the participation of Koreans in governing their country; and despatch business, industrial and educational groups to Seoul to help rehabilitate the southern zone. Doubts soon surfaced. At the War and State Departments, Hilldring and Vincent wanted Moscow to make the first move and felt Congress was 'going to require a lot of convincing in order for us to get the grant we want'. Chiang was also continually pestering a reluctant Washington for more aid. It was unlikely that Truman could deny aid to Chiang on the one hand and secure large funds for Korea on the other. Hodge nevertheless stepped up the pressure when in Washington doing his best to paint the darkest picture possible. At a press conference he described the 38th parallel as an 'iron curtain' and argued that the Soviets were conscripting a large army in their zone. To offset Hodge's negative remarks, on 10 March, Hilldring declared publicly at the Economic Club of Detroit, 'we have an important job to do, and we are going to stay until the job is done'.[63]

Four days later, the State Department (without prompting) briefed the British embassy on the special committee's plans for Korea. It was an encouraging sign in that Washington now seemed prepared to divulge its thinking to London on at least one East Asian issue, though policy recommendations on an issue that had practically no interest for the British was still a fairly safe gesture, avoiding the probability of interference from London. Now that Washington was in difficulties over Korea, it also subtly reminded the British that they too were tied to the future of Korea. This reminder came at a time when the Foreign Office was showing a reluctance to get involved at all in Korean affairs. While Dening was encouraged to see a positive US response to Korea and a tough attitude towards the Soviet Union, he was firm that at this stage 'we are not called upon, and would not wish, to intervene'. Dening worried the issue might come up at Moscow but with the Australians absent and US plans making trusteeship look more and more unlikely, the British, he felt, should steer clear. Sceptical that Congress would sign the cheque Dening, from the reports he had read, doubted the emergence of a competent administration in the American zone.[64]

Dening's suspicions were well founded. The figures for Congress were already being downsized ($540m), while Acheson recognised that if Moscow did suggest reconvening the Joint Commission, the whole aid package would need to be reassessed. Patterson's views were more black and white. He did not think any programme, 'no matter how enlightened', would satisfy the intense Korean desire for independence: the United States should 'pursue forcefully' a course to 'get out of Korea at an early date'. He did not want a badly presented case to Congress affecting more important plans for War Department spending. To Washington's surprise, on 19 April, Molotov agreed to restart the Joint Commission on 20 May. This time the British informed the Americans of their desire to remain aloof from Korean affairs. MacDermot told Drumright that the Foreign Office had instructed Bevin 'to keep clear of the Korean imbroglio'. The British had also ignored an effort from Nanking suggesting four-power consultation over Korea. Drumright reported back to Washington that Britain clearly saw Korea as a 'hot potato' and would rather see the Soviet-American powers settle their Korean differences themselves. The British did inform the Australians of developments, passing on the details of US plans but stressing that Britain had not been consulted over them. London also reassured Canberra that it still intended to pass responsibility for Korea to the Australians once a trusteeship proposal had been accepted by the four powers.[65]

For the first time since the war, the evidence began to suggest that Britain was striving to rid itself of any involvement in Korean affairs. Yet, even the smallest British presence there, such as Kermode's role as consul-general at Seoul, possessed the potential to draw Britain into the peninsula's affairs more deeply than it wished. Kermode's reports were certainly informative (and usually gloomy) but were often only read in the Foreign Office by a handful of desk officers. Kermode nevertheless could prove useful for Koreans in advancing their political agenda. Rhee, for example, called on Kermode to inform him he was sending one of his men, Byung Chic Limb, to London on a 'goodwill mission'. Rhee was simultaneously intending to tour the United States campaigning for independence. Had there been no British presence on the peninsula, this crude attempt by Rhee to garner wider recognition would not have been available. More disturbingly, all the reports from Kermode indicated that the 72-year-old Rhee was a 'megalomaniac', a dictator, and an extremist who sought to become the first president of an independent Korea at any cost and in a hurry using, if necessary, the 'blood of his deluded followers' who were no more than 'a band of "patriotic" assassins'. Unsurprisingly, Limb's visit proved embarrassing. He was completely unknown in Britain and given no official recognition, especially as Rhee's party was against trusteeship to which Britain was pledged. Limb told a sceptical Foreign Office, who received him informally, that Rhee was the only man to unite Korea and that the latter should become independent immediately and join the UN.[66]

Limb had ostensibly travelled to Britain to talk about trade but when the Americans announced the re-opening of private trade with southern Korea in June 1947, six months later the Board of Trade reported that all enquires about trading there had 'come to nothing'. There were only faint hopes Hong Kong might open up a trading route to the peninsula.[67] Stuck in Seoul with little to do other than receive what at times must have been alarming reports from the Americans (usually in the vein that the Soviets were carrying out sabotage and infiltration, biding their time waiting to strike south), Kermode looked for ways to be proactive. Alerted to the fact that Rhee was intending to boycott the Joint Commission and organise 'popular' demonstrations, the British consul-general called on the Korean to persuade him against such action. Kermode attempted to convince Rhee that he would be far more likely to win world sympathy by supporting the Commission than flatly refusing to have anything to do with it. Kermode made little impact but explained to the Foreign Office he was motivated by the fear that if Rhee persisted in his endeavours the result would be a landslide for Moscow or, at Rhee's instigation, bloody civil strife. Keeping in line with a desire to remain aloof from Korean affairs, the Foreign Office scolded Kermode, which led MacDermot to write 'it is in our interests to steer very clear of Korean politics at this stage. Dr Rhee is a puppet in a more important quarrel.' As Kermode's reports became increasingly disturbing they briefly caught the attention of senior Foreign Office officials: Sargent minuted 'things may blow up there [Korea]' and 'we must not be caught unawares', yet there was little follow up and it was not exactly clear what the British response should be. A Foreign Office paper was drawn up outlining the current situation but again there was no suggestion for British involvement.[68]

Although the Joint Commission reconvened in May, it was soon deadlocked. Joseph Jacobs, the new US political adviser in Korea, informed Kermode, 'every point so far has produced a pitched battle', with the Soviets still fighting to exclude Rightist elements. Both Rhee and Kim Ku carried out their initial threats with anti-trusteeship demonstrations staged in Seoul and various districts. Hodge, Kermode considered 'unwisely', even ordered US tanks to disperse the main demonstration in Seoul. If the Joint Commission failed (which seemed likely) Hodge anticipated terrorism by both Rightist and Leftist factions to begin on a scale that 'may approach an oriental style civil war' and an early attempt by the Communists to carry out their much talked about 'spontaneous uprising of the masses'. The Soviets were also, he claimed, re-equipping Chinese Communist forces in Manchuria and training a North Korean army of at least 150,000, most being 'battle-seasoned' in Manchuria. When Jacobs visited Pyongyang, he noted that the fundamentals of a Communist state were clearly in place: rampant fear; the liquidation of opposition; and photos of Stalin and the 'Korean stooge' Kim Il-sung everywhere. Jacobs thought, however, the Korean Communist state was 'not yet as well organized as Balkan satellites'. 'In the south, Rhee and his gang', Hodge declared, were engaged in 'all-out opposition' to the Soviets, the Joint Commission, himself and the US military government, using the 'war cry' of 'anti-trusteeship' and 'alleged' high-level promises of a separate government for southern Korea.[69]

Even though the situation in Korean was degenerating, in late June 1947 Senator Arthur Vandenberg, the influential Republican leader and chairman of the Senate Foreign Relations Committee, made it clear to Acheson that he would oppose any more schemes for foreign assistance during the remaining Congressional session. Vincent despondently told the British embassy in Washington that he was now pessimistic about large-scale aid for Korea but asked for the information to be kept confidential, as it was essential for the success of US policy that the Soviets should continue to contemplate the probability of American aid. With the Joint Commission deadlocked, Jacobs spoke of the need for a 'major reorientation' of US policy and presumed the announcement of Wedemeyer's fact-finding mission to both China and Korea indicated a new approach. The bad news was that the announcement encouraged Rhee to push for a separate South Korean state. Jacobs lamented the fact that the United States 'for reasons of expediency' (i.e. opposition to the Soviet Union) might be compelled to support extreme Rightist leaders such as Rhee, who nursed a 'violent and unreasoning hatred' towards Hodge. Kermode soon wired back to London that the United States had to make a declaration of policy quickly to prevent 'a confused and frustrated people' taking desperate action. Moscow might also seize the initiative. MacArthur told Gairdner (who had paid a short visit to Seoul) that the Soviets were pulling out troops from Korea and there was a possibility that Moscow might push for a mutual withdrawal. As the cries for a sense of direction in US policy increased, on 23 July, John Allison, the assistant chief of the Division of Northeast Asia Affairs, finished work on a paper aimed at breaking the deadlock. It recommended four-power consultation, the proposal of free elections under UN supervision and the withdrawal of troops after the establishment of a Korean government.[70]

Unaware of Allison's recommendations, the British nevertheless feared the question of British involvement in Korea might raise its head as the Soviet–American powers reached an impasse over the peninsula. What if Nanking revived its proposal for four-power consultations? *The Times* had already called for the UN to intervene to revise the whole concept of joint occupation. The British felt trapped. John Killick, a very junior official at the Japan and Pacific Department, spoke of Britain's international obligations – the only reference point was the Cairo Declaration, which had hitherto been ignored by the two superpowers in respect of Britain – and worried about Australia. Dening came to the point: Britain, as a great power, had to participate and he would not countenance the idea of Australia taking Britain's place in any four-power negotiations. The unsuccessful experiment in Japan of letting Australia assume responsibilities for the British Commonwealth had clearly left a sour taste in Dening's mouth. There is little indication that Dening wanted Britain to play a role in Korea for the sake of the Korean people. He seemed more worried about a further erosion of British power in an international arena and would only agree to the attachment of an Australian observer to any British delegation. In setting out his stall so rigidly, Dening's position conflicted with Montgomery's plea for Australia to take on a larger share in regional planning and the Foreign Office desire to rid itself from the Korean imbroglio. Dening's final remark – 'let's hope it [four-power talks] won't happen' – suggests an uneasiness over his stance, considering Korea was such a low priority.[71] It is perhaps reasonable to speculate that if the British had had a happier experience with Macmahon Ball on the Allied Council for Japan, London might have been more amenable to handing over Korea to Australia, especially as they had been willing to do so with the administration of a (what now seemed unlikely) trusteeship for that country.

On 4 August, an ad hoc committee of SWNCC accepted Allison's plan: the United States could not withdraw and abandon Korea – it would 'discourage those small nations now relying upon the U.S. to support them in resisting internal or external Communist pressure'. The irony was that Forrestal and Patterson believed Allison's solution *would* allow for a speedy withdrawal, liquidating the American commitment. The Americans first informed the British of their plans for four-power consultation. Dening reluctantly informed Sargent that as a signatory of the Cairo declaration 'I don't think we can refuse' the State Department's invitation.[72] The Foreign Office relayed to its Washington embassy that it was not 'sanguine' about the US proposals. It had hoped large-scale grant-in-aid would have helped unify Korea by attracting northern Korea into democratic collaboration (now not possible) but accepted there were few other options.The request for four-power consultation by the State Department with representatives from each embassy was communicated formally in late August. London told Washington it was 'impracticable' (code for unacceptable) for Australia to represent the Commonwealth but requested they attach an observer, which Evatt accepted on the proviso he could intervene if appropriate. Molotov, however, rejected the US approach, arguing it was not in accordance with the Moscow declaration of 1945. Frank Roberts soon learnt from the Americans in Moscow that the United States would now play its next card: referral of the Korean problem to the UN.[73]

On the ground, Kermode's position still seemed questionable. When Wedemeyer visited Korea, the British consul-general was totally ignored. He consoled himself with the fact that the British embassy in Washington would 'hear something of the story', which rather defeated the point of his presence in Seoul. Wedemeyer's report reiterated much Washington knew already: there could be no 'ideological retreat' in Korea; the Soviets aimed to dominate East Asia; and the creation of genuine democracy in the south of Korea would not be easy but if the United States provided both economic and military assistance, southern Korea could emerge as a 'bulwark of freedom'. Francis Stevens, the assistant chief of the Division of Eastern European Affairs, also thought Korea was 'a symbol to the watching world both of the East-West struggle for influence and power and of American sincerity in sponsoring the nationalistic aims of Asiatic peoples'. 'If we allow Korea to go by default and to fall within the Soviet orbit', Stevens argued, 'the world will feel that we have lost another round in our match with the Soviet Union, and our prestige and hopes of those who place their faith in us will suffer accordingly'. Stevens addressed his thoughts to Kennan and Allison, concerned over what appeared to be fairly unanimous agreement to abandon the Koreans to their fate. The Joint Chiefs of Staff, for example, continued to claim that the United States had little strategic interest in maintaining present troops and bases in Korea. The only worry for them was that for reasons of prestige, they might have to stay in Korea because a departure could have repercussions in both China and Japan.[74]

On 23 September, the Korean question was formally adopted on the agenda of the UN General Assembly. As the Joint Commission came to its sorry end, in early October, Shtikov proposed the withdrawal of all occupational forces from Korea. Aware that the Soviets would leave behind a well-armed force of Koreans in the north, in a *volte face*, Rightist demonstrations in Seoul now urged the continued US occupation of Korea. The Americans pressed ahead with their plans at the UN. On 6 October, Inverchapel reported that the United States was preparing a UN resolution, recommending a committee be appointed to supervise elections in both zones to help facilitate the establishment of a provisional government. The Committee would also arrange for the occupying powers to determine the procedure for the withdrawal of forces. The Foreign Office considered the whole idea unworkable and that the Soviets would oppose the plans. It would be impossible to hold free elections in the north and a sweeping Communist victory there would no doubt be counterbalanced by a Right-wing victory in the south preventing the formation of a central government. What was next? Some British officials thought the Americans would cut their losses and evacuate Korea while others thought they would hang on for as long as they could 'for reasons of prestige', preventing possible repercussions in China and Japan.[75]

The Australians agreed with the British that American plans were unlikely to succeed, and objected to Korea being discussed at the UN instead of through the forum of a wider Japanese peace settlement. Evatt told Marshall it should be discussed by the states directly concerned and that he had even sounded the British out over replacing them as the power to represent British Commonwealth interests. Marshall replied such a procedure could only 'confuse matters' as Korean independence was separate from the issue of a Japanese peace treaty. Given Dening's earlier private feelings, it was no surprise that the Foreign Office rebuffed Evatt's pitch to replace them in any talks on Korea, and only reiterated the British assurance that Australia would replace it 'on any ultimate trusteeship body'. At the UN, London reminded Canberra that Australia could at least speak in its own right. The British also disagreed that Korea 'must await our settlement with the aggressor state from whom we have freed her'. These discussions were overtaken when, on 17 October, the US delegation tabled a draft resolution (which the British had seen beforehand), calling for the holding of UN-supervised elections no later than 31 March 1948 in both zones of Korea through a temporary commission – United Nations Temporary Commission on Korea (UNTCOK), and then the withdrawal of Soviet-American military forces after the formation of a provisional government. Killick told Sargent that the British would go along with it but remained pessimistic: 'the hard facts were that it is strategically necessary for Russia to hold Korea, and that she has made the necessary dispositions to that end – a solid Soviet north, a disunited and discontented south'. The American proposal, he stated bluntly, was cover for their retreat.[76]

British suspicion of American motives was confirmed when Walter Bedell Smith told his British opposite number in Moscow, Sir Maurice Peterson, that US policy towards Korea was little more than 'a face saving device'. Smith was certain Korea would fall under Communist domination once American troops withdrew. The underlying reason for American policy, explained Smith, was financial: Washington could not afford a large grant-in-aid scheme for Korea. British officials were aghast: Killick wrote 'this depressing statement has the merit of being frank & realistic', but 'there is no disguising', minuted MacDermot, 'that it is a major American capitulation'. Others in the Foreign Office saw wider repercussions, stating 'this will much encourage the Russians to dig their toes in in Europe ... in their forthcoming discussions about Germany'.[77] It left the British once again to declare their determination to 'steer clear of this imbroglio' and they were against heavy Commonwealth representation in UNTCOK, something the Australians and New Zealanders had pressed for through the argument that the UN commission should consist of Far Eastern Commission powers because they had done the fighting against the Japanese and Korea was essentially part of a Japanese peace settlement. This, the Foreign Office thought, was 'undesirable' as it might force the British government into 'a position of major involvement'. In the final resort, the Foreign Office would not support the Australians against the Americans.[78]

In early November the resolution was adopted and UNTCOK would consist of members from China, France, Canada, Australia, India, El Salvador, Syria, the Philippines and the Ukrainian SSR. On the ground the Koreans were unhappy. The Americans had promised elections earlier, which did not materialise, and now the UN was seen as another vehicle to 'defraud' the Koreans of independence. Kermode concluded:

> we are not responsible for the tragic muddle that has developed, but it is uncomfortable to remember that at a time of our growing ascendancy in the war ours was one of the voices that promised freedom and independence to these people and that we now find ourselves unable to give effect to our valiant words.

It summed up beautifully the British dilemma. Rhee, meanwhile, had given qualified approval to the UN resolution on the assumption that the Soviet Union would oppose all solutions and that the UN, unable to force a settlement, would give their blessing to free elections in the south. What he did not bank on was the United States moving to force a supervised UN election in the south, even if the Soviets refused in the north, leaving Rhee unable to deploy coercive tactics, using the police and strong-arm youth pressure, to give him a resounding triumph. Kermode presumed Rhee would:

> do his utmost to sabotage the work of the United Nations Commission unless it opens the way or leaves the way open for him to achieve his personal ambition. The year that is drawing to a close has given its moment of anxiety, but there is an uncomfortably lurid look about the dawn of 1948.[79]

By the end of 1947, Britain had serious reservations about US policy towards the Far East. Dening told Sargent 'it becomes more evident every day that what is needed is a frank exchange of views with the Americans on an official level about the whole Far Eastern situation... The absence of an American policy is... endangering the whole position in the Far East'.[80] At this stage, as one commentator explains, Washington's policy makers followed a policy of drift in China 'not because public pressure forced a drawn out commitment to Chiang but because their own assessment of the baneful effects of a Communist China would not allow them to terminate it'. If US forces withdrew from Korea it would also indicate a weakness in American foreign policy already under fire in East Asia.[81] There was little the British could do to halt Communism inside China or Korea and confusion over exactly what sort of limited role Britain should play in the area remained. Emerging British criticism of American policy in East Asia also made it less likely for Washington to feel inclined to converse with London over the region's future. This was becoming more important as Britain worried about the direction of US policy towards Japan. Britain dreaded both Japan's economic collapse and complete recovery. A collapse could divert American aid from Western Europe and destabilise Southeast Asia, which provided important dollar earnings for the British, such as Malaya's rubber and tin. A complete recovery bred fear of Japan's military resurgence in Australia and New Zealand, and could see the United States augment Japanese economic intrusion into Southeast Asia to compensate for lost markets in China and Korea.

6
Going into Reverse

In 1948, Lord Inverchapel reported from Washington that Anglo-Americans relations were entering a new phase. US opinion on British and Soviet activities no longer followed the 'see-saw pattern', which was so 'astonishingly' constant during the war and in the years following it. In Churchillian language, the ambassador argued, 'responsible' Americans took it for granted that the destinies of Britain and the United States were 'inseparably bound together' by the 'coincidence' of moral and strategic interests. Harmonious relations also now existed in the embassy's dealings with members of the Truman administration, as exposure to problems in Greece, Palestine, and disturbances in India; along with the 'ultimatum-like "request"' for a US trusteeship over the former Japanese Mandated Islands[1] in 1947, had had 'a telling effect' on Britain's American critics. A distinction between 'imperialism' and safeguarding 'legitimate' overseas interests was, Inverchapel concluded, 'coming to be appreciated'.[2] Despite this analysis, it was US presidential election year, and the prospects for a Truman victory were not high, which meant a possible change of the administration and policy. Inverchapel was certainly no champion of Truman, while the ambassador's residency in Washington was marked by boredom, his inability to ingratiate himself with Washington society and leading American figures, and poor relations with the State Department.[3] These factors and the suspected imminence of Truman's departure went some way to explaining why US officials conversed rather guardedly with the British about the future of East Asia. The trouble was that the new direction of US policy was beginning to provoke Anglo-American divergences.

By 1948, as the Cold War intensified after the ruthless consolidation of Eastern Europe by Stalin and the Prague coup of February, the concept of directing a war against the Soviet Union centred on the Mediterranean and the Middle East. US strategy for East Asia and the Pacific assumed a secondary and largely defensive role. Korea was written off as indefensible: the danger of friction between the two superpowers and the cost of the occupation to the US taxpayer were thought to be disproportionately high in relation to Korea's strategic value. In addition, since the war, the United States had also contributed $1.5 billion in aid to China, which, Inverchapel noted, 'has disappeared with virtually nothing to show for it'. Present US policy was to administer just enough aid to keep the Nationalist regime afloat. US strategy for East Asia was now firmly centred on Japan: there was a desire to avoid an early peace treaty, leave occupation troops in place, revive heavy industry on its pre-war scale and increase Japanese exports to balance essential imports. Even a series of airfields had been built to accommodate the heaviest long-range bombers. It signified the end of a harsh peace for Japan, the realisation of China as a great power and a desire to see Korea become free, united and independent, in effect, a reversal of all US wartime and early post-war policies.[4]

Priorities, strategy and intelligence

In October 1948, Churchill, as leader of the Conservative opposition, told 4,000 people gathered at Llandudno in Wales that the Labour government had 'recklessly cast away' Britain's world interests and its duties. To loud cheers, Churchill argued that the survival of Britain and its Empire as a 'united power in the first rank among the nations' was at stake. Another Labour parliament would seal Britain's fate and close the story of British greatness. Yet, as he himself was forced to admit, Britain was dependent on 'American charity' for its 'daily bread', which tended to suggest that the final chapter on British primacy in the world had already been written. And when he spoke of the 'three majestic circles' of a multiracial British Commonwealth and Empire, a United States of Europe and the Anglo-American relationship (a policy Bevin had actually been pursuing), he tended to downplay how each circle might also diminish rather than enhance British power.[5]

Sir Edmund Hall-Patch, the leader of the British delegation to the nascent Organisation of European Economic Co-operation charged with distributing Marshall aid, argued that Britain could only survive its current economical plight 'by the good graces of America', which limited Britain's ability to carry out a truly independent foreign policy, especially where US interests were at stake. The successful outcome of the European Recovery Programme was therefore Britain's first priority. He also warned that the US vision of a fully integrated British-led tariff-free United States of Europe would signify the end of Britain's role as a world power. Sterling was the vehicle for half the world's trade in which the Commonwealth and Empire (not Europe) played a critical part. Hall-Patch believed many Americans saw the Sterling Area as 'a manifestation of the powers of evil' and a menace to US economic expansion but until Washington lowered its tariff barriers and the dollar was freely available, sterling would remain the only 'true international currency'. In short, Hall-Patch complained that most Americans did not understand the Commonwealth. Indeed, US criticism of Britain as an 'imperial' power could be invoked on the one hand yet exasperation expressed on the other if London did not keep its former dominions in line when the latter were critical of US policy, a frequent occurrence in East Asia.[6]

Propping up the empire, meanwhile, continued to drain Britain's overseas expenditure, especially once the Malayan Communist insurgency began in earnest that year. The Malayan Communist Party was essentially a Chinese movement that had little support amongst the Malays or the majority of Chinese in Malaya but the insurrection nevertheless put an additional strain on British resources. Attempts to lighten the burden met with mixed results. During the October 1948 Commonwealth conference, when Bevin aired the idea of regional political and economic co-operation in the Far East, his proposals received a rather lukewarm reception. India, Pakistan, Australia and New Zealand were all unwilling to do anything to support the European 'imperial' powers in their battle to maintain colonial rule in French Indo-China and Indonesia. The State Department too, as it watched the US position in China rapidly crumble, was reluctant to expend more dollars further south. Commonwealth defence co-operation also remained in its infancy and the handing over of strategic responsibility in wartime to other powers caused controversy when tabled by the British military. The Foreign Office argued that were Britain to relinquish its position in any respect, either in a period of 'uneasy peace', or in the event of war, to Australia in the Far East, it was 'no exaggeration to say that this would be likely to lead to the final extinction of United Kingdom influence in the area involved'. The Foreign Office spoke of 'surrendering' Britain's position to Australia in Japan, which had 'not been a success', yet forgot it had been prepared to let Canberra assume the onerous burden of administering a trusteeship for Korea as well if that had come to fruition. The Ministry of Supply argued that it was 'illogical' to limit Commonwealth help purely to local defence and wondered how exactly the Foreign Office proposed to uphold British prestige at all costs. Whether the Foreign Office deemed Australia's role in East Asia a success or not, Britain was in no position to pursue an independent role there.[7]

Britain's main responsibility in the Far East was to build up resistance to Communism in Southeast Asia. This had taken on greater emphasis when violence had broken out across Burma, Malaya and later Indonesia after a group of international Communists met at Calcutta in February–March 1948, where a large Soviet delegation had been sent. The key to British success would be on US support, maintaining a stable Malaya, settling the internal crises in Kashmir, French Indo-China and Indonesia, the promotion of economic and social welfare across the Far East, and the encouragement of political development with a view to self-government.[8] Southeast Asia, however, remained low on the list of Anglo-American priorities. Apart from Japan, the United States was trying to limit its commitments to the Far East. During a foreign affairs debate at the House of Commons in January, although Churchill spoke of 'all kinds of dangers', 'iron curtains' and 'points of collision' in both China and Korea, which 'we here in England find it baffling to measure', Labour's ministers did not dwell on the former prime minister's references to East Asia. Bevin made a brief reference to Japan, but neither he, Attlee nor Hector McNeil spoke much about the Far East in a debate dominated by European issues. At the last minute McNeil omitted all references to China and the Far East in his address, much to Dening's annoyance, especially as his department had gone to the trouble of briefing him. When one MP attacked US policy in China, Attlee did not rebut him.[9]

The British were in a difficult position: US policy towards East Asia was hard to defend. A former enemy, Japan, was in the process of being re-built, Korea seemed doomed and when Marshall went to Congress to 'beg' for $570m for Nationalist China, the journalist Alistair Cooke saw it as 'among the most pathetic expeditions in the history of lost causes'. Cooke also noted that some prominent Republicans were pushing for aid to Nanking not because they 'love China more' but because they 'love Europe less'. The Republican Walter Judd increased the tension and became one of the key figures in the 'China lobby', a group comprising members of Congress, businessman and high-profile media figures such as the publisher Henry Luce, who pressed for increased aid to Nationalist China. According to Butterworth (now Vincent's replacement at the State Department), Senator Vandenberg, a firm supporter of bipartisan policy towards Europe, let it be known that the chances of getting Marshall aid through Congress would be vastly improved if there was a China aid programme, however modest. Truman was also making it clear that he did not wish to see Communists participating in governments anywhere, a conclusion heightened by recent events in Czechoslovakia.[10]

The diversion of aid away from Western Europe was a major concern for London and dictated the British position on East Asian affairs. There could be no open criticism of the United States in East Asia at a time when the British wanted US help for what they deemed more important areas. Trouble in Palestine, continued US aid for Greece, the Communist coup in Prague and the Berlin Blockade (which started in June 1948) tended to indicate where those priorities lay. It was therefore down to the United States, as Dening made clear to Drumright in February, to hold the ring in East Asia. Britain was in no position to help Nationalist China and if the United States did not help Chiang, there was no one else who could. Dening argued that the European Recovery Programme could not be successful if the Far East turned Communist while Western Europe was rehabilitated through US aid. Dening was sure that the fall of Chiang would be 'disastrous' for the Anglo-American powers. Drawing on a paper Bevin laid before cabinet colleagues in January, Dening in Cold War and alarmist language claimed that Soviet policy was global and actively hostile to Anglo-American interests everywhere: if it came up against 'a stone wall' in Western Europe, it would probe elsewhere for weak spots such as China. It might then, he concluded, be too late to dislodge Moscow from a position of dominance in East Asia and the Far East.[11]

Dening's assessment was remarkably simplistic: it underestimated Soviet economic weakness, misunderstood the scale of aid (both military and economic) Chiang would need to turn events to his advantage, while underestimating the pressure local Communist leaders might exert on the future of East Asia. The controlling hand of Moscow was seen as a critical factor behind any potential Communist success. Small comfort, for example, was derived from doubts about how Moscow might fill a vacuum in Southeast Asia should the region turn 'red'. The threat of a Chinese Communist-led revolution in the region seemed a distant prospect: the British, like the Soviets and the Americans, underestimated the ability of Mao to rule even China.[12] One explanation for this attitude was the lack of good intelligence on the autonomy and methods of Mao and Kim Il-sung. Kim (like Rhee) continually attempted to use the occupying superpower to fulfil his own personal ambitions for unification, while Mao's relationship with Stalin remained as ambiguous as ever.[13] London and Washington had scant evidence of Mao being in receipt of financial help or the supply of military equipment and advisers from the Soviet Union.[14] Their principal sources of intelligence came from missionaries and travellers returning from Communist-held territory, which were often highly subjective descriptions of local conditions in limited areas. The State Department admitted they knew 'remarkably little' about the existence of any factions among Chinese Communists, the orientation and leadership of such factions, their relative strengths, and the status envisaged for Manchuria, Sinkiang, and other areas adjacent to the Soviet Union in Communist plans for China. The State Department hoped the CIA could help but this was a fledgling organisation born out of the break up of OSS and then SSU, and the latter, according to one member, had been staffed in China with low calibre personnel and was no more than 'a puny effort'.[15]

Its British counterpart, SIS was similarly operating from a position of weakness. British diplomats objected to the presence of SIS in East Asia and intelligence coverage was thin on the ground. SIS officers in China were beset by a lack of resources and overburdened with non-SIS work, while in Japan, SCAP's ruling that UKLM officials could have no contact with any Japanese and needed permission to travel outside Tokyo – a ruling ostensibly to block the Soviet mission indulging in such activity – naturally limited any SIS ability to conduct much in the way of its own intelligence gathering. Furthermore, in the midst of the re-constituted Far Eastern Department at the Foreign Office was a Soviet spy, Guy Burgess, a former SIS officer and private secretary to Hector McNeil, who would join the department in November 1948. Due to his knowledge of Communism, he became the department's political analyst on the Chinese revolution. Burgess argued that the Chinese Communists were neither agrarian reformers nor mere Soviet puppets but genuine Chinese revolutionaries. Unsurprisingly, he therefore peddled the line that the British government should not attack the Chinese Communists while firmly supporting moves to recognise a Communist China, but his impact is difficult to calculate and it is unclear what Stalin deduced from such secret intelligence, whether he trusted it and whether he passed any of it to Mao or Kim Il-sung.[16]

Similar doubts arise from the case of the double agent George Blake, imprisoned by the British for treachery after the Korean War. In 1948, Lieutenant-Colonel Neville Grazebrook, the officer responsible for intelligence in Singapore at General Headquarters, Far East Land Forces, told London that Korea was a 'closed book' to him. Kermode's reports, he explained, took weeks to reach him and the colonel enquired whether there was 'any way we can possibly step up our information sources'.[17] With the formation of a fragile South Korean state in August 1948 and the deteriorating position in China, SIS sent Blake to Seoul that October to gather information on Manchuria and the Soviet Maritime Provinces but his task proved hopeless, as there was no communication or trade routes to exploit between his base at Seoul and Communist territory in East Asia. What is difficult to ascertain is whether Blake was working for Stalin before the outbreak of the Korean War and his subsequent capture by the North Koreans. Failing to meet his initial objectives, Blake focused on widening contacts inside Korea in preparation for creating stay-behind networks ready for what seemed to the JIC an inevitable Soviet or Soviet-sponsored invasion of South Korea. That too made little progress and Blake's initial tasking and his Russian language skills indicated again the tendency to focus on Soviet rather than local intentions. Yet, why it was necessary to maintain Blake in Seoul is unclear, especially as there were few British interests in the extreme Northeast Asian region to defend.[18]

The Commonwealth and Korea

At the dawn of 1948, Kermode continued to report on the volatile situation inside Korea and the 'myopic vision' Rhee had in store for a South Korean state. Rhee aimed to rig elections to ensure that he was head of the government in the south, claim the extension of his authority over the whole of Korea and then secure UN recognition as the head of a Korean state. His plan was so transparent, Kermode observed, one is 'forgiven for thinking him crazed'. When John Allison, the State Department's Chief of the Division of Northeast Asian affairs, met Rhee, he left with the conviction he had been humouring a madman. The Foreign Office believed that even if Rhee's plan came off, it would live 'a short life' in the face of inevitable subjugation by the north. Rhee nevertheless remained determined, merging his party with a reluctant Ku and organising monster rallies. In January 200,000 Rightists attended a welcome rally at Seoul Stadium to impress members of UNTCOK.

What was clear to Kermode was that Hodge took too long to realise Rhee was 'determined to play nobody's hand but his own'. Rhee was now too well established as a national figure, which the US general discovered when he tried to build up Kim Kyu-sik (a moderate) instead. Kermode argued that Hodge's tendency, 'in common with many Americans', to treat anyone left of centre 'as a blood relation of the Communists' had seen many Koreans from the centre and moderate Left drawn towards Communism because they were 'sickened by the corruption, oppressive practices and utter selfishness of the Rightist political leaders'. The US 'ignorance of the nature of non-American peoples', Kermode concluded, had led them to make 'disastrous blunders'.[19]

The despatch indicated much frustration and the fact that there was little he or Britain could do to help the Americans. Nor were there any possibilities to develop trade. Kermode informed John Hutchinson, the commercial counsellor at Shanghai, that although Jardine's now operated ships between Hong Kong and Korea, it amounted to 'a trickle of trade', while the Korean yen was 'virtually valueless'. An economically viable South Korea, Kermode observed, would need 'billions of dollars' to keep it from progressive decline, and 'it is obvious that Congress is not going to pour that much down a bottomless funnel'. Strangulated by partition, South Korea had 'precious little' to export and Kermode saw no 'prospect whatever of a continuing and increasing foreign trade'. He therefore impressed upon Hutchinson that he would 'personally discourage any British firm from putting money into this country. Unless I have badly misread the situation they would almost certainly lose it.'[20] Kermode had not misread the situation: The State-Army-Navy-Air Force Co-ordinating Committee (SANACC), SWNCC's replacement body, had recognised there was no prospect of South Korea (essentially an agricultural area) sustaining itself without external aid. Its annual trade deficit was $100m and there was no likelihood of balancing trade without unification. The United States, the committee recommended, should therefore furnish the minimum amount of supplies to foster economic stability but make no commitments beyond 1948.[21]

SANACC concluded, and the Joint Chiefs of Staff agreed, that Korea possessed little strategic interest. There were no plans to train and equip a South Korean armed force within one year as Hodge suggested: MacArthur called such plans 'impracticable'. The balance of forces left little doubt over the result of a war between north and south. The Soviet-equipped North Korean People's Army numbered 125,000, which was in close touch with the Chinese Communist Army (the People's Liberation Army), faced a US-equipped South Korean constabulary of 17,000, a coastguard of 3,000 and a civil police force of 25,000. All in Washington accepted that the US position in Korea was untenable, even with a large expenditure of US money and effort, but could the United States leave with minimum damage to its prestige and prevent the abandonment of Korea to Soviet domination? The Joint Chiefs of Staff felt it should be accepted that once the 36,000 US forces withdrew, Communist domination of Korea would result, and references to a loss of US prestige should be crossed out of memorandums. Successful US extrication now focussed on the UN process: if the Soviets refused to allow the holding of elections in their zone, SANACC argued that Washington should then inform UNTCOK it proposed to proceed with zonal elections in South Korea only.[22] The Foreign Office was not privy to these papers but guessed the US plan of action and saw no alternative. British officials responsible for the area, however, felt there was a difference between using the UN 'to cover up one's failures and using it to "enforce" one's policies'. In the end, there appeared little prospect of a solution acceptable to either Moscow or Washington so long as the domination of the whole of Korea remained the objective of Soviet policy, which the British believed to be the case.[23]

The American plan faced immediate obstacles not just from Moscow but also members of the British Commonwealth. In Canada, participation in UNTCOK produced a cabinet crisis. Mackenzie King, the Canadian prime minister, 'thoroughly frightened' by the deterioration of East-West relations described to him by Bevin, believed that UNTCOK's work would be absolutely futile and bring the UN into greater disrepute.[24] King charged Lester 'Mike' Pearson, head of the Canadian delegation at the UN, to tell Lovett that no Canadian would ever serve on UNTCOK. Terribly 'amused' at the idea of a cabinet crisis over Korea, Hume Wrong, the Canadian ambassador in the United States, warned Pearson to expect a 'cold reception'. Lovett, worried that the Soviets and isolationists in Congress would exploit King's position, urged no public withdrawal and, as Pearson reported, 'didn't care whether we sent a messenger boy to Korea'. Truman kept on saying 'Surely Canada won't let us down' but then, in a rather crude attempt to calm Pearson, said, 'Don't worry, you won't get into any trouble over there, and if you do, we are behind you.' The Canadian was horrified. It was finally agreed that Truman should send a letter to King, attaching greater importance to the struggle against Communism in Europe and wider questions, to persuade the prime minister to change his mind. The State Department dismissed the idea of a phone call, as they felt Truman 'didn't know very much about this business' and King could 'overwhelm' him. Canada did eventually appoint its member to UNTCOK (George Patterson) but insisted on his withdrawal if Soviet co-operation did not materialise, code for the fact that Ottawa would have nothing to do with elections in South Korea only. King told Truman in no uncertain terms that he was not going to allow Canada to be used for enforcing one-sided American solutions 'merely to be cuffed over the head by the Russians'.[25]

King found support for Canada's stance from another member of the Commonwealth, Australia. Jacobs, the US political adviser in Korea, described the Australian UNTCOK delegate, S. H. Jackson, as anti-American, a Leftist sympathiser and determined to show the Americans up, his reaction spurred on by the small Australian role in the occupation of Japan. Jacobs alleged Kermode thought Jackson to be a man of 'wild' and radical ideas but the British diplomat had also described him as able, steady and responsible. In fact, Jackson initially received a reprimand from Patrick Shaw, the Australian mission head in Japan, fearful that after conversations with MacArthur he (Jackson) *was* prepared to broker something in South Korea only and use Rhee as a figurehead. Jackson's attitude undoubtedly changed once he arrived in Seoul and witnessed events at first hand, making him a firm advocate of his instructions from Canberra to stop elections in South Korea only. Jacobs and Hodge saw Jackson, along with the Canadian Patterson, at the heart of a British-led conspiracy to prevent an American withdrawal from Korea. There was no such conspiracy: both Jackson and Patterson were following instructions from Canberra and Ottawa not London. Shaw had even lobbied his friend Kumara Menon, the Indian delegate and chairman of UNTCOK, to follow Canberra's policy. The British were not issuing instructions to Delhi as Jacobs had again incorrectly assumed. Jacobs' conspiracy theory was probably fuelled by the fact that all three Commonwealth delegates (Jackson, Patterson and Menon) used the British consulate as a ciphering office, which Kermode complained, made 'constant inroads on my time for consultations'.[26]

American pressure on UNTCOK to push for elections in the south, Soviet non-co-operation with UNTCOK, the state of the Korean economy, Rightist corruption and violent Communist demonstrations were some of the major reasons why UNTCOK delegates felt they could not carry out the terms of the original UN resolution. Even Kermode thought it was right for the occupying power, and not the UN, to carry out US policy, which may have been hard to disguise in his exchanges with Jacobs. Washington, no doubt coloured by Jacobs' views, now wanted to know what the official British attitude was with regard to the US desire to hold elections in the south only. After speaking with MacDermot, Gallman, the US chargé in London, was confident that the British would follow US policy, as long as it could be shown every means had been taken to bring the north and south together. The Foreign Office privately felt that since British policy was one of non-involvement and the US was playing the hand on behalf of the democratic world ('perhaps not over adroitly'), there was no chance of Britain striking an independent line. Questions remained over the status of an elected 'national' assembly, even if some seats were left vacant for North Korean representatives, who were hardly likely to attend. The British seemed trapped and phrases such as 'we have no alternative' but to join the Americans in their 'wishful thinking' indicated London's dilemma. The Foreign Office was firm on one point, however: UNTCOK's report must be heard properly, not skirted over as the Americans had intimated. Commonwealth members were taking part in drawing up the report and their views could not be ignored. In view of the fact of the Kashmir dispute, for example, the British also did 'not wish to oppose without good cause any constructive suggestions which may be made by the Indian Chairman of the Commission'.[27]

On the ground, Hodge lost all patience with UNTCOK: he thought the Australians and Canadians had no concept of the developing Cold War and, along with the other UNTCOK delegates, were guilty of appeasing the Soviet Union. Kermode thought there was 'no sadder man in Korea today' than Hodge, whose hopes for an American-backed South Korean state as 'a bulwark against the red destroyer' now stood little chance of fruition. Soviet actions went some way to helping Washington's case: their refusal to receive UNTCOK and violent Communist demonstrations had, together with the announcement on North Korean radio of a draft constitution for a 'Democratic People's Republic of Korea' (which claimed jurisdiction over all Korea), 'blatantly' defied the UN according to the Foreign Office. The Americans, however, still remained sensitive. After talking with Foreign Office officials, Douglas, the US ambassador in London, told Marshall it was clear that Britain saw conditions in South Korea as 'chaotic' and had 'written off' Korea as lost to the Soviet Union. This negative despatch forced the Foreign Office to apologise to the State Department, confirming they had sent instructions to their UN delegation at New York 'generally to support' the United States in its policy for elections in the south and had 'intended no disparagement' of the US administration of its zone.[28]

In presenting their arguments at the UN for a resolution to hold elections in areas of Korea accessible to UNTCOK for a national assembly, the US delegation was also helped by the Communist coup in Czechoslovakia on 25 February, demonstrating the serious international situation, and also a general feeling of impatience with the Soviets over their failure to comply with UNTCOK. The Australians and Canadians still objected to what they saw as American bullying tactics but eventually thought better of tabling an alternative resolution and, on 26 February, the US resolution was passed 31 to 2 by the Interim Committee.[29] In Seoul, the Australian and Canadian delegates nevertheless did their best to derail the new resolution after Hodge had immediately approached UNTCOK and agreed on elections for May. The Canadian, Patterson, vigorously opposed such a move (he had been absent from this initial decision) and got Menon to reconsider it, after allegedly storming out of one session. Jackson then joined in but there was soon Canadian concern over Patterson's safety in Seoul and Pearson felt it was unwise form him to become the centre of such 'a violent controversy'. As a compromise, Zoki Djabi, the Syrian delegate, tabled a motion for elections to be held as long as the atmosphere was conducive to freedom of choice. Canada and Australia still disagreed but the Syrian motion was approved, which in effect discarded any hope of reunification.[30]

The atmosphere of freedom of choice was rather difficult to discern, a point Canberra was quick to impress upon the State Department, and they (the Australians) felt the elections were going to be 'a caricature of democracy' and should be declared 'null and void'.[31] Kermode also told London that the Koreans had no experience of democracy and were not up to governing themselves. Rightist pressure was applied to reluctant voters to persuade them to register, while North Korean radio called on all Communists to oppose the elections 'until death', which led to attacks on election officials and registration booths. In the Communist stronghold of Cheju Island, an island just south of mainland Korea, nearly 200 people died from such attacks. Meanwhile, considerable numbers of people followed Kim Ku (who had broken from Rhee) and Kim Kyu-sik, in opposing the elections, persuaded by their argument that the elections would prevent forever the unification of Korea. Kim and Ku's ill-fated trip to Pyongyang in April for the North-South conference unfortunately showed the redundancy of their belief in the possibility of a broad-based united front between political groups on either side of the 38th parallel and their failure to participate in the elections left the way open for Rhee.[32] Those elections took place on 10 May. UNTCOK agreed to observe them 5 to 0, with Syria, France and Canada abstaining. To the surprise and annoyance of Canberra, Jackson argued that conditions were much better on 1 May.[33] Yet, out of a total Korean population of 30 million (21 million in the south) only 6 million voted, and Soviet talk of a body of 10 million voters in opposition to the South Korean election was, the Foreign Office noted, 'no moonshine'. On 31 May, under the temporary chairmanship of Rhee, a largely conservative, ultra-nationalist 'national' assembly opened in Seoul.[34]

The American aim, enshrined in NSC 8 and approved by Truman in April, was to terminate the US military commitment in Korea by the end of 1948, to train and equip a Korean constabulary of 24,000 (to be expanded to 50,000 men), and to complete rehabilitation programmes for the fiscal year 1949 to forestall economic collapse. Upon the US military withdrawal, a US diplomatic mission would be established to make recommendations for continuing economic and military aid, while Washington would continue to encourage further UN interest. Even on this latter point, William Draper, the under-secretary of the army, worried the UN might request the United States to prolong its occupation on technical grounds. The War Department quite simply wanted out. Rhee, ironically, was now desperate for the US to stay until he had been given time to build up his own military forces to defend South Korea against an attack from the North.[35] The State Department would brief the sure-footed and judicious Sir Oliver Franks, who had recently replaced Inverchapel in Washington, on NSC 8, and on the need to recognise the new Korean government. The Foreign Office thought the US proposals 'remarkably unrealistic'. The South Korean state was an anomaly: MacArthur had assured the British that strategically Korea was a liability and London doubted the Americans were prepared to give substantial military and economic support. Leaving behind sufficient hostages by way of military advisers and missions to induce Soviet fears that an overt act of encroachment on their part would be regarded as a *casus belli* was, the Foreign Office concluded, 'playing a very risky game'.[36]

Concern turned to anxiety when the Foreign Office learned the United States was considering recognising the new South Korean government as the government of *all* Korea. The Foreign Office was unwilling to play ball, arguing such a course of action could 'not be justified', either by the terms of the UN resolutions on Korea or by the general principles that govern the recognition of new States. London was also aware that Australia, Canada and India would all object to endorsing a South Korean claim to have legitimacy for the whole of Korea, a claim that would be undoubtedly copied by the northern administration and its recognition by the Slav bloc. Such an outcome would then be 'getting dangerously near to direct incitement to civil war'. The whole idea, the Foreign Office concluded thunderously, was 'foolish and improper'. In slightly less colourful language, Hubert Graves visited the State Department to tell Butterworth that the United States might not get the support it desired.[37] The issue dragged on for the rest of the summer and Foreign Office fears were not without foundation when Rhee, elected president on 17 July, declared in his opening speech to the national assembly that his government represented the whole of Korea. On 12 August, Washington unilaterally decided to issue a statement decreeing that Rhee's government was entitled to be the government of Korea as envisaged by the UN resolutions. Bevin refused to follow suit. In North Korea, Kim Il-sung ordered a 'national' election on 25 August. Pyongyang declared that 99.7 per cent of the electorate had voted to elect 212 members to a People's Assembly and it also represented the whole of Korea. The British sympathised with the US position, and the fact that they were not as close to events on the ground in Korea, but they maintained that out of respect to the Commonwealth members in UNTCOK, Britain had to wait until that commission had delivered its assessment of the situation to the UN in the autumn.[38]

Before the UN General Assembly met, the State Department did its best to slow the US military withdrawal from Korea, to help expedite its programme for training and equipping South Korean security forces under the current US military advisory group, and arrange for the continuation of economic assistance. The department recommended an outlay of $410m but Draper doubted whether Congress would appropriate more than $125m, including electric power from specially equipped naval vessels. Deprived of access to northern electric power, coal and minerals and with the economies of Japan and China in turmoil, South Korea could barely survive. Inflation, black markets and limited US aid also stifled economic reconstruction. In North Korea, the removal of assets as 'Japanese reparations' and looting by Red Army troops had left the region in economic distress as well. Those Soviet troops, it was announced on 18 September, would be finally withdrawn by the end of December.[39] When the UN General Assembly met during September to December 1948, the US told the British that they were going to continue to press for the recognition of the South Korean government, in line with previous UN resolutions, where they could hand over all authority. Mac-Dermot could not understand why the United States wanted to force the issue, to which Erle Dickover, now responsible for Far Eastern matters at the American embassy in London, told him that the State Department simply wanted 'to shift the whole responsibility for Korea firmly from off his Government's neck on to that of the United Nations'.[40] The Foreign Office legal advisers eventually found away around the impasse, when the Americans inserted into their resolution a clause stating Rhee's government should be regarded as the government of Korea envisaged in the 1947 UN resolution but that it functioned as such with respect to those parts where UNTCOK could observe the elections.[41]

Jacobs, still bitter about over his whole experience with UNTCOK and currently the Far Eastern adviser to the US delegation, was certain that Australia would vote against any US resolution. Dening, however, after a meeting with Commonwealth delegations on 9 November was convinced that they would now take a more favourable approach to the US resolution and he told Jacobs that same day that if Evatt were allowed himself to move a resolution with which the Americans agreed, this might be the best way of enlisting his support, a ploy which received British ministerial approval.[42] The Americans did adopt this solution and an Australian–American draft resolution was tabled. It recommended the withdrawal of occupation forces as early as possible and that a new United Nations Commission on Korea (UNCOK) be established to bring about the unification of the country. The Americans did make concessions, much to Australian satisfaction: the resolution did not categorically imply whether the South Korean state was the declared government of the whole of Korea and members of the UN were *invited* to recognise the new state. The text was finally proposed by Australia, China and the United States and on 12 December the General Assembly adopted the resolution by 48 to 6 (the Soviet bloc). Britain supported UNCOK, keen that the UN should have a continuing interest in the Korean situation but there is no evidence to suggest that at this stage London had changed its mind from accepting the fact that Korea would eventually be 'lost' to Communism.[43]

China perceptions

The prospect of 'losing' China to Communism also began to look like a distinct possibility during 1948. The rather relaxed view from the State Department was that the 'loss' of China would have little impact on the Cold War. Marshall did not dismiss the need to furnish economic aid to Chiang but argued against the case for military aid, a position US military departments could not readily understand if the aim was to halt the tide of Communism worldwide. The reason for Marshall's stance, State Department officials told Inverchapel, was that military aid would only make more

Communists and antagonise large sections on the Chinese public. Kennan's Policy Planning Staff also argued that China was a 'vast poor house', lacking strategic resources and requiring huge economic assistance to recover from over a decade of war. Would the Soviets therefore necessarily benefit from such an acquisition? The Joint Chiefs of Staff thought so but even they came to accept limited military aid for Chiang (which they advocated) might not stem the Communist advance. There were no arguments, however, over the fact that China should be placed very low on the list of US Cold War priorities. In April, Congress nevertheless approved the China Aid Act, providing $338m for economic assistance and (against Marshall's advice) $125m for military aid.[44]

The British view was that such limited economic and military aid would not prove effective in preventing the spread of Communism down to the Yangtze but they hoped stabilisation might result thereafter. Like Kennan's Policy Planning Staff, the British JIC, whose interest began to quicken in China, doubted whether the Chinese Communists, who were experienced only in living off the countryside, could administer any large commercial or industrial area. Whether this assessment would turn out to be true or not, Brigadier Field was becoming more convinced that Chiang could now lose the civil war.[45] Relations between Nanking and London had also deteriorated during the first half of 1948 when, in January, Chinese mobs attacked British consular and commercial offices at Canton (Shameen Island) after the Hong Kong authorities evicted Chinese squatters from the walled-city of Kowloon. The Chinese Nationalists tried to claim jurisdiction over Kowloon in a populist effort to curb British treaty rights and deflect attention away from the domestic crisis. The incident briefly hit the news in Britain but faded as the Nationalists began rapidly to lose their control over China. Indeed, riots had also taken place in Shanghai as a protest against Chiang's failed political and economic policies. Militarily, ineffective commanders (mostly Chiang's 'old friends' and not fit for purpose), defective equipment and poor morale led the British and the Americans to believe it was 'absolutely beyond' the capacity of the Nationalists to restore the general Manchurian situation, even to where it was 18 months ago.[46]

The dire situation coloured the outlook of British diplomats who had to work on the ground. In February, Stevenson, the ambassador, enclosed copies of Chiang's New Year speech and Mao's report to the Central Committee of the Chinese Communist Party made on Christmas Day. The despatch contained one paragraph on Chiang's remarks and 12 on Mao's report. *The Times* had recently reported that Mao's party was carrying out the redistribution of land in the 'most arbitrary and violent manner' but Stevenson declared Mao would not show more hostility towards Britain than any other foreign country, except perhaps the United States. Hitherto, the embassy had stressed that Mao and his party was pursuing a cruel and Marxist policy, and would treat all capitalist countries alike, led by Soviet advice. Arthur Scott at the China Department hoped this *volte-face* was born from the frustration of the awful circumstances on the ground and he considered it dangerous to presume British commercial interests would be no worse off under Mao's rule. The long-term outlook was sure to be worse, as events had already proved in the north. The Chinese Communists, Scott argued, were not different from Communists elsewhere. While Peter Scarlett, the new head of the China Department, and Dening did not disagree, the latter took a more practical approach, arguing that if Britain could maintain its consular and embassy contacts inside a Communist China and merchants could contrive to trade, 'we should at any rate not discourage them from doing so'. Now, though, Dening concluded rather cautiously, this was not the time to discuss the question of recognition, as it would 'gravely complicate our relations' with the National Government and the United States.[47]

The embassy quickly set out to defend itself after Dening had written to Nanking expressing Foreign Office concern. The Minister, Lionel 'Leo' Lamb, in Stevenson's absence, explained that Chiang's speech was a 'replica' of so many others it did not seem to call for the same attention and Mao's speech, which tried to extend promises to the 'middle farmer' class and small capitalist, was seen as significant in its wider appeal. Reassuring London that they thought Communism was 'a vile and destructive ogre', the embassy did not think collectivist theories could stand up to the yearning of the Chinese peasant to own his land for the security of his family. The process to convert China to Communist orthodoxy could therefore be slow. The embassy did not expect any special treatment for British interests in a Communist China and there was no question of extending an olive branch to Mao but it was not worth provoking the Communists gratuitously, exposing British nationals and also consuls in Communist-held areas. There was a practical necessity of dealing with them *de facto* in areas under their control: 'we cannot afford to abandon our struggle to protect British interests'. If there was a chance to promote British trade, the embassy argued, 'we should surely not fail to take it up through over squeamishness about reddening our hands', and appealing to the 'commercial instinct of the Chinese may weaken his faith in the more sterile tenets of Sovietism'. An old China hand since 1921, Lamb was no doubt happy to sign off a letter that extolled the virtues of continuing trade with China.[48]

Speculation amongst British diplomatic and consular officials about the possibilities of long-term trade in a Communist China was a constant theme of 1948 and many remained divided over the potential outcome but there was never any question of blocking attempts to try. For the moment, there were only fleeting glimpses of what conditions might be like under Communist control (mostly discouraging, such as violent campaigns against landlords and rich peasants). Mao's armies, however, had still to secure Manchuria and it was considered premature to indulge in too much crystal gazing. Trying to assess the impact on the ground was difficult because, as Lamb explained, whatever the political complexion in China, xenophobia was 'a national characteristic'. One only had to read Chiang's *China's Destiny* (published in 1943) and witness the discriminatory practices carried out by the Nationalists against British trading interests to get a feel for the popular anti-foreign basis of *Kuomintang* policy. In the current Cold War climate, the issue (unlike other areas) was not, Lamb said, a clear-cut one between the Communists, 'whose hostility to us is patent, and their opponents whose friendship has been proved'. Recent evidence does not support such a view. Mao's ideological outlook was clear and he would place himself and his party firmly in the Soviet camp. Lamb tried to explain that for the Chinese man on the street there was only 'a choice between two evils'. Communism would probably not 'be a shock to a people that are already used to a secret police; arbitrary exactions and imposition and the disregard of *habeas corpus*'. Lamb did concede nevertheless that a Chinese Communist victory would usher no great benefits to the British.[49]

Like British diplomats on the ground, Stuart, the US ambassador in Nanking, was quickly losing much of his patience with Chiang. That irritation was being reciprocated by the Nationalist Chinese who delivered less than flattering assessments of US policy towards China. In June, the more liberal T. V. Soong, sent to Canton by Chiang to hold the south of China as a concession to hard liners in the *Kuomintang*, told Malcolm Mac-Donald, Britain's Commissioner-General for Southeast Asia, that Americans did not understand the Chinese; that Truman had been 'an unmitigated disaster' for the Chinese people; and that Marshall's mission was 'a grave misfortune'. The Chinese, Soong said, were not trained in democratic methods and it was a bad system of government for China, taking centuries to develop. Indeed, as one historian notes, there had been a continual belief in American discourse that a programme of modernisation for China meant Westernisation.[50] Furthermore, Chinese newspapers such as the *North China Daily News* noted that the US desire to build up Japan was provoking a violent repulsion amongst the Chinese. Stuart, meanwhile, described his talks with Chiang as futile, considering the Generalissimo incapable of change. Stuart and his US embassy colleagues also reported that a majority of Chinese people had privately had enough of the civil war. The trouble was that many Chinese people were convinced that the terrible destruction of their country only continued because of US aid to Chiang.[51]

As the blame game intensified and exasperated by what they saw as Nationalist incompetence, both Stuart and Stevenson soon began to re-advocate the idea of a coalition government, which accepted the fact (in Stevenson's words) that 'Communism in China is here to stay'. In London and Washington, the reaction to their ambassadors' views was one of disappointment. The Foreign Office thought both men had effectively 'written off' the Nationalist government, while Butterworth considered that the imposition of free speech and free elections in a coalition government aimed at neutralising Communist attempts at minority control was 'a pious hope'.[52] Marshall, having confronted increasing Soviet intransigence not just in East Asia but also in Europe, witnessing the coup in Czechoslovakia and, more recently, watching the blockade of Berlin, was at least clear about the American prospects of offering their good offices as mediator. He would not countenance such a suggestion and the secretary of state reminded Stuart of the 'engulfment' which had resulted from coalition governments in Eastern Europe.[53]

The State Department did not dispute the fact that the situation in China was reaching a critical stage but hoped it was 'not entirely beyond repair'. There was evidence that the Communists were experiencing difficulties due to the lack of qualified political and economic personnel, while 'the violence and brutality which had characterised their political activity continued to alienate many potential administrators'.[54] The British embassy in Nanking, however, continued to send out mixed signals about what to expect from the Chinese Communists. In a despatch signed off in Stevenson's name by Lamb, the embassy reported that the Chinese Communist Party had 'obediently' come out with a stock denunciation of the Yugoslav leader Marshal Tito and his split from Stalin, which the ambassador declared was 'a clear indication of their present subservience to Moscow'. Two months later, Lamb argued that it was only 'a cheap gesture' to please the Kremlin and did not indicate subservience to Moscow: Mao 'will take no more kindly to dictation from Moscow than does Tito'. London thought it remained to be seen whether Mao would act independently of Stalin but presumed his party would behave 'like Communist parties all the world over'.[55] This was the wiser counsel. Hector McNeil had already impressed upon members of the China Association at a lunch as the Savoy chaired by W. J. 'Tony' Keswick, the chairman of the China Association, that the Foreign Office would not appoint an unofficial representative to the Chinese Communists. The minister was also reluctant to promise that he would leave a member of the diplomatic community behind in Shanghai if it fell to the Communists: it was for British merchants to decide whether to trade with them – if they could then the Labour government would not stand in their way. In his notes from the meeting, Dening recorded that British merchant houses such as Shell, ICI, Unilever and BAT were determined to stay come what may.[56]

London and Washington often agonised over what to do about coming face to face with the Chinese Communists. British mercantile investment in China was greater than US investment (some £300m compared to the US investment of £87m) yet a more immediate problem was a possible attack by Mao's armies on Tsingtao, where US naval forces and its advisory group schools were based. Two schools of thought emerged. Admiral Oscar Badger, the US commander of Western Pacific naval forces, wanted to assist the Nationalists in their defence of the city. In the summer of

1948, US Marine forces stood at 3,600 and Badger considered it essential to protect US naval forces there and what he perceived as the general US position in the Far East. Horrified, the State Department felt it should be made 'unmistakably clear' that the defence of Tsingtao was a Nationalist and not an American responsibility. The State Department's wanted Badger to pull out his forces in an emergency, not stand and fight. During that summer, the Joint Chiefs of Staff argued against an immediate withdrawal, even thought the city was full of refugees and the morale of Nationalist troops was desperate. Forrestal also sanctioned a directive to Badger, in direct contravention of the State Department's wishes, which gave him freedom of action to defend his forces in an emergency, a 'weasel' phrase Butterworth noted. The issue of whether to intervene in Tsingtao or not dragged on for the rest of 1948 but as the Nationalist position in Manchuria crumbled, the NSC agreed to begin phasing out the US naval operation there at a desirable moment, while dependants and extraneous activities could be evacuated at once.[57]

Butterworth realised that the US could not maintain bases in Tsingtao or Shanghai once the Nationalists lost control as, apart from the obvious involvement in the civil war, Washington could face charges from the international community of maintaining them solely for reasons of 'power politics' and this would seriously 'weaken the moral leadership of the U.S. in world affairs'. Shanghai with its population of around six million was also likely to prove a testing ground for Communist administration and the hope was that the city's complex and highly integrated economy would still mean that the Communists would require essential imports from the West to prevent riots and chaos.[58] Whether or not this might provide Washington with some sort of lever over the Chinese Communists, the United States remained in a state of flux over its China policy. Butterworth told Dening during the latter's visit to Washington in June that the United States was no longer in a position to influence events on the ground. General Omar Bradley, the chairman of the Joint Chiefs of Staff, and Wedemeyer, now Director of Plans and Operations, all held serious doubts about placing advisers with Nationalist forces, while Kenneth Royall, US Army Secretary, even thought about stopping military supplies. The British noticed a marked reluctance on the part of the Americans to talk to them about China and Franks noted that the United States had 'no definite policy towards China'. Scarlett considered the whole US attitude 'defeatist' – the Americans considered him 'utterly old school tie' and 'inclined to be foxy' – and when Graves reported that the State Department rarely paid any attention to Stuart, the British saw one reason why the US was unable to influence local conditions.[59] There were also accusations Stuart could not keep a secret and had a Chinese secretary who told Chiang everything, the result being that the State Department did not trust the reports they were getting from their ambassador.[60] In Nanking,

Field meanwhile reported that US military assistance, administered through its advisory group in China, continued 'to get nowhere and achieve virtually no results'. There had, he noted, also been a noticeable deterioration in the quality of army staff arriving in China to administer the assistance.[61]

That August, the State Department told Stuart it was not likely that the situation on the ground would 'make it possible for us at this juncture to formulate any rigid plans for our future policy in China'. Washington had to preserve 'a maximum freedom of action'; a reference to whether aid should be switched to local commanders other than Chiang. Kennan simply felt that the Truman administration had to retain 'maximum flexibility' and then 'make our decisions as we go along'. There was certainly no question of a *rapprochement* with the Chinese Communists.[62] Two months later, the State Department maintained that it was still not possible to make any 'rigid plans for our future policy in China'.[63] By then, the Nationalist position in Manchuria had effectively collapsed and Chiang's armies were in danger of annihilation. During the last quarter of 1948, the Nationalist army would lose nearly one million men through death, desertion or capture, along with an enormous quantity of military equipment. Since there were no regular forces south of the Yangtze, the US embassy in Nanking reported that the People's Liberation Army could 'capture any city they wish' and the 'cessation' of large scale, formal military resistance by Nationalist armies was now 'only a matter of time'. One Communist column marched into Tsinan (Jinan) fully armed with US equipment. In addition, the Nationalist economy was falling apart after unsuccessful attempts to control prices and exchange rates by police-state methods. There were severe shortages of food and Chiang was as unpopular as ever. The only hope, and a view also held by the British, was that the Chinese Communists would be fully occupied maintaining the areas they already controlled.[64]

Stuart and John Cabot, the US consul-general at Shanghai, did not help quell the general feeling of panic when they recommended evacuation to American dependants connected with the US military advisory groups.[65] Yet, Alastair Cooke still could not work out whether the situation was serious or not. Truman was 'bantering' with newsmen in Florida; Marshall was busy at the UN General Assembly in Paris and nothing came out of news conferences with Lovett. The whole thing seemed a mess.[66] It was all too easy to criticise but alternative solutions were not readily forthcoming. In London, Scarlett told Dickover that the British held the same outlook as the Americans. China south of the Yangtze would dissolve into a multitude of warlord regimes, and it was difficult to see, Scarlett noted, what the West could do now, which rather undermined his harsh words of defeatism hurled at the Americans in private.[67] Franks also emphasised to Lovett that it was impossible for Britain to maintain a policy 'of a very positive nature towards China'. On enquiring upon future US intentions (on instructions from the

Foreign Office), Lovett accused the press of unjustly making great play with the charge that the State Department had no policy and that they had let matters drift. 'This was quite untrue', he said. The United States had given Chiang constant support and aid short of that which would embroil them in civil war. They were now confined to helping China within the limits set by Congress, which effectively meant waiting on events and redirecting aid to elements that fought the Chinese Communists.[68] At this stage, Truman, despite his growing antipathy towards the Nationalists, was not prepared to make a statement on the situation bearing out the true facts of the situation, which could, in Lovett's words, 'pull the rug from under Chiang Kai-shek's feet'.[69]

The likelihood of a Nationalist collapse forced the British to begin thinking about the future of Hong Kong if Chinese Communist armies struck south. Lamb was confident that Hong Kong would not be attacked even if Mao controlled all of China because of colony's economic value. In the short term, Lamb thought that some sort of 'bogus' coalition would emerge with the Communists at helm, a ploy in order to win a form of foreign recognition. His inescapable conclusion was that the Communist domination of China could not be prevented and he hoped the possibility of exploiting internal strains, 'which are sure to develop', might arise. Scarlett agreed that for the moment Hong Kong was not in direct danger, but he copied Lamb's telegram to the Service departments anyway. He disagreed, however, that an opportunity would arise to exploit internal strains within the Chinese Communist Party. The lesson to be learned from Yugoslavia, he noted, was that Communists 'whether orthodox or heterodox are equally hostile to non-Communist powers', and it was not wise to 'set our hopes too high'. Dening sat somewhere in the middle, hoping the strains might 'exploit themselves'. He thought orthodox Communists might be a bit 'thin on the ground' once they were spread all over China. 'I do not suggest', he concluded, 'that the stranglehold will not eventually be complete; merely that it is likely to take time'. Bevin read the internal debate with interest.[70]

By late 1948, Bevin had found himself increasingly drawn into Chinese affairs. In November he spoke to Marshall in Paris about China and the latter had explained how his government was at its 'wits end' over developments there. In a conversation that lasted an hour, Marshall said that he would continue to support Chiang for as long as he could but would resist the Generalissimo's attempts to drag the United States into the civil war. Bevin thought Marshall was 'not in the least panicky about the situation despite its gravity' though he intervened when the secretary of state said Chinese Communists were different from other Communists, a point with which he was unable to agree. That debate would continue into 1949 in both Washington and London. In the Foreign Office, there were discussions about a possible Mao–Stalin split over the future of Manchuria; which leader would profit from any Communist successes in Southeast Asia; and whether the British government should adopt a provocative attitude towards the Chinese Communists, which might react adversely against British merchants in China. If the British did nothing, for example, could it be seen as 'lily-livered' in the context of their fight against the Malayan Communists? Dening presumed that any British propaganda was hardly likely to work in China where he now accepted that most people wanted to be rid of Chiang, while the majority of people in Southeast Asia, he claimed, probably did not even understand what Communism was. They key was to provide stability and security to the region to make it more disposed to resist Communism. Merely pointing out how 'beastly' the Chinese Communists were, Dening concluded, was unlikely to have much effect in bolstering the British position in Southeast Asia.[71]

Recognising the seriousness of the situation, Bevin, with the help of his Foreign Office Far Eastern experts, laid a paper before cabinet that confronted the possibility of a potential Communist victory in China and assessed the economic difficulties Mao might face in running the country. During an initial brief period, Bevin explained, the Chinese Communists might be tolerant towards foreign trading interests but they would eventually work for the 'exclusion of the foreigner' from China. The foreign secretary, nevertheless, thought it sensible to try and keep 'a foot in the door'. Possible bargaining counters could be utilised by withholding certain essential imports to make sure Chinese Communists behaved while internal strains within the Chinese Communist Party could develop if Mao failed to exercise complete control. Bevin had no illusions that Mao would adopt orthodox Communist policies, a view that would prove to be correct. The cabinet paper also observed that if China was under Communist rule, the future of Hong Kong, a colony effectively living 'on the edge of a volcano', would depend on whether Mao deemed a stable port worthwhile to him. There would also be definite implications for Southeast Asia, with militant Communism close to Malaya's northern frontier, and Thailand and Indo-China as poor buffers. Across that region internal disorder could increase and Bevin recognised it was down to Britain to assume the lead there, as the Americans were not prepared to accept any responsibility for Southeast Asia. Ministers endorsed Bevin's recommendations.[72] Apart from informing the government of the China situation, Bevin also hoped that if the paper was passed to the Americans they could confide to the British how their own policy was developing. Bevin had complained to Marshall in Paris the difficulties in extracting information from the State Department, which Marshall promised to rectify. Dening was sceptical, telling Graves in Washington that any hope for increased transparency from the State Department was 'a vain one'. Dening moaned that Butterworth had proved less than forthcoming and he was waiting for him to use the situation in China as an excuse not to impart US thinking on Japan, now he could no longer use the presidential election, which Truman had won, as a reason.[73]

Japan and the next phase of the occupation

As the crisis degenerated in China, problems were also surfacing in Japan. At the end of 1947, Gascoigne told Bevin that the Japanese economy was 'deteriorating sadly'. UKLM thought MacArthur had 'to wake up to the true facts' and take 'strong remedial action' and wondered whether he was well informed on economic matters. Gascoigne considered the Finance Division of General William Marquat's Economic & Scientific Section 'a weak link', staffed with men possessing limited business experience. Many American businessmen were 'constitutionally allergic' to the kind of controls SCAP used and they, along with other British and Japanese financial experts, argued that MacArthur's economic experiment was no longer working. Gascoigne knew that SCAP would 'hotly resent any imputation' that anything was seriously wrong. Those responsible for Japan in Washington were unconcerned about any such backlash, and the ageing General Frank McCoy, the American chairman of the Far Eastern Commission, was instructed to tell the latter in January 1948 that the United States was seeking to rehabilitate Japan's economy and make it self-supporting. McCoy's remarks brought some satisfaction to the British, who since 1945 had advocated, amidst the Foreign Office remembered 'a good deal of harsh criticism', the need for a viable Japanese economy. Japanese industry had hardly reached more than half the 1930–4 levels set down by the Commission and London had no objection to the American desire to let Japan 'stand on her own feet economically' but there was slight concern that Washington might contemplate higher levels than anticipated to achieve viability 'at all costs'. How would other regional powers react to a resurgent Japan? The British hoped that if Anglo-American economic policy towards Japan could be co-ordinated, their commercial interests would be protected against the 'menaces' of Japanese economic competition.[74]

Such hopes for close economic consultation proved forlorn. In 1948, London continued to protest about the return of British business properties and licenses to trade were extremely restrictive. MacArthur told UKLM that until a peace treaty was signed the needs of his forces came first, which left the US Eighth Army in full or at least partial occupation of British premises (mostly in Yokohama) owned by companies such as Rising Sun Petroleum and Commercial Union Assurance, HSBC and Butterfield & Swire. The Board of Trade considered the position 'intolerable' but the Foreign Office was unwilling to apply 'firmness' or provoke a 'first-class row' over such an issue. A confrontation with General Walton Walker, the commander of the US Eight Army, was not one Gascoigne relished either and whose path, he imagined, it would 'not be pleasant' to cross.[75] The British move to secure a sterling area trade agreement with SCAP, which the State Department had sanctioned in January, also proved problematical. What Gascoigne thought would take 'a matter of weeks' to settle in February, dragged on for months.

Between the end of the war and December 1947, the British government had sold just under $25m worth of commodities (mainly salt) to SCAP and in return had bought just over $8.5m worth of Japanese products (mainly raw silk). Short of dollars, SCAP was in arrears on his British account and demanded an overdraft facility before any agreement was signed. He further pressed UKLM to agree to partial payments in dollars for Japanese textiles but they insisted payment had to be in sterling, forcing UKLM to exclude cotton textiles from the agreement reached in May. On this last point, SCAP reluctantly gave way in July albeit with strong reservations. The agreement would be worth just under $122m and would run from 1 Jul 1948 to 30 Jun 1949.[76]

The future of cotton textiles was of concern to the Labour government because of potential domestic implications. During the summer of 1948, Labour ministers such as McNeil and Harold Wilson, the young, competent and rather bureaucratic president of the Board of Trade, reminded Bevin of the grave concern within the Lancashire cotton industry about Japanese low cost competition, especially as the Attlee government had pledged full employment. Raymond Streat, the chairman of the British Cotton Board, wanted the government to make representations to the State Department and set limits on Japanese production. It was a course, considering that such light industry posed no security risks, that Bevin and Wilson recognised was 'not practical politics', especially at a time when US economic policy was 'running in the opposite direction' and by the fact Britain had already agreed that Japan must pay its own way and be self-supporting. Bevin would later tell Streat that his industry, whose unions and employers 'adhered stubbornly to old practices', had had a head start after the war, that the world was starved of textiles, and that he would not approach the State Department on this issue. A Whitehall-wide meeting of interested departments that October did agree half-heartedly, after pressure from the Board of Trade, to ask Washington to support an Anglo-American textile mission to Japan for talks on a non-governmental basis with SCAP and Japanese textile experts, yet made it clear that the British government was in no way committed. Streat faced an uphill battle and just one month before the outbreak of the Korean War, MacArthur finally though reluctantly received such a mission.[77]

For most of 1948, the British spent a large proportion of their time trying to ascertain what exactly the Americans intended for occupied Japan. The only thing they could be sure of was that a peace treaty seemed dead in the water, which to MacDermot at the Japan and Pacific Department was 'an attractive' short-term policy in the context of 'a general panic' about the Soviet Union but had 'disquieting' long-term political and strategic implications, not least by antagonising China and other Far Eastern powers worried by a Japanese resurgence but also perhaps the Japanese themselves who were unable to rid their occupier. Aware Marshall was preoccupied with the European Recovery Programme, the Foreign Office initially concluded any high-level pressure would be counter-productive. This attitude changed after the visit in March of two high-profile US officials from the State (Kennan) and Army (Draper) Departments to Japan. Kennan revealed little to Gascoigne about US thinking other than arguing that the State Department was 'over-burdened' and that a period of 'marking time' in Japan was necessary. Kennan actually saw MacArthur as a law unto himself and wanted Washington to have more direct control, to revive the *zaibatsu* and curtail the power of the labour unions, while also linking Japan to a regional containment programme, making Okinawa the centre of US 'offensive striking power' in the Western Pacific area. MacArthur was equally non-communicative with Gascoigne and said he knew nothing more than what was in the press about Draper's visit except that he was there to discuss with his experts a survey on reparations undertaken in 1947 by Clifford Strike, the head of an engineering consortium. With no concrete US proposals to report, Gascoigne could only surmise that the Americans were in 'a considerable quandary' about policy for Japan and this explained their reluctance to consult the British.[78]

The British were then in for a shock. Draper told journalists 'off the record' that the United States was preparing an aid programme whereby Japan would pay its way by 1952/3. The maximum US expenditure would be $580m per annum and this figure would decline as the programme neared its five-year deadline. The United States did not intend to hold the Japanese economy to any set level such as that of 1930/4, which was not an absolute maximum of production but represented the level of capacity to be left after reparations removals. If the Japanese could exceed this level with what was left it was permitted to do so, as long as it did not threaten the peace. Every effort would be made to stimulate Japan's trade with non-dollar nations, though the United States had no intention of releasing controls to a point where Japan would become an economic threat. Draper was also in favour of Japanese businessmen visiting foreign countries.[79] Almost simultaneously, MacArthur and the Army Department released a statement from him (SCAP) to Royall of 18 January 1948, which spoke of releasing restrictions as far as possible on trade and commerce and restoring the normal limits of diplomatic privilege and the right of Japanese citizenry to journey abroad to study and absorb cultural and scientific advances.[80] It appeared MacArthur had hoodwinked Gascoigne and the Foreign Office erupted arguing that all these statements paid 'scant attention' to other powers. Canberra thought MacArthur's statement 'discourteous' and 'disturbing'. Dickover paid a visit to the Foreign Office, stressing the burden on the US taxpayer but the damage was done: he still provided no more than generalisations and British officials lamented the lack of consultation.[81]

Kennan's actual recommendations laid before the State Department, envisaged a reduction in the scope of SCAP's operations; the building of an industrially revived Japan 'amenable to American leadership'; the retention of US tactical forces in Japan until the signing of a peace treaty; and a need for an offshore defensive perimeter which would include Okinawa. Kennan's whole paper was set against the backdrop of preventing Soviet penetration, which appeared to be making dramatic inroads within China and Korea. His proposals won widespread support in Washington,[82] while figures such as Forrestal, Royall and Draper even toyed with arguments for a limited degree of Japanese rearmament but they recognised this might put a strain on Japan's economy, undermine the Japanese constitution and bring forth outrage from most Far Eastern nations.[83] The British, however, were still left only with glimpses of American thinking and from Washington Graves told London that a 'hurried reconsideration' of US policy was being drawn up in the wake of events such as the coup in Czechoslovakia and the deterioration of the US position in China and Korea. What this meant for the 'allied' occupation of Japan was not clear and Graves worried that the British were bound 'to bump up' against the Americans over issues such as the future of the Far Eastern Commission, reparations, and acceptable levels for industry and shipbuilding. Indeed, Gascoigne had picked up from Kennan and Draper their dissatisfaction with the Far Eastern Commission (MacArthur simply wanted it liquidated) and UKLM's head remained downbeat, considerably discomfited over the failure of the Americans to divulge their thoughts to the British. Yet, he also recognised there was little the British could do now to change the US attitude and that it was still more desirable for the latter to decide the future of Japan.[84]

These may indeed have been the uncomfortable realities facing the British but Bevin wanted it stressed to Washington, when he heard the Defence Department wanted MacArthur to take sole charge of the 'next phase of the occupation', that he would not allow the Far Eastern Commission to become a rubber stamp for US decisions. The foreign secretary would sanction the 'freer use' of the interim directive (the State Department's preferred option) if needed in the face of obstruction by the Soviets and the Nationalist Chinese against the '*unanimous* wish of all other members of the Commission'. He would not, however, condone it in any other circumstances, especially if Commonwealth powers were in opposition to US policy, which would risk 'serious embarrassment' for Britain.[85]

That policy looked more disturbing after Draper released a report on 26 April by Percy Johnston, the Chemical Bank chairman, who he had taken with him to Tokyo to head a business delegation, which met *zaibatsu* representatives. The report stated that Japanese production should be accelerated by the relaxation of anti-*zaibatsu* measures, curtailing organised labour, controlling inflation, fixing the yen's foreign exchange value and increasing exports at the expense of domestic consumption. Johnston also recommended the cancellation of reparations and Japanese penetration into Far Eastern import markets, to help Japan achieve a nine-fold increase in exports. UKLM thought the report was well balanced from the point of view of Japan's economic needs, although it completely failed to understand SCAP's acute dollar problem. Despite State Department fears that the Johnston report might alienate allies, Draper, Royall and Kennan (the latter more aware of allied sensitivities) drove the new agenda forward to extend control over the occupation, securing funds from Congress, that would eventually lead to a new policy approved by Truman at the end of the year. Even MacArthur – after his stunning defeat in the presidential primary elections and also annoyed at the continuing criticism of his occupation at home, particularly amongst big business – began to devise his industrial deconcentration policies for the requirements of Japanese recovery.[86]

Britain, Dening claimed, could now no longer remain indifferent over the new trend in US policy for Japan. He recognised that the Americans considered Japan as their 'own particular reserve' and, as Britain was in no position to provide economic or financial aid for that country and had practically withdrawn from BCOF, London was 'on delicate ground' when it came to trying to influence Washington. The British nonetheless had to try, as East Asian issues affected not only Britain's position in Southeast Asia but also relations with the Commonwealth. Britain's close association with the United States meant that if the latter suffered a reverse in East Asia this could have an 'incalculable' impact on Britain's position in the Far East too. It was no longer enough, Dening concluded, to merely trust the running of East Asia to the Americans. Dening's solution was to travel to Washington to propose five-power talks on the subject of East Asia that would include Britain, the United States, Canada, Australia and New Zealand.[87] The general rancour in Australian–American relations worried Bevin, enhanced by the fact that in January, the CIA had reported on Australian security leaks from a series of intercepted Soviet communications (code-named 'Venona' by the British), which left serious doubts about Australian security. British concern over this matter was rather ironic considering figures such as Guy Burgess were leaking British secrets to Moscow. Bevin, nevertheless, agreed it was essential to establish some form of allied dialogue in order to determine Far Eastern policy and suggested, with Attlee's acceptance, that Dening should travel to Canberra, Wellington and Ottawa first for oral talks, stressing to them the need for secrecy, before then visiting Washington.[88]

Embarking on his whistle-stop tour in May–June, Dening considered his projected talks with the Americans would fail almost immediately after he visited Canberra. He found the attitude at the Department of External Affairs horrifying as figures such as Dr John Burton, its secretary, and Evatt, attacked US policy worldwide and argued that the Soviets were not as bad as they were painted. 'Appeasement of the Soviet Union', Dening noted, 'appeared to be their main aim'. Unlike the British who wanted to 'steer' the United States the right way, the Evatt–Burton combination seemed inclined to achieve it in an 'openly provocative' way. Dening thought Chifley more reasonable as he had no illusions about Soviet aims but as the actual conduct of foreign affairs remained in the hands of Evatt and Burton, Dening concluded that in their existing frame of mind, they would not keep the talks secret. Dening's trip to Wellington was little better and there too he recorded a distrust of US policy in the Far East, while Alastair McIntosh, the New Zealand secretary for external affairs, saw Butterworth as 'uncooperative' (Dening did not disagree) while considering 'intolerable' his attitude that as the United States was the only power to ensure security in the Pacific, it was up to the smaller power (i.e. New Zealand) to take it and not ask questions.[89]

Mutual suspicions remained high. Australian–American confrontation continued in the Allied Council for Japan even after Macmahon Ball's departure, a body Gascoigne thought had long fallen into 'desuetude', while Canberra sought to reduce its strength in BCOF to 2,750, considering its task virtually complete, which later drew complaints from the Americans that they would have to fill the gaps with US troops to cover the area.[90] In Washington, when Graves told Butterworth and Kennan about Dening's proposed visit, their immediate reaction was one of reluctance and they also asked why the latter needed to visit Australia, as they wanted him to be able to talk freely without reference to other powers, to which Graves retorted that 'discussions within the family were both natural and necessary'.[91] The signs for close collaboration were not encouraging. When Dening arrived in Washington in late May, Lovett made it clear that the United States was not ready for five-power talks and asked Dening point blank whether they could rely on Australian security. Dening could only reply he hoped so. Lovett then discoursed at length about the forthcoming US election and attitude of Congress, who, if they found out about five-power talks, would be immediately hostile. 'No one could say', he said, 'what policies a new administration would follow'. Lovett was not opposed to bilateral Anglo-American conversations but Dening responded that if concrete proposals emerged, his government would have to consult the Commonwealth. Lovett divulged little else to Dening, neither did Kennan nor Butterworth who were also present, except that they had 'abandoned all idea' of an early peace settlement.[92] Dening might have saved himself the trouble of journeying thousands of miles to ascertain such anodyne information. Further talks over the next few days produced no more than the British already knew. Back in London, although Sargent was worried about the 'hostile attitude' of the Australians towards the United States, he felt this 'accumulated resentment' was the result of 'domineering tactics' adopted by the Americans. It was time for the United States to stop indulging in unilateral action and consider the interests of other friendly powers.[93]

What Dening had tried to impress upon the Americans was that a peace treaty could not be deferred indefinitely, as this would lead to possible Japanese resentment and non-cooperation while Japan itself would be unable to start to regularise its relations with other countries. A resentful Japan could also provide opportunities for the Soviet Union. As a way out of the impasse, Dening thought the US position might be secured through a bilateral defence pact between Japan and the United States. He recalled with some satisfaction that Butterworth displayed interest in this exposition and 'obviously the Americans had not thought of such a solution to their problem'. Dening, however, was forced to admit that the Chiefs of Staff had 'not given detailed consideration' to the strategic situation in East Asia but he felt it could be safely assumed that they would not wish to see the US strategic position there weakened (Dening's assessment was later proved accurate). With regard to Dening's broader point, Kennan and Butterworth dismissed his assumption that the Japanese would want an early peace treaty. The Japanese, they suggested, were more alarmed by the prospect of being left unarmed against a Soviet-dominated Northeast Asia. This fact, according to the State Department, which could hardly be stated in public, required another phase of the occupation in order to strengthen Japan and rehabilitate its economy.[94] It was an argument that was clearly non-negotiable.

McNeil's call therefore for Bevin to tell Marshall that Britain would not agree to delay a peace treaty indefinitely or acquiesce in the new proposed policy for Japan was unlikely to work and rather cause resentment, whether it presented Britain with a 'nasty political mess' or not.[95] The British still needed US economic help and in conversation with Franks, Marshall felt an understanding of what the United States was seeking to do in Japan was important not only for broad American East Asian interests but also in relation to the European Recovery Programme. It was vital the latter be fully carried out over a four-year period, Marshall stated. He saw difficulties in doing this: so far the other competing demands of Central and South America on the US purse had been staved off but the United States was also pouring money into Japan at the rate of a billion dollars a year. Marshall then spiced up his talk with Franks by dropping subtle hints and mild threats. The US secretary of state, for example, warned that a Republican administration would tend to lean towards measures of financial economy. It was necessary to reduce the costs of the occupation but it was also impossible to clear out of Japan – the resulting vacuum would be filled by the Soviet Union. Marshall warned the British ambassador that what could begin as an issue of spending fewer dollars in Japan might over the coming months be broadened out by a chain reaction into a less favourable attitude in the United States to the European Recovery Programme. This, he felt, was important to avoid. It did not take the astute Franks long to recognise the implicit threat behind Marshall's language and the ambassador was in 'little doubt' that Britain should be seen to be 'constructive and helpful' using its good offices to persuade other members of the Commonwealth, particularly Australia, to support US policy.[96]

Dening, while scathing of American East Asian policy, was not blind to the broader picture and Britain's more important interests. He was prepared to face realities and accept the reorientation of US policy. Furthermore, if

Britain did not accept the new US policy, Dening knew the Americans would go ahead anyway. The Americans could not, he nevertheless argued, claim they had no other choice. Lovett, for example, had warned him that a new administration might be isolationist and could draw in their horns (a rather unappealing alternative), leaving the smaller powers in the Pacific exposed to the danger of Soviet penetration and aggression. Could therefore indefinite US protection be assured? And, if not, why should other powers, such as Australia and New Zealand, give 'carte blanche' to the United States? Dening was clearly still smarting from his recent experience in Washington and wrote frustratingly, 'the American thinks that the United States is the sole power which can ensure security in the East, to which the other powers should be satisfied with any measures they think appropriate'. Some comfort lied in the fact that the United States considered Britain (and Canada) to be in the 'inner circle', though this was awkward from the point of view of the Australasian powers, still less India and Pakistan. Yet, Dening deemed it 'so valuable' to be in the 'inner circle' that Britain would be foolish to jeopardise this position through open clashes with the Americans, when an exchange of views, however modest, could benefit the whole Commonwealth anyway.[97]

The British did impart the results of the Dening–State Department conversations on Japan to Commonwealth capitals, arguing that the US position in the Far East should not be weakened further, although explaining that London still thought it best to conclude an early peace treaty early.[98] Chifley responded by telling Attlee that the Americans seemed 'obsessed' by the fear of Soviet motives and designs to the exclusion of all other important considerations. If they built up Japan's economy as contemplated, Chifley argued, the US could provoke the Soviet Union and also 'restore Japan to a position of power and assertiveness in which she would soon want to be entirely rid of American control, however administered' and then free to pursue aggressive policies. The Australians wanted the Americans to agree to fix economic levels, which would make Japan 'self-sufficient but not dangerous'. Japan should also not be built up out of proportion with the economies of Southeast Asia: Australian security depended on the stability of the region. In a subsequent telegram, Canberra did hint that it might be flexible on Japan's economic levels so long as its security was safeguarded. Evatt had written along such lines in the *New York Times* in April, seeing it as 'short-sighted to set out to deliberately depress Japanese standards'. What he objected to was the United States turning Japan into its own private 'bastion'. Wellington did not want levels to surpass those set by the Far Eastern Commission either but accepted that there must be some flexibility if the Americans wanted to relieve their own financial burden. New Zealand would therefore not insist on their own estimates so long as the US did not make 'excessive concessions to its own business groups' and made genuine attempts to meet the main security arguments and reparation claims of other countries. At the other end of the scale were the Canadians, who saw no need to challenge US policy, especially as Ottawa had often suggested the upward revision of figures for the Japanese economy.[99]

Japan, with its skilled manpower and industrial war making potential, constituted a critical basis of power in Asia that the United States could not allow the Soviet Union to control. Consequently, although East Asia ranked behind Europe and the Middle East in US strategic priorities, Washington was not prepared to write Japan off and wanted it to form part of a strategic defensive position in the East.[100] The British JIC did not quarrel over the strategic significance of the Japanese Islands and considered that under Soviet control, they could play a most useful part in the defence of the latter's Northeast Asian provinces.[101] Bevin realised that for the Commonwealth, security in the Pacific, whether the potential aggressor was Japan or the Soviet Union, depended to a major extent on the United States. Although he did not wish to see levels rise beyond Japan's 1930–34 standard of living, if the Americans set them higher, he was prepared to consider them. It was also becoming increasingly difficult to conduct discussions in any forum in which the Russians had a seat, such as the Far Eastern Commission.[102] The fact had to be faced that in the last resort the United States could and would take unilateral action with regard to Japan. The Americans had not, for example, submitted their new proposals through the Commission, nor would they agree with the British contention that the Japanese building of merchant ships for export constituted a security threat.[103]

In October 1948, the NSC concluded (NSC 13/2) that the question of Japanese security should only be formulated in the light of the prevailing international situation and degree of internal stability in Japan. It recommended retaining US forces and advised against pressing for an early peace treaty. Rearmament was considered impractical but, contrary to British Commonwealth suspicions, distrust of Japan remained a feature of US planning.[104] After his election triumph in November, Truman committed his full authority to the so-called 'reverse course'. In December, he issued an economic directive that consolidated the themes of NSC 13/2, the Johnston Report and measures to build up Japanese industry. He named a special emissary, Detroit banker Joseph Dodge, to implement a stabilisation programme.[105] Despite Truman's endorsement of the 'reverse-course', US strategic priorities towards Europe, such as lifting the Berlin Blockade, and the Middle East were maintained. MacArthur, for example, complained to the British that reductions in his forces were worrying him. With Chinese Communist successes in Manchuria, MacArthur told the British that if the Soviets did build air bases in North China, he would be encircled from Vladivostok to the Yangtze, in what he termed a serious situation, especially if further reductions were made from his forces. A quarter of his Air Force had already been transferred for work in Germany. MacArthur argued that he could hold his own with what he had got now but if another 25 per cent were to be taken his position would be very dangerous.[106]

The success of the US stabilisation plan depended upon a US aid package for Asia of $165 million, no international trade discrimination and the ability of Japan to conduct freely its own foreign commerce and merchant shipping. The problem was that any programme depended on Japan gaining access to East and Southeast Asian markets, areas currently wracked by instability and emerging Communist threats.[107] In his annual report on Japan for 1948, Gascoigne concluded that there seemed little hope of an early peace while the economic situation remained unsatisfactory. Japan's productive capacity remained below two-thirds of the 1930–34 average and inflation threatened to harm even modest industrial recovery. He was also sceptical that the Japanese had accepted democracy and presumed the latter were, in part, playing along with the Americans to gain as much economic bounty as possible. Gascoigne, distrustful of the Japanese, thought the latter wanted to regain their primacy in world commercial markets, exploit rivalries between the allies, and secure armed forces again. Evatt, for example, was convinced that the recent war crimes trials had shown there had been little real change of heart on the part of the Japanese. The future, according to Gascoigne, did not look rosy.[108]

At the end of 1948, Dening complained bitterly to Graves that 'unless there is a concerted Far Eastern policy soon, the future can only develop to our comment detriment'. American policy, he continued had, 'failed in China because they failed to appreciate Chinese intransigence; it has virtually failed in Korea because they failed to appreciate Korean intransigence; and it is my personal view that it will eventually fail in Japan because they fail to appreciate Japanese intransigence. Where we shall all be then I shudder to think.' Royall had even recently told Montgomery that the best form of allied defence in the Far East would be to abandon Japan and defend a line much farther south. 'I wonder', Dening noted, 'how long it will be before this defeatist outlook finds more general expression. I have an uneasy feeling that, having burnt their fingers, the Americans are adducing reasons to themselves why they should abandon the Far East', an outcome Australia and New Zealand always feared. 'This is, of course, just letting off steam, since you cannot say any of it to the Americans', Dening finished off his letter to Graves, but he was sure some fresh attempt in the New Year 'will have to be made by us to bring home the realities of the situation'.[109]

7
The Road to War

During the first half of 1949, the *Manchester Guardian* told its readers that the Communist success in China was 'speeding up all the revolutionary movements in Asia'. Changes were rapidly taking place and it was now 'a race between the West and the Communists to see who will have most hand in shaping them'. The *Sunday Observer* argued that a Communist victory in China would be a blow similar to that struck by the Japanese in 1941–2 and was astonished by the lack of a Western response, compared to the reaction after the Czechoslovakian coup in February 1948. As with the war against Japan, the *Observer* noted that events in the Far East were seen as far off local events that meant little to the 'man in the street'. But the Cold War was no less global than the Second World War, especially when Dutch and French armies were tied up in Southeast Asia draining the military strength of Western Europe. Both newspapers argued that it was therefore of paramount importance to put an end to the struggles for independence in Indonesia and French Indo-China. The *Manchester Guardian* claimed that the French and the Dutch, with their 'out-of-date [colonial] policies', were ruining the whole cause of the West in the Far East. It was for Britain, the United States, Australia and India to produce a social and economic plan for Southeast Asia. Collaboration was vital.[1]

Collaboration, however, was the one factor in short supply throughout the Far East. After China seemed 'lost', the Americans appeared disinterested in Southeast Asia and reluctant to defend more than a perimeter around Japan as a basis for its Far Eastern strategy.[2] The Truman administration aimed to give priority to Europe, just as during the war Roosevelt refused to allow the clamour of the 'Pacific Firsters' to divert him from his strategy of concentration against Germany rather than Japan.[3] The US embassy in London also noticed that at Labour's Blackpool party conference in July 1948, Bevin, apart from a few remarks about China, barely mentioned the Far East in his speech on foreign affairs.[4] In response to a request from the tenacious Dean Acheson, the new US secretary of state, who wished to have a 'matey' exchange of views on the Far East with Bevin, the latter told Ambassador

Douglas that with the British now out of Palestine, he wanted to secure the Near and Middle East first before becoming too deeply involved in the Far East.[5]

Although the Bevin–Acheson relationship was close,[6] there remained Anglo-American discord over the future of China and Japan. Disunity arose in particular over the British desire to push for the early recognition of the Chinese Communist state, supporting a policy of keeping a foot in China's commercial door, and the refusal to accept US attempts to place embargoes on a variety of key goods to China. Washington hoped a policy of controlled trade would induce the Chinese Communists to want more and then develop a sense of dependence on the United States.[7] Regarding Japan, the Americans conversed little with the British over their economic and financial policies, aware no doubt that Britain objected to some of the proposed lifting of restrictions on the Japanese economy. The defence aspects attached to a possible treaty were also rarely discussed but this was down principally to the American inability to decide the best course to adopt in order to protect Japan from Communist infiltration or attack. Washington worried that other powers would not agree to the US determination to stay in Japan in some form at a peace conference. It meant the latter would not take place until after the outbreak of the Korean War.

Regional collaboration and defence

By 1949, the Far East remained an extremely unstable region. Tension was high in Kashmir, while Burma, Thailand, Malaya and French Indo-China all suffered from internal disorders and the Indonesian situation still needed to be resolved. Now, the prospect of a Communist-controlled China seemed to threaten further the stability of the region, providing a 'grave danger to Malaya', leading, for example, to an improvement in the morale of the Malayan Communists, and allowing more Chinese Communist agents to be infiltrated into Malaya. Thailand and French Indo-China were seen as poor buffer states to prevent the tide of Communism.[8] Throughout 1949, Malcolm MacDonald reinforced the dangers. As the British commissioner-general in Southeast Asia, he tried to impress upon London the urgency of the situation and the importance of the region in Britain's global Cold War strategy. 'We need', MacDonald argued, 'Asian equivalents of the Marshall Plan and the Atlantic Pact', which could offer aid to resist Communism, ensure economic progress and provide political and military stability. The difficulty, which MacDonald recognised, was that, 'In London, the spirit is willing, but the flesh is weak. In Washington, the flesh is strong, but the spirit has so far been unwilling.' His calls for an immediate Commonwealth conference, however, met with the response from London that such a gathering could wait until the autumn or even 1950.[9]

The Colonial Office explained that the achievement of social progress, based on economic development, in relatively underdeveloped countries – as opposed to highly developed Western countries receiving Marshall Aid – was 'a laborious process'. Apart from a shortage of money, there was also a lack of materials and technical staff to help implement a Marshall aid-type programme for Southeast Asia. The Colonial Office barely possessed enough resources to carry out programmes of development for Malaya.[10] There was no doubt Britain had a position of influence in Southeast Asia but it was still tarred with the stigma of imperialism while the Americans seemed to be retreating from China and Korea, withdrawing their forces to Japan.[11] Efforts at regional collaboration by various powers highlighted the inherent difficulties and complexities confronting any initiatives. In the summer of 1949, the New Zealanders tabled ideas for a Pacific pact that contained only 'peoples of European origin'. The pact would exclude India, Japan, Thailand and, for political reasons, the French and Dutch as well. The idea was quite simply to secure a US military guarantee for Australia, New Zealand and British territories in Southeast Asia.[12] When the Filipino President, Elpidio Quirino, proposed a regional Pacific pact, he demanded the United States provide money and leadership. Quirino's idea won few friends once Chiang came aboard.[13] Finally, Pandit Nehru, the Indian leader, tried to develop a 'united Asian front' but his effort too met with a somewhat lukewarm response throughout the whole region. Indian leadership attracted the Americans as it did the British – the Attlee government was sensitive to Indian representations, proud of overseeing its independence – but it could also signify the eclipse of Britain's power in the region. The Indians were also unlikely to follow a US or British lead, fearing involvement in another Western-led power bloc against the Soviet Union.[14]

In August 1949, the new British Permanent Under-Secretary's Committee (PUSC), similar to the Kennan's Policy Planning Staff, produced two long papers assessing the prospects for regional collaboration in the Far East. The PUSC observed that nationalism remained 'rampant' from Afghanistan to the China Sea, and its intensity made for prickly international relationships, distrust between Asiatic neighbours and an abnormal sensitivity to 'anything which savours of Western domination or dictation'. The memories of British defeats in 1941–2 at the hands of the Japanese had not yet faded, leaving those to view British policy more critically and with less confidence. Doubts were reiterated about Indian leadership (the problem of Kashmir remained) and US involvement in the region was seen as essential. If the British used a Commonwealth approach to the idea of establishing regional collaboration, it might garner less suspicion. Yet, the vastness of the Far Eastern area and the slenderness of Britain's military resources made any question of direct intervention in an anti-Communist struggle, whether of a Cold War nature or in a general world war, out of the question. Ultimately, the PUSC argued, the responsibility for the defence of Southeast Asia had to rest with those countries themselves but there was little hope of any wide strategic co-operation between all the countries concerned. The most that could be aimed for was that each country individually put its armed forces in the best possible shape to maintain internal security or infiltration from outside.[15] These PUSC papers were assimilated into a despatch for Nanking and handed to Guy Burgess for onward transmission: they went missing. If they did fall into Soviet hands it would have confirmed to Moscow general British weakness in the region.[16]

Cabinet calls to reduce British military expenditure had not abated, even though Montgomery complained Britain was not able to fight with what it had and that it was simply 'not on' for the Chiefs of Staff to make pro- posals for three balanced armed services within a limitation of £600m.[17] British forces were still in Austria, Trieste and Greece while Malaya had ushered in an unforeseen commitment. The cabinet agreed that defence esti- mates for 1949–50 should total £760m (later revised upwards to £780m), and the reduction in military personnel would only gradually be reduced from 793,000 in 1949 to 750,000 in 1950.[18] British military and intelligence papers argued that Stalin still sought to avoid a major war but, after the onset of the Berlin crisis, the risks appeared greater. Truman's 1949 decision to put a $15 billion ceiling on defence spending for the fiscal year 1950, for example, also led Forrestal to complain that the United States could not retain troops in Korea, meet emergencies in Greece and Italy, provide forces for the Middle East or carry on the Berlin airlift.[19] Conscious of the need to be financially stringent, the Chiefs of Staff commissioned a report by an inter-service working party, under the chairmanship of the civil servant Sir Edmund Harwood, to limit the size of armed forces to no more than £700m annually. The proposals made uncomfortable reading. They recommended major cuts across the globe, effectively stripping away a British military pres- ence in the Far East, leading to a reliance on the United States and Australia for the defence of the region. The political fall out was deemed so severe that the report's recommendations for the Far East were to put one side.[20]

Some belated progress was at least made in getting the Australasian powers to agree to consider planning responsibility for an area comprising Malaya, Indonesia, Australasia, the Southeast Indian Ocean and Southwest Pacific Ocean, which later became known as the ANZAM arrangement. Canberra formally endorsed ANZAM in 1950 and the Americans also accepted the boundaries for planning purposes. Once this principle had been accepted the Chiefs of Staff had hoped that as the Soviet danger in the Far East could be neutralised by US air and naval power in the Pacific, the Australians could be encouraged to divert forces to the Middle East, where from the Cairo-Suez area, and along with Okinawa and Britain, the allies hoped to launch atomic strikes against the Soviet Union if war broke out. Remember- ing their experience in 1942 and unsure of US plans for the Pacific or the British ability to obtain base rights in Egypt, the Australians hesitated over sending forces to the Middle East and the issue remained fluid even after the outbreak of the Korean War. Canberra was more sympathetic to a Middle East commitment once it had signed the ANZUS agreement with the United States in September 1951, a Pacific Pact that excluded Britain (much to its initial dismay), but led to US security guarantees for the region, and a price Washington was willing to pay for Canberra's acceptance of a 'soft' Japanese peace treaty.[21]

British strategic planning for the Far East, however, continued to be a low priority, especially after the formation of the North Atlantic Treaty Organisation (NATO) in April 1949, which, along with the successful testing of a Soviet atomic bomb that August, would see the gradual reorientation of British strategy away from the Middle East to the defence of Western Europe. It also signified the demise of Bevin's attempts to create an independent third force comprising allies in Europe and the Commonwealth. Britain simply could not help pay to revive Europe or develop colonial regions.[22] The British quest for some form of a regional federation in the Far East was also a long way from being realised, a fact revealed when Bevin travelled to the Commonwealth foreign ministers meeting at Colombo, Ceylon, in January 1950. There, plans for economic development in order to promote regional collaboration were reinforced but the area's political problems signalled the difficulties of achieving quickly anything like a NATO pact for the Far East.[23] Even after the creation of the Peoples Republic of China on 1 October 1949, as the United States began to look more carefully at the situation in Southeast Asia in Cold War terms, the NSC remained cautious.[24] Just months before the outbreak of the Korean War, the British were still arguing for the Commonwealth and the United States 'to take their full share of the burden' in the Far East.[25] The Chiefs of Staff in a major review of defence policy in May 1950 continued to speak of the need to reduce the garrisons in Malaya and French Indo-China (there was some brighter news here with the promise of US assistance to the French) in order to release forces for the 'really vital end' – the defence of Western Europe. The Chiefs of Staff made it clear that in war Southeast Asia was not vital to Britain's survival, as was 'proved' during 1941–5, and there would be no diversion of resources there. Yet, the Chiefs lamented the fact that allied policy in the Far East still seemed to be at cross purposes, causing controversy and Anglo-American divergence.[26]

Peace treaty stalemate

The volatile situation in the Far East, the potential 'loss' of China and the precarious nature of the South Korean state brought a new impetus to the American focus on Japan's economic recovery in 1949. The Japanese government had already announced that its economy could not reach 1930–4 levels of production by 1953. A self-sustaining Japan would now require the United States to increase Japanese exports from $600 million in 1949 to $1.5 billion in 1953 but the prospects were not encouraging as nationalist uprisings in Southeast Asia damaged the flow of trade, increased food shortages and forced Japanese reliance on US supplies. Gascoigne thought Yoshida, the new Japanese prime minister, who he saw as 'an intriguer and a trouble-maker', was simply not up to the challenge of guiding his country through such demanding times. It was an assessment that underestimated the new Japanese leader, who would stay in power until 1954.[27] Sir William Strang, on a visit to Tokyo during 12–21 February before he took up his new role as permanent under-secretary at the Foreign Office, meanwhile realised that British exporters would have to face increased competition from the Japanese. US pressure to relax restrictions on Japan's economy and merchant shipping, left Strang in little doubt that the Japanese would once again attempt to attain economic predominance over those areas which they seized during the war.[28]

Anticipating the next US moves for Japan proved a difficult business for the British, hampered by a lack of consultation with the State Department and a policy of drift in Washington. US Army Secretary Royall attempted to concentrate minds by announcing in February that in the event of world war, the United States was under no obligation to defend Japan and US troops would withdraw. Royall's outburst confused the British, shocked Yoshida and infuriated MacArthur, who along with Acheson tried to reassure Britain's diplomats. MacArthur was suspicious, complaining to Max Bishop, an old friend and the Chief of the Division of Northeast Asian Affairs at the State Department, about the gradual transference of naval forces from his command to the Atlantic, the reduction of his air forces and the policy of the US military to 'scuttle the Pacific'. SCAP felt many senior US figures with a military background, such as Acheson's predecessor, Marshall, were convinced that the Pacific was only of minor significance compared to the Atlantic and Europe. Bishop tried to buoy the general by affirming that the State Department was in full support of the military development of Okinawa, contrary to SCAP's alleged impressions. Royall later publicly confirmed that the US garrison would remain at Okinawa.[29]

Whatever Royall's motives, they certainly did little to instil confidence. Dening felt that Royall's comments left lingering doubts about the US commitment to Japan, while Franks sarcastically remarked that Butterworth's assurances of no change in US policy were only worthwhile if Britain knew exactly what that strategy was, which of course it did not. As Dening told Bevin in the spring of 1949, he was none the wiser about US policy for Japan since his visit to Washington the previous summer. The British remained worried about whether the Japanese would co-operate with the West once the occupation was over, while UKLM was unsure if the new Japan was really that new at all, although it stressed that the British did not regard the Japanese with the blank hatred sometimes encountered amongst the

Australians.[30] After a brief visit to Japan, Max Bishop, too, recognised that many Japanese were becoming tired of the occupation and their benevolence was 'wearing rather thin'. Yoshida had become a symbol of Japan's ability to stand up to the occupation. Japan would either develop a desire for revenge or a sense of independence and co-operation with the United States; and its economy would either collapse or stabilise. Bishop was horrified to find a 'deep-rooted sense of complacency' and 'permanency' amongst SCAP officialdom. He therefore concluded that it was essential to bring about the 'immediate and obvious beginnings of a change in the character of the occupation' and realise the full implementation of NSC 13/2.[31]

The arrival of Dodge in Japan during February 1949 went some way to achieving this required change. He oversaw a revitalisation of the *zaibatsu*, restricted inflation, promoted exports, increased workers living standards and, along with help from Yoshida, limited the rights of unions to bargain and strike. By implementing these measures, Dodge hoped to contain Communism and encourage Japan to align itself, commercially and ideologically, with the West. Reeling from his political setback in the presidential primaries, MacArthur placed few obstacles in the way of Dodge's far-reaching measures.[32] In May, NSC 13/3 recommended that the United States should advise the Far Eastern Commission that all industrial facilities, including the so-called 'primary war facilities', presently designated for reparations be utilised as necessary. Furthermore, there would be no limitations on Japan's production for peaceful purposes or on levels of Japanese productive capacity in industries devoted to peaceful purposes.[33] Acheson knew these measures would disturb certain Far Eastern countries – principally Australia, New Zealand and the Philippines – but he accepted them and had Truman's backing, who shared his commitment to the struggle against Communism. Acheson warned US diplomatic posts that if through their own 'short-sightedness' these countries alienated a now friendly disposed Japan, they might make it easy prey to Communist ideologies.[34]

In reply, Andrew Foster, the US chargé at Canberra, warned Washington that the Australians still objected to American policy for Japan, such as most-favoured nation treatment for Japanese commerce, Japanese levels of industry and reparations. There was a 'lingering hatred and fear' of the Japanese amongst the Australian people and the latter overrode the 'logic of the situation'. They, with Evatt leading the way, insisted on the primacy of the Far Eastern Commission over SCAP and feared Japanese economic competition. It was also election year in Australia and this, Foster concluded, 'did not predispose either the Government or the electorate toward a dispassionate view of international problems'.[35] When the United States announced the new measures at a session of the Far Eastern Commission, the British were also miffed. There was no consultation beforehand and Franks put this down to an American conviction that no other countries had a definite right to be consulted. Franks, who had an excellent relationship with Acheson, did try to excuse this behaviour by blaming Washington's cumbersome political machinery, whereby the NSC or the president could suddenly override State Department decisions, making the latter reluctant to discuss policy issues with the Foreign Office.[36] Frank Tomlinson, the assistant head of the Far Eastern Department, thought the United States was nevertheless heading towards a position, which would make it positively dangerous for them to countenance a peace treaty, especially as a treaty might reverse previous US decisions.[37]

Indeed, the Joint Chiefs of Staff thought it was premature to consider a peace treaty for this very reason. Japan was of high strategic importance, with its skilled manpower and industrial potential, and was also integral to the control of an offshore island chain (the US Navy, for example, preferred Yokosuka on the mainland to Okinawa) being built for the defence of the Western Pacific against a possible Soviet attack. The Joint Chiefs also recommended the creation of a Japanese army in time of war to enhance Japan's capability for self-defence.[38] Although MacArthur and the State Department felt that Japanese rearmament was inadvisable during peacetime, there were no objections to considering the idea in secret, if war between the Soviet Union and the United States broke out.[39] The British commanders-in-chief, Far East, did not dispute that Japan and Okinawa could provide valuable air bases within strategic bombing range of Soviet Far Eastern industrial areas. In addition, they recognised it was prudent to deny to the Soviet Union Japanese manpower and their military and technical ability. If the latter was combined with forces from a Communist-controlled China, Britain's Far Eastern commanders argued that the US-British Commonwealth position in the Far East and the Pacific might become untenable.[40]

One of those commanders, Admiral Sir Patrick Brind, commander-in-chief, Far East Station, was told by MacArthur on a visit to Tokyo that he wanted Japan to remain strictly neutral. The general had long held the belief that Japan should become the 'Switzerland' of the Far East and SCAP had no intention of converting the Japanese, whom he still distrusted, into allies against the Soviet Union. To secure Japan against Soviet attack, SCAP preferred using bases in the Pacific, such as Okinawa, Manila, Guam, the Aleutian Islands and Alaskan bases. To Brind's suggestion that an atomic bomb might wipe out bases on Okinawa, where airfields were concentrated in small vulnerable areas, MacArthur produced the rather unconvincing reply that if they had such bombs they would use them on more important targets. MacArthur's remarks were one of the few instances that provided the British with an indication of US military thinking for Japan. MacArthur's grip on the formulation of US policy, however, had slipped (a fact with which the British were aware) and could not be relied upon as a true guide to the views of the Truman administration.[41]

In fact, Kennan told Dening in July that the defence aspects of a possible peace treaty, which he said the United States was now seriously considering, continued to be a major sticking point for American policy makers. He explained that the United States did not want Japan for offensive operations but merely to deny it to the enemy and was looking at the possibilities of a bilateral agreement with the Japanese (Dening's suggestion). Dening believed that allowing Japan to re-enter the comity nations would be sufficient inducement for them to voluntarily concede bases for US security and ensure their (Japan's) friendship. Kennan, according to the British record, worried about the Soviet Union and a Communist China. He felt no agreement could be reached with them present at the peace table yet, conversely, if excluded, they might make their own treaty with Japan, which was more favourable.[42] There was not much the British could do to force the American hand on the question of the defence aspects for a peace treaty but these were not the only problems. The Foreign Office disagreed with American attempts to allow the Japanese to participate in international affairs, and remained uncomfortable with American reparations and economic policy. They also thought making strikes illegal by law was an unwise method to combat Communism. If Britain permitted Japan unrestricted production, after a few years of full-scale industrial rehabilitation, Japan could be free to exploit its increased capacity or fall under influence of the Soviet Union with this considerable industrial power. All these issues were so serious that Bevin hoped to address them with Acheson in September 1949 when he was due to travel to Washington.[43]

Discord in China

Nowhere were Anglo-American divergences more apparent than in China. As one scholar has pointed out, during 1949, this was not necessarily due to a lack of communication – as the two governments began to converse frequently about China – but rather because the more Washington and London set out their positions, 'the further apart the two were driven'.[44] The prospect of a Chinese Communist state demanded British ministerial decisions over recognition, the future of the trading communities, the defence of Hong Kong, and the status of Formosa (Taiwan), where Chiang eventually set up a government in December 1949 after his failed efforts to build a bastion of resistance in south and southwestern China. At the turn of 1949, there was at least Anglo-American agreement that Chiang's continuation in power was undermining any hope of a dwindling Nationalist bargaining position in possible coalition negotiations with the Communists. The Generalissimo had supposedly 'retired' on 21 January, handing over power to his vice-president, Li Tsung-jen (Li Zongren), a rival, but it soon became clear Chiang had no intention of transferring any real power. Nationalist schemes in January for the great powers to sponsor coalition negotiations under Li were ignored by Washington, London and Paris. They would not trust Soviet participation, and might find themselves responsible for bringing into power a

Communist-dominated coalition, while the Western powers all agreed that Chiang was simply attempting to play for time.[45]

Stalin was equally suspicious though he ignored Mao's request to reject the offer outright, fearing that the United States might use this as an excuse for armed intervention. As a compromise Mao put forward eight conditions for negotiations, which all proved unacceptable to the Nationalists. Stalin remained cautious and made it clear that if Chinese Communist forces crossed the Yangtze and the Americans intervened, he would not come to Mao's assistance. Refusing a request from Mao to visit him personally, considering it a crucial juncture of the civil war, Stalin sent Politburo member Anastas Mikoyan to China instead. Historians have debated the extent to which strains existed in the Mao–Stalin relationship, but Mikoyan's visit was significant in that it marked the first formal contact between Moscow and the Chinese Communist Party.[46] While not privy to these exchanges, the British JIC still hoped for potential rifts between Stalin and Mao. They felt the Soviet occupation of Port Arthur and Dairen was one point of conflict and wondered: 'whether Chinese Communists will remain loyal to Moscow when Chinese national interests and the policy of the Kremlin are in conflict'. They were sure, however, that Chinese Communist and Soviet aims in the Far East would at least strive to remain identical.[47]

Gauging Mao's attitude towards foreign interests soon became a prime British concern. By the end of January, the British had heard nothing from Walter Graham, their consul-general at Mukden, cut off since 18 November 1948. The Americans and the French had not heard from their consular officials either. Angus Ward, the US consul-general, was blockaded in his consulate after refusing to hand over his radio transmitter. Since 22 January 1949, the British had also lost contact with Scott Burdett, their consul-general at Tientsin, after Chinese Communist forces had occupied the city. Mao's aim was to squeeze out Western interests and redefine the basis of China's external relations. As one historian notes, Mao strove to see the Chinese treated as 'equals', which sprung from a profound 'victim mentality', yet it was a position both the British and the United States would find hard to accept in a historical-cultural sense, particularly as Mao wished the Western powers to apologise for their past demeanours. Sir Eric Beckett, the Foreign Office legal adviser, nevertheless argued that Communists had to be recognised by consulates as *de facto*, otherwise it would be impossible to deal with them (the Nationalists could still be recognised as *de jure* of the whole of China). Dening was willing to accept such an argument but wanted to wait until the position had been 'clarified'. He and Scarlett thought other powers would be 'outraged' if Britain pressed ahead with some form of recognition so soon and without consultation: it would look like the British were only interested in securing their commercial interests first. The evidence suggests that Mao was in no hurry and even unwilling to pursue the issue of Western recognition.[48]

Unbeknown to the British, Soviet representatives in the northeast had expressed to Chinese Communist Party members that they must maintain their distance from Western countries and cautioned against establishing any commercial contacts with them. When the British established contact with their consul-general at Tientsin, Burdett's reports indicated that the British community there was 'in desperate straits'. Stevenson, the British ambassador, seemed powerless to do anything apart from protesting through the press, which he was reluctant to do. Patrick Coates, responsible for Chinese issues at the Far Eastern Department, wondered whether the British had perhaps overestimated the Chinese Communists being 'desperately anxious' to trade with the outside world. Scarlett tried to remain optimistic, hopeful that these reports of hardship were the result of the city being under military occupation.[49]

A month later the news was little better: Chinese Communists indulged in anti-imperialist slogans and ignored foreigners although there was no active hostility. Trade was at a complete standstill and employers could not dismiss employees, even when they were unable to give the employees work to do. A representative of Butterfield and Swire reported that the foreign population had become known as the 'invisible men'.[50] Indeed, Mao would tell the Seventh Central Committee in March 1949 that bringing the remaining foreign presence under control was a foremost concern. He would not concede a privileged status to diplomats accredited to the Nationalists, nor would he recognise objectionable treaties while foreign trade would come under government control.[51] Unaware of Mao's pronouncements, Bevin informed the cabinet that his advice to merchants was still to try and engage in trade with the Communists, to which there was general agreement, provided it was made clear the government would not foot the bill for any losses merchants might incur.[52]

As Chiang's attempts to broker a favourable peace petered out, figures such as Wedemeyer recognised it would no longer be a question of if Mao crossed the Yangtze but when; and the general thought that it was certainly 'worse than useless' to send any aid to Nationalist areas.[53] By the spring of 1949, the New York Times observed that the United States was following in China a policy of what Rudyard Kipling called 'judicious leaving alone'. The Truman administration believed, the article noted, that the dam had broken and it was 'waiting for the waters to recede'. Alluding to remarks by State Department officials, James Reston, the author of the article, stated that they remained convinced that China was not a 'strategic springboard but a strategic morass' and hoped the Communists would become 'bogged down' in trying to run the country. Whether Mao would then move to a brand of 'Titoism' and defy Moscow was debateable but 'top' US officials thought not.[54] These officials may well have been influenced by a recent CIA report that spoke of the internal challenges facing Mao but argued (as the British JIC had earlier) that his diplomatic measures would be calculated 'to advance the ends of Soviet foreign policy'. Any pledge that the Chinese Communists would like foreigners to continue 'business as usual', the CIA argued, was only calculated to win recognition and minimise foreign opposition to regime change. Guy Burgess saw this report, which had been handed to the Far Eastern Department, and it is likely that its conclusions were passed to Moscow.[55] Whether it gave any hint of future US policy remained a moot point, especially as the British themselves were unclear.

On the ground, Robert Urquhart, Britain's new consul-general at Shanghai who lacked any China experience, desperately hoped for splits in the Chinese Communist Party and opportunities to 'wean' Mao and his followers away from traditional Communist practices to help foster British trade. Coates, though, remarked sarcastically that he had not lately found any Marxist–Leninists 'weanable'. Tito's quarrel with Moscow had not suddenly found the Yugoslav leader ready to accept the benefit of Britain's experience in labour–capital relations. The Chinese Communists would therefore show open hostility as soon as they dared do so. Scarlett agreed.[56] Mao's 'lean to one side' speech in the summer of 1949, in which he declared his party would 'march with the Soviet Union', seemed to confirm Coates' reservations and the ideological drawing of lines.[57] The evidence indicates that Mao was determined to make Chinese Communist foreign policy compatible with Soviet aims, and formal contacts continued when a prominent Chinese Communist official, Liu Shao-ch'i (Liu Shaoqi), visited Moscow, discussing the 'division of labour' in promoting world revolution. The Soviet Union would remain at the centre, while a Communist China would be responsible for spreading revolution in the Far East.[58]

Deliberate confusion was sown once more, however, when the British and Americans received rumours that there were splits in the Chinese Communist Party: articles appeared in *The Times* (8 August) together with information from Michael Keon, an Australian journalist, who had been in contact with Chou En-lai. The latter had apparently alleged that there was a violently pro-Soviet faction (headed by Liu Shao ch'i) and another faction (headed by Chou En-lai) that sought peace, highlighting the need to reconstruct China and diplomatic relations with the West, that is pushing in a Titoist direction. Whether this was considered a plant or not, the British decided it did not affect current policy but if it was true Dening argued it did seem to confirm the correctness of British policy of keeping a foot in the door. Dening's focus then quickly returned to the Americans once more, exasperated by their failure to discuss these alleged Communist splits with London, especially as Washington had known about them for some time. Dening was also sure that if the United States began to move towards an evacuation of China (which he began to suspect), this could only play into the hands of Chou's supposed opponents.[59]

The continued US policy of 'waiting until the dust has settled' had worried the Foreign Office, as they believed that the State Department would be forced into making 'ill-advised' and 'hasty' ad hoc measures, such as the recent American desire to impose sanctions and the threats addressed to the Communists at Hong Kong, as revenge for Communist treatment of US consuls.[60] The Truman administration was under pressure from the Republicans, who saw a promising field for discontent over the president's failed policies for China, and demanded some sort of action. Rumours of Republican threats to obstruct appropriations for arms in Europe under the North Atlantic Pact soon surfaced and, on 14 April, Congress decided to release $54m of unexpended China aid for use at Truman's discretion in non-Communist China.[61] Yet, when Mao's forces crossed the Yangtze that month, Stalin's concerns that such a move might provoke an American response proved unfounded. Indeed, the British were far more worried about a complete US withdrawal from China.[62]

Now, as in 1941, British interests in Shanghai and Hong Kong could be immediately threatened. Hong Kong was handling £20m worth of goods every month, providing storage, insurance, banking and shipping facilities for transiting this trade. The total value of capital invested in Hong Kong was in the order of £250m (£156m British), while British investment in Shanghai was £250m and the community there still numbered between 4 and 5,000.[63] A Foreign Office telegram to Franks wanted the latter to impress upon the State Department that withholding supplies from the Shanghai area was 'inadvisable'. Such a move might cause a breakdown of public utilities and the total collapse of law and order, especially as the economy was already in a 'parlous' state. If the Nationalists also chose to fight it out in the city of six million (as SIS sources indicated), the whole situation for the welfare of the people would be 'disastrous', and the Western powers could be held responsible for such a breakdown by imposing sanctions.[64] Graves, who visited the State Department immediately, was assured that the United States had made no decision to cut off supplies from Shanghai but wished to keep to a minimum the quantity of such commodities like cereals and fuel to avoid them falling into Communist hands. They explained that China aid legislation made it mandatory that shipments ceased as soon as the Communists gained control of Shanghai but the United States would not stop private trade.[65]

As panic amongst the international community increased, Urquhart reported that one member of the China Association had told him that many of his associates were behaving like 'a pack of old women' and thinking only of 'retreat'.[66] With fear spreading across the city, Urquhart came under intense pressure from the British community to do something for 'psychological reasons', and he recommended that a local commander be appointed to protect British and other Western interests by force. Both the Foreign Office and Stevenson rightly saw that such a move would be perceived as an 'outrageous attempt by the old Treaty Powers to restore their old position in China'. The best method, they argued, was to keep the Shanghai police on duty by promising monetary rewards borne by the business community. If emergency plans were activated, forces – HMS *Belfast* was on standby at Hong Kong to take two companies of infantry to guard points of embarkation – would only act in a humanitarian role to evacuate and protect British nationals.[67] In London, the China Association lobbied MPs to highlight the British commercial stake in Shanghai, arguing that merchants *were* determined to stay put, but it was forced to fall back on pre-war statistics to make its case because of the disruption to trade caused by China's internal strife.[68] Urquhart's American opposite number, John Cabot, was also hopeful he could extract guarantees from the Communists for the protection of US property and citizens (even without US recognition). He could not contemplate how the Communists could refuse 'even to discuss' the question of trade so vital for Shanghai. But what he feared was that the eagerness of foreigners to trade (as shown in Tientsin) might undermine any bargaining position, such as withholding supplies for good behaviour.[69] Cabot later recalled that many American businessmen in China hated the Nationalists, wanted to retain the old unequal treaties, and after the fall of Shanghai declared how glad they were to see the Communists in the city.[70]

By the summer of 1949, the situation seemed desperate. The HMS *Amethyst* incident – in which the British frigate delivering supplies to the British community in Nanking became trapped in the Yangtze in April, making a dramatic escape in July under Communist artillery – did not improve the prospects for friendly relations with Mao. The stand-off lasted over a hundred days and the escape was followed enthusiastically in the British press with the crew receiving a rapturous homecoming.[71] After the consequent withdrawal of British warships from the Whangpoo River, a tributary of the Yangtze, and the Communist occupation of Shanghai, it was difficult to see what the British could now do to protect their remaining nationals and commercial interests in the city. There was no official link to the Chinese Communist hierarchy and British consular officials were ignored. Faced with unreasonable sums of taxation, unruly labour and a subsequent Nationalist blockade of the China coast, British trading firms were drawing on reserves of £375,000 a month.[72] The Americans were also unwilling to negotiate with the British the end of a Nationalist blockade, and British ministers would not authorise orders for warships to protect merchant vessels inside Chinese territorial waters, even after the British merchant ship s.s. *Anchises* was attacked. As Stevenson argued, it was surely not in the British interest to help the Communists obtain supplies by 'running the blockade' and the British should not appear 'over-eager' to trade with the Communists. The Foreign Office agreed: if the Chinese Communists showed a need to utilise British trade, that would be 'very salutary', but there was no indication so far that they did. The Foreign Office was not about to offer advice to British merchants that would immediately saddle them with responsibility for success. That was the duty of the China Association.[73]

Whether or not London agreed with Urquhart's assertion that the 'fiction' the Nationalists were the government of China 'must come to an end' and the British should work to defeat 'the last vicious kicks of a dying mule',[74] Bevin accepted Stevenson's and Brind's advice that breaking the blockade would be seen as a 'betrayal'. Armed clashes with the Nationalists or the Communists could be twisted by both parties as an infringement of sovereignty or 'imperialism', and Bevin needed little persuading that it was best to 'keep out of this'. If both sides (along with the United States) agreed to let relief ships in that might be another matter but Bevin advised his officials not to 'press it'.[75] That was not good news for the China Association, who were pressing Hector McNeil to send relief ships for the desperate British community. The Association's pleas did make an impact, however, and in July the cabinet accepted that if both the British and the Americans wished to 'keep a foot in the door', which was still believed to be the case, then some effort should be made to support the British community otherwise there might be nothing left to bargain with.[76] The Americans were unresponsive and Kennan told Dening that he saw members of the US community as 'hostages', having little sympathy for them. They had stayed to make money, Kennan said, and the Truman administration regarded them as an 'embarrassment' not meriting much consideration.[77] When the British embassy formally approached the State Department, the latter stated they wanted to send in ships for the purposes of evacuation rather than the delivery of relief supplies. The State Department felt that the blockade was causing great damage to the Chinese Communists and that Mao had overrated his bargaining position. It was a sobering assessment, leaving the Foreign Office convinced that it now looked like the Americans were prepared to 'cut their losses', a course diametrically opposed to British policy.[78]

Not all British officials, however, agreed with a policy of keeping a foot in the door. Gerald Tyrrell, the new consul-general at Canton, was rather inclined to accept the American prognosis. Although Tyrrell had served in China for 11 years from 1930, since 1941 he had spent the rest of his diplomatic service in the United States. It probably explained his tendency to look more favourably upon the US position. Tyrrell claimed that the concept of keeping a foot in the door no longer held water; that the blockade was hurting the Communists; and that neither the latter nor the Nationalists were 'in the least concerned about enabling foreign trading interests to survive'.[79] The Far Eastern Department, with Burgess quick to lead the way, disagreed and Dening remarked the 'the best thing to do' with Tyrrell's letter was 'to ignore it'.[80] At the War Office, there were also private concerns about established policy and a view that the British should pull out before the Chinese Communists 'throw us over-board'. Overestimating Britain's leverage, it was hoped such a course would deny the Communists the initiative, cause 'a wave of disillusion among the wavering Chinese' and manifestly increase Mao's economic difficulties, forcing Moscow to waste money on

China, as London and Washington had done. Stay-behind networks of secret agents could prevent the complete lowering of the 'bamboo curtain', one War Office official wrote, rather than commercial contacts.[81] Such networks would never materialise. Although these opposing views to stated British policy had some merit, the political fall out of leaving the British community to its own devices by failing to attempt an accommodation with the Chinese Communists over trade (particularly at a time of economic crisis in Britain) was deemed by the Labour government to be too great. Supporting a provocative attitude could also leave Hong Kong in a precarious position (another valuable commercial asset) and, in short, Bevin arguments to the cabinet in December 1948 were unlikely to be modified.

By August, no British ships were calling at Shanghai and the American President Lines were the only way out. Yet John Keswick, the doyen of the British business community, refused to be swept away by American hysteria.[82] The British cabinet hesitated, awaiting a law officer's report on whether it was feasible to send in relief ships.[83] But up until the outbreak of the Korean War, that legal advice recommended against breaking the blockade by naval intervention, despite intense pressure from companies such as Jardine Matheson and Butterfield & Swire. The State Department proved equally reluctant, worried about getting into 'a hornets nest with Congress', while the Chinese Communists seemed indifferent.[84] The Nationalist blockade of China also became tied in with discussions about the future status of Formosa. US military planners (particularly MacArthur) saw Formosa occupying an important strategic position in the Pacific. By the end of 1949, however, the State Department, disillusioned with Chiang, persuaded the Joint Chiefs of Staff to disavow the use of overt military force to protect the island, in favour of moderate economic and political help. The British protested to the Americans that continued military aid (such as aircraft) to the Nationalists on Formosa could fall into the hands of the Communists and be turned on Hong Kong. The JIC even concluded that a Chinese Communist occupation of Formosa would lift the present Nationalist blockade of Shanghai, improve the possibilities of trade and reduce the likelihood of an attack on Hong Kong.[85]

Throughout 1949, the British worried intensely about a direct attack on Hong Kong and internal unrest there through Communist-influenced trade unions, a large influx of refugees or Communist-inspired aggression by guerrilla bands. In April, the BDCC (Far East) requested the three battalions at Hong Kong be reinforced by a brigade group and the Chiefs of Staff agreed.[86] On 5 May the cabinet authorised the despatch of reinforcements and an announcement was made in the House of Commons. On Alexander's recommendations, by the end of that month, the cabinet had approved further reinforcements, which by the autumn aimed to see the colony's defences comprise four brigades, one light fleet carrier (plus one replenishment aircraft carrier), three cruisers, up to 15 destroyers or frigates, one flying boat squadron and three (one long-range) fighter squadrons. It meant diverting forces from the Western Union, leaving no effective reserve in Britain, reducing air forces in Germany and leaving no operational aircraft carrier in the Mediterranean during August–September. It was a staggering a commitment but felt necessary as the Chiefs of Staff estimated the Chinese Communist army could attack the island with 40,000 men and 50–60 aircraft. These reinforcements were not announced publicly for the fear of being seen as openly provocative towards the Chinese Communists and there was no indication yet of Commonwealth views either, who could see the whole enterprise as a 'relic of colonialism'.[87] British officials nevertheless felt that such reinforcement was particularly vital after the *Amethyst* incident, which they presumed had weakened British prestige.[88]

The cabinet agreed that if Britain did not defend the colony it would have a disastrous effect on Britain's position in the Far East (particularly Malaya) and amongst countries such as Burma, Thailand and French Indo-China. But Bevin and Attlee shied away from making a provocative statement that Britain would never leave Hong Kong and focused instead on the theme of deterring aggression, which the cabinet supported. This approach was seen as necessary to garner international support.[89] That support was decidedly mixed, even amongst the Commonwealth. Louis St. Laurent, the Canadian prime minister, regarded colonialism as 'repugnant' when Hong Kong was raised; India, Pakistan and Ceylon for similar reasons did not issue any public declarations of support; Australia was reluctant to provide material help, which the British saw as particularly disappointing in view of plans for regional defence in the area; and the United States (while seeing the colony's value in intelligence terms) confirmed a commitment to help Hong Kong was out of the question, especially at a time when NATO was under consideration and Congress might question the boundaries of the pact.[90] Despite this disappointing response, Hong Kong would remain on full alert against attack until the outbreak of the Korean War. There was no indication of the extent of duration of the military commitment, even though the garrison was reduced in April 1950 and secret intelligence began to indicate the Chinese Communists had no plans to mount a direct attack on the colony.[91]

By the late summer of 1949, US policy seemed to be moving towards withdrawing all US officials from China and assisting other US nationals to evacuate; while refusing to establish diplomatic relations with the Chinese Communist until a majority of other governments agreed that it was advantageous to do so and that adequate guarantees had been offered. Washington also wished to place embargos on trade with Communist China; 'discourage' such trade wherever possible by denying credits, facilities and protection; continue to the recognise Nationalists but limit assistance to them until they showed increased capability of successful resistance; provide whatever assistance was possible to Chiang on Formosa; and provide assistance to non-Communist elements in China.[92] When Acheson sought Bevin's views on

China, the foreign secretary told Ambassador Douglas that he was preoccupied with an upcoming Middle East conference, clearly indicating where
he considered China to be on his list of priorities. Douglas retorted that
China was a matter of urgency, to which Bevin reluctantly agreed and he
promised to give Dening the benefit of his views. Dening told Douglas not
to expect too much as the present atmosphere in London was unfavourable
for a discussion of China because Bevin and other cabinet ministers were
taking leave in August during which it would be practically impossible to
get a decision on important matters. 'British generally feel', Douglas sur-
mised, 'China [is] primarily [an] American problem and will expect US to
take lead in negotiations'. He incorrectly assumed (though he had little
reason to think otherwise considering Bevin's disinterest) that the British
would go along with US policy except over the question of trade with the
Communists. The British are 'obsessed with necessity of exporting wherever
possible', Douglas concluded.[93]

The Americans tried to defend their position on China in August 1949,
when the Truman administration produced a 1,100 page White Paper, entitled *United States Relations with China with Special Reference to the Period
1944–1949*. It hoped to place the facts about Nationalist rule in China before
the US public. In Acheson's letter of transmittal, drafted by Dr Philip Jessup,
the State Department emphatically declared that the Nationalist failure in
China did not stem from the inadequacy of US aid. It also stated that the
Chinese Communist leaders 'have publicly announced their subservience to
a foreign power, Russia'. It made the possibility of a wedge strategy look less
likely, only highlighting ideological divisions. Republican senators assailed
the White Paper as a whitewash and 'a wishful do-nothing' policy which
succeeded only in placing Asia in danger of Soviet conquest. As a compromise, during September, the administration accepted a proposal by Congress
that $75 million should be used on a confidential basis by Truman in 'the
general area of China'.[94]

Depressed, Bevin told the cabinet that beyond indicating their anxiety
about control of flow of strategic raw materials to China the United States
had given no clear indication of its policy. Furthermore, while the United
States had been previously disposed to agree that nationals should remain
in China and jointly follow a policy of keeping 'a foot in the door', now,
the foreign secretary told his colleagues, without warning US policy 'seems
to have taken a sharp turn in the direction of retreat'. While on the one
hand the State Department had issued a White Paper which sought to justify the past policy of the United States in China and liberally castigated
the Nationalists, on the other they appeared to have decided that it was no
longer attractive to keep 'a foot in the door' and to be desirous of evacuating
their nationals from China as soon as possible. On the positive side, the fact
that the United States had asked the British to take charge of their consulates
and US interests was interpreted by Bevin to mean that the United States did

not quarrel with Britain's decision to remain in China. He lamented that it was easier for the Americans to cut their losses: the total loss meant less to the United States than Britain in its current state of economic and financial crisis. There would be no hasty decisions, however, and Bevin proposed (and the cabinet agreed) that Stevenson should be withdrawn as soon as a Chinese Communist central government was about to be set up, otherwise the latter could demand immediate recognition or his immediate withdrawal and force the British to make a decision before they were ready to do so.[95]

Instability in Korea

The establishment of a South Korean state was now a reality. The United States opened an embassy in Seoul, with John Muccio assuming the position as ambassador. Muccio had served in the Far East, South America and more recently Berlin, in what was generally considered the frontline of the Cold War. He had immediately endorsed Rhee's appeals for the retention of at least some US forces to help maintain the new government in the initial stages, which the State Department had agreed to, even though the Pentagon was still willing to write the peninsula off as a strategic asset. Max Bishop and Niles Bond at the State Department, however, argued that Northeast Asia was 'one of the four or five significant power centres in the world'. If Korea fell to Communism, might not Japan follow suit, especially considering the situation in China? The whole US position in the Far East and the Pacific could then be at stake.[96] While the British would not disagree with State Department views, unclear of US intentions, they had hitherto come to adopt the outlook of the Pentagon, accepting the inevitable loss of Korea in the near future and that US assistance programmes were part of face-saving devices. The British JIC also confessed that its intelligence on Korea remained 'meagre'.[97] MacArthur had already told General Gairdner that if the Soviet Union attacked Korea his plans were to get Hodge's army out 'as quickly as he could'.[98]

The new man now charged with keeping an eye on developments in Korea after Kermode's departure was Captain Vyvyan Holt, who would hold the rank of British minister at Seoul. A man of great charm and an eccentric, Holt possessed a wealth of Middle Eastern experience but he had no knowledge of the Far East.[99] His despatches soon resembled those of his predecessor, Kermode, and he kept London informed of continual Communist incursions into South Korea. In October 1948, Holt reported that in Sunchon, south of Seoul, Communist rebels, junior officers and non-commissioned officers, within the XIV and XV regiment of constabulary, had butchered over 300 police and non-Communist civilians before South Korean forces eventually pressed the Communist guerrillas back further south to the Yosu peninsula. Everywhere the rebels went they put up the flag of North Korea and displayed Communist slogans. All the available evidence pointed to a carefully planned Communist uprising.[100] The Yosu revolt starkly demonstrated the vulnerability of the Seoul government and its inability to govern the southern provinces effectively. It also highlighted the need for the retention of at least some US troops, which the national assembly agreed to support in November. The result was not a foregone conclusion. Only 103 of 198 members were present in the assembly, and of these, 16 abstained on grounds of principle. As in 1945, most Koreans still wanted to be rid of foreign control and influence but Rhee knew he could not ignore the superiority in numbers, training and weapons of the North Korean forces.[101]

Rhee therefore readily seized upon and publicised statements of his conversations with MacArthur in which the latter stated he would defend South Korea, as he would 'protect the United States and California against aggression'. MacArthur told Gascoigne, who wondered if the US envisaged a new policy for Korea, that the statement should have been made with a further explanation to the effect that he would defend South Korea in his present capacity as commander of US forces in the Pacific. The Foreign Office considered Gairdner's earlier private conversation with MacArthur as a much more authentic expression of the latter's views. If the statement had been designed to 'frighten' the Soviets, Tomlinson doubted it had much effect.[102] Due to the lack of consultation over Korea, it is clear the Foreign Office was initially unaware of the emerging resolve that the State Department was beginning to show towards Korea. The British view in early 1949 remained that a South Korean army, whatever its numbered strength, could not hold out against a determined attack by the North Koreans, either by inspired risings or by invasion over the border, and that Korea had been written off in highest US strategic circles.[103]

In March 1949, meanwhile, Pyongyang and Moscow concluded an arms pact whereby the latter committed to supply munitions to the North Korean army. The rapid collapse of the Nationalist Chinese armies also meant that Korean troops fighting in China were more likely to return sooner than anticipated. Some units had already begun to return home in 1948 and were quickly incorporated into the North Korean army.[104] Could the US deter an attack from the North? The CIA recommended the continued presence of a moderate number of US forces to act as a deterrent but MacArthur, the Joint Chiefs of Staff and Louis Johnson, the new Secretary of Defense, all advocated withdrawal, due to pressing commitments elsewhere and through a belief that Korea was not favourable terrain upon which to fight a war if war should come.[105] The latest NSC estimates put the North Korean army at between 75 and 95,000 and the South Korean army (formerly the constabulary) at 65,000, of which 50,000 were US-equipped. In addition, the South Koreans had 45,000 police and 4,000 in the coastguard. The North Koreans, however, could call on another 30,000 for internal security forces, while the Korean units attached to People's Liberation Army equalled or exceeded the strength of the combined army and security forces in North Korea. The sums made grim reading.[106]

In March, the NSC agreed that the most immediate objective was to withdraw the remaining 7,500 US troops from Korea as early as possible with the minimum bad effects as set out in NSC 8. The NSC nevertheless accepted that a unified Korean state under Communist control could only 'enhance' the strategic position of the Soviet Union in the Far East with respect to Japan and reflect badly on US international standing. Complete American disengagement might be seen as a US betrayal of its friends and allies in the Far East, possibly contributing to a fundamental realignment of forces in favour of the Soviet Union. The NSC therefore recommended that it should implement present and projected programmes of training, equipping and supplying the South Korean security forces, both during 1949 and 1950, while also implementing existing plans for economic and technical assistance to Korea through 1950 and possibly 1951–2 as well. As MacArthur had stated that the establishment of Korean security forces within the current programme was now substantially complete, the NSC agreed to withdraw US troops from Korea by 30 June 1949 subject to consultation with the UN. When reading the initial NSC drafts, the US military were keen to remove references to the projection of a military commitment into 1950, wanted reference to a 'Navy' removed, reverting to the word 'coastguard' (they would not support a Korean Navy), and only wished to equip a 35,000 police force (not 45,000 as originally stated).[107]

Despite these caveats and a desire to avoid a direct military embroilment in South Korea – the Americans would still not guarantee South Korean territory in a local or global conflict – US military officials endorsed the NSC's recommendations. They too recognised that total disengagement from Korea could undermine an already damaged US credibility in the Far East. American diplomats therefore tried to reassure Rhee that troop withdrawals reflected no lessening of the US commitment. The Americans also seemed more upbeat. Drumright, now the chargé of the US embassy in Korea, informed Acheson that the South Korean government was settling down and economic conditions were improving. The inflationary spiral had slowed, prices remained stable and currency circulation was declining while increased coal and power production was assured during the next few months. Although the grain collection programme had failed, food stocks were believed to be adequate for the immediate future. Drumright's positive assessment, however, did not gloss over the fact that corruption and inefficiency was still at large.[108] Even so, the State Department now led efforts to elicit large-scale economic aid for Korea, totalling $150 million for fiscal year 1950. Truman was persuaded to present this request to Congress but no legislative action was taken on the Korean aid bill during 1949, although two interim appropriations did provide $60m up to February 1950.[109]

In late April 1949, Holt reported on the gradual shift in the US attitude regarding Korea. Muccio seemed particularly upbeat, the latter telling
the British minister that he was convinced that his government firmly
intended to continue giving substantial military and financial aid to the
South Koreans. Holt reported back to London that the Americans in Seoul
were now 'quite happy about the future' and that the 100,000 armed troops
and police in the south were 'well able' to deal with any probable threat
of aggression from the north or Communist uprisings in the south. Holt
concluded that the Americans were evidently prepared to help on a very
substantial scale, and were confident that it would be adequate. He admitted,
though, that he did not have enough information to form his own 'emphatic
opinion' and that the Washington embassy would be better placed to find
out about US policy than Seoul.[110] Tomlinson was not entirely convinced of
the turn around in South Korea's fortunes and noted that the Foreign Office
would not modify its views, except to the extent of agreeing the weight of
evidence indicated that in a purely Korean struggle the South could now
hold its own, provided the United States continues to supply a substantial
quantity of material help.[111]

The final US troop withdrawals from Korea in the summer of 1949 soon
ushered in widespread concern. Before the withdrawal, Rhee pleaded for
American guarantees of defence and independence. As well as a standing
army of 65,000 men, Rhee had wanted a reserve of 200,000 men fully
equipped with US weapons. Not surprisingly, these requests were ignored
by Washington and no guarantees were forthcoming.[112] By mid-1949, Rhee
faced a significant rural partisan force in five of his eight provinces. In
contrast, North Korea appeared more stable than the South. Kim Il-sung's
leadership was still under threat but factionalism within the government did
not disrupt internal order. Rhee was also faced with economic crisis, corruption amongst his ministers and found himself in disputes with the national
assembly. His autocratic rule and intractability, shown in his formation of
a cabinet that failed to represent various groups within the assembly, further undermined his position. Communist guerrilla attacks and unrest along
the 38th parallel, meanwhile, forced the UN to adopt another American-
sponsored resolution, which called on UNCOK to carefully monitor the
border. The localities of Ongjin, Kaesong and Chunchon suffered the worst
disturbances. Attacks varied in strength from small skirmishes to planned
operations by as many as 2,000 men. Cheju Island was almost entirely in
the hands of Communist insurgents.[113]

In early July, when *The Times* reported that the last US troops had left
Korea they were confident this did not indicate a lessening US interest,
yet that confidence eroded during the ensuing months with the newspaper
doubting that the South Koreans could hold their own against serious invasion. Concern grew with the end of the fighting in China, which *The Times*
recognised would allow for the release of Korean Communist troops back

home. It led UNCOK to report that there was now a grave danger of civil war. *The Times* correctly concluded, however, that until the word was given from the Kremlin, the North was unlikely to invade the South.[114] Bevin was not ignorant of the dangers. On his way to the Colombo Conference aboard HMS *Kenya*, he addressed the ships' company on the problems of resisting aggression, and surprised them by remarking that he was 'very worried about the precarious situation in Korea ... If you ask me where I think we might all be in for further trouble, I believe Korea is the place.'[115] Bevin's comments are interesting as they suggested that the British would in some way be involved in a Korean conflagration even though throughout much of 1949 the British paid little attention to the peninsula. His remarks proved chillingly correct.

The drift towards regional conflict

In early September 1949, Dening flew into the United States to join a British ministerial delegation that had arrived in Washington for financial talks, against the background of another sterling crisis. Dening's arrival, *The Times* recognised, indicated the importance which Far Eastern affairs were likely to play in the forthcoming ministerial talks.[116] In preliminary discussions at the State Department with Butterworth and Livingston Merchant, the US deputy assistant secretary of state for Far Eastern Affairs, Dening did not mince his words. He expressed concern over what he termed the relatively minor emphasis of US foreign policy on the Far East as opposed to Europe. Dening claimed that Bevin intended to point this out frankly to Acheson, especially the lack of a clear Anglo-American Far Eastern policy, which was placing the foreign secretary in an increasingly difficult political position, with his parliamentary critics making the most of this issue prior to probable early general elections. Such lecturing must have made for an uncomfortable meeting. Butterworth conceded that US Far Eastern policy lacked the community of approach of its European policy but argued that this has been due to the vast area involved and to the backwardness, factionalism, poverty and strife among and within many countries that made up the region. He nevertheless considered the sum of US aid to the Far East had been 'formidable', even though it suffered in comparison with Marshall aid 'wrapped up in one conspicuous package'.[117]

Before Acheson and Bevin met, Dening raised three more issues with Butterworth: the need for an early Japanese peace treaty; close Anglo-American consultation over the question of recognition of a Chinese Communist state; and US views on the status of Formosa. Butterworth's responses were firm. He remained sceptical over whether Commonwealth countries would embrace key clauses for a generous peace treaty and he thought the United States would not proceed unless the conference was 'rigged' beforehand. Butterworth also cautioned the British about making the first move over recognition, since 'first come would not be first served', while Merchant thought Mao would surely insist on a rupture of relations with the Nationalists, which the United States was not prepared to contemplate. Regarding Formosa, Merchant pointed out that although he felt there was only a slight chance of the Nationalists retaining the island, the US military considered it possessed strategic importance. They wanted therefore to continue aid to Chiang to render Formosa less susceptible to Communism. Butterworth nevertheless deplored the situation in which the administration had $80–90m to spend in China until February 1950 and Congress trying to force another $75m upon them, when the fact of the matter was that conditions were far too unstable to allow the money to be spent with any hope of success.[118]

These blunt conversations set the tone for Acheson's meeting with Bevin a few days later. Acheson, showing his ideological hostility towards Mao, thought it was unwise to give the appearance of 'running after' the Chinese Communists; 'conciliatory gestures' would not be acceptable to the American public. Acheson's aim was to let Mao learn that the position of being a Soviet satellite had little to recommend it. Every effort, Acheson argued, should be made to show up Soviet actions which were contrary to China's interests. In response, Bevin retorted that he was in a difficult position. The British community had been advised to stay and his government could not now ask them 'to clear out'. To do so would have a very demoralising effect on Hong Kong and the rest of the area. Bevin accepted that the grant of recognition would have to depend on how the Communists behaved but, at the same time, he thought there was a risk, if the Western powers remained 'too obdurate', that the Chinese would be driven further into the arms of Moscow. It was important to avoid doing anything which would discourage them from being Chinese 'first and foremost', the foreign secretary declared. Acheson agreed that the objective must be to encourage a split with Moscow though he made it quite clear that he thought premature recognition would serve to discourage the anti-Communist forces in China.[119]

Moving on to Japanese affairs, Bevin expressed sympathy for a liberal, non-punitive treaty for Japan, and offered the suggestion once more that American strategic needs be met through a separate US–Japan agreement providing for the retention of US security forces and bases in Japan in the post-treaty period. Acheson agreed it was important to proceed with a peace treaty and promised a paper on US policy before Bevin set off for the Colombo Conference. The Bevin–Acheson exchanges were frank if nothing else and Butterworth was hopeful that at least the United States and other friendly Far Eastern powers might now be able to agree on a way forward. Dening too came away encouraged by the fact that violent disagreements had been averted.[120] The Australians were left less than happy, immediately complaining that yet again major discussions had taken place on the Far East without their involvement. On instructions from Evatt, Norman Makin, the Australian ambassador in Washington, told Acheson that Australia's close association with the United States during the war and the 'important' part it had played in the Pacific theatre, as well as the important part it was playing now in Far Eastern affairs, 'entitled it to be present'. Acheson remarked sarcastically that it would be quite impossible 'for us to undertake that we would discuss no matter affecting the Far Eastern area except in the presence of a representative of Australia'. Makin, Acheson recorded, was 'somewhat apologetic' about the message he had to deliver. Attlee was furious and told Chifley that Bevin had been trying hard for the last two years to establish confidence between the American–Australian powers and this move had not helped.[121]

Although Anglo-American officials had been positive about the Washington talks, there remained obstacles to overcome. Stevenson told Bevin that the question of recognising a Communist China had to be based on practical, not ideological, grounds. Britain could not abandon its great commercial stake, the ambassador argued, and the new regime would have to be judged on its actions. Yet, Stevenson's theory, that protests against Chinese Communist behaviour could be stepped up if the latter misbehaved, proved unrealistic. Stevenson left China in November leaving behind John Hutchinson, the chargé, to carry on the embassy's affairs.[122] Nehru, meanwhile, applied pressure on the British to recognise the new Communist government that same month, championing what he saw as progressive nationalism. When British Far Eastern representatives convened at Bukit Serene for a conference during early November 1949 to discuss regional affairs, they also advocated recognition, decreeing that what happened in China was the business of the Chinese, and the British would be merely recognising an accomplished fact. Despite US objections, the Attlee government decided that on balance it was in British interests to recognise the People's Republic of China, and they did so in January 1950, hoping it would protect Britain's Far Eastern imperial position by reducing the threat to Hong Kong, Malaya and Singapore, encouraging trade and undermining Soviet influence over the Chinese Communists.[123] The decision did not pay off: Mao was non-responsive and little changed to alleviate the plight of Britain's commercial community. After the Labour government was returned to power with a majority of just six and Parliament reconvened in March 1950, opposition MPs attacked the policy, calling it 'a blunder', and an act of panic, while Eden spoke of the opportunities now available to Mao in playing off Britain against the United States.[124]

Despite the domestic fallout for the Labour government, inside Whitehall, the consensus remained, with the Foreign and Colonial Offices leading the way, that a total break in relations would only promote a further deepening of the division between East and West, a development that could bolster the Communist cause across Southeast Asia where important British interests resided.[125] There were also small signs that the seeds for dissension were beginning to be sown. Mao's trip to Moscow between December 1949 and

January 1950 was uneasy and Hutchinson even received information that the talks were going badly for the Communist leader. The Foreign Office noted the financial settlement did not appear generous and they wondered correctly whether Stalin would find pretexts to stay in Manchuria, such as the non-signature of a Japanese peace treaty. Mao had, however, received security guarantees from Stalin and the signing of a new Sino-Soviet alliance in February 1950 would certainly help the Chinese Communist leader secure his 'post-victory revolution at home'.[126]

Unlike the British, Acheson was in no mood to see whether Mao could or could not be trusted. The US secretary of state, though, did not consider Formosa was a platform from which to counter the Chinese Communists, who could only use the issue to express their nationalist credentials and attack the United States.[127] Indeed, on 5 January 1950, Truman stated that although economic aid to Chiang would continue, the United States would not intervene militarily in Formosa. It was a statement that helpfully overshadowed Britain's recognition of China. Seven days later, during his speech at the National Press Club on 12 January 1950, Acheson similarly spoke of the US abstaining from 'foolish adventures' in Formosa. The British, concerned about military equipment falling into the hands of the Chinese Communists if Formosa fell, could nevertheless not persuade the State Department to halt the residue of war material (some $7m) being shipped to the island purchased out of the $125m made available under the China aid act of 1948.[128]

The Nationalist blockade also continued with the China Association increasing the pressure upon the Attlee government for it to be broken. The Association described Shanghai as 'a shadow of its former self. The river is empty, godowns and offices show little signs of activity, industrial production is sadly restricted. There is idleness and unemployment.' Trade was at a standstill, shipping was 'a dead loss' and the Chinese Communist authorities refused to discuss difficulties such as exorbitant taxation and labour issues. Yet in a meeting with China Association representatives, Bevin was unwilling to change current policy and re-stressed the many political difficulties involved in breaking the blockade.[129] Across the Atlantic, however, the Truman administration was beginning to rethink one of its policy decisions: the defence of Formosa. Pressure from the Pentagon and 'McCarthyites', led by Senator Joseph McCarthy – who claimed there were 205 card-carrying members of the Communist Party in the State Department – began to force a change. MacArthur also sent a passionate memorandum to Washington re-emphasising the strategic importance of the island. Two days after the outbreak of the Korean War, Truman declared Formosa must now be denied to the Communists. Franks despondently concluded that the possibility of the United States reaching a *modus vivendi* with Peking was dead. Whether it had ever really existed was doubtful.[130]

With regard to a Japanese peace treaty, again little progress was being made. MacArthur had immediately poured scorn on Acheson's promises in

September 1949 regarding an early peace treaty, telling Gascoigne it was no more than a 'smoke screen' to satisfy Allied concerns.[131] There is no evidence to suggest that Acheson's remarks were other than genuine, and the secretary of state appeared distressed when he had to tell Franks privately that he was unable to give an indication of US requirements for a peace treaty to Bevin before the Colombo Conference. Acheson would not say why but Franks guessed the trouble lay with the Pentagon and the security clauses.[132] The Joint Chiefs of Staff would not accept a peace treaty with Japan unless both the Communist Chinese and the Soviets accepted their provisions for a chain of Pacific bases and permanent military facilities throughout Japan's four main islands. They feared that if Moscow and Peking did not legally bind themselves to a treaty, they could use it as an excuse to enter Japan free of US command.[133] Flabbergasted, Acheson confronted the General Omar Bradley, chairman of the Joint Chiefs of Staff, deriding the military's attempts to gain Soviet and Chinese Communist support for their policies, while trying to explain the damage it was inflicting on US relations with its allies.[134]

In a subsequent letter to Franks, Acheson confirmed that on the matter of security the United States had been unable to reach agreement. It was essential to retain US forces in Japan, including the Ryukyu and Bonin Islands. Yet, if these arrangements were to be maintained through a bilateral arrangement as suggested by Bevin, it would be necessary to specify a time period for their retention and size. Because of uncertainties in the Far East, the time limit and size of forces would 'have to be on the maximum side', which could lead to 'unfortunate psychological reactions in Japan and other Far Eastern countries'. Acheson explained that neutrality was 'illusory' in the context of East–West relations; there were no UN security forces; while the re-arming of Japan was not an acceptable political alternative. Clearly in a difficult position, Acheson laid emphasis on the fact that these were not conclusions but the problems that confronted them.[135] Consequently, by the end of 1949, British policy was effectively marooned, unable to influence US strategy for Japan and in no position to consult with the Commonwealth because it lacked precise information on the direction of US planning. Truman was the only person who could resolve the dispute over the Japanese peace treaty but was unwilling to do so until the dust had settled over the issue of recognising Communist China. Johnson, the defence secretary, had also been a stalwart supporter of the president when most people had written him off to win a second term and the president took his views seriously.[136]

At the Commonwealth meeting in Colombo Conference in January 1950, all foreign ministers stressed the need for an early peace treaty and that Japan must remain outside the Soviet bloc but there remained divergences over the restrictions to be imposed on Japan. As predicted, Australia and New Zealand emphasised the continuing danger of a Japanese military resurgence. On the other hand, India, Pakistan and Ceylon wanted minimum restrictions. Bevin stressed the 'unwisdom' of going into an international meeting if differences of opinion continued unresolved. It was therefore accepted that a working party of Commonwealth high commissioners be set up in London with a view to reconciling these differences.[137] There would be plenty of time to discuss such matters. By March 1950, Tomlinson told US Ambassador Douglas in London that the British failure to receive US views was causing the government 'increasing embarrassment'.[138] There were no signs of the impasse being resolved either. When Acheson was due to visit London for talks in May, Defense Department officials wanted the secretary of state to delete any references to an 'early' peace treaty, still desirous of Soviet and Chinese Communist compliance, even though Truman had told the NSC in December that a peace treaty could proceed without the Soviet Union. The president, along with Acheson, realised the political implications of delay and appointed in April 1950 John Foster Dulles, the Republican lawyer and politician, with responsibility for negotiating a treaty, which would be finally signed in September 1951.[139]

All these East Asian issues would receive unexpected impetus with the outbreak of the Korean War. Unbeknown to London and Washington, Kim Il-sung had been pressing Stalin throughout 1949 for permission to unify the country by force. Attempts to ignite a takeover in the South by guerrilla warfare had failed but Kim still hoped for a successful uprising once his troops had broken through the defences of the South. He claimed that a swift victory would then ensue. Stalin was concerned with the wider picture. As a Communist victory in China appeared imminent, Stalin told Kim that 'the Americans will never agree to be thrown out of [Korea and] lose their reputation as a great power'. Stalin, nevertheless, realising that the United States was in retreat in China and Korea, did not dismiss the possibility entirely. He also read Acheson's speech at the National Press Club carefully and NSC 48, on which it was based, courtesy of British spies in Washington, which excluded Korea from the US defensive perimeter in the Pacific. A week later Congress rejected the administration's Korean aid bill. Stalin therefore told Kim to consult Mao and the latter agreed to provide assistance. By the spring of 1950, Mao had sent back to Korea nearly 70,000 soldiers and it was unlikely that he would have vetoed Kim's plan to unify his own country through revolutionary war.[140]

In London there was no formal pre-war JIC assessment of the situation in Korea. A JIC team had visited Washington in 1949 and asked their US colleagues for information on Korea. This had been withheld because of policy differences between the two governments over China. Washington held the view that Korea and Formosa laid outside Anglo-American agreements on intelligence exchanges. The British were left to guess the likely American reaction. At the end of 1949, the War Office was firmly convinced that the North Korean Army could advance into South Korea with little difficulty. Yet, a North Korean invasion was considered unlikely in the immediate future.

It was thought that the North Koreans would pursue 'the well-tried tactics of preparing the country within rather than resort to open aggression'. If an invasion did occur, the War Office argued that the Americans were unlikely to become involved. The War Office concluded that 'the possession of South Korea is not essential for allied strategic plans, and although it would be obviously desirable to deny it to the enemy, it could not be of sufficient importance to make it the cause of World War Three'.[141] Compared to the American presence in Korea, the British interest in Korea remained small. There was a Church of England mission and branches of two trading firms – Jardines and Butterfield & Swire – endeavouring to develop general trading between Hong Kong and Korea.[142]

Just two months before the outbreak of the Korean War, Dening remained in a critical mood of US policy towards the Far East just as he had since 1944. Recent talks with the Americans had led to nothing. With regard to China, it was 'crystal clear' that the Americans had devoted 'no thought to this subject at all, and their attitude is completely negative and defeatist'. The Americans aimed 'to keep their face firmly averted from China in the hope that while it is in that position some miracle will occur to change the situation in their and our favour'. There remained no consultation on the Far East comparable to that which took place over Europe and the Middle East, and this stemmed from developments in China and the US inability to resolve their difficulties over Japan. Quite simply, Dening concluded, the Americans did not have a policy for China and Japan: 'the fact of the matter is that the United States have neglected and are neglecting the Far East, and that unless and until they can be moved from their inertia, the rest of us will be in very acute danger'.[143] His dramatic words seemed realised in June 1950.

That the Anglo-American powers were caught by surprise with Kim Il-sung's invasion of South Korea in June 1950 is not disputed by historians. The response of both Britain and the United States to the crisis is, however, fascinating, considering the low priority that both powers attached to Korea's strategic importance. Upholding the UN, which had sponsored the creation of a South Korean state, was one reason for a firm response. Standing up to aggressors and the 'Munich' syndrome was another: no one wanted to see a repeat failure of the 1930s and the fate that befell the League of Nations. The Soviet testing of an atomic bomb in August 1949 had also intensified the dangers of a general world war. In addition, in the spring of 1950, Paul Nitze, the new head of the State Department's Policy Planning Staff, had overseen a new document drawn up by the State and Defense Departments. The report, NSC 68, stated that Moscow sought 'to impose its absolute authority over the rest of the world'. The United States, the report concluded, needed to adopt a 'flexible response' and respond swiftly to any Soviet aggression, which had grown bolder because of relative US military weakness. In this context, Washington's reaction – immediately sending ground forces and seeking international support – is not a surprise. Franks also later recalled that the British government accepted the crisis in Korea was 'not a local episode', and had wider implications.[144]

The British cabinet therefore accepted a UN Security Council resolution tabled by the United States urging all members to assist South Korea. The cabinet (after seeking advice from an ill Bevin) was not prepared, however, to broaden the UN resolution out to include the phrase 'Communist imperialism', which could be used to encompass the future of Formosa. Furthermore, the Chiefs of Staff, while content to send naval units to help US forces, considered it impossible to send troops to Korea given Britain's already burdensome commitments. The cabinet accepted this advice and the decision was in keeping with Britain's existing global strategy. Increasing pressure to send ground troops occurred when it appeared that South Korea was about to collapse in July 1950. After Attlee and Truman agreed to official Anglo-American exchanges in Washington on the strategic situation in the Far East, Franks, who had been present, suggested that the Americans saw the British as 'the only dependable ally and partner'. The ambassador invoked Britain's world position – if Britain came on board (that is, it sent ground troops), other powers would follow.

Franks then referred to the strength of the Anglo-American partnership during the Second World War, which was undeniable, but looked rather less convincing if one analysed that relationship in the Far East. Finally, Franks told London that 'the United States Administration faces and shares the expectation of the American people that we shall show we are with them on the ground in Korea'. If the British did not it might impair the relationship indefinitely. Again, the Americans had shown no concern for a British presence on the ground in Korea after the end of the war against Japan, and seemed only to turn to London when problems arose on the peninsula and they sought British support for their actions. Franks was prepared to dismiss any past history of rivalry or disagreements in the Far East: his point was that it did not matter in this context. What did matter was US help for more important British interests, such as the defence of Western Europe, economic rehabilitation and solidifying the Anglo-American relationship in general, which might be in jeopardy if Britain did nothing.[145] Franks' arguments certainly struck a cord with the cabinet and they helped to tip the balance over sending a ground force, leading the British to make preparations for a Commonwealth division, comprising forces from Australia, New Zealand, Canada and South Africa.[146]

Conclusion

This book has explored why Britain twice sent its armed forces to a region that was extremely low on the list of British global priorities. Considering the impact East Asia and the Pacific had on the outcome of the Second World War in the Far East, the origins of the Cold War, and the Anglo-American relationship, the historiography on the origins of these British decisions remains remarkably small. Britain's interaction with the United States in East Asia was dictated by a mixture of political, commercial and economic rivalry, declining British power, emerging Communist threats in China and Korea, Soviet policy, and relations with the Commonwealth (principally Australia). For both Britain and the United States, however, the East Asian region was a backdrop to more important strategic priorities.

East Asia and the wider Far East were always considered a secondary theatre in the allied fight against Fascism and the critical objective of liberating Europe. Anglo-American co-operation in the Far East was also less consensual than elsewhere, principally because Washington wished to distance itself from the stigma of being associated with British imperialism in the region. The American objective was to defeat Japan and liberate the Asian peoples from oppression (thereby furthering US commercial interests), while the British wanted to beat the Japanese and re-establish their colonial rule over lost Far Eastern territories (which, in turn, would further British commercial interests). In a bold move to dampen Anglo-American tension in the region, the British attempted to eradicate American suspicions of their alleged imperialist designs by sending forces to help in the main assaults against the Japanese homeland. If the British could be seen to be fighting alongside the Americans in the assaults on Japan, just as the two powers had fought together in mainland Europe, the 'special relationship' could be further cemented into the post-war world. Although Churchill obtained Roosevelt's agreement to accommodate British forces in American invasion plans, the United States was, in general, far from convinced of the need to utilise Britain's military help in an area that was designated an American responsibility.

American military planners clearly felt they alone had the men and material required to carry out an invasion of Japan and saw the arrival of British resources as a complicated and time-consuming political exercise. Furthermore, any British contribution, unlike a Soviet one with their far larger resources, could not significantly advance a Japanese surrender. The reason that neither London nor Washington drew back from the various pledges made for the main assaults against Japan was that a failure to make a stab at a collaborative enterprise in the region could create long-standing resentment between the two powers that might impede their working relationship in other more vital areas. It was telling that Attlee, a man who would seek to challenge all of Britain's global commitments, foresaw political dangers if he withdrew the British component from invasion planning, despite his own serious reservations and that of cabinet colleagues such as Bevin.

The evidence suggests, nevertheless, that the political benefits to be derived from British participation were small if not non-existent. In 1944–5, the United States sought to dominate East Asian affairs from a position of strength. It had done the bulk of the fighting in the Pacific and endeavoured to manage the post-war occupation of Japan with little outside help, while aiming to rebuild China as a great power orientated towards Washington, obtaining certain commercial privileges in the process. There seemed little desire on the part of the Americans to acquire allies in order to achieve their post-war East Asian objectives. The United States was certainly reluctant to work with an imperial power, Britain, in trying to create a new world order for the region, especially as that power was also a commercial rival in China and across the Far East. The American attempt (initiated by Roosevelt) to try to work with the Soviet Union in China and Korea (not Japan), to the exclusion of the British, also waxed and waned from 1944, never really gaining momentum once the United States came to the conclusion that the considerable political costs for Moscow's co-operation in East Asia greatly outweighed the potential benefits.

This chain of events showed how Britain had slid down the East Asian regional pecking order, where before 1941 it had been a major player. Now, all the British could do was to claw back lost commercial assets in China and Hong Kong, and weigh up whether it was worth pitching for an international role in Korea and Japan. Considering Britain's declining power and financial difficulties, Soviet-American indifference towards a British role in the region, and Britain's more important commitments in Southeast Asia, it is not surprising that British attempts to play some sort of international role in East Asia foundered. Yet, as the East Asian region remained a US responsibility and a low priority in British foreign and defence policy, the failure to achieve greater influence in the reconstruction of Japan, and the American desire to exclude the British from Chinese and Korean affairs, was not viewed too tragically by London, except where exclusion affected Britain great power status and began to threaten British interests further south. Parliament, the press and the British public also rarely interested themselves in events in East Asia. This was fortunate as the British post-war East Asian experience was littered with disappointments.

In China, the British struggled to reclaim their property and commercial assets, fill all their consular posts or work with the Americans, who seemed extremely reluctant to co-operate with an 'imperialist' Britain inside that country. After Marshall's unsuccessful efforts at mediation to prevent civil war, the United States was even less inclined to talk to Britain about an apparently failing China policy. In Korea, the Americans rarely discussed the peninsula's affairs with the British and only sough their help (e.g. at the UN), when US occupation policy ran into trouble in the face of what was perceived to be a strong Soviet-backed state north of the 38th parallel. International bodies for post-war Japan were also ineffective in the face of a US determination to control the occupation, forcing the British to create a direct line to MacArthur through the United Kingdom Liaison Mission. The latter initially proved useful but UKLM's ability to gauge American intentions gradually diminished as Washington began to tighten its grip on US policy towards Japan. Then the British became increasingly reliant on the good offices of the State Department for information and the results were mixed at best.

Why, then, did the British decide to send troops for the occupation of Japan as part of BCOF? They arrived late, were stationed in an unimportant part of Japan and within months were almost all pulled out and relocated elsewhere for more urgent tasks. One reason formed part of a major sub-plot to the Anglo-American story in East Asia: the role of Australia. Since the Second World War Canberra had been pushing for a greater say in the region's affairs, which for Australia was the Near North and not the Far East. That desire in its rawest form strove to replace Britain as the main Commonwealth power in the region. The dilemma for the British, in trying to alleviate some of their burdensome post-war commitments, was to assess how much damage might be inflicted upon Britain's great power status if Commonwealth responsibility for countries such as Japan and Korea devolved onto the Australians. The initial British conclusion was that the experiment should be attempted, and the Attlee government agreed to Australian leadership for BCOF with Canberra representing interested Commonwealth capitals on the Allied Council for Japan. It was also agreed that the Australians could pursue a similar Commonwealth role if a four-power trusteeship for Korea materialised.

By 1947, the Foreign Office clearly regretted the decision, watching with horror open Australian attacks on US policy in East Asia, at a time when Britain was looking for American political, economic and military help in the Cold War rapidly unfolding in Europe and the Middle East. This is not to say that Britain did not share Australian misgivings about American East Asian policy, but London always tried to iron out disagreements with Washington behind closed doors. To make matters worse, Washington deemed that it was London's responsibility to keep Canberra in line. The Australian claim to be able to represent the British Commonwealth in the region also looked less credible as they ran into difficulties in maintaining BCOF and shied away from taking the lead for regional defence planning in the Far East. On this last point, the Foreign Office was very reluctant to devolve any responsibility to Australia (in peace or war) for defence planning, fearful that this would finally extinguish the Britain's ability to call itself a truly global world power. Other Whitehall departments wondered how exactly Britain could spread its sparse resources everywhere.

Unwilling and unable to devolve ultimate responsibility for the region's affairs to Australia, by 1948 Britain also anxiously watched as the American position on the East Asian continent continue to weaken. From 1944 onwards, Britain had always been concerned that the United States might not fulfil its new post-war responsibilities as a world power of the first rank if those responsibilities became too costly. With chaos inside China exacerbated by civil war and internal strife inside Korea, the British worried that their prophecy was about to come true as the Americans seemed as though they might retreat from the East Asian mainland. Britain was also concerned that the United States, in covering its retreat, was intent on building up a former enemy, Japan, as a bulwark against the spread of Communism in East Asia. London therefore felt unable to stand on the sidelines any longer and in an effort to tackle the emerging threats confronting allied strategy for the Far East pressed Washington for greater Anglo-American consultation over East Asian problems. The British were not prepared blindly to support what seemed to be a reorientation of all American wartime and early post-war policies.

The British could not hide their disappointment, though criticism was conducted in private. Nor were the Americans afraid to tell the British that if they did not fall into line over their new policy for Japan, it could impact on the US ability to continue to fund recovery in Europe where Britain was at the front of queue for financial help. London did not demur, especially when it viewed events in East Asia against the background of heightening Cold War tensions in Europe (epitomised by the Czechoslovakian and Berlin crises), its own financial difficulties, and a policy of trying to garner US support for its policies in the Middle East. Britain therefore reluctantly went along with what they saw as a flawed US policy for East Asia: offloading the Korean problem onto the UN, propping up the Chinese Nationalist regime with limited aid and reversing the course for Japan. They hoped they could at least act as a restraining influence on what they saw as any wilder aspects of US policy, but London offered no alternative solutions to combat the emerging crises in China and Korea. British reaction to the American reverse-course policy in Japan, for example, seems short-sighted in retrospect, especially when one views Japanese post-war development. As *The*

Times reminded its readers, if the State Department had appeared too ready in East Asia to back the 'wrong side for the right reasons' (a reference to Chiang Kai-shek and Syngman Rhee) it should not be forgotten that it was forced to work with inadequate material. However exasperating the governments of Western Europe had sometimes appeared to Washington, they were infinitely stronger than the so-called 'democratic regimes' in East Asia. If there was now little left of the crumbling wall the Truman administration tried to build between itself and the Soviet Union, *The Times* concluded, 'it is extremely doubtful whether any other Government or any other policy could have done better'.[1]

The Times article betrayed a certain simplicity in its assessment but one that British policy had to contend with during the post-war period. The reference to the State Department understated the complexity of US foreign policymaking but it is interesting to note that Foreign Office–State Department exchanges were the principal conduit through which London learnt of American intentions for East Asia. This left a necessarily incomplete picture of American thinking. State Department officials and diplomats had limited control and co-ordination over US foreign policy. The White House, Congress and its committees, the Defence Department (from 1947) and the CIA (also from 1947) all made an impact on determining the American response to overseas problems and, unlike Britain, there was no cabinet to formulate a common US policy. In addition, during the first three years of the only forum that attempted to co-ordinate policy, the NSC, Truman rarely attended its meetings. This meant that American policy was inevitably fragmented: the State Department therefore had to be careful in what it said to the British in case those pronouncements were undermined by a plethora of other internal influences.[2] The flip side for the Americans was that British ministers rarely involved themselves in East Asian affairs and Britain's response to US policies in the region was kept ticking along by Foreign Office. What the Foreign Office decreed was likewise not always the wish of the Ministry of Defence or the cabinet, although Bevin's powerful influence more often than not meant the Foreign Office view was respected.

Indeed, the power of individuals and their ability to work with their opposite numbers also dictated how Anglo-American relations developed in the region. In this respect, Sir Esler Dening played a key role for the Foreign Office. He was a staunch imperialist and unlikely to countenance any erosion of British influence, yet his lecturing and condescending tone towards the Americans must have grated with State Department officials, and particularly Walton Butterworth. Dening's time in SEAC undoubtedly shaped his view of Americans, which unfortunately was not an ideal environment to make such an assessment. Butterworth's attitude did not help matters either and his oft-repeated assertion that the future of East Asia was best left to the Americans to which other powers should be grateful was a move hardly calculated to endear himself to Foreign Office officials or other members of the British Commonwealth. Butterworth's outlook was little different to his predecessors. John Carter Vincent was equally prepared to dismiss the necessity for British involvement in East Asia much to John Sterndale Bennett's annoyance but in this outlook the American was only aping Roosevelt who often sidelined Churchill over the region's key post-war issues. Lord Inverchapel's arrival in Washington as British ambassador in 1946 also did little to enhance the Foreign Office–State Department relationship, a man bored by his surroundings and unwilling to ingratiate himself with leading Americans figures.

There were brighter spots. In Japan, the MacArthur–Gascoigne relationship was extremely close and the head of UKLM kept the British well-informed of developments in Japan. In China, the Stevenson–Stuart relationship was similarly intimate but both relationships had limited utility in the fact that US policy was made in Washington, not Tokyo and Nanking. With the departure of Inverchapel and the arrival of Franks in May 1948, there were better prospects for a closer understanding between London and Washington and the new British ambassador struck up an excellent relationship with Acheson. Relations between Acheson and Bevin were also close. However good personal relationships may or may not have been, the British could not hide the fact that they saw US policy for East Asia as a failure and the more the British complained (albeit in private) the less the Americans were prepared to listen.

By 1950 Anglo-American tension in East Asia was reaching a high point. With the formation of the Chinese Communist state in October 1949, the US retreat from mainland China was complete and the drawing of ideological lines left Washington disinclined to engage with the Chinese Communists. This meant non-recognition, no support for what was left of the American business community inside China, a US refusal to help lift the Nationalist blockade of Chinese ports, and a reluctance to cut off aid to the Chinese Nationalists in Formosa. To illustrate the divergence in Anglo-American policy towards China, the British contemplated recognition, were prepared to try to help their business community inside China (as long as there were no financial implications for the government), wanted the Nationalist blockade lifted to relieve the pressure on that community, and for that very reason, wanted the flow of US supplies to Formosa stopped. They argued that they had to look at the problem from a practical, not an ideological, viewpoint. By keeping a foot in the door, the British hoped to persuade the Chinese Communists of the benefits of trade and maintaining a relationship with the West, while helping to lessen tension in the region, which could affect the future of Hong Kong and British Far Eastern interests, especially the latter where Communism was on the rise in several Southeast Asian countries. Meanwhile, after the final US troops had left South Korea in the summer of 1949, by 1950 most commentators considered it only a matter of time before the Korean peninsula fell under complete Communist control too. With the American refusal to countenance an early peace treaty for Japan, the allied position in East Asia appeared in disarray and Anglo-American collaboration on the key issues looked unrealisable.

Yet, by the second half of 1950, Britain and the United States would be fighting side by side in Korea, an amazing occurrence given that, as one scholar has observed writing about the Far East, the 'so-called "special relationship" hardly seemed to work at all in this vast area'.[3] With the Cold War seemingly about to turn hot, however, Franks' convincingly laid out arguments for British involvement on the ground in Korea that won the day. They were arguments remarkably similar to those employed by one of his predecessors in Washington, Lord Halifax, when the latter spoke of the necessity for British forces to take part in the invasion of Japan. The trouble was that the background to both of those decisions were made against the landscape of previous American indifference to British actions in the Far East and sometimes even a blank refusal to entertain British wishes at all. What was striking, therefore, was Britain's ability to put these differences with the Americans in the Far East to one side in the belief that sending British forces to the East Asian area, a region that was low on the list of priorities, could help sustain their relationship in more important areas and potentially reinforce Britain's self-perceived status as a great power.

Notes

Introduction

1. See, for example, C. Thorne, *Allies of a Kind: The United States, Britain, and the War Against Japan, 1941–1945* (Oxford: Oxford University Press, 1978); Wm. R. Louis, *Imperialism at Bay: The United States and the Decolonisation of the British Empire, 1941–1945* (Oxford: Clarendon Press, 1977); J. Sbrega, *Anglo-American Relations and Colonialism in East Asia, 1941–1945* (New York: Garland, 1983); and R. Aldrich, *Intelligence and the War Against Japan: Britain, America and the Politics of Secret Service* (Cambridge: Cambridge University Press, 2000).
2. The only study to look at British early post-war policy in a regional East Asian context is P. Lowe, *Containing the Cold War in East Asia: British Policies towards Japan, China and Korea, 1948–1953* (Manchester: Manchester University Press, 1997). Other studies have focused on either Japan or China. See, for example, R. Buckley, *Occupation Diplomacy: Britain, the United States and Japan 1945–1952* (Cambridge: Cambridge University Press, 1982); N. Yokoi, *Japan's Postwar Economic Recovery and Anglo-Japanese Relations, 1948–62* (London: Routledge, 2003); B. Porter, *Britain and the Rise of Communist China: A Study of British Attitudes, 1945–1954* (London: Oxford University Press, 1967); and L. Xiang, *Recasting the Imperial Far East: Britain and America in China, 1945–1950* (London: M. E. Sharpe, 1995).
3. S. Ashton, G. Bennett and K. Hamilton (eds.), *Documents on British Policy Overseas* (hereafter *DBPO*), *Series I, viii, Britain and China, 1945–1950* (London: Frank Cass, 2002), p.vii.
4. See S. Dockrill, 'Britain's Grand Strategy and Anglo-American Leadership in the War against Japan' in B. Bond and K. Tachikawa (eds.), *British and Japanese Military Leadership in the Far Eastern War 1941–1945* (London: Routledge, 2004), pp.6–12 and A. Shai, *Britain and China, 1941–47: Imperial Momentum* (London: Macmillan, 1984), p.33.
5. For good accounts of British policy in the region before the attack on Pearl Harbor, see A. Best, *Japan and Pearl Harbor: Avoiding War in East Asia, 1936–41* (London: Routledge, 1995); P. Lowe, *Great Britain and the Origins of the Pacific War: A Study of British Policy in East Asia, 1937–1941* (Oxford: Clarendon Press, 1977); N. Tarling, *Britain, Southeast Asia and the Onset of the Pacific War* (Cambridge: Cambridge University Press, 1996); and A. Trotter, *Britain and East Asia, 1933–1937* (Cambridge: Cambridge University Press, 1975).
6. A. Toynbee, *The World After the Peace Conference* (London: H. Milford, Oxford University Press, 1925).
7. The widely acclaimed C. Bayly and T. Harper, *Forgotten Armies: The Fall of British Asia 1941–1945* (London: Allen Lane, 2004) has, for example, made a significant impact. See my review in *The Journal of Strategic Studies*, 29 (2006), pp.938–40. See also M. Hastings, *Nemesis: The Battle for Japan, 1944–45* (London: Harper Collins, 2007).
8. See, for example, H. P. Willmott, *Grave of a Dozen Schemes: British Naval Planning and the War Against Japan* (London: Airlife, 1996); N. E. Sarantakes, 'The Royal Air Force on Okinawa: The Diplomacy of a Coalition on the Verge of Victory',

Diplomatic History, 27 (2003), pp.479–502; idem, 'One Last Crusade: The British Pacific Fleet and its Impact on the Anglo-American Alliance', *English Historical Review*, 121 (2006), pp.429–66; T. Hall, ' "Mere Drops in the Ocean": The Politics and Planning of the Contribution of the British Commonwealth to the Final Defeat of Japan, 1944–45', *Diplomacy and Statecraft*, 16 (2005), pp.93–105; and C. Baxter, 'In Pursuit of a Pacific Strategy: British Planning for the Defeat of Japan, 1943–45', *Diplomacy and Statecraft*, 15 (2004), pp.253–77.

9. It is not my intention here to recite in detail the available literature on why the Japanese surrendered, suffice to say that T. Hasegawa's *Racing the Enemy: Stalin, Truman, and the Surrender of Japan* (London: Harvard University Press, 2005) has recently sparked a new debate over the ending of the war against Japan. See also idem (ed.), *The End of the Pacific War: Reappraisals* (Stanford: Stanford University Press, 2007); R. Frank, *Downfall: The End of the Imperial Japanese Empire* (New York: Random House, 1999); Y. Koshiro, 'Eurasian Eclipse: Japan's End Game in World War II', *American Historical Review*, 109 (2004); and the H-Diplo Roundtable Review, 7 (2006), http://www.h-net.org/~diplo/roundtables/

10. See C. Baxter, 'The Foreign Office and Post-war Planning for East Asia, 1944–45', *Contemporary British History*, 21 (2007), pp.149–72.

11. See, for example, N. Tarling, *Britain, Southeast Asia and the Onset of the Cold War, 1945–50* (Cambridge: Cambridge University Press, 1998); T. Remme, *Britain and Regional Co-operation in South-East Asia, 1945–49* (London: Routledge, 1995); P. Dennis, *Troubled Days of Peace: Mountbatten and South East Asia Command, 1945–46* (Manchester: Manchester University Press, 1987); R. Spector, *In the Ruins of Empire: The Japanese Surrender and the Battle for Postwar Asia* (New York: Random House, 2007); and C. Bayly and T. Harper, *Forgotten Wars: Freedom and Revolution in Southeast Asia* (Cambridge, MA: Harvard University Press, 2007).

12. See R. Ovendale, *The English-Speaking Alliance: Britain, the United States, the Dominions and the Cold War, 1945–1951* (London: Allen & Unwin, 1985) and K. Srinivasan, *The Rise, Decline and Future of the British Commonwealth* (Basingstoke: Palgrave Macmillan, 2005), chp. 1.

13. See J. Kent, *British Imperial Strategy and the Origins of the Cold War, 1944–49* (Leicester: Leicester University Press, 1993) and M. Hopkins, 'A British Cold War?', *Intelligence and National Security*, 7 (1992), pp.479–82.

14. See, for example, O. A. Westad, *Cold War & Revolution: Soviet-American Rivalry and the Origins of the Chinese Civil War* (New York: Columbia University Press, 1992); idem (ed.), *Brothers in Arms: The Rise and Fall of the Sino-Soviet Alliance, 1945–1963* (Stanford: Stanford University Press); idem, *Decisive Encounters: The Chinese Civil War, 1946–1950* (Stanford: Stanford University Press, 2003); S. Goncharov, J. Lewis, and X. Litai, *Uncertain Partners: Stalin, Mao and the Korean War* (Stanford: Stanford University Press, 1993); M. Hunt, *The Genesis of Chinese Communist Foreign Policy* (New York: Columbia University Press, 1996); C. Jian, *China's Road to the Korean War: The Making of the Sino-American Confrontation* (New York: Columbia University Press, 1994); idem, *Mao's China and the Cold War* (London: University of North Carolina Press, 2001); S. Qing, *From Allies to Enemies: Visions of Modernity, Identity, and U.S.-China Diplomacy, 1945–1960* (Cambridge, MA: Harvard University Press, 2007); Weathersby, 'Soviet Aims in Korea and the Origins of the Korean War, 1945–1950: New Perspectives from Russian Archives', *Cold War International History Project: Woodrow Wilson Center for Scholars* (1993); and idem, 'Stalin and the Korean War' in M. Leffler and D. Painter (eds.), *Origins of the Cold War: An International History* (London: Routledge, 2005), pp.265–81.

1   Defeating Japan

1. For Australian accounts of their part in the Pacific War see, for example, D. Day, *The Great Betrayal: Britain, Australia and the Onset of the Pacific War, 1939–42* (New York: Norton, 1988); idem, *Reluctant Nation: Australia and the Allied Defeat of Japan, 1942–45* (New York: Oxford University Press, 1992); D. Horner, *High Command: Australia and Allied Strategy, 1939–1945* (Sydney: George Allen & Unwin, 1982); and idem, *Inside the War Cabinet: Directing Australia's War Effort, 1939–45* (St. Leonards: Allen & Unwin, 1996).

2. Churchill, minute, 31 Dec 1944 and Eden, minute, 8 Jan 1945, PREM 4/31/4, The National Archives, Kew, London (TNA); Dockrill, 'Grand Strategy', pp.6–17; and L. Allen, 'The Campaigns in Asia and the Pacific', *The Journal of Strategic Studies*, 13 (1990), p.163.

3. W. Kimball, *Forged at War: Churchill, Roosevelt and the Second World War* (London: Harper Collins, 1997), pp.188–91.

4. Mountbatten to Eden, 26 Nov 1943, F757/757/61, FO 371/41739, TNA and Thorne, *Allies*, chp. 11.

5. Cadogan's remarks are noted in Cavendish-Bentinck, minute, 26 Nov 1943, A10965/361/45, FO 371/34182, TNA.

6. Ismay to Auchinleck, 27 Jul 1944, 4/9/7, Ismay papers, Liddell Hart Centre for Military Archives, King's College London (KCL).

7. W. Churchill, *The Second World War*, v, *Closing the Ring* (London: Cassell, 1952), p.366 and Bayly and Harper, *Forgotten Armies*, pp.269–81.

8. The standard work on Mountbatten is P. Ziegler, *Mountbatten: The Official Biography* (London: Phoenix Press, 2001). For a critical assessment, see A. Roberts, *Eminent Churchillians* (London: Weidenfeld & Nicolson, 1994), chp. 2.

9. Churchill, minute, 31 Dec 1944, PREM 4/31/4, TNA; Churchill to Ismay, 12 Sep 1944 in W. Churchill, *The Second World War*, vi, *Triumph and Tragedy* (London: Cassell, 1954), p.146; and G. Kennedy, 'Lord Halifax: Wartime Ambassador to the United States, 1941–1946' in C. Baxter and A. Stewart (eds.), *Diplomats at War: British and Commonwealth Diplomacy in Wartime* (Leiden: Martinus Nijhoff Publishers, 2008), pp.118–19.

10. Diary entries for 14 Jul, 8 Aug and 9 Sep 1944 in A. Danchev and D. Todman (eds.), *War Diaries 1939–1945: Field Marshal Lord Alanbrooke* (London: Weidenfeld & Nicolson, 2001), pp.570, 578–9 & 590. On Churchill's health, see Grigg to his father, 10 Apr 1944, PJGG 9/6/27, Grigg papers, Churchill Archives Centre, Cambridge University (CAC); and diary entries for 19 Apr, 17 Jul and 3 Aug 1944 in D. Dilks (ed.), *The Diaries of Sir Alexander Cadogan, O.M. 1938–1945* (London: Cassell, 1971), pp.621, 647 & 653.

11. Washington tel. 430, 2 May 1944, F2300/993/61, FO 371/41746, TNA.

12. See, for example, diary entry for 1 Aug 1944 in T. H. White (ed.), *The Stilwell Papers* (New York: Sloane, 1949), p.286.

13. M. Howard, *Grand Strategy*, iv, *August 1942–September 1943* (London: HMSO, 1972), p.542.

14. Brooke to Dill, 30 Mar 1944, 6/3/10, Alanbrooke papers, KCL.

15. Washington tel. 430, 2 May 1944, F2300/993/61, FO 371/41746, TNA.

16. Cavendish-Bentinck, minute, 26 Nov 1943, A10965/361/45, FO 371/34182, ibid.

17. Roosevelt's remarks are in Churchill, minute for Ismay, 14 Mar 1944, CHAR 20/188B, Churchill papers, CAC.

18. On the possibility of the Chiefs of Staff resigning, see diary entry for 3 Mar 1944 in Danchev and Todman (eds.), *War Diaries*, p.528.

19. For Brooke's and the Chiefs of Staff's views, see Ismay to Churchill, 16 Mar 1944, CHAR 20/188B, Churchill papers, CAC; Chiefs of Staff to Churchill, 28 Mar 1944, ibid.; and Brooke to Dill, 30 Mar 1944, 6/3/10, Alanbrooke papers, KCL. The desire to maintain the Combined Chiefs of Staff system is in 'Report on COS(44)51', Jebb, minute, 19 Feb 1944, U1751/748/G, FO 371/40740, TNA. On MacArthur's views of the British, see C. Thorne, 'MacArthur, Australia and the British, 1942–1943: the secret journal of MacArthur's Liaison Officer' (Parts I & II) in *Australian Outlook*, 29 (1975), pp.53–67 & 197–210; and M. Schaller, 'General Douglas MacArthur and the Politics of the Pacific War' in G. Bischof and R. L. Dupont (eds.), *The Pacific War Revisited* (Baton Rouge: Louisiana State University Press, 1997), pp.17–40.
20. Hastings, *Nemesis*, pp.365–6.
21. F. Shedden, 'The United Kingdom Government's Demands for the British Pacific Fleet Ignore the Australian Limits to Possible Aid', chp. 53, pp.1–2 (hereafter Shedden 'British Pacific Fleet'), The Shedden Collection (1937–71), 771/8, A5954/69, National Archives of Australia, Canberra (NAA).
22. Curtin to Churchill, 17 May 1944, in W. J. Hudson (ed.), *Documents on Australian Foreign Policy* (hereafter *DAFP*), 1944, vii (Canberra: Australian Government Publishing Service, 1988), doc. 153.
23. King to MacArthur, 21 Jul 1944 (Navy, 28 Jun 1944 – 8 Feb 1945), Folder 6, Box 10, RG 4, MacArthur Memorial Archives, Norfolk, Virginia (MMN).
24. MacArthur to King, 5 Aug 1944, ibid.
25. Marshall to MacArthur, 19 Aug 1944 (War Department, 9 Aug – 28 Dec 1944), Folder 2, Box 17, RG 4, ibid.
26. MacArthur to Marshall, 27 Aug 1944, ibid. See also Curtin's review of his discussions with Churchill in the summer of 1944 in Curtin to Churchill, 1 Sep 1944, in Hudson (ed.), *DAFP*, 1944, vii, doc. 265. On Curtin's role in the war, see D. Day *John Curtin: A Life* (Sydney: Harper Collins, 1999); J. Edwards, *Curtin's Gift: Reinterpreting Australia's Greatest Prime Minister* (Sydney: Allen & Unwin, 2005); and P. Edwards, 'Curtin, Macarthur and the "Surrender of Sovereignty": a Historiographical Assessment', *Australian Journal of International Affairs*, 55 (2001), pp. 175–85.
27. R. D. Buhite, *Douglas MacArthur: Statecraft and Stagecraft in America's East Asian Policy* (Plymouth: Rowman & Littlefield Publishers, 2008), p.64.
28. 'Political Implications of Far Eastern Strategy', Dening memo., 17 Feb 1944, F1040/100/23, FO 371/41795, TNA. On Mountbatten's remark, see Mountbatten to Dening, 9 Sep 1943, MISC 251(3480), Dening papers, Imperial War Museum, London (IWM). See also 'Dening's Daisyfield', *News Review*, 13 Dec 1945.
29. See Cadogan, minute, 18 Feb 1944, F1040/100/23, FO 371/41795, TNA; Eden, minute, 21 Feb 1944, ibid., Sterndale Bennett, minute, 3 Jul 1945, F4056/69/23, FO 371/46440, ibid. and 'British Participation in the War against Japan', Bevin memo., DO(45)3, 8 Aug 1945, PREM 8/29, ibid.
30. Dening, minute, 17 Feb 1944, F1040/100/23, FO 371/41795, ibid.
31. See Clarke, minute, 5 May 1944, F2151/100/23, FO 371/41797, ibid.; Butler, minute, 6 May 1944, ibid.; Dockrill, 'Grand Strategy', pp.20–1; and H. W. Baldwin, 'Confusion over Burma Warfare', *New York Times*, 12 Apr 1944. For the highly volatile atmosphere in which British and American intelligence agencies operated in the Far East, see Aldrich, *Intelligence*.
32. Chungking tel. 1380, 20 Dec 1944, F234/127/61, FO 371/46325, TNA.
33. See Jebb, Cavendish-Bentinck and Cadogan minutes, 14 & 16 Dec 1944, F5802/993/61, FO 371/41746, ibid.

34. Diary entry for 14 Jul 1944 in Danchev and Todman (eds.), *War Diaries*, p.570 and Earl of Avon, *The Eden Memoirs: The Reckoning* (London: Cassell, 1965), pp.461–2.
35. See Winant to Hopkins, 1 Sep 1944 in *Foreign Relations of the United States: Diplomatic Papers* (hereafter *FRUS*): *The Conference at Quebec 1944* (Washington: US Government Printing Office, 1972), pp.254–6; Hopkins to Winant, 4 Sep 1944, ibid., pp.256–7 and Hull to Roosevelt, 8 Sep 1944, *FRUS*, 1944, iii, *The British Commonwealth and Europe, 1944* (Washington: United States Government Printing Office, 1965), pp.53–6.
36. MacArthur to King, 5 Aug 1944 (Navy, 28 Jun 1944 – 8 Feb 1945), Folder 6, Box 10, RG 4, MMN and MacArthur to Marshall, 27 Aug 1944 (War Department, 9 Aug – 28 Dec 1944), Folder 2, Box 17, ibid.
37. Churchill's message is in Churchill to Lumsden, 6 Sep 1944 (Official Correspondence, Jul-Oct 1944), Folder 9, Box 2, RG 3, ibid.
38. MacArthur's message reported by Lumsden to Churchill, 6 Sep 1944, ibid.
39. 'British Participation in the War Against Japan', US Chiefs of Staff memo., CCS 452/25, 8 Sep 1944, *FRUS: Quebec 1944*, p.257.
40. Marshall to MacArthur, 12 Sep 1944 (Navy, 28 Jun 1944 – 8 Feb 1945), Folder 6, Box 10, RG 4, MMN.
41. See mtg. of the Combined Chiefs of Staff with Churchill and Roosevelt, 13 Sep 1944, *FRUS: Quebec 1944*, pp.312–18; minutes of the Combined Chiefs of Staff meeting, 14 Sep 1944, ibid., pp.330–41; Leahy, minute, JCS 175th mtg., 13 Sep 1944. Folder CCS334 JCS mtgs 168-85 (7-4-44), Box 198, Central Decimal File 1942-5, RG 218, National Archives and Records Administration, College Park, Maryland (NARA); and R. J. Marshall to MacArthur, 28 Sep 1944 (War Department, 9 Aug – 28 Dec 1944), Folder 2, Box 17, RG 4, MMN. On understanding King's attitude see M. Coles, 'Ernest King and the British Pacific Fleet: The Conference at Quebec, 1944 ("Octagon")', *The Journal of Military History*, 65 (2001), pp.105–29.
42. See Curtin's views contained in Octagon tel. GUNFIRE 143, 15 Sep 1944, CHAR 20/171, Churchill papers, CAC.
43. See Octagon tel. GUNFIRE 251, 18 Sep 1944, ibid. and The Earl Mountbatten of Burma, *Report to the Combined Chiefs of Staff by the Supreme Allied Commander South-East Asia 1943–1945* (London: HMSO, 1951), pp.76–7 & 83–4.
44. J. Ehrman, *Grand Strategy*, v, *August 1943–September 1944* (London: HMSO, 1956), pp.493–524. On Marshall's thoughts about an invasion of Japan at this time, see idem, *The Atomic Bomb: An Account of British Policy in the Second World War* (London: Cabinet Office, 1953), p.232 in CAB 101/45, TNA.
45. D. Rees, *The Defeat of Japan* (London: Praeger, 1997), p.64.
46. 'Moscow Conference: Far Eastern Questions', Clarke memo., 20 Sep 1943, F5138/294/61, FO 371/35947, TNA.
47. W. A. Harriman and E. Abel, *Special Envoy to Churchill and Stalin 1941–1946* (London: Random House, 1976), pp.364, 371.
48. Ashton, Bennett and Hamilton (eds.), *DBPO, Series I*, viii, p.ix.
49. Churchill, minute for Cadogan, 23 Apr 1944, F2115/1358/23, FO 371/41823, TNA.
50. Rees, *Defeat*, pp.68–9.
51. Diary entry for 15 Oct 1944 in Danchev and Todman (eds.), *War Diaries*, pp.607–08.

52. Cairo tel. HEARTY 262, 21 Oct 1944, CHAR 20/173, Churchill papers, CAC; Rees, *Defeat*, p.69; and Harriman and Abel, *Special Envoy*, p.364.
53. 'Probable Post-War Tendencies in Soviet Foreign Policy as Affecting British Interests', Foreign Office memo., 29 Apr 1944, N1008/183/38, FO 371/43335, TNA; 'An Estimate of Russian Aims in the Far East, Far Eastern Department memo', 5 Oct 1944, F9836/8854/61, FO 371/54073, ibid.; 'Russia's Strategic Interests and Intentions from the point of view of her security', JIC(44)467(0)(Final), 18 Dec 1944, CAB 81/126, ibid.; and 'Strategic Interests in the Far East', JP(44)278)(Final), 1 Jan 1945, CAB 79/28, ibid.
54. See Westad, *Cold War*, pp.8–9 and Hasegawa, *Racing*, pp.25–7.
55. 'Russia's Strategic Interests and Intentions from the point of view of her security', JIC(44)467(0)(Final), 18 Dec 1944, CAB 81/126, TNA and Eden, minute, 6 Jan 1945, N678/20/38, FO 371/57860, ibid.
56. V. Zubok and C. Pleshakov, *Inside the Kremlin's Cold War: From Stalin to Khrushchev* (London: Harvard University Press, 1997), pp.27–34 and D. Reynolds, *Summits: Six Meetings That Shaped the Twentieth Century* (New York: Basic Books, 2007), pp.108–11, 115–6 & 126.
57. Deane to Marshall, 2 Dec 1944, Box 5, Safe Files, Roosevelt papers, Franklin D. Roosevelt Library, Hyde Park, New York (FDRL) and Marshall memo. for Roosevelt, 3 Jan 1945, ibid.
58. Ehrman, *Grand Strategy*, v, pp.377–403, 524–33.
59. See Mountbatten to Churchill, 2 Oct 1944, CHAR 20/172, Churchill papers, CAC and Churchill to Mountbatten, 5 Oct 1944, ibid.
60. Leahy memo. for Roosevelt, 11 Jan 1945, Box 1, Safe Files, Roosevelt papers, FDRL and C. Brower, 'Sophisticated Strategist: General George A Lincoln and the Defeat of Japan, 1944–45', *Diplomatic History*, 15 (1991), p.324.
61. Reynolds, *Summits*, p.123.
62. Westad, *Cold War*, p.29.
63. Churchill, *Second World War*, vi, p.342; Earl of Avon, *Memoirs*, p.514; Dilks (ed.), *Diaries*, p.715; and Harriman and Abel, *Special Envoy*, p.399; and Reynolds, *Summits*, pp.128–9.
64. Churchill, minute, 10 Mar 1945, F8854/-/61, FO 371/54073, TNA.
65. R. H. Spector, *Eagle Against the Sun: The American War with Japan* (London: Cassell, 2001), p.540.
66. See M. Schaller, *The American Occupation of Japan: The Origins of the Cold War in Asia* (Oxford: Oxford University Press, 1985), pp.8–13; Hasegawa, *Racing*, pp.62 & 65; and M. Sherry, *Preparing for the Next War: American Plans for Postwar Defense, 1941–45* (London: Yale University Press, 1977), pp.159–90.
67. 'Co-ordination of British Organisations in China', JIC(45)111(0)(Final), 3 Apr 1945, CAB 81/128, TNA. For the intelligence rivalries on the ground in China regarding the coast-watching organisation, see Mountbatten to Donovan, 26 Jun 1944, Folder 2, Box 357, Entry 210, RG 226, NARA; McGivern to Hoffman, 1 & 7 Aug 1944, ibid.; and F. Wakeman, *Spymaster: Dai Li and the Chinese Secret Service* (London: University of California Press, 2003), chp. 22.
68. Curtin to Bruce, 9 Nov 1944, *DAFP*, 1944, vii, doc. 339.
69. Shedden, 'British Pacific Fleet', chp. 53, pp.3–11.
70. Sarantakes, 'One Last Crusade', pp.450–8.
71. Hastings, *Nemesis*, 434–6.
72. 'Manpower-Answer to Prime Minister's Directive', JP(45)108(Final), 2 May 1945, CAB 79/33, TNA and COS minutes, COS(45)117, 4 May 1945, ibid.

73. See Portal and Cunningham minutes, COS(45)103, 19 Apr 1945, CAB 79/32, ibid.; Brooke, minute, COS(45)143, 4 Jun 1945, CAB 79/34, ibid.; 'British Partic-ipation in V.L.R. Bombing of Japan', CCS 691, 18 Sep 1944, Folder CCS 373.11 Japan (9-18-44) Sec.1, Box 114, Geographic File, 1942–5, RG 218, NARA; 'British Participation in V.L.R. Bombing of Japan', JCS 1120, 19 Oct 1944, ibid.; 'British Participation in V.L.R. Bombing of Japan', decision on JCS 1120/1, note by JCS secretaries, 30 May 1945, ibid.; and 'British Participation in V.L.R. Bombing of Japan', Chiefs of Staff representatives memo., CCS 691/3, 5 Jun 1945, ibid. MacArthur's objections are in MacArthur to War Department, tel. CA51492, 10 Apr 1945, ibid.
74. Portal to Kuter, 1 Feb 1945, ibid.; Lincoln, minutes, JPS 200th–201st mtgs, 5 & 9 May 1945, ibid.; and 'British Participation in V.L.R. Bombing of Japan', JCS 1120/1, 10 May 1945, ibid. See also Sarantakes, 'Royal Air Force', pp.479–502.
75. 'British Part in the Final Phase of the War Against Japan', JP(45)69(Final), 8 May 1945, CAB 84/70, TNA and S. W. Kirby, *The War Against Japan*, v, *The Surrender of Japan* (London: HMSO, 1969), pp.83–92.
76. Portal and Cunningham minutes, COS(45)124, 11 May 1945, CAB 79/33, TNA.
77. Minutes of mtg. held at the White House, 18 Jun 1945, Folder CCS 334 JCS meetings 186–94 (2-2-45), Box 198, Central Decimal File, 1942–5, RG 218, NARA.
78. Joint Staff Mission (Washington) tel. JSM 902, 14 Jun 1945, F4030/69/23, FO 371/46440, TNA.
79. 'Proposals for British Participation in the War Against Japan', JP(45)155(Final), 26 Jun 1945, CAB 84/73, ibid.; 'War Against Japan – British Proposals', JP(45)157(Final), 28 Jun 1945, F4236/69/23, FO 371/46440, ibid.; and Allen, minute, 29 Jun 1945, ibid.
80. See Sterndale Bennett, minute, 29 Jun 1945, ibid. and his remarks on 'British Participation in the War Against Japan', COS(45)423(0), 30 Jun 1945, in Stern-dale Bennett, minute, 3 Jul 1945, F4056/69/23, ibid. Dening's undated memo. was entitled, 'Political Factors Affecting British Participation in the War Against Japan after the Fall of Singapore', F4056/69/23, ibid. For the situation in South-east Asia's rice-producing countries, see 'British Part in the Final Phase of the War Against Japan', JP(45)69(Final), 8 May 1945, CAB 84/70, ibid. See also Tarling, *Britain*, pp.45–6.
81. Washington tel. 4673, 5 Jul 1945, F4057/69/23, FO 371/46440, TNA.
82. Sterndale Bennett to Hollis, 10 Jul 1945, ibid.
83. Snyder, Rosenmam and Allen memo., 4 Jul 1945, *FRUS: The Conference of Berlin (The Potsdam Conference)*, 1945, i (Washington: US Government Printing Office, 1960), i, p.228.
84. Diary entry for 4 Jul 1945 in Danchev and Todman (eds.), *War Diaries*, p.702.
85. Churchill to Curtin, 4 Jul 1945 in W. J. Hudson and W. Way (eds.), *DAFP*, 1945, viii (Canberra: Australian Government Publishing Service, 1989), doc. 126.
86. 'Man-Power in the Second Half of 1945', CP(45)53, 29 Jun 1945, CAB 66/67/3, TNA and Cherwell, minute, 12 Jul 1945, CHAR 20/232, Churchill papers, CAC.
87. Brooke, minute, CCS 194th mtg., 17 Jul 1945, Folder CCS 370 Great Britain (7-15-44) Sec.2, Box 82, Geographic File, 1942–5, RG 218, NARA.
88. Marshall to MacArthur, 7 Jul 1945, Folder CCS 370 Great Britain (7-15-44) Sec.1, ibid.
89. 'British Participation in the War Against Japan', United States Chiefs of Staff memo., CCS 889/1, 17 Jul 1945, Folder CCS 370 Great Britain (7-15-44) Sec.2,

ibid. and 'British Participation in the War Against Japan', US Chiefs of Staff memo., CCS 889/2, 18 Jul 1945, ibid.

90. See D. Ford, 'Planning for an Unpredictable War: British Intelligence Assessments and the War Against Japan, 1937–45', *The Journal of Strategic Studies*, 27 (2004), pp.159–60.

91. Diary entries for 17 and 18 Jul 1945 in Danchev and Todman (eds.), *War Diaries*, pp.706–07 and Marshall, minute, CCS 194th mtg., 17 Jul 1945, Folder CCS 370 Great Britain (7-15-44) Sec.2, Box 82, Geographic File, 1942–5, RG 218, NARA.

92. Ehrman, *Atomic Bomb*, pp.256–8.

93. See Rees, *Defeat*, pp.119–20; Baxter, 'In Pursuit', p.270; and Portal, minute, CM(45)18, 7 Aug 1945, CAB 128/1, TNA.

94. Truman to his wife, 20 Jul 1945 in R. Ferrell (ed.), *Dear Bess: The Letters from Harry Truman to Bess Truman 1910–1959* (Columbia: University of Missouri Press, 1998), pp.519–20.

95. J. Byrnes, *Speaking Frankly* (New York: Harper and Bros., 1947), p.208; R. L. Messer, *The End of an Alliance: James F. Byrnes, Roosevelt, Truman, and the Origins of the Cold War* (Chapel Hill: University of North Carolina Press, 1982), p.13; Koshiro, 'Eurasian Eclipse', p.437; W. Miscamble, *From Roosevelt to Truman: Potsdam, Hiroshima, and the Cold War* (Cambridge: Cambridge University Press, 2007), pp.240–9; and Hasegawa, *Racing*, pp.153, 202 & 297–8. Churchill's views can be found in diary entry for 23 July 1945 in Danchev and Todman (eds.), *War Diaries*, p.709 and Churchill, minute for Eden, 23 Jul 1945, FO 954/7, TNA.

96. See, for example, E. Lindley, 'Defeat of Japan: Allies Role in the Pacific', *Washington Post*, 15 Sep 1944; idem, 'Britain's Role Against Japan', *Newsweek*, 25 Sep 1944; 'Let's Lick Japan Ourselves', *Washington Times Herald*, 16 Sep 1944. See also Somerville to Mountbatten, 27 Mar 1945, SMVL 9/2, Somerville papers, CAC, on the poor exposure in the press of the British Pacific Fleet's exploits.

97. D. M. Horner, 'MacArthur, Douglas (1880 – 1964)', *Australian Dictionary of Biography* (Canberra: Australian National University, 2006), www.adb.online.edu.au.

98. Attlee to Chifley in Hudson and Way (eds.), *DAFP*, 1945, viii, doc. 150.

99. 'British Participation in the War Against Japan', British Chiefs of Staff memo., CCS 889/4, 5 Aug 1945, Folder CCS 370 Great Britain (7-15-44) Sec.2, Box 82, Geographic File, 1942–5, RG 218, NARA.

100. See, for example, Dening to Sterndale Bennett, 13 Jul & 2 Aug 1945 in R. Butler and M Pelly (eds.), *DBPO, Series I, i, The Conference at Potsdam 1945* (London: HMSO, 1984), docs. 132 & 599.

101. See 'British Participation in the War Against Japan', Bevin memo., DO(45)3, 8 Aug 1945, PREM 8/24, TNA; and Bevin and Attlee minutes, DO(45)2, 8 Aug 1945, CAB 69/7, ibid.

102. 'British Participation in the War Against Japan', US Chief of Staff memo., CCS 889/5, 9 Aug 1945, Folder CCS 370 Great Britain (7-15-44) Sec.2, Box 82, Geographic File, 1942-5, RG 218, NARA.

103. See Australia (Govt.) tels 197 & 205 of 1 Aug 1945 paraphrased in Australia (Govt.) tel. 305, 21 Sep 1945, 115, A2937/1, NAA.

104. See C. Thorne, *The Issue of War: States, Societies, and the Far Eastern Conflict of 1941–1945* (London: Hamish Hamilton, 1985), p.120; and Dudley, minute, 21 Aug 1945, F5023/69/23, FO 371/46440, TNA.

105. Coles, 'Ernest King', p.128 and Hastings, *Nemesis*, p.436.

106. Mountbatten to MacArthur, 16 Aug 1945, 5/11, Penney papers, KCL.

2 Post-War Planning in Wartime

1. Cavendish-Bentinck, minute, 3 Mar 1945, U890/36/70, FO 371/50774, TNA. Cavendish-Bentinck was also head of the Foreign Office's Services Liaison Department, which had been created in 1943.
2. Tarling, *Britain*, chp. 1.
3. 'Machinery for the Planning and Coordination of Far Eastern Policy', Sterndale Bennett memo., 5 Aug 1944, F4307/955/61, FO 371/41744, TNA and Sterndale Bennett to Dening, 30 Aug 1944, MISC 251(3480), Dening papers, IWM.
4. See minutes in FE(44)1, 15 Nov 1944, CAB 96/5, TNA.
5. Sterndale Bennett, minute, 26 Dec 1944, F5868/168/61, FO 371/41727A, ibid. and 'Organisation for Dealing with Far Eastern Affairs', Sterndale Bennett memo., 8 Jun 1945, F3943/149/61, FO 371/46328, ibid.
6. H. Borton, *Spanning Japan's Modern Century: The Memoirs of Hugh Borton* (Oxford: Lexington Books, 2002), pp.83–4, 93–7, 103–4 & 120–1.
7. Schaller, *Occupation*, p.7.
8. State Department tel. 744, 30 Jan 1945, 890.00/1-1945, Roll 1, C0045, Central Files, The Far East, 1945–9, RG 59, NARA.
9. London tel. 678, 19 Jan 1945, ibid.
10. Sterndale Bennett, minute, 16 Jan 1945, F214/127/61, FO 371/46325, TNA.
11. Gore Booth to Sterndale Bennett, 30 Jul 1945, F4797/4664/61, FO 371/46383, ibid.
12. Grew to Byrnes, 20 Jul 1945, 890.00/7-2045, Roll 1, C0045, Central Files, The Far East, 1945–9, RG 59, NARA and Byrnes to Grew, 25 Jul 1945, ibid.
13. See diary entries for 4 Aug 1944, 5 Oct 1944, 30 Oct 1944, 7 Dec 1944, 20 Dec 1944, 11 Jan 1945 and Cadogan to his wife, 8 Feb 1945 in Dilks(ed.), *Diaries*, pp.670, 675, 685, 688–9, 694–5 & 706.
14. Cadogan, minute, 9 Jun 1944, U6253/758/G, FO 371/40740, TNA. On the torrid history of the Post-Hostilities Planning Committee, see A. Gorst, 'British Military Planning for Postwar Defence' in A. Deighton(ed.), *Britain and the First Cold War* (London: St. Martin's Press, 1990), pp.91–108 and J. Lewis, *Changing Direction: British Military Planning for Post-War Strategic Defence* (London: Frank Cass, 2003), chps. 3 & 4.
15. Ismay to Pownall, 14 Mar 1944, 4/26, Ismay papers, KCL.
16. See K. Sansom, *Sir George Sansom and Japan: A Memoir* (Tallahassee: The Diplomatic Press, 1972), p.138; Hudson's obituary in *The China Quarterly*, 58 (1974), pp.229–30; G. N. Clark, 'Webster, Sir Charles Kingsley', *Oxford Dictionary of National Biography* (Oxford: Oxford University Press, 2004–8), www.oxforddnb.com; Buckley, *Occupation*, pp.23–6; and C. Thorne, 'Chatham House, Whitehall and Far Eastern Issues, 1941–1945', *International Affairs*, 54 (1978), pp.1–29.
17. J. Fenby, *Generalissimo: Chiang Kai-shek and the China He Lost* (London: Free Press, 2005), pp.372–3.
18. Ashton, Bennett and Hamilton (eds.), *DBPO, Series I*, viii, p.x and diary entries for 21 & 23 Nov 1943 in Danchev and Todman (eds.), *War Diaries*, p.477–80.
19. Churchill, minute, 23 Aug 1944, F4046/34/10, FO 371/41581, TNA; K. Sainsbury, *Churchill and Roosevelt at War: The War They Fought and the Peace They Hoped to Make* (London: Macmillan, 1994), pp.160–78; and Hasegawa, *Racing*, p.24.
20. Roosevelt to Mountbatten, 8 Nov 1943, Box 36, Great Britain Diplomatic Files, Roosevelt papers, FDRL; H. J. van de Ven, *War and Nationalism in China*,

1925–1945 (London: Routledge, 2003), pp.61–3; and Spector, *Eagle*, pp.352–3 & chp. 17. Dening's retrospective comments are in Dening to Bevin, 25 Mar 1946, MISC 251(3480), Dening papers, IWM. For the American flirtation with Mao, see M. Sheng, 'America's Lost Chance in China? A Reappraisal of Chinese Communist Policy toward the United States before 1945', *The Australian Journal of Chinese Affairs*, 29 (1993), pp.153–7.

21. Diary entry 24 Nov 1943 in Lord Moran, *Churchill at War 1940–45* (London: Robinson, 2002) p.159.
22. See notes of mtg. between Ogden and the China Association, 5 Apr 1944, CHAS/MCP/45, China Association papers, School of Oriental and African Studies Library, London (SOAS); and 'British Rehabilitation in China', Ogden memo., 19 Aug 1944, F3923/120/10, FO 371/41604, TNA.
23. Chungking tel. 1019, 19 Sep 1944, F4608/120/10, ibid.
24. Ashton, Bennett and Hamilton (eds.), *DBPO, Series I*, viii, p.viii, ix and doc. 1.
25. Eden to Seymour, 6 Dec 1944, F1903/57/10, FO 371/46180, TNA.
26. Thorne, *Allies*, chps. 6, 12, 19 & 26; Spector, *Eagle*, chp.16 and Aldrich, *Intelligence*, chps. 14–15 & 19.
27. 'Anglo-American-Soviet Policy toward China', Vincent memo., 11 Jan 1945, Folder 'Vincent, John Carter', Box 1, Lot File 110, Records of Division of Chinese Affairs, RG 59, NARA; 'China and the Kremlin', Davies memo., 4 Jan 1945, 893.00/1-445, Roll 1, LM 69, Internal Affairs of China 1945–9 (hereafter IAC 1945–9), ibid.; Hurley's comments in Stettinius memo. for Roosevelt, 4 Jan 1945, ibid.; and State Department memo. sent by SWNCC to Joint Chiefs of Staff, 1 Feb 1945, SFE 107–112, Roll 2, T1205, Records of the Subcommittee for the Far East, 1945–8 (SFE 1945–8), RG 353, ibid.
28. Vincent to Ballantine and Grew, 25 Jan 1945, Folder 'Vincent, John Carter', Box 1, Lot File 110, Records of Division of Chinese Affairs, RG 59, ibid.
29. See Xiang, *Recasting*, p.10 and Aldrich, *Intelligence*, pp.7–9, 286–7 & 360–2.
30. J. Osterhammel, 'Imperialism in Transition: British Business and the Chinese Authorities, 1931–37', *The China Quarterly*, 98 (1984), pp.260–86 and Shai, *Britain*, pp.7 & 77–8.
31. Wilkinson to Sansom, 28 Dec 1944, F222/57/10, FO 371/46178, TNA; Sansom to Far Eastern Department, 29 Dec 1944, ibid.; Wallinger to Eden, 24 Jan 1945, F962/57/10, FO 371/46179, ibid. and Chungking tel. 93, 14 Feb 1945, ibid.
32. Shai, *Britain*, pp.69–75; 'British Policy towards China', Sterndale Bennett memo., 2 Mar 1945, F1331/409/10, FO 371/46232, TNA; Sterndale Bennett, minute, 4 Mar 1945, ibid. and Scott, minute, 27 Jan 1945, F492/57/10, FO 371/46178, ibid.
33. Young, minute, ASE(C)(45)1, 7 Mar 1945,F1482/12/10, FO 371/46129, ibid.
34. Hall-Patch, minute, 10 Mar 1945, F1331/409/10, FO 371/46232, ibid.; Cavendish-Bentinck, minute, 13 Mar 1945, ibid. and 'British Commercial Policy in China', Anderson memo., APW(45)51, 5 Apr 1945, F2181/57/10, FO 371/46181, ibid.
35. Shai, *Britain*, p.33.
36. Record of mtg. held at the FO, 3 May 1945, CHAS/MCP/8, China Association papers, SOAS; Mitchell to Butler, 3 Jul 1945, CHAS/MCP/45, ibid. and Sterndale Bennett to Mitchell, 26 Jul 1945, ibid.
37. Quoted from Xiang, *Recasting*, p.30.
38. 'Co-ordination of British Organisations in China', JIC(45)111(0)(Final), 3 Apr 1945, CAB 81/128, TNA.

39. London tel. 2160, 2 Mar 1945, 893.00/3-245, Roll 1, IAC 1945–9, LM 69, RG 59, NARA.
40. Gallman to Stettinius, 9 Apr 1945, 893.00/4-945, ibid. and memo. of conversation held at the FO, 6 Apr 1945, ibid.
41. Churchill note, 11 Apr 1945, CHAR 20/197B, Churchill papers, CAC; Sterndale Bennett to Seymour, 24 Apr 1945, F2263/127/61, FO 371/46325, TNA; and Hurley to Truman, 14 Apr 1945, *FRUS*, 1945, vii, *Far East: China* (Washington: United States Government Printing Office, 1969), pp.329–32.
42. London tel. 3990, 19 Apr 1945, 893.00/4-1945, Roll 1, LM 69, IAC 1945–9, RG 59, NARA; State Department tel. 3269, 26 Apr 1945, 890.00/4-2645, Roll 1, C0045, Central Files, The Far East, 1945–9, ibid.; and London tel. 4326, 28 Apr 1945, 890.00/4/-2685, ibid.
43. Willoughby to Lockhart, 26 May 1945, 893.00/5-2645, Roll 2, LM 69, IAC 1945–9, ibid.
44. R. Sherwood, *The White House Paper of Harry L. Hopkins*, ii, *January 1942–July 1945* (London: Eyre & Spottiswoode, 1949), pp.891–3 & 903.
45. Ashton, Bennett and Hamilton(eds.), *DBPO, Series I*, viii, p.2.
46. Hayes to Seymour and Carton de Wiart, 26 Jul 1945, WO 208/291, TNA.
47. Hurley's remarks in Leahy to Stettinius, 29 May 1945, 893.00/5-2945, Roll 2, LM 69, IAC 1945–9, RG 59, NARA.
48. 'Politico-Military Problems in the Far East: Treatment by U.S. Occupation Forces of Special Areas: Hong Kong', SWNCC 111/2, 14 Jun 1945, SFE 107–112, Roll 2, T1205, SFE 1945–8, RG 353, ibid.
49. See 'The Future of Korea', FO memo., 8 Sep 1945, F6911/2426/23, FO 371/46476, TNA for these pre-war trading figures.
50. J. Matray, *The Reluctant Crusade: American Foreign Policy in Korea, 1941–1950* (Honolulu: University of Hawaii Press, 1985), pp.17–18; and record of discussion between Sansom, Hornbeck and Clarke, 13 Oct 1943, F5471/723/23, FO 371/35956, TNA.
51. Borton, *Spanning*, pp.122–3.
52. P. Lowe, *The Origins of the Korean War* (London: Longman, 1997), pp.7–12.
53. MacDermot, minute, 1 Aug 1944, F3299/102/23, FO 371/41801, TNA and Sterndale Bennett to Allison, 4 Sep 1944, ibid.
54. Hudson, minute, 3 Nov 1943, F5471/723/23, FO 371/35956, ibid.
55. Harriman and Abel, *Special Envoy*, pp.261–2 & 275 and Lowe, *Origins*, p.14.
56. The committee was composed principally of Toynbee (chairman), Hudson, Charles Webster and Sir Paul Butler who served extensively in East Asia during the First World War and inter-war periods.
57. 'Korea: Political Problems: Provisional Government', area committee memo., 4 May 1944, *FRUS*, 1944, iii, pp.1240–1.
58. E. van Ree, *Socialism in One Zone: Stalin's Policy in Korea, 1945–1947* (Oxford: Berg Publishers, 1989), p.37.
59. W. Leahy, *I Was There: The Personal Story of the Chief of Staff to Presidents Roosevelt and Truman Based on Notes and Diaries Made at the Time* (London: Gollancz, 1950), pp.478–9.
60. Webster, minute, 27 Dec 1944, F6012/102/23, FO 371/41801, TNA.
61. 'Future of Korea', Research Department memo., 20 Dec 1944, ibid.
62. Sterndale Bennett, minute, 8 Jan 1945, ibid.
63. Ward, minute, 10 Jan 1945, ibid. and Jebb, minute, 12 Jan 1945, ibid.
64. Butler, minute, 22 Jan 1945, ibid.

65. Diary entry for 13 Jan 1945, Webster diary, x, Webster papers, Archives, London School of Economics and Political Science, University of London (LSE).
66. Roosevelt-Stalin mtg., 8 Feb 1945, *FRUS: The Conference at Malta and Yalta, 1945* (Washington: United States Government Printing Office, 1955), pp.766–71.
67. Rhee, *Socialism*, pp.38–40; Earl of Avon, *Memoirs*, p.438; Kimball, *Forged in War*, p.314; Weathersby, 'Soviet Aims', p.7; and R. Slusser, 'Soviet Far Eastern Policy, 1945–50: Soviet Goals in Korea' in Y. Nagai and A. Iriye (eds.), *The Origins of the Cold War in Asia* (New York: Columbia University Press, 1977), pp.128–30.
68. Harriman and Abel, *Special Envoy*, p.471 and Sherwood, *Hopkins*, ii, p.892.
69. M. Paul, 'Diplomacy Delayed: The Atomic Bomb and the Division of Korea, 1945' in B. Cumings (ed.), *Child of Conflict: The Korean–American Relationship, 1943–1953* (London: University of Washington Press, 1983), pp.67–91; J. Matray, 'Captive of the Cold War: The Decision to Divide Korea at the 38th Parallel', *Pacific Historical Review*, 50 (1981), pp.145–68.
70. Record of 6th mtg. at Potsdam, 22 Jul 1945 in Butler and Pelly (eds.), *DBPO*, *Series I*, i, doc. 226; and Ree, *Socialism*, pp.38–47.
71. 'United Nations Plan for Organising Peace', Eden memo., WP(43)300, 7 Jul 1943, CAB 66/38, TNA. For Webster's influence, see 'Regional Organisation', Webster memo., 17 Jun 1943, Webster Papers, 11/8, LSE.
72. R. V. A. Janssens, *'What Future for Japan?' U.S. Wartime Planning for the Post-war Era, 1942–1945* (Amsterdam: Rodopi, 1995), pp.80–2; G. Sansom, *Postwar Relations with Japan* (New York: Institute of Pacific Relations, 1942), pp.6 & 12–13; and idem, *Japan* (London: H. Milford: Oxford University Press, 1944), pp.29–32.
73. See, for example, de la Mare, minute, 28 Mar 1944 and Blackburn, minute, 29 Mar 1944, F1461/168/61, FO 371/41727A, TNA after reading a pamphlet issued by the American Universities Committee on Post-War International Problems, entitled *Post-War Treatment of Japan*. Regarding the Post-Hostilities Planning Committee. See also Butler, minute, 17 Apr 1944, ibid.; Sterndale Bennett, minute, 10 Oct 1944, U7658/748/G, FO 371/40741A, ibid.; and J. Embree, 'Military Occupation of Japan', *Far Eastern Survey*, 13 (1944), pp.173–6.
74. Janssens, *'What Future for Japan?'*, pp.65–8, 80 & 144.
75. See 'Japan: Occupation and Military Government', Area Committee memo., 13 Mar 1944, *FRUS*, 1944, v, *The Near East, South Asia, and Africa, The Far East* (Washington: United States Government Printing Office, 1965), pp.1202–5 and 'Japan: The Post-War Objectives of the United States in Regard to Japan', Area Committee memo., 17 Apr 1944, *FRUS*, 1944, iii, pp.1230–1.
76. Sterndale Bennett to Anderson, 2 Mar 1945 and enclosure, F1834/364/23, FO 371/46447, TNA.
77. Anderson to Sterndale Bennett, 21 Mar 1945, ibid.
78. Ward, minute, 10 Apr 1945, ibid.
79. Cavendish-Bentinck, minute, 11 Apr 1945, ibid.
80. 'Occupation and Control of Japan', Far Eastern Department revised memo., Apr 1945, ibid.
81. 'Establishment of a Far Eastern Advisory Commission', SWNCC 65/2, 30 Apr 1945, SFE 107–112, Roll 2, T1205, SFE 1945–8, RG 353, NARA.
82. King memo, 22 Mar 1945, ibid. and Train memo., undated, ibid.
83. Borton, *Spanning*, pp.125–30 and Schaller, *Occupation*, pp.7–8.
84. See minutes in SWNCC (SFE), 18th mtg., 16 Apr 1945, Roll 1, T1198, Minutes of Meetings of the Subcommittee for the Far East, 1945–7, RG 353, NARA.

85. For this approach, see 'National Composition of Forces to Occupy Japan Proper in the Post-Defeat Period', SWNCC 70/2, 23 Jun 1945, SFE 100–106, Roll 1, T1205, SFE 1945–8, ibid.
86. Sterndale Bennett, minute, 27 Apr 1945, F1834/364/23, FO 371/46447, TNA.
87. Sargent's view is recorded in Sterndale Bennett, minute, 30 Apr 1945, ibid.
88. Sansom to Sterndale Bennett, 3 May 1945, F2774/364/23, ibid.; Eden, minute for Churchill, 26 May 1945, F3220/364/23, FO 371/46447, ibid. and Churchill, minute for Eden, 30 May 1945, ibid.
89. Washington tels 3754–5, 29–30 May 1945, F3238/364/23, ibid. See also memo. by the office of the chief of naval operations, 1 May 1945, *FRUS*, 1945, vi, p.536 and report by the SWNCC Subcommittee for the Far East, 11 Jun 1945, ibid., pp.549–54.
90. Foulds, minute, 31 May 1945, F3220/364/23, FO 371/46447, TNA and Cadogan to Machtig, 4 Jul 1945, F3766/364/23, ibid.
91. Sansom, minutes, 28 & 29 May 1945, F3620/364/23, ibid. and Schaller, *Occupation*, pp.10–13.
92. 'Policy towards Japan', Sansom memo., 20 Jun 1945, F3768/364/23, FO 371/46447, TNA.
93. Allison to Stettinius, 22 Jun 1945, 890.00/5-2245, Roll 1, C0045, Central Files, The Far East, 1945–9, RG 59, NARA.
94. There remain reservations about Sansom's stature within the British government and commentators highlight the fact that he was not asked to travel to Potsdam to advise ministers. See Buckley, *Occupation*, pp.10–13 and G. Daniels, 'Sir George Sansom: Pre-eminent Diplomat and Historian' in H. Cortazzi (ed.), *British Envoys in Japan, 1859–1972* (Folkestone: Global Oriental, 2004), p.255–6.
95. 'An Estimate of Conditions in Asia and the Pacific at the Close of the War in the Far East and the Objectives and Policies of the United States', State Department policy paper, 22 Jun 1945, *FRUS*, 1945, vi, p.579.
96. X. Liu, *A Partnership for Disorder: China, the United States, and Their Policies for the Postwar Disposition of the Japanese Empire, 1941–1945* (Cambridge: Cambridge University Press, 1996), pp.30–1, 48–9 & 53–4 and Thorne, *Issue*, p.136.
97. 'National Composition of Forces to Occupy Japan Proper in the Post-Defeat Period', SWNCC 70/2, 23 Jun 1945, SFE 10–106, Roll 1, T1205, SFE 1945–8, RG 353, NARA and 'National Composition of Occupation Forces for Japan Proper', Joint Staff Planners memo., JPS 674/3, 27 Jun 1945, ibid.
98. Sterndale Bennett to Hollis, 4 Jul 1945, F3998/364/23, FO 371/46447, TNA and extract from COS(45)175, 12 Jul 1945, ibid.
99. Sterndale Bennett, minute, 21 Jul 1945, F4396/364/23, ibid.
100. Foulds to Sterndale Bennett, 24 Jul 1945, ibid.; FO tel. 7943, 29 Jul 1945, ibid.; and for American press allegations, de la Mare, minute, 17 Jul 1945, F4783/364/23, ibid.
101. Hasegawa, *Racing*, pp.83 & 86.
102. Combined Chiefs of Staff minutes, 9 Feb 1945, *FRUS*, 1944, *Malta and Yalta*, p.826.
103. Hudson, minute, 13 Jan 1944, F931/94/23, FO 371/41793, TNA; Foulds, minute, 10 Nov 1944, F5234/94/23, FO 371/41794, ibid.; Sterndale Bennett, minute, 22 Jun 1945, F3620/364/23, FO 371/46447, ibid.; and 'The Japanese Attitude to Unconditional Surrender', JIC(45)204(0)(Final), 27 Jun 1945, CAB 81/129, ibid.
104. R. Butow, *Japan's Decision to Surrender* (Stanford: Stanford University Press, 1954), pp.96–102 and L. Freedman and S. Dockrill, 'Hiroshima: A Strategy of Shock' in

S. Dockrill (ed.), *From Pearl Harbor to Hiroshima: The Second World War in Asia and the Pacific, 1941–45* (London: St. Martin's Press, 1994), p.201.

105. Grew to Stettinius, 3 Jan 1945, *FRUS*, 1945, vi, *The British Commonwealth, The Far East* (Washington: US Government Printing Office, 1969), p.516; Sansom, minutes, 28 & 29 May 1945, F3620/364/23, FO 371/46447, TNA; Truman, minute, mtg. held at the White House, 18 Jun 1945, Folder CCS 334 JCS meetings 186–94 (2-2-45), Box 198, Central Decimal File, 1942–5, RG 218, NARA; and Schaller, *Occupation*, pp.15–16.

106. Marshall, minute, JCS 196th mtg., 17 Jul 1945, Folder CCS334 JCS mtgs 195–203 (7-2-45), Box 198, Central Decimal File 1942–5, RG218, NARA; McFarland memo. for the Joint Chiefs of Staff, 17 Jul 1945, Folder CCS 387 Japan (5-9-45), Box 136, Geographic File, 1942–5, ibid.; Ismay to Churchill, 17 Jul 1945, PREM 3/397/5, TNA and Churchill conversation with Truman, 18 Jul 1945 in Butler and Pelly(eds.), *DBPO, Series I*, i, doc. 184.

107. Foulds to Sterndale Bennett, 24 Jul 1945, F4396/364/23, FO 371/46447, TNA; FO tel. 7943, 29 Jul 1945, ibid.; Marshall, minute, JCS 196th mtg., 17 Jul 1945, Folder CCS 387 Japan (5-9-45), Box 136, Geographic File, 1942–5, RG218, NARA; and Hasegawa, *Racing*, p.156.

108. Balfour to Dunn, 2 Aug 1945, *FRUS*, 1945, vi, pp.582–84.

109. Australian (Govt.) tel. 209, 1 Aug 1945, F4762/364/23, FO 371/46447, TNA.

110. Bevin, minute, CM(45)9, 9 Aug 1945, CAB 128/1, ibid.

3   Japan Surrenders

1. COS tel. COSSEA 314, 13 Aug 1945, F5399/630/23, FO 371/46454, TNA; 'British Action Upon Japanese Surrender', US Chiefs of Staff memo., CCS 901/5, 17 Aug 1945, Folder CCS 386.2 Japan (4-9-45) Sec. 4, Box 136, Geographic File 1942–5, RG 218, NARA; and War Department tel. WARX 47513, 10 Aug 1945, 893.00/11–1345, Roll 2, LM 69, IAC 1945–9, RG 59, ibid.

2. See SACSEA tel. SEACOS 461, 3 Sep 1945, F6417/630/23, FO 371/46457, TNA; Tarling, *Britain*, pp.53–5; and Dennis, *Troubled Days*, pp.20–1.

3. Evatt to Addison, 9 Aug 1945 in Hudson and Way (eds.), *DAFP*, 1945, viii, doc. 164.

4. Attlee and Bevin reply to Winant, 10 Aug 1945, F4975/630/23, FO 371/46453, TNA; FO tel. 8294, 11 Aug 1945, F4974/630/23, ibid.; diary entry for 11 Aug 1945 in Dilks(ed.), *Diaries*, p.781.; and Australian legation to State Department, 13 Aug 1945, *FRUS*, 1945, vi, pp.650–5.

5. Truman to Attlee, Chiang and Stalin, 11 Aug 1945, Folder CCS 387 Japan (2-7-45) Sec. 2, Box 137, Geographic File 1942-5, RG 218, NARA; Moscow tels 3522, 3524 & 3525, 11 Aug 1945, F4977/630/23, FO 371/46453, TNA; and Stalin to Truman, 12 Aug 1945, *FRUS*, 1945, vi, p.643.

6. Washington tel. 5579, 13 Aug 1945, F5510/630/23, FO 371/46453, TNA.

7. Diary entries for 11 and 14 Aug 1945 in P. Dixon, *Double Diploma: The Life of Sir Pierson Dixon: Don and Diplomat* (London: Hutchinson, 1968), pp.180–1.

8. Diary entry for 11 Aug 1945 in Dilks(ed.), *Diaries*, p.781.

9. COS tel. COSSEA 314, 13 Aug 1945, F5399/630/23, FO 371/46454, TNA.

10. General Order Number 1 can be found in Truman to MacArthur, 15 Aug 1945, *FRUS*, 1945, vii, pp.530–1. See also Attlee to Truman, 18 Aug 1945, ibid., p.504; and Truman to Attlee, 18 Aug 1945, Folder CCS 386.2 Japan (4-9-45) Sec. 4, Box 137, Geographic File 1942-5, RG 218, NARA.

11. 'Summary of Impressions Received at Manila', Penney memo., 23 Aug 1945, 5/13, Penney papers, KCL; War Department tel. WARX 53785, 23 Aug 1945, Folder CCS 386.2 Japan (4-9-45) Sec. 5, Box 136, Geographic File 1942–5, RG 218, NARA; MacArthur to War Department, tel. CX 36419, 24 Aug 1945, ibid.; Chungking tel. 931, 24 Aug 1945, F5714/1147/10, FO 371/46253, TNA; and Wedemeyer to War Department, tel. CFB 6222, 28 Aug 1945, Folder CCS 387 Japan (2-7-45) Sec. 3, Box 137, Geographic File 1942-5, RG 218, NARA.

12. SACSEA tel. SEACOS 448, 20 Aug 1945 (rec'd 21 Aug), Folder CCS 386.2 Japan (4-9-45) Sec. 4, ibid.; and 'British Action in Southeast Asia Command', Chiefs of Staff memo., CCS901/8, 21 Aug 1945, ibid.

13. Penney to his wife, 25 Aug 1945, 4/33, Penney papers, KCL; Kandy tel. 369, 20 Aug 1945, F5458/630/23, FO 371/46454, TNA; and minutes in COS(45)203, 22 Aug 1945, CAB 79/38, ibid. On the OSS mission to Korea, see Evans report, 3 Sep 1945, Folder 6, Box 223, Entry 210, RG 226, NARA.

14. FO tel. 875, 13 Aug 1945, F5193/917/10, FO 436/14, TNA; Chungking tel. 861, 17 Aug 1945, F5234/917/10, ibid.; and FO tel. 940, 20 Aug 1945, ibid.

15. Ogden autobiography, PPMS 47, File 145, Ogden papers, SOAS.

16. Wallinger to Sterndale Bennett, 15 Aug 1945, F6489/186/10, FO 436/14, TNA.

17. Carton de Wiart to Ismay, 23 Aug 1945, PREM 8/485, ibid.

18. Chungking tel. 932, 24 Aug 1945, F6652/917/10, FO 436/14, ibid.; FO tel. 999, 27 Aug 1945, F5751/22/510, ibid.; and Chungking tel. 996, 1 Sep 1945, F6196/225/10, ibid.

19. D. Heinzig, *The Soviet Union and Communist China 1945–1950: The Arduous Road to the Alliance* (London: M. E. Sharpe, 2003), pp.54–5 and Harriman and Abel, *Special Envoy*, pp.472–3 & 495–7. For the British justification of returning to Hong Kong, see Alexander to Attlee, 4 Sep 1945, F6859/1147/10, FO 371/46254, TNA; Cadogan, minute, 6 Sep 1945, ibid.; and Bevin, minute, DO(45)5, 7 Sep 1945, CAB 69/7, ibid.

20. Wedemeyer to Marshall, 19 Aug 1945, *FRUS*, 1945, vii, pp.531–4 and Westad, *Cold War*, pp.101–2.

21. Hurley to Byrnes, 16 Aug 1945, *FRUS*, 1945, vii, pp.445–6; S. Goncharov, Lewis and Litai, *Uncertain Partners*, pp.7–10; Hunt, *Genesis*, pp.162–3; and Jian, *Mao's China*, pp.28–30. On the British position, see 'British Policy Towards China', Sterndale Bennett memo., 2 Mar 1945, F1331/409/10, FO 371/46232, TNA and Prideaux-Brune, minute, 13 Jun 1945, F3065/36/10, FO371/46170, ibid.

22. Wedemeyer to War Department, tel. CFBX 4352, 12 Aug 1945, Folder CCS 386.2 Japan (4-9-45) Sec. 4, Box 136, Geographic File 1942-5, RG 218, NARA; Wedemeyer to War Department, tel. CFBX 4580, 14 Aug 1945, ibid.; and MacArthur to War Department, tel. CX 33449, 14 Aug 1945, ibid.

23. War Department to MacArthur, Nimitz and Wedemeyer, tel. WARX 49334, 14 Aug 1945, ibid.; McFarland memo. for SWNCC, 14 Aug 1945, Folder CCS 387 Japan (2-7-45) Sec. 2, Box 137, ibid.; Marshall to MacArthur, 14 Aug 1945, ibid.; War Department to MacArthur, Nimitz and Wedemeyer, tel. WARX 50181, 15 Aug 1945, Folder CCS 386.2 Japan (4-9-45) Sec. 4, ibid.; and Hasegawa, *Racing*, pp.267–75.

24. Price to Sterndale Bennett, 20 Aug 1945, F5586/364/23, FO 371/46448, TNA; Peck to Sterndale Bennett, 26 Aug 1945, F5939/364/23, ibid.; Dominions Office tel. 1572, 1 Sep 1945, F5413/364/23, ibid.; Churchill to Peck, 27 Aug 1945, PREM

8/28, ibid.; and Australia (Govt.) tel. 255, 28 Aug 1945 in Hudson and Way (eds.), *DAFP*, 1945, viii, doc. 221.

25. Dunn to Byrnes, 30 Aug 1945, Roll 1, T1205, SFE 100–106, SFE 1945–8, RG 353, NARA.
26. Marshall to MacArthur, 15 Aug 1945, Folder CCS 387 Japan (2-7-45) Sec. 2, Box 137, Geographic File 1942–5, RG 218, ibid.
27. Australia (Govt.) tel. 245, 21 Aug 1945, 115, A2937/1, NAA; Attlee to Chifley, 25 Aug 1945, in Hudson and Way (eds.), *DAFP*, 1945, viii, ibid., doc. 217.
28. War Department tel. WARX 51397, 18 Aug 1945, Folder CCS 387 Japan (2-7-45) Sec. 3, Box 137, Geographic File 1942–5, RG 218, NARA.
29. See Bruce to Chifley, 25 Aug 1945; Attlee to Chifley, 25 Aug 1945; and Chifley to Attlee, 27 Aug 1945 in Hudson and Way (eds.), *DAFP*, 1945, viii, docs. 216–17 & 219.
30. COS to SACSEA, tel. COSSEA 314, 13 Aug 1945, F5399/630/23, FO 371/46454, TNA; 'British Action Upon Japanese Surrender', US Chiefs of Staff memo., CCS 901/5, 17 Aug 1945, Folder CCS 386.2 Japan (4-9-45) Sec. 4, Box 136, Geographic File 1942-5, RG 218, NARA; 'British Action upon Japanese Surrender', Joint Staff Planners report, JCS 1464/1, 16 Aug 1945, CCS 901/5, 17 Aug 1945, ibid.; and MacArthur to War Department, tel. 36421, 24 Aug 1945, Folder CCS 386.2 Japan (4-9-45) Sec. 5, ibid.
31. Dominions Office tel. 170, 13 Aug 1945, PREM 8/27, TNA; and Australia (Govt.) tel. 245, 21 Aug 1945 in Hudson and Way (eds.), *DAFP*, 1945, viii, doc. 207.
32. See minutes in COS(45)210, 30 Aug 1945, CAB 79/38, TNA.
33. Attlee to Chifley, 1 Sep 1945 in Hudson and Way (eds.), *DAFP*, 1945, viii, doc. 230 and MacArthur to War Department, tel. 36421, 24 Aug 1945, Folder CCS 386.2 Japan (4-9-45) Sec. 5, Box 136, Geographic File 1942–5, RG 218, NARA.
34. McFarland memo. for SWNCC, 14 Aug 1945, Folder CCS 387 Japan (2-7-45) Sec. 2, Box 137, Geographic File 1942–5, RG 218, NARA.
35. 'British Action Upon Japanese Surrender', memo by US Chiefs of Staff, CCS 901/5, 17 Aug 1945, Folder CCS 386.2 Japan (4-9-45) Sec. 4, Box 136, ibid.; Churchill confirmed to Attlee he had not discussed Korea at Yalta. Peck to Sterndale Bennett, 26 Aug 1945, F5586/364/23, FO 371/46448, TNA; Churchill to Peck, 27 Aug 1945, PREM 8/28, ibid. See also 'Occupational Forces for Japan and Korea', JP(45)217(Final), 28 Aug 1945, CAB 79/38, ibid.; and COS tel. COS(W)85, 30 Aug 1945, F6257/2426/23, FO 371/46476, ibid.
36. J. Gaddis, *We Now Know: Rethinking Cold War History* (Oxford: Clarendon, 1998), pp.57–8; Ree, Socialism, p.67; and MacArthur to War Department, tel. 36421, 24 Aug 1945, Folder CCS 386.2 Japan (4-9-45) Sec. 5, Box 136, Geographic File 1942-5, RG 218, NARA.
37. 'International Agreements as to Occupation of Korea', SWNCC 176/1, 24 Aug 1945, ibid.
38. J. Young, *Britain and the World in the Twentieth Century* (London: Arnold, 1997), pp.145–6.
39. Washington tel. 1038, 23 Aug 1945, AN2560/22/45, FO 371/44557, TNA.
40. Donnelly, minute, 5 Sep 1945, ibid. and Tarling, *Britain*, pp.51–2.
41. Diary entry for 31 Jul 1945 in Dilks (ed.), *Diaries*, p.778; diary entry for 9 Oct 1945 in Dixon, *Double Diploma*, p.196; and P. Boyle, 'The British Foreign Office View of Soviet-American Relations, 1945-46', *Diplomatic History*, 3 (1979), p.308.

See also A. Bullock, *Ernest Bevin: Foreign Secretary 1945–1951* (London: W. W. Norton, 1983).

42. H. Dalton, *High Tide and After: Memoirs 1945–1960* (London: Frederick Muller, 1962), p.70; diary entry for 17 Oct 1945 in Dalton diary, xxxiii (Jul–Dec 1945), Dalton papers, LSE; and 'Our Overseas Financial Prospects', Dalton note, CP(45)112, 14 Aug 1945, CAB 129/1, TNA.
43. Barnett, *Lost Victory*, pp.43–4.
44. M. Leffler, *A Preponderance of Power: National Security, the Truman Administration, and the Cold War* (Stanford: Stanford University Press, 1992), p.61.
45. R. Pollard, 'The national security state reconsidered: Truman and economic containment, 1945–1950' in M. Lacey (ed.), *The Truman presidency* (Cambridge: Cambridge University Press, 1989), pp.207–8; and J. Gaddis, 'The insecurities of victory: the United States and the perception of the Soviet threat after World War II', in ibid., pp.244–5.
46. Boyle, 'Foreign Office', p.310 and J. Kent, 'British Policy and the Origins of the Cold War' in Leffler and Painter (eds.), *Origins*, pp.156–61.
47. Bevin, minute, 28 Sep 1945, CM(45)36, CAB 128/1, TNA.
48. Sterndale Bennett, minute, 17 Sep 1945, F6911/2426/23, FO 371/46476, ibid.
49. See 'Far Eastern Commission', Sterndale Bennett memo., 29 Sep 1945, F7613/364/23, FO 371/46449, ibid. and Dominions Office tel. 1988, 24 Oct 1945, F8518/364/23, ibid.
50. Hurley to Byrnes, 1 Sep 1945, *FRUS*, 1945, vii, p.545; COS minutes in COS(45)222, 13 Sep 1945, CAB 79/39, TNA; 'British Representation with U.S. Forces at Chinese Ports', US Chiefs of Staff memo., CCS 901/12-13, 15 & 26 Sep 1945, Folder 386.2 Japan (4-9-45) Sec. 5, Box 136, Geographic File 1942–5, RG 218, NARA; COS minutes in COS(45)240, 3 & 9 Oct 1945, CAB 79/40, TNA; and Harcourt to Alexander, 7 Nov 1945, AVAR 5/10/70(c), Alexander papers, CAC.
51. Washington tel. 6196, 13 Sep 1945, F6922/760/10, FO 436/14, TNA.
52. Bevin to Seymour, 17 Sep 1945, F7205/186/10, ibid.
53. FO tel. 1114, 17 Sep 1945, F6182/186/10, ibid.; FO tel. 1222, 30 Sep 1945; and Chungking tel. 1054, 5 Oct 1945, F8592/1147/10, ibid.
54. Harcourt to Alexander, 7 Nov 1945, AVAR 5/10/70(c), Alexander papers, CAC.
55. 'The Economic Importance of Hong Kong', Boehringer memo., 15 Oct 1945, Folder Hong Kong 1945, Box 7, Lot File 110, Records of Division of Chinese Affairs, RG 59, NARA and 'The Policy of the United States in regard to foreign enclaves in China', Secretary's staff committee, 18 Dec 1945, ibid.
56. *The Times*, 20 Oct 1945.
57. FO tel. 1114, 17 Sep 1945, F6182/186/10, FO 436/10, TNA; Seymour to Sterndale Bennett, 1 Nov 1945, F10179/186/10, FO 371/46215, ibid.; and Xiang, *Recasting*, pp.58–9. The US decision to halt aid to British internment camps is in diary entries for 22 & 27 Oct 1945, 3/4, Jacobs-Larkcom papers, KCL. See also China Association general committee mtg., 5 Dec 1945, CHAS/MCP/8, China Association papers, SOAS.
58. 'Internal Situation in China', JIC(45)314(Final), 10 Nov 1945, F10436/186/10, FO 371/46215, TNA.
59. Wedemeyer to War Department, tel. CM-IN 22159, 27 Sep 1945, 893.00/11-1345, Roll 2, LM 69, IAC 1945-9, RG 59, NARA; War Department tel. WARX 77563, 20 Oct 1945, ibid.; Wedemeyer to War Department, tel. CM-IN 12147, 26 Oct 1945, ibid.; War Department tel. WARX 80362, 1 Nov 1945, ibid.;

and minutes of mtg. of Secretaries of State, War and Navy, 6 Nov 1945, 893.00/11-645, ibid.

60. 'U.S. Military Advisory Group to China', JCS 1330/10, 22 Oct 1945, Roll 5, T1205, SFE 119-124, SFE 1945-8, RG 353, ibid.; Vincent memo., 12 Nov 1945, *FRUS*, 1945, vii, pp.614–17; 'Factors Affecting Inactivation of China Theater', Freeman Matthews memo., 13 Nov 1945, 893.00/11-1345, Roll 2, IAC 1945–9, RG 59, NARA; and Vincent to Acheson, 15 Nov 1945, 893.00/11-1545, Roll 2, ibid. On Vincent, see G. May, *China Scapegoat: The Diplomatic Ordeal of John Carter Vincent* (Washington: New Republic Books, 1979), chps. 2 & 3.

61. 'The Situation in China', Drumright memo., 16 Nov 1945, Folder 306.001 'US Policy Toward China Jul-Dec 1945', Box 8, Lot File 110, Records of Division of Chinese Affairs, RG 59, NARA and Vincent to Acheson and Cohen, 17 Nov 1945, ibid.

62. Chungking tel. 1291, 16 Oct 1945, WO 208/206, TNA; London tel. 11385, 31 Oct 1945, 893.00/10-3145, Roll 2, LM 69, IAC, 1945-9, RG 59, NARA; and London tel. 11934, 14 Nov 1945, 893.00/11-1445, ibid. See also Spector, *Ruins*, pp.32–3.

63. Goncharov, Lewis and Litai, *Uncertain Partners*, p.11; Westad, *Cold War*, pp.83–92; and Jian, *Mao's China*, p.31. For British intelligence reaction to the events in Manchuria, see Chungking tel. 1158, 22 Sep 1945, WO 208/206, TNA; 'China', CX report, 22 Sep 1945, WO 208/4399, ibid.; SACSEA tel. SAC 25335, 15 Oct 1945, ibid.; London tel. 6315, 19 Oct 1945, WO 208/206, ibid.; and 'Internal Situation in China', JIC(45)314(Final), 10 Nov 1945, F10436/186/10, FO 371/46215, ibid.

64. Wedemeyer to Eisenhower, 20 Nov 1945, *FRUS*, 1945, vii, pp.650–60.

65. Hurley to Truman, 26 Nov 1945, Folder 030.003, 'Hurley Mission 1945-6', Box 1, Lot File 110, Records of Division of Chinese Affairs, RG 59, NARA; Spector, *Ruins*, pp.70–1; Xiang, *Recasting*, pp.52–4 and D. Acheson, *Present at the Creation: My Years in the State Department* (London: W. W. Norton & Co., 1969), pp.133–4.

66. Hayes to Wallinger, 26 Nov 1945, F11795/1147/10, FO 436/14, TNA; Chungking tel. 1206, 30 Nov 1945, ibid.; London tel. 12430, 28 Nov 1945, 893.00/11-2845, Roll 3, LM69, IAC 1945–9, RG 59, NARA; and Xiang, *Recasting*, p.54.

67. Vincent memo., 9 Dec 1945, 893.00/11-12-945, Roll 3, LM 69, IAC 1945–9, RG 59, NARA; Spector, *Ruins*, pp.71–2; Leffler, *Preponderance*, pp.86–7; and Qing, *Allies*, pp.61–2.

68. 'United States Initial Post-Defeat Policy Relating to Japan', SWNCC 150/4, 6 Sep 1945, Roll 2, T1205, SFE 107–112, SFE 1945–8, RG 353, NARA.

69. Sterndale Bennett, minute, 23 Sep 1945, F7331/364/23, FO 371/46449, TNA and Allison to Vincent, 28 Sep 1945, 890.00/9-2845, Roll 1, C0045, Central Files, The Far East, 1945–9, RG 59, NARA.

70. Foulds, minute, 23 Aug 1945, F5559/584/61, FO 371/46347, TNA and Hudson, minute, 1 Sep 1945, F6312/584/61, ibid.

71. Atcheson to Seymour, 10 Nov 1945, SEYR 3/4, Seymour papers, CAC.

72. M. Schaller, *Altered States: The United States and Japan Since the Occupation* (Oxford: Oxford University Press, 1997), p.8 and J. Dower, *Embracing Defeat: Japan in the Aftermath of World War II* (London: Allen Lane, 1999), pp.47–8.

73. Sterndale Bennett, minute, 11 Sep 1945, F6699/364/23, FO 371/46449, TNA.

74. Sansom to Sterndale Bennett, 11 Sep 1945, F7150/630/23, FO 371/46459, ibid.

75. Atcheson to Acheson, 7 Nov 1945, *FRUS*, 1945, vi, pp.838–41.

76. P. Lowe, 'Great Britain and Douglas MacArthur: War and Peace in the Pacific and Asia, 1941–1951' in K. G. Robertson (ed.), *War, Resistance and Intelligence: Essays*

in Honour of M. R. D. Foot (Barnsley: Leo Cooper, 1999), pp.54–5; and Schaller, *Altered*, pp.7–10.

77. Gairdner, minute, COS(45)249, 12 Oct 1945, CAB 79/40, TNA and Chifley to Evatt, 31 Oct 1945 in Hudson and Way (eds.), *DAFP*, 1945, viii, doc. 353.

78. The Australians also pressed for the establishment of a Joint Chiefs of Staff in Australia. See Evatt to Chifley and Beasley, 14 Sep 1945, 115, A2937/1, NAA; Chifley to Attlee, 21 Sep 1945, ibid.; COS minutes in COS(45)232, 24 Sep 1945, CAB 79/39, TNA and COS minutes in COS(45)249,12 Oct 1945, CAB 79/40, ibid. On the Australian–Americans negotiations over BCOF's role, see Anderson to Northcott, 13 Nov 1945, 843/13, A5954/69, NAA; Chifley to Evatt, 29 Nov 1945, ibid.; Evatt and Levarack to Chifley, 30 Nov 1945, ibid.; Northcott to Shedden, 15 Dec 1945, ibid.; Beasley memo., 15 Dec 1945, ibid.; and Australia (Govt.) tel. 462, 19 Dec 1945. For Fraser's remarks, see New Zealand (Govt.) tel. 221, 19 Dec 1945, ibid. See also P. Bates, *Japan and the British Commonwealth Occupation Force, 1946–52* (London: Brassey's, 1993).

79. Gairdner, minute, COS(45)250, 15 Oct 1945, CAB 79/40, TNA and Buckley, *Occupation*, p.72.

80. FO tel. 11726, 22 Nov 1945, F11569/8564/23, FO 371/46526, TNA; Sterndale Bennett, minute, 4 Dec 1945, ibid.; and H. Cortazzi (ed.), *Japan Experiences: Fifty Years, One Hundred Views: Post-War Japan through British Eyes, 1945–2000* (Surrey: Japan Library, 2001), p.7.

81. Cadogan, minute, 11 Sep 1945, F6699/364/23, FO 371/46449, TNA and Addison, minute, CM(45)35, 25th Sep 1945, CAB 128/1, ibid.

82. Dixon, minute, 16 Sep 1945, F7090/364/23, FO 371/46449, ibid.

83. Bevin to Byrnes, 28 Sep 1945, *FRUS*, 1945, vi, p.725; Byrnes to Bevin, 29 Sep 1945, ibid., p.726; Byrnes to Molotov, 29 Sep 1945, ibid., pp.726–7.

84. 'Far Eastern Commission', Sterndale Bennett memo., 29 Sep 1945, F7613/364/23, FO 371/46449, TNA.

85. Evatt to Bevin, 25 Sep 1945, 115, A2937/1, NAA.

86. Sargent, minute, 9 Oct 1945, N13432/18/38, FO 371/47856, TNA; Moscow tel. 4640, 21 Oct 1945, F8717/1665/61, FO 371/46362, ibid.; Harriman to Byrnes, 16 Oct 1945, *FRUS*, 1945, vi, pp.755–6; Page memo., 25 Oct 1945, ibid., pp.787–95; Harriman to Byrnes, 30 Oct 1945, ibid., pp.808–9; Harriman to Byrnes, 13 Nov 1945, ibid., pp.849–51; 'Far Eastern Advisory Commission', SWNCC 65/12, 18 Oct 1945, Roll 2, T1205, SFE 107-112, SFE 1945-8, RG 353, NARA; War Department tel. WAR 77672, 21 Oct 1945, ibid.; MacArthur to War Department, tel. CA 53682, 22 Oct 1945, ibid.; and Schaller, *Occupation*, pp.59–60.

87. Moscow tel. no. 4759, 30 Oct 1945, F9237/364/23, FO 371/46451, TNA and Harriman to Byrnes, 29 Oct 1945, *FRUS*, 1945, vi, pp.804–6.

88. Moscow tel. 3664, 26 Oct 1945, Roll 7, C044, US State Department Special Files: Northeast Asia, 1943–56, RG59, NARA; and minutes of mtg. of Secretaries of State, War and Navy, 6 Nov 1945, 893.00/11-645, Roll 2, LM 69, IAC 1945–9, ibid.

89. Harriman to Byrnes, 6 Nov 1945, *FRUS*, 1945, vi, pp.831–2 and Moscow tel. no. 4955, 14 Nov 1945, F10102/364/23, FO 371/46451, TNA; Cadogan, minute, 16 Nov 1945, ibid.; and Bevin, minute, 17 Nov 1945, ibid. Sterndale Bennett, minute, 19 Nov 1945, ibid.; Cadogan, minute 19 Nov 1945, ibid.; and Sterndale Bennett, minute, 22 Nov 1945, ibid.

90. 'Future of Korea', FO memo., 8 Sep 1945, F6911/2426/23, FO 371/46476, ibid.

91. See minutes in SWNCC 39–40th mtgs, 7 & 11 Sep 1945, Roll 1, T1198, minutes of meetings of the Subcommittee of the Far East, 1945-7, RG 353, NARA and 'Structure and Composition of Civil Affairs Administration in Korea', SWNCC 79/1, 27 Sep 1945, Roll 5, T1205, SFE 119-124, SFE 1945–8, ibid.
92. Washington tel. 6193, 13 Sep 1945, F6911/2426/23, FO 371/46476, TNA and Vincent to Ballantine, 13 Sep 1945, Folder Korea 1945–6, Box 7, Lot File 110, Records of Division of Chinese Affairs, RG 59, NARA.
93. Foulds, minute, 15 Sep 1945, F6911/2426/23, FO 371/46476, TNA.
94. Sterndale Bennett, minutes, 17 & 22 Sep 1945, ibid.; Ward, minute, 17 Sep 1945, ibid.; Broadmead, minute 20 Sep 1945, ibid.; Cadogan, minute, 22 Sep 1945, ibid.; and Bevin, minute, n.d., ibid. The draft statement prepared for Truman (released 18 Sep 1945) is in *FRUS*, 1945, vi, p.1048. For Dominion Office views, see James, minute, 12 Oct 1945, DO 35/2003, TNA; Shannon, minute, 13 Oct 1945, ibid.; Stephenson to Addison, 17 Oct 1945, ibid.; and Addison, minute, 19 Oct 1945, ibid. See also minutes of 25 Oct 1945 in FE(M)(45)3, CAB 96/9, ibid. for the ministerial decision.
95. Dominions Office tel. D2016, 30 Oct 1945 in Hudson and Way (eds.), *DAFP*, 1945, viii, doc. 354 and FO tel. 10906, 30 Oct 1945, DO 35/2003, TNA.
96. Report by SWNCC's subcommittee on the Far East, SWNCC 101/4 (approved by SWNCC on 24 Oct 1945), *FRUS*, 1945, vi, pp.1096–1103 and Vincent to Vittrup, 7 Nov 1945, ibid., pp.1113–4.
97. Benninghoff to Byrnes, 15 Sep 1945, ibid., pp.1049–53; Hodge to MacArthur, 24 Sep 1945, ibid., pp.1054–7; Hodge to MacArthur, 12 Oct 1945, ibid., pp.1072–3; Langdon to Byrnes, 21 Nov 1945, ibid., pp.1130–3; and Langdon to Byrnes, 26 Nov 1945, ibid., pp.1134–6. On Soviet policy, see Weathersby, 'Soviet Aims', p.13. See Matray, *Crusade*, pp.53–5 and B. Cumings, *The Origins of the Korean War*, i, *Liberation and the Emergence of Separate Regimes 1945–19547* (Princeton, NJ: Princeton University Press, 1981), p.123 for an assessment of Hodge's character.
98. Byrnes to Langdon, 29 Nov 1945, *FRUS*, 1945, vi, pp.1137–8.
99. Byrnes' and Halifax's views are in Dominions Office tel. 2125, 17 Nov 1945, DO 35/2003, TNA.
100. Winant to Byrnes, 14 Nov 1945, *FRUS*, 1945, vi, pp.1124–5.
101. Australia (Govt.) tels 443 & 263, 6 Dec 1945, *DAFP*, 1945, viii, doc. 434.
102. Evatt to Makin, 7 Dec 1945 in Hudson and Way (eds.), *DAFP*, 1945, viii, doc. 435.
103. Bevin's remarks are in Duncan to Chifley, Makin and Evatt, 7 Dec 1945, in Hudson and Way (eds.), *DAFP*, 1945, viii, doc. 438.
104. Evatt to Makin, 9 Dec 1945, ibid., doc. 441 and Evatt to Makin, 15 Dec 1945, ibid., doc. 455.
105. Cadogan to his wife, 17 & 20 Dec 1945, ACAD 3/16, Cadogan papers, CAC.
106. Diary entry for 23 Dec 1945 in Jacob diary, JACB 1/25, Jacob papers, ibid.
107. Sterndale Bennett, minute, 27 Dec 1945 in Ashton, Bennett and Hamilton (eds.), *DBPO, Series I*, viii, doc. 6 and British record of thirteenth mtg. of the Moscow Conference of foreign ministers, 26 Dec 1945 in R. Bullen and M. E. Pelly (eds.), *DBPO, Series I*, ii, *Conferences and Conversations 1945: London, Washington and Moscow* (London: HMSO, 1985), doc. 349.
108. Bevin, minute, CM(46)1, 1 Jan 1946, CAB 128/5, TNA.
109. Minutes of the First Formal Session of the Moscow Conference of foreign ministers, 16 Dec 1945, *FRUS*, 1945, vii, pp.835–9.
110. British record of first mtg. of Moscow Conference of foreign ministers, 16 Dec 1945, Bullen and Pelly(eds.), *DBPO, Series I*, ii, doc. 289; 'Unified Administration

of Korea', US delegation memo., 17 Dec 1945, *FRUS*, 1945, ii, pp.641–3; 'Regarding Korea', Soviet delegation memo., 20 Dec 1945, *FRUS*, 1945, ii, pp.699–700; and 'Korea', Sterndale Bennett, minute, 20 Dec 1945, F1697/199/23, FO 371/54249, TNA.

111. British record of fourth and fifth mtgs of Moscow Conference of foreign ministers, 19 & 20 Dec 1945 in Bullen and Pelly (eds.), *DBPO, Series I*, ii, docs 307 & 313.

112. See US memos, 19 Dec 1945, *FRUS*, 1945, ii, *General: Political and Economic Matters* (Washington: United States Government Printing Office, 1967), pp.677–80; British record of seventh (informal) mtg. of Moscow Conference of foreign ministers, 21 Dec 1945 in Bullen and Pelly(eds.), *DBPO, Series I*, ii, doc. 320; and Schaller, *Occupation*, p.61.

113. Australia (Govt.) tel. 465, 19 Dec 1945, *DAFP*, 1945, viii, doc. 464. Moscow tel. 344, 19 Dec 1945, *DAFP*, 1945, viii, doc. 466; Dominions Office tel. 537, 21 Dec 1945, ibid., doc. 472; Bevin's comments are in Dominions Office, tel. 542, 24 Dec 1945, ibid., doc. 478; and Evatt to Dunk, radio message, 2 Jan 1946, W. J. Hudson and W. Way(eds.), *DAFP*, ix, *January–June 1946* (Canberra: Australian Government Publishing Service, 1991), doc. 5.

114. Bullock, *Bevin*, pp.199–200 & 218 and Cadogan to his wife, 17, 20 & 21 Dec 1945, ACAD 3/16, Cadogan papers, CAC.

4   Occupation and Civil War

1. 'The Way We Have Gone', Vansittart letter, *Manchester Guardian*, 5 Jan 1946.

2. Bevin, minute, CM(46)14, 11 Feb 1946, CAB 128/5, TNA.

3. Thailand had declared war on Britain and the United States in January 1942 under pressure from the Japanese but Washington, unlike London, was inclined to ignore its significance.

4. Tarling, *Britain*, pp.108–28; Dening to Bevin, 25 Mar 1946, MISC 251 (3480), Dening papers, IWM; and Sterndale Bennett, minute, 18 Feb 1946, F2805/203/61, FO 371/54056, TNA.

5. Ibid. and R. Craigie, 'Looking Eastwards', *The Sunday Times*, 17 Mar 1946.

6. Mason to Wright, 22 Dec 1945, AN 205/5/45, FO 371/51627, TNA; Balfour to Mason, 11 Jan 1946, ibid.; Mason, minute, 25 Jan 1946, ibid.; and Gage, minute, 4 Feb 1946, F2129/2129/61, FO 371/54052, ibid.

7. See 'Estimate of British Post-War Capabilities and Intentions', JIC 340/1, 13 Feb 1946, Folder CCS 000.1 Great Britain (5-10-45) Sec. 2, Box 82, Geographic File 1942–5, RG 218, NARA and Truman to Byrnes, letter (unsent), 5 Jan 1946, R. H. Ferrell (ed.), *Off the Record: The Private Papers of Harry S. Truman* (London: University of Missouri Press, 1997), pp.79–80.

8. Boyle, 'Foreign Office', p.311.

9. V. Mastny, *The Cold War and Soviet Insecurity: The Stalin Years* (Oxford: Oxford University Press, 1996), pp.23–6; Kent, 'British Policy, p.162; and Leffler, *Preponderance*, pp.121–7.

10. H. Friedman, 'The "Bear" in the Pacific? US Intelligence Perceptions of Soviet Strategic Power Projection in the Pacific Basin and East Asia, 1945–1947', *Intelligence and National Security*, 12 (1997), pp.75–101.

11. Kennan to Byrnes, 22 Feb 1946 in *FRUS*, 1946, vi, *Eastern Europe; The Soviet Union* (Washington: United States Government Printing Office, 1969), pp.696–709; Roberts to Bevin, 14, 17 & 18 Mar 1946 in M. E. Pelly, H. J. Yasamee and

K. A. Hamilton (eds.), *DBPO, Series I*, vi, *Eastern Europe 1945–1946* (London: HMSO, 1991), docs 80 & 82–3; and. J. Zametica, 'Three Letters to Bevin: Frank Roberts at the Moscow Embassy, 1945–6' in J. Zametica (ed.), *British Officials and British Foreign Policy, 1945–50* (Leicester: Leicester University Press, 1990), pp.39–97.

12. B. F. Smith, *The War's Long Shadow: The Second World War and Its Aftermath: China, Russia, Britain, America* (New York: Simon and Schuster, 1986), pp.152–3.

13. FO memo., 1 Apr 1946, R. Bullen and M. Pelly(eds.), *DBPO, Series I*, iv, *Britain and America: Atomic Energy, Bases and Food, 12 December 1945–31 July 1946* (London: HMSO, 1987), doc. 59; 'Strategic Aspect of British Policy' FO memo. attached to COS(46)239(0), 5 Oct 1946, U2930/2930/10, FO 371/57315, TNA; M. Dockrill and M. Hopkins (eds.), *The Cold War* (Basingstoke: Palgrave, 2006), p.33; and R. Merrick, 'The Russia Committee of the British Foreign Office and the Cold War, 1946–47', *Journal of Contemporary History*, 20 (1985), pp.453–68.

14. 'British Foreign Policy in the Far East', Far Eastern Civil Planning Unit memo., GEN 77/94, 14 Jan 1946, CAB 130/5, TNA.

15. Fraser to Alexander, 23 Jan 1946, AVAR 5/11/7(a), Alexander papers, CAC.

16. ' "Strikes" in the RAF', Stansgate memo., CP(46)25, 27 Jan 1946, CAB 129/6, TNA.

17. M. Murfett, *In Jeopardy: The Royal Navy and British Far Eastern Defence Policy 1945–1951* (Oxford: Oxford University Press, 1995), chps.1–2.

18. Diary entry for 18 Feb 1946 in Dalton diary, xxxiv (Feb–Dec 1946), Dalton papers, LSE.

19. R. Aldrich and J. Zametica, 'The Rise and Decline of a Strategic Concept: the Middle East, 1945–51' in R. Aldrich (ed.), *British Intelligence, Strategy and the Cold War, 1945–51* (London: Routledge, 1992), pp.239–52 and Leffler, *Preponderance*, pp.122–7.

20. Mastny, *Cold War*, pp.23–6; Kent, 'British Policy', p.162; and Leffler, *Preponderance*, pp.121–7.

21. Roberts to Bevin, 30 Aug 1946, F12910/12653/23, FO 371/54335, TNA.

22. MacDermot to Bevin, 14 Dec 1946, F559/95/23, FO 371/54126, ibid.

23. Sansom to Sterndale Bennett, 14 Mar 1946, F4579/95/23, FO 371/54131, ibid.

24. Sansom to his wife, 19 Apr 1946 in Sansom, *Sansom*, p.160.

25. Diary entries for 29 Dec 1945 and 1, 10, 11, 14 & 15 Jan 1946 in ibid., pp.144–50. The full diary extracts of Sansom's visit to Tokyo in January are deposited in F3595/2/23, FO 371/54086, TNA.

26. Diary entries for 15, 22, 28 & 29 Jan 1946 in Sansom, *Sansom*, pp.151–5. Gairdner's reaction is in diary entry for 10 Apr 1946 in A. Rix (ed.), *Intermittent Diplomat: The Japan and Batavia Diaries of W. Macmahon Ball* (Melbourne: Melbourne University Press, 1988), p.24.

27. See Buckley, *Alliance*, pp.12–13 & 19; Schaller, *Occupation*, chp.2; and J. Dower, 'Occupied Japan and the Cold War in Asia' in Lacey (ed.), *Truman*, pp.375–84.

28. R. Storry, *A History of Modern Japan* (London: Penguin, 1990), pp.240–1.

29. Morland to Far Eastern Department, 21 Feb 1946, F4591/95/23, FO 371/54131, TNA.

30. See 'Now Isn't that Nice of the Hollywood General!' *Sunday Pictorial*, 6 Jan 1946; 'US Troops and Japanese Women: Authorities Condone Mass Fraternisation', *Madras Mail*, 22 Jan 1946; and Cortazzi (ed.), *Japan*, pp.10–11.

31. Sterndale Bennett, minute for Sargent, 28 Mar 1946, F4199/2/23, FO 371/54089, TNA.

32. 'Policy towards Japan', Japan and Pacific Department memo., 18 Apr 1946, F7671/2/23, FO 371/54095, ibid.
33. Cabinet minutes, CM(46)20, 4 Mar 1946, CAB 128/5, ibid. and cabinet minutes, CM(46)22, 8 Mar 1946, ibid.
34. 'Estimate of British Post-War Capabilities and Intentions', JIC 340/1, 13 Feb 1946, Folder CCS 000.1 Great Britain (5-10-45) Sec. 2, Box 82, Geographic File 1942–5, RG 218, NARA and 'British Capabilities Versus the USSR', JIC 342/2, 27 Mar 1946, ibid.
35. See 'Interests and Policies of Canada, Australia and New Zealand in the Far East and the Pacific', DO memo., n.d., Dec 1945, F290/290/61, FO 371/54015, TNA.
36. Chifley, minute, PMM(46)7, 20 Apr 1946 in W. J. Hudson and W. Way(eds.), *DAFP*, ix, *January–June 1946* (Canberra: Australian Government Publishing Service, 1991), doc. 200.
37. Sturdee to Chifley, 10 Apr 1946, ibid., doc. 182.
38. See 'United Kingdom Military Representation in the Dominions', Hollis note, COS(46)111(0), 10 Apr 1946, CAB 21/1799, TNA and minutes of PMM(46)4, 25 Apr 1946, Hudson and Way(eds.), *DAFP*, 1946, ix, doc. 210.
39. See minutes of PMM(46)5, 26 Apr 1946, ibid., doc 213 and Chifley to Evatt and Forde, 1 May 1946, ibid., doc. 227.
40. Cabinet minutes, CM(46)41, 3 May 1946, CAB 128/5, TNA; Bevin to Attlee, 5 May 1946, CAB 130/4, ibid.; Attlee, minute for Bevin, 6 May 1946, ibid.; and Bullock, *Bevin*, pp.200–01.
41. Chifley to Evatt, 28 Jun 1946, Hudson and Way(eds.), *DAFP*, 1946, ix, doc. 332.
42. FO tel. 296, 15 Jun 1946, F8808/405/G, FO 371/54281, TNA.
43. Ball had had two brief stints as an adviser at the 1945 San Francisco Peace Conference and as Australia's representative to the Dutch East Indies. See Beasley to Evatt, 30 Jan 1946, A98, A2908/15, NAA; Bevin, minute for Attlee, 16 Feb 1946, F3066/2/23, FO 371/54085, TNA; Attlee to Chifley, 20 Feb 1946, PREM 8/191, ibid.; Tokyo tel. 422, 20 Apr 1946, F5985/2/23, FO 371/54092, ibid.; diary entry for 19 Sep 1946 in Rix (ed.), *Diplomat*, p.111; and K. Dermody, 'Officer, Sir Frank Keith (1889–1969)', *Australian Dictionary of Biography* (Canberra: Australian National University, 2006), www.adb.online.edu.au.
44. Evatt to Makin, 25 Apr 1946, Hudson and Way (eds.), *DAFP*, 1945, ix, doc. 211; Graves to Foulds, 6 Aug 1946, F11714/857/23, FO 371/54288, TNA; Dening, minute, 15 Aug 1946, F11591/857/23, ibid.; Ball to Evatt, 29 Jul 1946, W. J. Hudson and W. Way (eds.), *DAFP*, x, *July–December 1946* (Canberra: Australian Government Publishing Service, 1993), doc. 41; Tokyo tel. 1234, 21 Oct 1946, F15304/2/23, FO 371/54108, TNA; and Attlee to Gairdner, 19 Nov 1946, F16837/2/23, FO 371/54112, ibid.
45. Diary entry for 26 Nov 1945 in Alanbrooke diary (9 May–23 Dec 1945), 5/11, Alanbrooke papers, KCL; and Bevin, minute, 13 Jun 1946, F8997/2/23, FO 371/54097, TNA.
46. Keswick to Dening, 9 Aug 1946, CHAS/C/3, China Association papers, SOAS.
47. See 'Cinderella Role for British in Japan: Army Protests', *Daily Mail*, 3 Aug 1946; 'Drab Winter for AIF in Japan', *Melbourne Herald*, 23 Sep 1946 and 'Men of BCOF have Reason to Complain', *Melbourne Herald*, 25 Sep 1946. BCOF's public relations officer, Colonel Gordon Jenkins, sent a riposte in BCOF tel. PRI3853, 25 Sep 1946, 609/12, A5954/69, NAA and BCOF tel. PRI5334, n.d., ibid. For an overview of the Australian press and BCOF, see P. Torney, ' "Renegades to Their

Country": The Australian Press and the Allied Occupation of Japan, 1946–1950', *War & Society*, 25 (2006), pp.89–110.

48. Montgomery, minute, COS(46)146, 27 Sep 1946, CAB 79/52, TNA.
49. Attlee to Chifley and Fraser, 11 Nov 1946 in Hudson and Way (eds.), *DAFP*, 1946, x, doc. 209.
50. Chifley to Attlee, 28 Nov 1946, ibid., doc. 255; Tedder to COS, tel. 1425, 1 Dec 1946, F17292/2/23, FO 371/54113, TNA.
51. See MacDermot draft memo., n.d., F14501/2/23, FO 371/54106, TNA; COS minutes in COS(47)46, 28 Mar 1946, DEFE 4/3, ibid.; and 'BCOF in Japan – Implications for Withdrawal', JP(47)24(Final), 20 Mar 1947, ibid.
52. COS minutes in COS(47)46, 28 Mar 1946, DEFE 4/3, ibid.; Tokyo tel. C68665, 31 Dec 1946, Folder 'ABC 014 Japan', ABC Correspondence, 1940-48, Box 31, Entry 421, RG 165, NARA; 'BCOF in Japan – Implications for Withdrawal', JP(47)24(Final), 20 Mat 1947, DEFE 4/3, TNA; 'Withdrawal of U.K. Army Component from British Commonwealth Forces Japan', JP(47)122(Final), 3 Sep 1947, DEFE 4/7, ibid.; and COS to Commonwealth Relations Office, 11 Oct 1947, ibid.
53. Tokyo tel. no. 781, 18 Jul 1946, F10513/2/23, FO 371/54100, ibid.
54. J. Hoare, *Embassies in the East: The Story of the British Embassies in Japan, China and Korea from 1859 to the Present* (Surrey: Curzon Press, 1999), pp.158–9; P. Lowe, 'Great Britain, Japan and the Future: The End of the Allied Occupation, 1948–52' in R. Aldrich and M. Hopkins (eds.), *Intelligence, Defence and Diplomacy: British Policy in the Post-war World* (London: Frank Cass, 1994), pp.180–2; idem, 'Great Britain and Douglas MacArthur', p.56; diary entry for 13 Aug 1946 in Rix(ed.), *Diplomat*, pp.92–3; and Atcheson to Seymour, 20 Aug 1946, SEYR 3/4, Seymour papers, CAC.
55. Gascoigne to Bevin, 7 Aug 1946, F13031/2/23, FO 371/54105, TNA and Gascoigne to Dening, 11 Sep 1946, F14696/198/23, FO 371/54248, ibid.
56. Gascoigne to Dening, 28 Oct 1946, F16601/2/23, FO 371/54111, ibid.
57. Hooper to de la Mare, 2 Aug 1946, F11310/252/23, FO 371/54300, ibid.; Mitchell to FO, 26 Aug 1946, F12474/252/23, ibid.; France to de la Mare, 24 Dec 1946, F18463/1252/23, FO 371/54301, ibid.; and de la Mare to France, 6 Jan 1947, ibid.
58. Tokyo tels 1257-8, 25 Oct 1946, F15640/2/23, FO 371/54109, ibid.
59. Gascoigne to Dening, 28 Oct 1946, F16601/2/23, FO 371/54111, ibid.
60. MacDermot and Dening, minutes, 30-1 Dec 1946, F18192/12653/23, ibid. and Jebb, minute, 18 Feb 1947, ibid.
61. Tokyo tel. 1219, 16 Oct 1946, F15144/2/23, FO 371/54107, ibid.
62. Memo. of conversation by Acheson, 4 Jan 1946, *FRUS*, 1946, viii, pp.606–7; Harriman and Abel, *Special Envoy*, pp.541–3; Cumings, *Origins*, i, chps.6 & 11; and Lowe, *Origins*, pp.25–30 & 33–6.
63. MacDermot to Bevin, 29 Dec 1945, F729/199/23, FO 371/54249, TNA and Hoare, *Embassies*, pp.195–6.
64. James, minute, 1 Feb 1946, DO 35/2005, TNA; Davies, minute, 22 Feb 1946, ibid.; De la Mare to Davies, 25 Feb 1946, F1936/199/23, FO 371/54249, TNA and Dominions Office tel. 87, 4 Mar 1946, ibid.
65. For Evatt's descriptions of Australia's place in the world, see Department of External Affairs tel. unnumbered, 7 Jan 1946 in Hudson and Way (eds.), *DAFP*, 1946, ix, doc. 11.
66. Hoare, *Embassies*, p.196.
67. On the closeness of this relationship, see W. B. Smith, *My Three Years in Moscow* (Philadelphia: J. B. Lippincott, 1950), p.106.

68. Roberts to Sterndale Bennett, 11 Apr 1946, F6082/199/23, FO 371/54250, TNA. Some of the original American reporting on their difficulties with the Soviets can be found in Benninghoff to Byrnes, 15 Feb 1946, *FRUS*, 1946, viii, pp.633–6 and a report from Hodge in MacArthur to Byrnes, undated, ibid., pp.640–2.

69. De la Mare, minute, 30 Apr 1946, F6082/199/23, FO 371/54250, TNA.

70. Van Ree, *Socialism*, pp.208–9.

71. Kermode to Far Eastern Department, 5 Jun 1946, F10408/199/23, FO 371/54251, TNA.

72. Tokyo tel. 517, 15 May 1946, F7415/199/23, FO 371/54250, ibid.; Moscow tel. 1749, 16 May 1946, F7298/199/23, ibid.; 'Korea' notes by Gairdner, 16 May 1946, F8835/199/23, ibid.; Roberts to Foulds, 24 May 1946, F7994/199/23, ibid.; and Tokyo tel. 689, 21 Jun 1946, F9247/199/23, ibid. For the original American reporting on the crisis during this period, see Langdon to Byrnes, 30 Apr 1946, *FRUS*, 1946, viii, pp.662–4; Langdon to Byrnes, 8 May 1946, ibid., pp.667–74 and Langdon to Byrnes, 14 May 1946, ibid., pp.677–9.

73. 'Korea', FO memo., 21 May 1946, F8060/199/23, FO 371/54250, TNA.

74. Kermode to Bevin, 6 May 1946, ibid. and Tokyo tel. 615, 6 Jun 1946, F8473/198/23, FO 371/54247, ibid.

75. Kermode to Bevin, 12 Jun 1946, F10352/199/23, FO 371/54251, ibid. and de la Mare, minute, 29 Jun 1946, F8835/199/23, FO 371/54250, ibid. See also Byrnes to Langdon, 5 Apr 1946, *FRUS*, 1946, viii, pp.657–8 for signs of doubts about trusteeship.

76. Kermode to Bevin, 12 Jun 1946, F10352/199/23, FO 371/54251, TNA; De la Mare, minute, 24 Jun 1946, F9219/199/23, FO 371/54250, ibid.; Foulds, minute, 27 Jun 1946, ibid.; and Dening, minute, 28 Jun 1946, ibid.

77. Langdon to Byrnes, 23 Aug 1946, *FRUS*, 1946, viii, pp.726–9 and Acheson to Langdon, 13 Sep 1946, ibid., pp.735–7.

78. Hodge to War Department, tel. TFGCG 352, 27 Apr 1946, Roll 4, T1205, SFE 114–118, SFE 1945–8, RG 353, NARA; War Department tel. WAR 87750, 11 May 1946, ibid.; and 'Proposed Negotiations with the USSR over Korea on a Governmental Level', SWNCC 176/22, 26 Jul 1946, ibid.; Truman to Pauley, 16 Jul 1946, *FRUS*, 1946, viii, pp.713–4; Hilldring to Operations Division, War Department, 6 Jun 1946, ibid., pp.692–9; and Acheson to Smith, 13 Jul 1946, ibid., pp.711–13.

79. The piece was in the 'The London Letter', *The Scotsman*, 12 Jul 1946.

80. De la Mare, minute, 30 Jul 1946, F10974/199/23, FO 371/54251, TNA and Tokyo to FO, tel. 923, 14 Aug 1946, F11876/199/23, ibid. On de la Mare, see A. de la Mare, *Perverse and Foolish: A Jersey farmer's son in the British Diplomatic Service* (Jersey, La Haule, 1994).

81. Sansom to Dening, 12 Sep 1946, F13840/199/23, FO 371/54251, TNA.

82. Washington tel. 5641, 14 Sep 1946, F13553/199/23, ibid.; Lloyd, minute, 19 Sep 1946, ibid.; and Sawbridge, minute, 19 Sep 1946, ibid.

83. 'Monthly Report on Korea for June 1946', despatch no. 14, 13 Jul 1946, F12585/199/23, ibid.; de la Mare, minute, 5 Sep 1946, ibid.; Kermode to Bevin, 14 Aug 1946, F13224/199/23, ibid.; and Lloyd, minute, 16 Sep 1946, ibid.

84. See *The Times*, 24 Oct 1946; 'Disorders in Korea', *The Times*, 14 Nov 1946; *The Times*, 5 Dec 1946; and P. Warner, 'Maclean, Sir Fitzroy Hew Royle (1911–1996)' in, *Oxford Dictionary of National Biography* (Oxford: Oxford University Press, 2004–08), www.oxforddnb.com.

85. Tokyo tel. 1283, 1 Nov 1946, F1733/54/81, FO 371/63831, TNA. Hodge's actual report is in MacArthur to Eisenhower, 28 Oct 1946, *FRUS*, 1946, viii, pp.750–1.

86. Vincent to Hilldring, 4 Nov 1946, ibid., p.764 and Hilldring to Vincent, 8 Nov 1946, ibid., pp.764–5.
87. Wallinger to Bevin, 11 Dec 1945, F67/25/10, FO 371/53561, TNA and 'British Foreign Policy in the Far East', Far Eastern Civil Planning Unit memo., GEN 77/94, 14 Jan 1946, CAB 130/5, ibid.
88. Chungking tel. 24, 6 Jan 1946, WO 208/4399, ibid.; Seymour to Bevin, 7 Jan 1946, F1364/384/10, FO 371/53670, ibid.; and Seymour to Bevin, 24 Jan 1946, F2291/384/10, ibid. On Chou's link with SIS, see Aldrich, *Intelligence*, p.289.
89. Dreyer, *China*, pp.316–17; Hunt, *Genesis*, pp.168–9; Jian, *Mao's China*, p.34; Patterson to Byrnes, 18 Feb 1946, *FRUS*, 1946, x, *The Far East: China* (Washington: United States Government Printing Office, 1972), pp.278–9; and Chungking tel. 456, 25 Mar 1946, N4192/605/38, FO 371/56831, TNA. See also S. Levine, 'A New Look at American Mediation in the Chinese Civil War: The Marshall Mission and Manchuria', *Diplomatic History*, 3 (1979), pp.349–75.
90. Byrnes memo., 5 Jan 1946, Roll 5, T1205, SFE 119–126, SFE 1945–8, RG 353, NARA and Joint Chiefs of Staff memo., 13 Feb 1946, ibid.
91. Chungking tel. 188, 30 Jan 1946, 893.00/1-3046, Roll 3, LM 69, IAC 1945-9, RG 59, ibid.; Chungking tel. 189, 30 Jan 1946, ibid.; and Vincent to Acheson, 2 Feb 1946, ibid.
92. Chungking tel. 290, 23 Feb 1946, F2979/757/10, FO 371/53684, TNA.
93. 'The Position in Manchuria', Foulds memo., 23 Feb 1946, F2954/757/10, ibid.; Warner, Sterndale Bennett and Mason, minutes, 26 Feb 1946, ibid.; Winant to Byrnes, 20 Feb 1946, *FRUS*, 1946, x, pp.1108–9; Gallman to Byrnes, 9 March, ibid., pp.1116–19; and Marshall memo., 10 Mar 1946, *FRUS*, 1946, ix, *The Far East: China* (Washington: United States Government Printing Office, 1972), pp.528–9.
94. Bevin, minute, CM(46)23, 11 Mar 1946, CAB 128/5, TNA.
95. Chungking tel. 467, 28 Mar 1946, F4954/757/10, FO 371/53686, ibid.; Winant to Byrnes, 9 Apr 1946, *FRUS*, 1946, x, p.1112; Moscow tel. 1519, 23 Apr 1946, F6090/757/10, FO 371/53687, TNA; and Fenby, *Generalissimo*, p.466.
96. Dreyer, *China*, pp.318–9; Westad, *Cold War*, pp.158–62; Marshall to Soong, 29 May 1946, *FRUS*, 1946, ix, p.912; Marshall to Truman, 26 Jun 1946, 893.00/6-2646, Roll 4, LM 69, IAC 1945–9, RG 59, NARA; and Acheson to Marshall, 4 Jul 1946, 893.00/7-446, ibid.
97. Wm. Roger Louis, *Ends of British Imperialism: The Scramble for Empire, Suez and Decolonization – Collected Essays* (London: I.B. Tauris, 2006), pp.339–78; Ashton, Bennett and Hamilton (eds.), *DBPO, Series I*, viii, pp.41–2, fn.1; and COS minutes, COS(46)176, 3 Dec 1946, CAB 79/54, TNA.
98. See articles in the *Financial Times*, 10 & 11 July 1946; Seymour to Bevin, 9 May 1946, F8331/25/10, FO 371/53564, TNA; Hall to Seymour, 30 Apr 1946, F9360/51/10, FO 371/53548, ibid.; and Ogden to Wallinger, 12 Jul 1946, F11581/33/10, FO 371/53575, ibid.
99. See 'China: Some Current Trends and Recent Developments', Kitson memo., 23 May 1946, F7701/25/10, FO 371/53564, ibid.; 'China Policy', Kitson memo., 17 Jun 1946, F8984/25/10, FO 371/53565, ibid.; Scott, minute, 4 Jul 1946, F9715/25/10, ibid.; Killearn to Sargent, 11 Jun 1946, ibid.; and 'China', China Department memo., 1 Sep 1946, F13295/384/10, FO 371/53672, ibid.
100. Stevenson to Bevin, 3 Sep 1946, F13592/25/10, FO 371/53568, ibid.; Vincent to Marshall, 11 Apr 1946, Folder 'Vincent, John Carter', Box 1, Lot File 110, Records of Division of Chinese Affairs, RG 59, NARA; and N. B. Tucker, *China*

Confidential: American Diplomats and Sino-American Relations, 1945–1996 (New York: Columbia University Press, 2001), pp.23–6.

101. FO tel. 29 Aug 1946, F11597/25/10, FO 371/53566, TNA.
102. 'Situation in China', Vincent memo., 3 Sep 1946, Folder 'Vincent, John Carter', Box 1, Lot File 110, Records of Division of Chinese Affairs, RG 59, NARA; Washington tel. 5482, 4 Sep 1946, F12949/515/10, FO 371/53678, TNA; Kitson, minute, 9 Sep 1946, ibid.; Dening, minute, 14 Sep 1946, F13295/384/10, FO 371/53672, ibid.; and Butterworth memo., 6 Sep 1946, *FRUS*, 1946, x, pp.147–50.
103. Mitchell to FO, 18 Jan 1946, F1124/116/10, FO 371/53641, TNA; FO tel. 65, 7 May 1946, F6741/116/10, FO 371/53643, ibid.; Kitson to Blaker, 26 Aug 1946, F12139/116/10, FO 371/53645, ibid.; and Stevenson to Attlee, 7 Nov 1946, F17040/25/10, FO 371/53571, ibid. See Qing, *Allies*, pp.34–56 for an excellent survey of Sino-American discussions for a commercial treaty, which many Chinese believed was a new unequal treaty.
104. 'British Policy towards China', China Department memo., 18 Oct 1946, F15359/384/10, FO 371/53672, TNA.
105. Vincent to Acheson, 5 Nov 1946, *FRUS*, 1946, x, pp.879–82; Carter to Marshall, 3 Dec 1946, ibid., p.887; Stevenson to Bevin, 30 Nov 1946, F17289/25/10, FO 371/53571, TNA; Stevenson to Attlee, 23 Nov 1946, F17620/25/10, ibid.; Nanking tel. 887, 19 Dec 1946, F18180/384/10, FO 371/53673, ibid.; Nanking tel. 143, 10 Feb 1947, F1870/37/10, FO 371/63302, ibid.; Kitson, minute, 13 Feb 1947, ibid.; and Dreyer, *China*, p.319.
106. F. Maclean, 'Japan: MacArthur's Task', *Sunday Observer*, 20 Oct 1946; idem, 'Japan Under MacArthur', *The Scotsman*, 23 Oct 1946; idem, 'Far Eastern Survey: China', *The Observer*, 3 Nov 1946; Gascoigne to MacArthur, 26 Oct 1946, Folder 'British File No.1', Box 107, RG 5, NMM; Gascoigne to MacArthur, 28 Oct 1946, ibid.; and Drumright to Byrnes, 12 Nov 1946, 893.00/11-1246, Roll 4, LM 69, IAC 1945–9, RG 59, NARA.

5   Questioning Engagement

1. 'The Far East', *Manchester Guardian*, 28 May 1947; Dening, minute for Sargent, 16 Dec 1947, F16907/1382/23, FO 371/63784, TNA; Tarling, *Britain*, pp.188–94; and K. Hack, 'South East Asia and British Strategy, 1944–51' in Aldrich (ed.), *Intelligence*, p.318.
2. See Killearn to MacDonald, 3 & 13 Sep 1947, 17/2/33 & 65, MacDonald papers, DUL.
3. Cabinet minutes, CM(47)13, 28 Jan 1947, CAB 128/9, TNA and diary entry for 28 Jan 1947 in Dalton diary, xxxv (Jan–Oct 1947), Dalton papers, LSE.
4. Attlee, minute, DO(47)20, 18 Sep 1947, CAB 131/5, TNA; DO minutes, DO(47)22, 29 Sep 1947, ibid.; 'Defence Estimates 1948/9', Alexander memo., CP(48)2, 2 Jan 1948, CAB 129/23, ibid.; Barnett, *Lost Victory*, chp.4; and Murfett, *Jeopardy*, chp. 3.
5. 'British Commonwealth Occupation Forces in Japan', JCS 1398/27, 30 Apr 1947, Folder 'ABC 014 Japan', ABC Correspondence, 1940–48, Box 31, Entry 421, RG 165, NARA; COS minutes, COS(47)69, 30 May 1947, DEFE 4/4, TNA; 'Withdrawal of Indian Forces', JP(47)41(Final), 27 May 1947, ibid.; and K. Hack, 'South East Asia and British Strategy, 1944–51' in Aldrich (ed.), *Intelligence*, p.318.
6. Gascoigne to Bevin, 1 Jan 1948, F2199/2199/23, FO 371/69914, TNA.

7. Leffler, *Preponderance*, chp. 4. Halifax, Britain's retired ambassador, thought Marshall far more consistent than Byrnes. Halifax to MacDonald, 5 Jul 1947, 15/9/2, MacDonald papers, Durham University Library (DUL).

8. R. Frazier, 'Did Britain Start the Cold War? Bevin and the Truman Doctrine', *Historical Journal*, 27 (1984), pp.715–27; Leffler, *Preponderance*, p.142–7; J. Gaddis, *The Cold War* (London: Allen Lane, 2005), p.95; A. Defty, *Britain, America and Anti-Communist Propaganda, 1945–53: The Information Research Department* (London: Routledge, 2004), p.46; and X (G. Kennan), 'The Sources of Soviet Conduct', *Foreign Affairs*, 26 (1947), pp.566–82.

9. Zubok and Pleshakov, *Cold War*, pp.50–1 and Gaddis, *Cold War*, p.32.

10. Eisenhower to Joint Chiefs of Staff, 16 May 1947, JCS 1776/1, MF 51, RJCS, 1946–53, KCL and 'Military Importance of Korea', JSP report for JCS, JCS 1483/44, 22 Sep 1947, ibid.

11. See Forrestal memo., 29 Sep 1947, *FRUS*, 1947, vi, *The Far East* (Washington: United States Government Printing Office, 1972), pp.817–18; and Matray, *Crusade*, pp.115–16.

12. Inverchapel's remarks were an assessment of 1947 drawn up in 1948, see Inverchapel to Bevin, 16 Feb 1948, AN669/6/45, FO 371/68013B, TNA.

13. Bevin remarks to the House of Commons are in Gascoigne to MacArthur, 18 May 1947, Folder 'British File No. 1', Box 107, RG 5, MMA.

14. Drumright to Byrnes, 28 Jan 1947, 893.00/1-2847, Roll 5, LM 69, IAC 1945–9, RG 59, NARA.

15. *The Times*, 30 May 1947.

16. 'British Commonwealth Strategy – Allocation of Areas of Strategic Responsibility', Montgomery memo., COS(47)99(0), 7 May 1947, DEFE 5/4, TNA; 'Future Defence Policy', DO(47)44, 22 May 1947, DEFE 4/4, ibid.; Attlee and Bevin minutes, COS(47)74, 11 Jun 1947, DEFE 5/4, ibid.; Aldrich and Zametica, 'The Middle East', pp.252–4; and R. Aldrich and M. Coleman, 'Britain and the Strategic Air Offensive Against the Soviet Union: The Question of South Asian Air Bases, 1945–9', *History: The Journal of the British Historical Association*, 74 (1989), pp.400–26.

17. 'Operational Responsibility for China', JP(47)72(Final), 9 Jun 1947, DEFE 4/4, TNA; COS minutes, COS(47)124, 6 Oct 1947, DEFE 4/7, ibid.; SEALF tel. PEPPER 82, 29 Jun 1947, BLM 181/15, Reel 17, PP/MCR/C30, Montgomery papers, IWM; SEASEC 8th Misc Mtg., 3 Aug 1947, BLM 181/16, ibid.; Boyd to Cunningham, 1 Jul 1947, BLM 181/22, ibid. and Montgomery diary, part viii, tour no. 3, Australia and New Zealand (21 Jun-8 Aug 1947), chp. 53, BLM 181/1, ibid. See also Murfett, *Jeopardy*, pp.45–9.

18. Drumright to Byrnes, 28 Jan 1947, 893.00/1-2847, Roll 5, LM69, IAC 1945–49, RG 59, NARA. See also G. Samson, 'British Policy in China: The Need for Better Representation', *Manchester Guardian*, 8 Apr 1947. The Foreign Office had suffered a 10 per cent cut in manpower but claimed Nanking and Shanghai were sufficiently staffed. Kennedy, minute, 19 May 1947, F4903/28/10, FO 371/63285, TNA. See also Kitson to Mitchell, 27 May 1947, CHAS/C/3, China Association papers, SOAS and Barclay to Mitchell, 31 Jul 1947, ibid.

19. Bevin, minute for Attlee, 2 Jan 1947, PREM 8/485, TNA.

20. Under the terms of the agreement announced on 23 January 1946 by Alexander, the British loaned HMS *Petunia*, a sloop; HMS *Mendip*, a destroyer; HMS *Aurora*, a light cruiser; two submarines and eight harbour defence motor launches for a five-year period. *Aurora* and eight motor launches were later transferred to Nationalist China. See M. Murfett, 'Old Habits Die Hard: The Return of British Warships to

Chinese Waters after the Second World War' in J. Hattendorf and M. Murfett (eds.), *The Limitations of Power: Essays presented to Professor Norman Gibbs on His Eightieth Birthday* (London: Macmillan, 1990), pp.204–5 and DO(48)11, 15 Jul 1948, CAB 131/5, TNA.

21. Grose to Kitson, 30 Aug 1946, F12762/119/10, FO 371/53652, ibid.; Nanking tel. 528, 18 Sep 1946, F13859/119/10, ibid.; Dening, minute for Sargent, 23 Sep 1946, ibid.; Sargent, minute, 26 Sep 1946, ibid.; Cabinet minutes, CM(46)86, 14 Oct 1946, CAB 128/8, ibid.; and FO tel. 910, 16 Oct 1946, F13859/119/10, FO 371/53652, ibid.

22. Field to Howman, 20 Dec 1946 & 10 Jan 1947, WO 208/4922, ibid.; Field to Wallinger, 17 Jan 1947, F2051/13/10, FO 371/63271, ibid.; Stevenson to Bevin, 14 March 1947, F4490/4490/10, FO 371/63439, ibid.; and T. C. Jesperson, *American Images of China, 1931–1949* (Stanford: Stanford University Press, 1996), p.146. See also Field's memoirs entitled 'That's The Way It Was', written in c. 1970, P149, Field papers, IWM.

23. Kitson, minute, 4 Jan 1947, F371/86/10, FO 371/63332, TNA and Dening, minute, 4 Jan 1947, ibid. Bevin's views are in Sargent, minute, 6 Jan 1947, ibid.

24. Field to Howman, 20 Jan 1947, WO 208/4922, ibid.

25. ibid.; Nanking tel. 143, 10 Feb 1947, F1870/37/10, FO 371/63302, ibid.; Kitson, minutes, 12–13 Feb 1947, ibid.; Nanking tel. 150, 13 Feb 1947, F2014/37/10, FO 371/63303, ibid.; Nanking tel. 151, 13 Feb 1947, F2007/37/10, FO 371/63302, ibid.; Kitson, minute, 15 Feb 1947, ibid.; Drumright to Marshall, 11 Feb 1947, 893.00/2-1147, Roll 5, LM69, IAC 1945–49, RG 59, NARA; and Penfield to Vincent, 12 Feb 1947, 893.00/2-1247, ibid.

26. Washington tel. 1160, 22 Feb 1947, F2459/37/10, FO 371/63302, TNA and Moscow tel. 114, 15 Mar 1947, F3569/76/10, FO 371/63320, ibid.

27. Kitson, minute, 25 Feb 1947, F2459/37/10, FO 371/63302, ibid.

28. Stevenson to Dening, 7 Mar 1947, F4120/76/10, FO 371/63321, ibid.

29. Ibid.; Scott, minute, 8 Mar 1947, F2357/76/10, FO 371/63318, ibid.; Scott, minute, 27 March 1947, F4120/76/10, FO 371/63321, ibid.; and Jian, *China's Road*, pp.19–20.

30. Dening, minute, 27 Mar 1947, F4120/76/10, FO 371/63321, TNA; Acheson to Smith, 2 Apr 1947, *FRUS*, 1947, vii, *The Far East: China* (Washington: United States Government Printing Office, 1972), pp.814–815; minutes of conference concerning China, 20 Feb 1947, ibid., pp.946–50; Acheson to Patterson, 28 Mar 1947, ibid., p.811; Forrestal to Marshall, 26 May 1947, pp.966–8; Ringwalt to Vincent, 5 May 1947, Folder 'John Carter Vincent', Lot File 110, Box 1, Records of Division of Chinese Affairs, RG 59, NARA; memo. of conversation by Sprouse, 27 May 1947, Folder 'British Far Eastern Relations', ibid.; Scott to Kentish, 16 May 1947, F6427/13/10, FO 371/63272, TNA; Scott, minute, 29 May 1947, ibid. F7362/76/10, FO 371/63323, ibid.; Kitson, minute, 30 May 1947, ibid.; and Scott, minute, 30 Jun 1947, F7375/13/10, FO 371/63272, ibid. On Chiang's view, see Westad, *Decisive*, pp.160–1.

31. FO tel. 5324, 1 Jun 1947, F7185/13/10, FO 371/63272, TNA; Bevin, minute, CM(47)60, 8 Jul 1947, CAB 128/10, ibid.; Dening, minute, 6 Oct 1947, F13972/13/10, FO 371/63273 ibid.

32. Haynes to Scott, 15 Dec 1947, F16504/13/10, ibid.; and Scott, minute, 23 Dec 1947, ibid.

33. Sargent, minute for Attlee, 1 Jan 1948, ibid.; Farrell to Scott, 4 Feb 1948, F2182/34/10, FO 371/69551, ibid.; Scott, minute, 10 Feb 1948, ibid.; Scarlett,

minute, 11 Feb 1948, ibid.; Scarlett, minute, 25 Mar 1948, F5192/34/10, ibid.; Haynes to Scott, 30 & 31 Mar 1948, ibid., and Dening, minute, 5 Apr 1948, ibid.

34. Drumright to Marshall, 15 May 1947, 893.00/5-1547, Roll 6, LM 69, IAC 1945–9, RG 59, NARA; Butterworth to Marshall, 16 May 1947, 893.00/5-1647, ibid.; Mukden tel. 78, 30 May 1947, 893.00/5-3047, Roll 7, ibid.; Stuart to Marshall, 30 May 1947, 893.00/5-3047, ibid.; Stuart to Marshall, 4 Jun 1947, 893.00/6-447, ibid.; Nanking tel. 541, 28 May 1947, F7181/76/10, FO 371/63323, TNA; Nanking tel. 549, 29 May 1947, F7362/76/10, ibid.; Kitson, minute, 29 May 1947, ibid.; Westad, *Decisive*, p.164; and Dreyer, *China*, pp.325, 330–1.

35. Vincent to Marshall, 5, 6 & 10 Jun 1947, 893.00/6-547-757, Roll 7, LM 69, IAC 1945–9, RG 59, NARA.

36. 'United States Policy Towards China', JSSC memo. for the JCS, JCS 1721/4, 21 May 1947, RJCS: 1946–1953, MF 44, KCL; 'United States Policy Toward China', JCS memo. for SWNCC, 9 Jun 1947, *FRUS: The Far East, China*, 1947 (Washington: United States Government Printing Office, 1969), vii, pp.838–8; Marshall to Lovett, 2 July 1947, ibid., pp.635–6; and Vincent to Marshall, 20 Jun 1947, 893.00/6-2047, Roll 7, LM 69, IAC, 1945–9, RG 59, NARA.

37. Forrestal to Marshall, 20 Jun 1947, *FRUS*, 1947, vii, pp.968–70; Marshall to Forrestal, 23 Jul 1947, ibid., pp.970–1; and Vincent to Marshall, 18 Jul 1947, 893.00/7-1847, Roll 7, LM 69, IAC, 1945–9, RG 59, NARA.

38. Westad, *Decisive*, pp.162–8.

39. May, *China Scapegoat*, chps. 5–10.

40. Dening, minute, 10 Jul 1947, F9179/76/10, FO 371/63325, TNA and Kitson, minute, 30 Jul 1947, F10121/76/10, ibid.

41. Memo. of conversation by Ringwalt, 2 Jun 1947, 893.00/6-247, Roll 7, LM 69, IAC, 1945–9, RG 59, NARA; State Department tel. 682, 9 Jun 1947, ibid.; Drumright to Marshall, 20 Jun 1947, 893.00/6-2047, ibid.; and 'Operational Responsibility for China', JP(47)72(Final), 9 Jun 1947, DEFE 4/4, TNA.

42. Christensen, *Useful Adversaries*, pp.61–6; Nanking tel. 695, 17 Jul 1947, F9732/76/10, FO 371/63325, TNA; Kitson, minute, 24 Jul 1947, ibid.; Washington tel. 3973, 16 Jul 1947, F9956/76/10, ibid.

43. Kitson, minute, 28 Jul 1947, ibid.; Dening, minute, 28 July 1947, ibid.; Sargent, minute, 28 Jul 1947, ibid.; and Bevin, minute, n.d., ibid.

44. 'Report on the Financial and Fiscal Situation in China', memo. for Wedemeyer, 22 Aug 1947, *FRUS*, 1947, vii, p.739; and 'Present Situation in China', Sprouse memo. for Wedemeyer, 23 Aug 1947, ibid., pp.741–59. See also Sprouse oral history interview, 11 Feb 1974, Harry S. Truman Library, Independence, Missouri (HSTL) and Westad, *Decisive*, p.161 on Chiang's embarrassment over Wedemeyer's visit.

45. Kitson, minute, 11 Aug 1947, F10250/85/10, FO 371/63327, TNA.

46. Nanking tel. 949, 4 Oct 1947, F13467/37/10, FO 371/63309, ibid.; Dening, minute, 25 Oct 1947, ibid.; Field to Howman, 5 Aug 1947, WO 208/4922, ibid.; Ringwalt to Carter, 3 Sep 1947, 893.00/9-347, Roll 7, LM 69, IAC, 1945–9, RG59, NARA; and Mukden tel. 297, 3 Oct 1947, 893.00/10-347, Roll 8, ibid.

47. Scott, minute, 7 Oct 1947, F13467/37/10, FO 371/63309, TNA; Scott, minute, 11 Nov 1947, F14773/76/10, FO 371/63328, ibid.; minutes of the meeting of the Committee of Two, 3 Nov 1947, *FRUS*, 1947, vii, pp.908–912; Dening, minute, 17 Nov 1947, F14773/76/10, FO 371/63328, TNA; Nanking tel. 1141, 11 Dec 1947, F16337/76/10, FO 371/63330, ibid.; and Field to Tarver, 2 & 16 Dec 1947, WO 208/4922, ibid.

48. Clerk to Butterworth, 10 Dec 1947, 893.00/12-1047, Roll 8, LM69, IAC (1945–9), RG59, NARA; Drumright to Marshall, 4 Dec 1947, 893.00/12-447, Roll 8, ibid.; 'The Chinese Conflict', *The Times*, 3 Dec 1947; and 'China's Tepid War', *The Economist*, 20 Dec 1947.

49. Tokyo tel. 254, 4 Mar 1947, F2963/1382/23, FO 371/63766, TNA; MacDermot, minute, 6 Mar 1947, ibid.; and Douglas to Marshal, *FRUS*, 1947, vi, p.451. The issue of allowing British businessmen to enter Japan was still dragging on in 1947. See Gascoigne to MacArthur, 9 Jul 1947, Folder 'British File No.1', Box 107, RG 5, MMA. In July, some 20 trade services personnel were finally allowed to enter Tokyo to prepare to the ground. See Marquat conference with Gascoigne, 13 Jul 1947, ibid.

50. Washington tel. 1485, 10 Mar 1947, F3272/1382/23, FO 371/63766, TNA.

51. Schaller, *Altered*, pp.12–13; idem, *Occupation*, pp.95–7; J. Dower, *Japan in War and Peace:Eessays on History, Culture and Race* (London: Harper Collins, 1996), p.173; and Acheson, *Present*, pp.227–9.

52. Dening to Gascoigne, 8 May 1947, F6171/1382/23, FO 371/63768, TNA.

53. Kennan memo. for Lovett, 12 Aug 1947, *FRUS*, 1947, vi, pp.486–7; MacArthur to Joint Chiefs of Staff, 1 Sep 1947, Folder 'Japanese Peace Treaty, 1947–48 Vol.1', Roll 8, C0044, US State Department Special Files: Northeast Asia, 1943–56, RG 59, NARA; Schaller, *Occupation*, pp.98–9; and 'Peace Treaty with Japan – Military Requirements', Stapleton note, COS(47)120(0), 7 Jun 1947, DEFE 5/4, TNA.

54. Sansom to Dening, 11 Apr 1947, F5525/1382/23, FO 371/63767, ibid.; Washington tel. 3892, 11 Jul 1947, F9330/1382/23, FO 371/63772, ibid.; Tokyo tel. 1081, 31 Jul 1947, F10365/1382/23, FO 371/63775, ibid.; and Borton, *Spanning*, pp.211–13.

55. Tokyo tels 1087–8, 1 Aug 1947, F10453/1382/23, FO 371/63775, TNA; Tokyo tel. 1092, 1 Aug 1947, F10455/1382/23, ibid.; and diary entry for 6 Aug 1947 in Dix (ed.), *Diplomat*, pp.231–4.

56. Montgomery diary, part viii, tour no. 3, Australia and New Zealand (21 Jun–8 Aug 1947), chp. 54, BLM 181/1, Reel 17, PP/MCR/C30, Montgomery papers, IWM and Melbourne tel. PEPPER 96, 4 Jul 1947, BLM 181/41, ibid.

57. See record of conference in Burton's room, 8 Jul 1947, W. J. Hudson and W. Way (eds.), *DAFP*, 1947, xii, *Australia and the Post War World* (Canberra, Australian Government Publishing Service, 1995), doc. 332; and 'United Kingdom Strategy at the Canberra Conference', CJT(47)5, 25 Aug 1947, CAB 21/1757, TNA.

58. Dening, minute for Bevin, 6 Oct 1947, F13769/1382/23, FO 371/63781, ibid.

59. Dening, minute, United Kingdom delegation, CJT(47)5, 1 Sep 1947, CAB 21/1758, ibid.; and 'Japanese Peace Settlement', FO memo., 16 Dec 1947, F16907/1382/23, FO 371/63784, ibid.

60. Davies memo., 11 Aug 1947, *FRUS*, 1947, vi, pp.485–6; Kennan memo. for Lovett, 12 Aug 1947, ibid., pp.486–7; and Schaller, *Occupation*, pp.102–6.

61. See Atcheson to Marshall, 24 Jun 1947, *FRUS*, 1947, vi, p.238–9; Evatt to Marshall, 16 Oct 1947, Folder 'Japanese Peace Treaty, 1947–48 Vol.1', Roll 8, C0044, US State Department Special Files: Northeast Asia, 1943–56, RG59, NARA; Marshall to Evatt, 23 Oct 1947, ibid.; note of discussion between Bevin and Marshall, 24 Nov 1947, F15947/1382/23, FO 371/63783, TNA and Noel-Baker to Bevin, 25 Nov 1947, ibid.; Dening, minute for Sargent, 28 Nov 1947, F15948/1382/23, ibid.; Dening to Gascoigne, 3 Dec 1947, F15976/1382/23, FO 371/63783, ibid.; Bevin, minute, CM(47)92, 2 Dec 1947, CAB 128/10, ibid.; 'Japanese Peace Settlement',

FO memo., 16 Dec 1947, F16907/1382/23, FO 371/63784, ibid.; and Schaller, *Occupation*, p.101.

62. Vincent to Marshall, 27 Jan 1947, *FRUS*, vi, *The Far East, 1947* (Washington: United States Government Printing Office, 1972), pp.601–3; Marshall to MacArthur, 7 Feb 1947, ibid., pp.605–6; and memo. and draft report of the special inter-departmental committee on Korea, 25 Feb 1947, ibid., pp.608–18.

63. Ibid.; memo. by Hilldring and Vincent to Marshall, 28 Feb 1947, ibid., pp.618–9; editorial note in ibid., p.620; Matray, *Crusade*, p.116; and Chancery to North American Department, 14 Mar 1947, F4084/54/81, FO 371/63832, TNA.

64. Washington tel. 1602, 14 Mar 1947, F3550/54/23, ibid. and Dening to Dixon, 26 Mar 1947, ibid.

65. Acheson to Patterson, 28 Mar 1947, *FRUS*, 1947, vi, pp.621–3; Patterson to Acheson, 4 Apr 1947, ibid., pp.625–8; Molotov to Marshall, 19 Apr 1947 ibid., pp.632–5; and Drumright memo., 24 Apr 1947, ibid., pp.636–8. The Chinese note is in Stuart to Marshall, 15 Apr 1947, ibid., pp.631–2; and Dominions Office tels 91 & 99, 2 & 14 May 1947 in Hudson and Way (eds.), *DAFP*, 1947, xii, doc. 533 & 535.

66. Seoul tel. 7, 6 Feb 1947, F1712/54/81, FO 371/63831, TNA; de la Mare, minute, 11 Feb 1947, ibid.; and FO tel. 17, 27 Feb 1947, F2095/54/81, ibid.

67. FO tel. 68, 13 Dec 1947, BT 11/3560, ibid.

68. Kermode to Bevin 28 Mar 1947, F5826/5826/81, FO 371/63850, ibid.; Dening, minute, 3 May 1947, ibid.; Seoul tel. 36, 30 Apr 1947, F6038/54/81, FO 371/63834, ibid.; Seoul tel. 44, 19 May 1947, F6931/54/81, ibid.; MacDermot, minute, 23 May 1947, ibid.; Sargent, minute, 6 May 1947, F5826/5826/81, FO 371/63850; and 'Korea', Japan and Pacific Department memo., 22 May 1947, F7634/54/81, FO 371/63835, ibid.

69. Seoul tel. 66, 28 Jun 1947, F8715/54/81, ibid. Hodge's report is in MacArthur to Marshall, 2 Jul 1947, *FRUS*, 1947, vi, pp.682–4. See a similar report by Hodge in MacArthur to Marshall, 9 Jul 1947, ibid., pp.696–7 and also Hodge to Marshall, 16 Jul 1947, ibid., pp.703–4; and Jacobs to Marshall, 7 Jul 1947, ibid., pp.690–1. See also Cumings, *Origins*, i, chps. 6 & 7 and idem, *The Origins of the Korean War*, ii, *The Roaring of the Cataract 1947–1950* (Princeton, NJ: Princeton University Press, 1990), pp.185–208.

70. Matray, *Crusade*, p.116; Washington tel. 4006, 18 Jul 1947, F9827/54/81, FO 371/63836, TNA; and Jacobs to Marshall, 21 Jul 1947, *FRUS*, 1947, vi, pp.710–11; and Seoul tel. 72, 21 Jul 1947, F9942/54/81, FO 371/63836, TNA. Gairdner's views were reported in Tokyo tel. 990, 13 Jul 1947, F9362/54/81, ibid. See also memo. by Allison, 23 Jul 1943, *FRUS*, 1947, vi, pp.713–4.

71. Killick, minute, 15 Jul 1947, F9362/54/81, FO 371/63836, TNA; Dening, minute, 16 Jul 1947, ibid.; and 'Difficulties in Korea', *The Times*, 30 Jul 1947.

72. Dening, minute for Sargent, 11 Aug 1947, F10470/54/81, FO 371/63836, TNA.

73. 'United States Policy in Korea', report by the ad hoc committee on Korea, 4 Aug 1947, *FRUS*, 1947, vi, pp.738–41; Hilldring to Marshall, 6 Aug 1947, ibid., pp.742–3; Matray, *Crusade*, pp.120–1; FO tel. 8339, 18 Aug 1947, F10470/54/81, FO 371/63836, TNA; Lovett to Molotov, 26 Aug 1947, *FRUS*, 1947, vi, pp.771–4; Clark to Marshall, 28 Aug 1947, ibid., pp.774–5; Australian High Commission tel. 683, 2 Sep 1947, F12044/54/81, FO 371/63837, TNA; Hankinson to Burton, 9 Sep 1947, Hudson and Way (eds.), *DAFP*, 1947, xii, doc. 537; Bevin to Douglas, 5 Sep 1947, F12044/54/81, FO 371/63837, TNA; Molotov to Marshall, 5 Sep 1947,

FRUS, 1947, vi, pp.779–81 and Moscow tel. 2009, 6 Sep 1947, F12408/54/81, FO 371/63837, TNA.

74. Kermode to Graves, 10 Sep 1947, F13823/6462/81, FO 371/63851, ibid.; Matray, *Crusade*, pp.126–7; 'United States Policy on Korea', Stevens memo., 9 Sep 1947, *FRUS*, 1947, vi, pp.784–5; and 'The Interest of the United States in Military Occupation of South Korea from the Point of View of the Military Security of the United States', draft memo. for the Secretary of Defence in 'Military Importance of Korea', JSP memo., 1483/44, 22 Sep 1947, RJCS: 1946–1953, MF 51, KCL. This memo. was approved by the Secretary of Defence on 29 Sep 1947, JCS 1483/46, ibid.

75. Seoul tel. 98, 3 Oct 1947, F13473/54/81, FO 371/63839, TNA; Washington tel. 258, 6 Oct 1947, F13571/54/81, ibid.; Killick, minutes, 8 & 16 Oct 1947, ibid.; Brimelow, minute, 9 Oct 1947, ibid.; and Rundall, minute, 17 Oct 1947, ibid.

76. Evatt to Marshall, 16 Oct 1947 in Hudson and Way (eds.), *DAFP*, 1947, xii, doc. 370; Marshall to Evatt, 23 Oct 1947, Folder 'Japanese Peace Treaty, 1947–48 Vol.1', Roll 8, C0044, US State Department Special Files: Northeast Asia, 1943–56, RG 59, NARA; New York tel. 2955, 17 Oct 1947 F14064/54/81, FO 371/63839, TNA; FO tel. 3586, 21 Oct 1947, ibid.; and Killick, minute for Sargent, 28 Oct 1947, F14683/54/81, FO 371/63840, ibid.

77. Moscow tel. 2347, 29 Oct 1947, F14555/54/81, ibid.; Killick, minute, 31 Oct 1947, ibid.; MacDermot, minute, 31 Oct 1947, ibid.; and Hankey, minute, 1 Nov 1947, ibid.

78. New York tel. no. 3144, 31 Oct 1947, F14643/54/81, ibid.; Australian delegation (UN) tel. UN1041 (New York), 28 Oct 1947, in Hudson and Way(eds.), *DAFP*, 1947, xii, doc. 538; and FO tel. 3752, 3 Nov 1947, F14643/54/81, FO 371/63840, TNA.

79. Kermode to Bevin, 2 Dec 1947, F594/511/81, FO 371/69937, ibid. and Kermode to Bevin, 12 Dec 1947, F595/511/81, ibid.

80. Dening, minute for Sargent, 16 Dec 1947, F16907/1382/23, FO 371/63784, ibid.

81. R. Buhite, ' "Major Interests": American Policy toward China, Taiwan, and Korea, 1945–1950', *Pacific Historical Review*, 47 (1978), p.430 and CINCFE tel. 56266, 22 Oct 1947, MF 51, RJCS 1946–53, KCL.

6 Going into Reverse

1. The Japanese Mandated Islands comprised Marshall, Caroline and Mariana Islands.

2. Inverchapel to Bevin, 16 Feb 1948, AN669/6/45, FO 371/68013B, TNA.

3. M. Hopkins, *Oliver Franks and the Truman Administration: Anglo-American Relations 1948–1952* (London: Routledge, 2003), p.17.

4. Inverchapel to Bevin, 21 May 1948, AN2076/6/45, FO 371/60814, TNA and Lowe, 'MacArthur', p.57.

5. 'Mr. Churchill's Warning to Western World', *The Times*, 11 Oct 1948.

6. Hall-Patch, minute, 9, Mar 1948, AN669/6/45, FO 371/68013B, TNA and D. Reynolds, *Britannia Overruled: British Policy and World Power in the Twentieth Century* (Harlow: Pearson, 2000), p.182.

7. 'Australian Defence Co-operation', Sargent memo., 14 Oct 1948, DEFE 5/8, TNA; Bullock, *Bevin*, p.631; Hack, 'Southeast Asia', p.323; and Murfett, *Jeopardy*, pp.75–80.

8. 'The Strategic Position of Malaya', Stapleton note, COS(49)43(0), 23 Feb 1948, DEFE 5/10, TNA; 'Communist Influence in the Far East', JIC(48)113(Final), 17 Dec 1948, DEFE 4/19, ibid.; 'Communist Strategy in S. E. Asia', FO memo., 12 Nov 1948, F15863/727/61, FO 371/69695, ibid.; and Tarling, *Britain*, pp.270–1.
9. Gallman to Marshall, 30 Jan 1948, 893.00/1-3048, Roll 9, IAC 1945–9, RG 59, NARA and Drumright to Marshall, 5 Feb 1948, 893.00/2-548, ibid.
10. A. Cooke, 'Republicans Tip-Toe Away From An Avalanche', *Manchester Guardian*, 23 Feb 1948; Butterworth oral history, 6 Jul 1971, HSTL; and Lowe, *Containing*, p.87.
11. Drumright to Marshall, 5 Feb 1948, 893.00/2-548, Roll 9, IAC 1945–9, RG 59, NARA. Bevin's arguments are in 'Future Foreign Publicity Policy', Bevin memo., CP(48)8, 4 Jan 1948, CAB 129/23, TNA and 'Review of Soviet policy', Bevin memo., CP(48)7, 5 Jan 1948, ibid.
12. 'Soviet Interests, Intentions and Capabilities', JIC(48)9(0)Final, 23 Jul 1948, DEFE 4/5, ibid.; 'Communist Strategy in S. E. Asia', FO memo., 12 Nov 1948, F15863/727/61, FO 371/69695, ibid.; Coates, minute, 30 Dec 1948, F17873/33/10, FO 371/69548, ibid.; and Blackham, minute, 3 Jan 1949, ibid. See also State Department (Office of Intelligence Research) memo., 2 Jul 1948, MF 515, OSS/State Department Intelligence and Research Reports, KCL.
13. R. Aldrich, G. Rawnsley and M-Y. Rawnsley, 'Introduction: The Clandestine Cold War in East Asia, 1945–65' in Special Issue: The Clandestine Cold War in Asia, 1945–65: Western Intelligence, Propaganda and Special Operations, *Intelligence and National Security*, 14 (1999), p.3; Cumings, *Origins*, ii, pp.365–9; and Y. Kim, 'The Origins of the Korean War: Civil War or Stalin's Rollback?', *Diplomacy & Statecraft*, 10 (1999), pp.186–214.
14. See Leys, minute, 1 Jul 1948, WO 208/4753, TNA and 'Communism in Countries Outside the Soviet Orbit', Bevin note, CP(48)223, 13 Sep 1948, CAB 129/29, ibid.
15. See 'China' unreferenced intelligence report, 10 Jan 1948, WO 208/4747, ibid.; Freeman to Butterworth, 13 Oct 1948, 893.00/9-848, Roll 11, IAC 1945–9, RG 59, NARA and Moscrir to George, 1 Aug 1946, Box 329, Entry 210, RG 226, ibid.
16. See T. Driberg, *Guy Burgess: A Portrait with Background* (London: Weidenfeld and Nicolson, 1956),.80–1; A. Purdy and D. Sutherland, *Burgess and Maclean* (London: Secker & Warburg, 1963), p.79; G. Blake, *No Other Choice: An Autobiography* (London: Jonathan Cape, 1990), pp.117; Lowe, *Containing*, p.186; and S. Kerr, 'Burgess, Guy Francis de Moncy (1911–1963)' in *Oxford Dictionary of National Biography* (Oxford: Oxford University Press, 2004–2008), www.oxforddnb.com.
17. Grazebrook to Tarver, 1 Apr 1948, WO 208/4833, TNA.
18. Blake, *Choice*, pp.110–14; E. H. Cookridge, *George Blake: Double Agent* (London: Hodder, 1970), pp.70–2; 'Soviet Interests, Intentions and Capabilities', JIC(48)9(0)Final, 23 Jul 1948, DEFE 4/5, TNA; and 'Communist Influence in the Far East', JIC(48)113(Final), 17 Dec 1948, CAB 158/5, ibid.
19. Scott, minute, 15 Jan 1948, F595/511/81, FO 371/69937, ibid.; Tomlinson, minute, 15 Jan 1948, ibid.; Kermode to Bevin, 17 Jan 1948, F2829/511/81, FO 371/69939, ibid.; and report on the activities of UNTCOK for the period, 8 Jan–15 Feb 1918, Jackson memo., 17 Feb 1948, 3123/4/5 Part 1, A1838/278, NAA.
20. Kermode to Hutchinson, 12 Feb 1946, BT 11/3560, TNA.
21. 'United States Policy in Korea', note by Secretaries to JCS, JCS 1483/49, 15 Jan 1948, RJCS: 1946–1953, MF 51, KCL.

22. Ibid. and 'United States Policy in Korea', report by the JSSC to the JCS, JCS 1483/50, 30 Jan 1948, ibid.
23. Tomlinson, minute, 23 Jan 1948, F1373/1373/81, FO 371/69954, TNA.
24. Lovett memo., 3 Jan 1948, *FRUS*, vi, *The Far East and Australasia, 1948* (Washington: United States Government Printing Office, 1974), pp.1079–81.
25. Pearson memo., 11 Jan 1948 in H. M. Mackenzie (ed.), *Documents on Canadian External Relations (DCER)*, xiv, 1948 (Ottawa: Department of Foreign Affairs and International Trade, 1994), doc. 92; Truman to King, 5 Jan 1948, *FRUS*, 1948, vi, pp.1081–3; New York tel. 9, 6 Jan 1948, ibid., doc.93; King to Truman, 8 Jan 1948, ibid., doc.98; Wailes memo. for Lovett, 9 Jan 1948, *FRUS*, 1948, vi, p.1084; and Ottawa tel. 45, 16 Jan 1948, F1373/1373/81, FO 371/69954, TNA. See also J. Munro and A. Inglis (eds.), *Mike: The Right Honourable Lester B. Pearson: Memoirs 1948–1957*, ii, *The International Years* (Toronto: University of Toronto Press, 1973), pp.135–45.
26. Jacobs to Marshall, 5 Feb 1948, *FRUS*, 1948, vi, pp.1093–4; Jacobs to Marshall, 8 Feb 1948, ibid., pp.1095–7; Jacobs to Marshall, 12 Feb 1948, *FRUS*, 1948, vi., pp.1105–09; and Lowe, *Containing*, p.176. On the Australian attitude, see Department of External Affairs tel. 33, 28 Jan 1948, 3123/4/5, Part 1, A1838/278, NAA; Tokyo tel. 83, 15 Feb 1948, ibid.; Canberra (DEA) tel. 580, 18 Feb 1948, ibid.; and R. O'Neill, *Australia in the Korean War*, i: *Strategy and Diplomacy* (Canberra: Australian Government Publishing Service, 1981), pp.7–8. On the views of Shaw and Jackson, see 'Korean Commission', Jackson memo., 6 Jan 1948, 3123/4/5 Part 1, A1838/278, NAA; Tokyo despatch 3/48, 9 Jan 1948, ibid.; and Shaw to Jackson, 9 Jan 1948, ibid. On the use of Kermode's office as a ciphering office, see Kermode to Bevin, 16 Mar 1948, F4990/511/81, FO 371/69940, TNA and Jackson memo., 16 Feb 1948, 3123/4/5 Part 1, A1838/278, NAA.
27. Kermode to Bevin, 7 Feb 1948, F2918/511/81, FO 371/69939, TNA; Tomlinson, minute, 24 Feb 1948, ibid.; Seoul tel. 13, 9 Feb 1948, F2191/511/81, FO 371/69937, ibid.; and Scott, minute, n.d., ibid. See also Butler to Marshall, 12 Feb 1948, *FRUS*, 1948, vi, p.1104; St. Laurent to Patterson, 11 & 13 Feb 1948, *DCER*, 1948, xiv, doc. 105 & 107; Gallman to Marshall, 12 Feb 1948, *FRUS*, 1948, vi, p.1105; Tomlinson, minute, 11 Feb 1948, F 2191/511/81, FO 371/69337; MacDermot, minute, 12 Feb 1948, ibid.; New York tel. 439, 11 Feb 1948, F2280/511/81, ibid.; Scott, minute, 13 Feb 1948, ibid.; MacDermot, minute, 13 Feb 1948, ibid.; and FO tel. 658, 13 Feb 1948, ibid.
28. Hodge to Marshall, 14 Feb 1948, *FRUS*, 1948, vi, pp.1110–13; Hodge to Marshall, 22 Feb 1948, ibid., pp.1125–7; Kermode to Bevin, 12 Feb 1948, F3983/511/81, FO 371/69940, TNA; Kermode to Bevin, 19 Feb 1948, F3986/29/81, FO 371/69936, ibid.; Tomlinson, minute, 18 Feb 1948, F2825/29/81, ibid.; 'Korea', MacDermot, minute, 18 Feb 1948, F2631/511/81, FO 371/69938, ibid.; Douglas to Marshall, 20 Feb 1948, *FRUS*, 1948, vi, p.1121; and Marshall to embassy in the United Kingdom, 21 Feb 1948, ibid., pp.1124–5 and fn.1.
29. New York tel. 155, 20 Feb 1948, P. Andre (ed.), *DAFP*, 1948–9, xvi, *Australia and the Postwar World – Beyond the Region* (Canberra: Australian Government Publishing Service, 2001), doc. 138; New York tel. 170, 24 Feb 1948, ibid., doc. 139; Pearson to King, 25 Feb 1948, *DCER*, 1948, xiv, doc. 113; Riddell to Pearson, tel. 229, 25 Feb 1948, ibid., doc. 114; New York tel. 260, 25 Feb 1948, ibid., doc. 115; and Ottawa tel. 238, 26 Feb 1948, ibid., doc. 117. See also Butterworth to Marshall, 4 Mar 1948, *FRUS*, 1948, vi, pp.1137–9; Austin to Marshall, 1 Mar 1948, ibid. pp.1134–6; Matray, *Crusade*, pp.144–5; Lowe, *Containing*, p.176; and

W. Stueck, *The Korean War: An International History* (Princeton, NJ: Princeton University Press, 1995), p.26.

30. See Langdon to Marshall, 10 Mar 1948, *FRUS*, 1948, vi, pp.1146–8; Marshall to Austin, 11 Mar 1948, ibid., pp.1149–50; Langdon to Marshall, 12 Mar 1948, pp.1150–3; St. Laurent to Patterson, 3 Mar 1948, *DCER*, 1948, xiv, doc. 120; Tokyo tel. 74, 5 Mar 1948, ibid., doc. 121; Pearson memo., 11 Mar 1948, ibid., doc. 125; and Matray, *Crusade*, p.145.

31. Canberra (DEA) tel. 235, 6 Mar 1948, *DAFP*, 1948–9, xvi, doc. 141 and McIntyre note, 1 Apr 1948, *DAFP*, 1948–9, xvi, doc. 145.

32. Kermode to Bevin, 16 Mar 1948, F4990/511/81, FO 371/69940, TNA; Crowther to Bevin, 29 Apr 1948, F7341/511/81, FO 371/69941, ibid.; Jacobs to Marshall, 29 Mar 1948, *FRUS*, 1948, vi, pp.1162–3; Lovett to Jacobs, 5 Apr 1948, ibid., pp.1170–2; and Jacobs to Marshall, 9 Apr 1948, ibid., pp.1177–8; and Matray, *Crusade*, p.147.

33. McIntyre, minute for Shann, 7 May 1948, *DAFP*, 1948–9, xvi, doc. 147.

34. Jacobs to Marshall, 19 May 1948, *FRUS*, 1948, vi, pp.1201–2; Seoul tel. no.40, 8 May 1948, F6718/511/81, FO 371/69941, TNA; Scott, minute, 10 May 1948, ibid.; Scott, minute, 11 May 1948, F6654/511/81, ibid.; Seoul tel. 46, 25 May 1948, F7485/511/81, ibid. and Cumings, *Origins*, ii, pp.379–407.

35. 'United States Policy in Korea', SANACC 176/39, 22 Mar 1948, RJCS: 1946–1953, MF 51, KCL; 'The Position of the United States with Respect to Korea', note by secretaries to JCS, JCS 1483/54, 9 Apr 1948, ibid.; 'Report by the National Security Council on the Position of the United States with Respect to Korea', NSC 8, 2 Apr 1948, *FRUS*, 1948, vi, pp.1164–9; Draper to Lovett, 3 May 1948, ibid., pp.1186–8; Jacobs to Marshall, 6 May 1948, ibid., pp.1191–2; and Butterworth to Marshall and Lovett, 11 May 1948, ibid., pp.1192–5.

36. Butterworth to Gross, 25 May 1948, ibid., pp.1204–06; Tomlinson, minute, 3 Jun 1948, F7836/511/81, FO 371/69941, TNA; MacDermot, minute, 4 Jun 1948, ibid.; and Sargent, minute, 8 Jun 1948, ibid.

37. FO tel. 6718, 22 Jun 1948, F7836/511/81, FO 371/69941, ibid.; Washington tel. 3076, 24 Jun 1948, F8868/511/81, FO 371/69942, ibid.; Tomlinson, minute, 28 Jun 1948, ibid.; FO tel. 7215, 3 Jul 1948, ibid.; and FO tel. 7216, 3 Jul 1948, ibid.

38. Washington tel. 3337, 8 Jul 1948, F9317/511/81, ibid.; FO memo. handed to US embassy, 14 July 1948, F9509/511/81, ibid., FO tel. 89, 20 Jul 1948, F9802/511/81, FO 371/69943, ibid.; Nielson to Marshall, 14 Jul 1948, *FRUS*, 1948, vi, pp.1241–2; Donovan to Marshall, 19 Jul 1948, ibid., p.1246; Douglas to Marshall, 19 Jul 1948, ibid., pp.1247–8; Jessup to Marshall, 20 Jul 1948, ibid., pp.1249–51; Holt to Bevin, 6 Jul 1948, F9317/511/81, FO 371/69942, TNA; Holt to MacDermot, 15 Jul 1948, F10201/29/81, FO 371/69936, ibid.; Lowe, *Containing*, pp.178–9; idem. *Origins*, pp.56–8; and Farrar-Hockley, *Korean War*, i, pp.20–2. On the British refusal to issue a statement, see FO tel. 626, 13 Aug 1948, F/511/81, FO 371/69944, TNA and Douglas to Marshall, 13 Aug 1948, *FRUS*, 1948, vi, p.1273.

39. Jacobs to Marshall, 12 Aug 1948, ibid., p.1272; Butterworth memo., 17 Aug 1948, ibid., pp.1276–8; Marshall to Certain Diplomatic and Consular Officers Abroad, 10 Jul 1948, ibid., pp.1235–7; Butterworth memo., 17 Aug 1948, ibid., pp.1276–9; 'Future Economic Assistance to Korea', Saltzman memo., 7 Sep 1948, ibid., pp.1292–8; Marshall to Royall, 17 Sep 1948, ibid., pp.1302–03; Hoffman to Marshall, 1 Oct 1948, ibid., pp.1312–13; and 'The New Government in South

Korea: Its Form and Chances for Survival', State Department memo., 17 Aug 1948, RJCS: 1946–1953, MF 515, KCL.

40. FO tel. 9946, 4 Sep 1948, F12493/511/81, FO 371/69945, TNA.

41. Cheke to Graves, 28 Sep 1948, F12637/511/81, ibid. and CRO tel. 944, 28 Sep 1948, F13376/511/81, FO 371/69946, ibid.

42. Minutes of a meeting of the Commonwealth delegations, Paris, 9 Nov 1948, F13357/511/81, FO 371/69945, ibid. and 'Korea', Dening, minute, 9 Nov 1948, F15883/511/81, FO 371/69947, ibid.

43. UNCOK's new members were Australia, China, El Salvador, France, India, the Philippines and Syria. See Draft Resolution on Korea for the UN General Assembly, 8 Nov 1948, *FRUS*, 1948, vi, pp.1321–22; 'Korea', Dening, minute, 9 Nov 1948, F15883/511/81, FO 371/69947; Paris (Australian UN delegation) tel. 303, 1 Dec 1948, *DAFP*, 1948–9, xvi, doc. 157; Paris tel. 363, 12 Dec 1948, ibid., doc. 159; Canberra (DEF) tel. 26, 2 Feb 1949, doc. 162; and Farrar-Hockley, *Korean War*, i, p.26.

44. Policy Planning Staff memo., 7 Sep 1948, *FRUS*, viii, *The Far East: China, 1948* (Washington: United States Government Printing Office, 1973), pp.146–65; Washington tel. 1069, 6 Mar 1948, F3611/190/10, FO 371/69584, TNA.; Leffler, *Preponderance*, p.249; and T. J. Christensen, *Useful Adversaries: Grand Strategy, Domestic Mobilization, and Sino-American Conflict, 1947–1958* (Princeton, NJ: Princeton University Press, 1996), pp.60–1. For the United States debate over the grant of aid to China, see *FRUS*, 1948, viii, pp.442–685.

45. 'China-Military Situation', JIC(48)30(0), 13 May 1948, CAB 158/3, TNA and Field to Tarver, 24 May 1948, WO 208/4922, ibid. See also P. Cradock, *Know Your Enemy: How the Joint Intelligence Committee Saw the World* (London: John Murray, 2002), p.83.

46. Under the 1898 Anglo-Chinese Convention, Chinese claims for jurisdiction over Kowloon City were correct. But after disturbances in 1899 by repeated attacks on British forces, the latter occupied the city in 1899 and refused to recede on this position. Nanking tel.18, 9 Jan 1948, F1764/35/10, FO 371/69552, TNA; Canton tels 13–15, 17–18 Jan 1948, 893.00/1-1748 & 1848, Roll 8, IAC 1945–9, RG 59, NARA; London tel. A-288, 26 Jan 1948, 893.00/1-2648, Roll 9, ibid.; Clark to Butterworth, 17 Feb 1948, 893.00/2-1748, ibid.; Ringwalt to Butterworth, 2 Apr 1948, 893.00/3-2248, ibid.; Canton to Nanking, tel.1A, 22 Jan 1948, F2019/361/10, FO 371/69605, TNA; Canton to Nanking, tel.2A, 22 Jan 1948, F1900/361/10, ibid.; Scarlett minute, 10 Mar 1948; F3602/154/10, FO 371/69580; Hong Kong tel.956, 20 Oct 1948, F14784/154/10, FO 371/69583, ibid.; Field to Tarver, 4 Feb & 3 Mar 1948, WO 208/4922, ibid.; and 'China-Military Situation', JIC(48)30(0), 13 May 1948, DEFE 4/13, ibid.

47. 'Communism in China', *The Times*, 12 Feb 1948; Stevenson to Bevin, 2 Feb 1948, F2535/33/10, FO 371/69527, TNA; Scott, minute, 24 Feb 1948, ibid.; Scarlett, minute, 27 Feb 1948, ibid.; and Dening, minute, 9 Mar 1948, ibid. These decisions were conveyed to the China Association. See Scarlett to Mitchell, 31 Mar 1948, CHAS/C/3, China Association papers, SOAS.

48. Lamb to Dening, 25 May 1948, F8032/33/10, FO 371/69534, TNA.

49. Stevenson to Bevin, 7 Apr 1948, F6117/33/10, FO 371/69531, ibid. and Lamb to Bevin, 25 May 1948, F8050/33/10, FO 371/69534, ibid. On Mao's outlook see Jian, *Mao's China*, pp.39–41.

50. MacDonald to Stevenson, 16 Jun 1948 (sent 10 Jul 1948), 22/2/61, MacDonald papers, DUL; Westad, *Decisive*, p.164; and Qing, *Allies*, p.7.

51. Herndon to Allison, 12 Aug 1948, 893.00/6-848, Roll 10, IAC 1945–9, RG 59, NARA. See summaries of Stuart's comments in Butterworth to Marshall, 8 Jul 1948, 893.00/6-1448, ibid.; Butterworth to Marshall, 21 Jul 1948, 893.00/7-2148, Roll 11, ibid.; Butterworth to Marshall, 27 Jul 1948, 893.00/7-1748, ibid.; Butterworth to Marshall, 27 Jul 1948, 893.00/7-2748, ibid.; Butterworth to Marshall, 30 Jul 1948, 893.00/6-3048, Roll 10, ibid. and Stuart to Marshall, 17 Jul 1948, 893.00/7-1748, Roll 11, ibid.

52. Nanking tel. 544, 1 Jul 1948, F9228/33/10, FO 371/69535, TNA; Nanking tel. 567, 7 Jul 1948, F9585/33/10, FO 371/69536, ibid.; Scott, minute, 13 Jul 1947, ibid.; Nanking tel. 1473, 10 Aug 1948, 893.00/8-1048, Roll 11, IAC 1945–9, RG 59, NARA and Butterworth to Marshall, 16 Aug 1948, 893.00/7-3048, ibid.

53. Butterworth to Marshall, 9 Aug 1948, 893.00/6-3048, Roll 10, ibid.; State Department tel. 1164, 12 Aug 1948, 893.00/6-3048, ibid.; and State Department tel. 1038, 16 Jul 1948, 893.00/7-1448, ibid.

54. Butterworth to Marshall, 21 Jul 1948, 893.00/7-2148, Roll 11, ibid.

55. Nanking tel. 585, 14 Jul 1948, F9876/33/10, FO 371/69536, TNA; Scott, minute, 19 Jul 1948, F9833/33/10, ibid.; Lamb to Scott, 10 Sep 1948, F13826/33/10, FO 371/69539, ibid.; and Scott, minute, 8 Oct 1948, ibid.

56. Dening, minute, 19 Mar 1948, F4392/33/10, FO 371/69529, ibid. and Scarlett, minute, 14 Jun 1948, F8226/6139/23, FO 371/69927, ibid.

57. Marshall to Butterworth, 14 May, 893.00/5-1448, Roll 10, IAC 1945–9, RG 59, NARA; 'Action by U.S. Forces at Tsingtao in Defense of U.S. Lives and Property', Souers note, NSC 11, 24 May 1948, ibid.; Butterworth to Marshall, 24 May 1948, 893.00/5-2448, ibid.; Marshall to Forrestal, 28 May 1948, 893.00/5-2848, ibid.; Butterworth to Marshall, 8 Jun 1948, 893.00/6-848, ibid.; Nanking tel. 1044, 9 Jun 1948, 893.00/6-948, ibid.; Forrestal to Marshal, 17 Jun 1948, 893.00/6-1748, ibid.; Butterworth to Marshall, 8 Jul 1948, 893.00/6-1448, ibid.; State Department note, 28 Aug 1948, 893.00/6-1748, ibid.; and Butterworth to Lovett, 1 Oct 1948, 893.00/10-148, Roll 11, ibid.

58. State Department tel. 96, 24 Oct 1948, 893.00/10-2348, ibid.; Butterworth to Lovett, 2 Dec 1948, 893.00/12-248, ibid.

59. Memo of conversation, 2 Jun 1948, 893.00/6-248, Roll 10, ibid.; Washington tel. 222, 5 Jun 1948, F8226/6139/23, FO 371/69927, TNA; Scarlett, minute, 14 Jun 1948, ibid.; and Dening, minute, 15 Jun 1948, ibid. See also memo. of conversation by Marshall, 11 Jun 1948, *FRUS*, 1948, viii, pp.90–9. For US views on Scarlett, see Ringwalt to Merchant, 7 Feb 1950, 790.00/2-50, Roll 1, Central Files, The Far East, 1950–54, C0046, RG 59, NARA.

60. Cabot oral history, 18 Jul 1973, HSTL.

61. Field to Tarver, 24 May 1948, WO 208/4922, TNA.

62. State Department tel. 1180, 13 Aug 1948, 893.00/8-1048, Roll 11, IAC 1945–9, RG 59, NARA and Kennan to Marshall, 12 Aug 1948, 893.00/8-1248, ibid.

63. State Department tel. 96, 24 Oct 1948, 893.00/10-2348, ibid.

64. Nanking tel. 1807, 30 Sep 1948, 893.00/9-3048, ibid.; Stuart to Marshall, 14 Oct 1948, 893.00/10-1448, ibid.; Nanking tel. 1010, 18 Nov 1948, F16258/33/10, FO 371/69542, TNA; and Dreyer, *China*, pp.336–40.

65. Nanking tel. 2053, 1 Nov 1948, 893.00/11-148, Roll 11, IAC 1945–9, RG 59, NARA; State Department tel. 1534, 2 Nov 1948, 893.00/11-248, ibid. and Field to Tarver, 15 Nov 1948, WO 208/4922, TNA.

66. A. Cooke, 'Chinese Government in Greater Danger: Search for American Policy', *Manchester Guardian*, 12 Nov 1948.

67. London tel. 4724, 2 Nov 1948, 893.00/11-248, Roll 11, IAC 1945–9, RG 59, NARA.
68. FO tel. 12050, 11 Nov 1948, F15941/33/10, FO 371/69541, TNA and Washington tel. 5240, 17 Nov 1948, F16203/33/10, FO 371/69542, ibid.
69. Marshall to Lovett, 26 Nov 1948, 893.00/11-2648, Roll 12, IAC 1945–9, RG 59, NARA; Washington tel. 5437, 29 Nov 1948, F16909/190/10, FO 371/69587, TNA; and Fenby, *Generalissimo*, p.480.
70. Nanking tel. 1010, 18 Nov 1948, F16258/33/10, FO 371/69542, TNA; Scarlett, minute, 23 Nov 1948, ibid.; and Dening, minute, 23 Nov 1948, ibid.
71. Paris tel. 109, 19 Nov 1948, F16331/190/10, FO 371/69586, ibid.; Lamb to Scarlett, 29 Nov 1948, F17873/33/10, FO 371/69548, ibid.; Coates, minute, 30 Dec 1948, ibid.; Blackburn, minute, 3 Jan 1949, ibid.; Scott, minute, 11 Jan 1949, ibid.; Mackenzie, minute, 14 Jan 1949, ibid.; Coates, minute, 22 Dec 1948, F17966/33/10, ibid.; Scarlett, minute, 23 Dec 1948, ibid.; and Dening, minute, 3 Jan 1949, ibid.
72. 'Recent Developments in the Civil War in China', Bevin memo., CP(48)299, 9 Dec 1948, CAB 129/31(Part I), ibid. and cabinet minutes, CM(48)80, 13 Dec 1948, CAB 128/13, ibid.
73. Dening to Graves, 29 Dec 1948, F18545/33/10, FO 371/69550, ibid. The paper was summarised for the Americans by Franks. See Satterthwaite to Butterworth, 5 Jan 1949, 893.00/1-549, Roll 13, LM 69, IAC 1945–9, RG 59, NARA and Franks to Lovett, 5 Jan 1949, ibid.
74. Gascoigne to Bevin, 19 Dec 1947, F64/60/23, FO 371/69802, TNA and Green, minute, 10 Jan 1948, ibid. See also Lowe, 'Allied Occupation', p.181 and H. Schonberger, 'The Japan Lobby in American Diplomacy, 1947–1952', *Pacific Historical Review*, 46 (1977), pp.327–59. On McCoy's announcement to the Far Eastern Commission, see Cheke, minute, 7 Jan 1948, F207/4/23, FO 371/69802, TNA; Washington tel. 322, 21 Jan 1948, F1187/4/23, ibid.; Scott, minute, 23 Jan 1948, ibid.; and Cheke, minute, 23 Jan 1948, ibid. See also Lowe, *Containing*, p.15 and idem, *Origins*, p.84.
75. Gairdner to MacArthur, 10 Jan 1948, F1464/4/23, FO 371/69803, TNA; Gascoigne to MacDermot, 11 Jan 1948, ibid.; Gascoigne to MacDermot, 8 Mar 1948, F4830/4/23, FO 371/69806, ibid.; Gascoigne to MacDermot, 7 May 1948, F7351/4/23, FO 371/69808, ibid.; Eichelberger to Gascoigne, 22 May 1948, ibid.; Gascoigne to MacDermot, 27 May 1948, ibid.; Gilbert to MacDermot, 2 Jun 1948, ibid.; and Gascoigne to Dening, 9 Oct 1948, F14952/44/23, FO 371/69825, ibid.
76. CRO tel. 25, 27 Jan 1948, F1484/4/23, FO 371/69803, ibid.; CRO tel. 71, 4 Mar 1948, ibid.; Interdepartmental Committee for Trade with Japan, TJ(48)12, 18 Feb 1948, F2134/2134/23, FO 371/69913, ibid.; Gascoigne to Bevin, 31 May 1948, F8311/4/23, FO 371/69809, ibid.; Gascoigne to MacArthur, 1 Jun 1948, ibid.; Canberra tel. 18, 4 Jun 1948, P. Andre (ed.), *DAFP*, 1948–9, xiv, *The Commonwealth, Asia and the Pacific* (Canberra: Australian Government Publishing Service, 1998), doc. 374; Report by Clark, Wrigley and McWatters, 17 Aug 1948, ibid., doc. 375; and Tokyo tel. 790, 29 Jul 1948, F10499/4/23, FO 371/69813, TNA. See also Buckley, *Occupation*, pp.166–70 and Yokoi, *Anglo-Japanese Relations*, chp.2.
77. McNeil, minute for Bevin, 3 Jun 1948, F8332/6139/23, FO 371/69927, TNA; Wilson to Bevin, 8 Jul 1948, F10090/4/23, FO 371/69812, ibid.; Bevin to Wilson, 17 Jul 1948, ibid.; Bevin, minute, 18 Aug 1948, F10929/60/23, FO 371/69814, ibid.; minutes of a meeting held at the Foreign Office, 4 Oct 1948, F13779/60/23,

FO 371/69815B; Cheke, minute, 4 Oct 1948, ibid.; and Bevin to Wilson, 4 Nov 1948, F15008/4/23, FO 371/69815C, ibid. See also Lowe, *Origins*, pp.85–6 and idem, *Containing*, p.60.

78. MacDermot, minute, 24 Jan 1948, F1187/4/23, FO 371/69802, TNA; CRO tel. 7, 14 Feb 1948, F471/46/23, FO 371/69829, ibid.; Tokyo tel. 248, 11 Mar 1948, F4043/662/23, FO 371/69885, ibid.; Tokyo tel. 270, 17 Mar 1948, F4213/662/23, ibid.; FO tel. 239, 18 Mar 1948, F4215/662/23, ibid.; and Tokyo tel. 278, 20 Mar 1948, F4352/66/23, ibid. See also conversation between MacArthur and Kennan, 5 Mar 1948, *FRUS*, 1948, vi, pp.699–706; Kennan to Marshall, 14 Mar 1948, 711.90/3-1048, Roll 1, C0045, Central Files, The Far East, 1945–9, RG 59, NARA; Schaller, *Altered*, p.16; and idem, *Occupation*, chp.6 & 7.

79. Tokyo tel. 302, 28 Mar 1948, F4638/662/23, FO 371/69885, TNA.

80. Tokyo tel. 311, 1 Apr 1948, F4839/662/23, ibid.

81. Cheke, minute, 3 Apr 1948, F4638/662/23, ibid.; MacDermot to Graves, 5 Apr 1948, ibid.; FO tel. 277, 3 Apr 1948, ibid.; Australia (Govt.) tel. 86, 6 Apr 1948, F4829/662/23, ibid.; Tomlinson, minute, 13 Apr 1948, F52336/662/23, ibid.; and FO tel. 320, 17 Apr 1948, F5236/662/23, FO 371/69886, ibid.

82. 'Recommendations with Respect to U.S. Policy toward Japan', Kennan memo., PPS 28, 25 Mar 1948, *FRUS*, 1948, vi, pp.691–719; conversation between MacArthur and Kennan, 5 Mar 1948, ibid., pp.699–703; Cargo memo. for Gerig, 5 Apr, ibid., pp.722–24; Thorp memo. for Butterworth, 6 Apr 1948, ibid., pp.964–66; Saltzman memo. for Butterworth, 9 Apr 1948, ibid., pp.727–36; and Schaller, *Altered*, pp.15–16.

83. Conversation between MacArthur, Draper and Kennan, 21 Mar 1948, *FRUS*, 1948, vi, pp.706–9; Allison memo. for Hamilton, 30 Apr 1948, ibid., pp.742–3; Schaller, *Occupation*, p.124; Dower, *Japan*, p.174; and idem, 'Occupied Japan', pp.390–1.

84. Graves to MacDermot, 8 Apr 1948, F5789/662/23, FO 371/69886, TNA and Gascoigne to Bevin, despatch no.87, 10 Apr 1948, F6048/662/23, ibid.

85. Graves to Dening, 17 Apr 1948, F6104/662/23, ibid.; Tomlinson, minute, 3 May 1948, ibid.; Inverchapel to Bevin, 27 Apr 1948, F6489/662/23, FO 371/69887, ibid. and Bevin to Balfour, 27 May 1948, ibid.

86. See 'Comments on the Reparation Section of the Johnston Report', Shearer, minute, n.d., F8309/4/23, FO 371/69809, ibid.; Gascoigne to Bevin, 28 May 1948, ibid.; Sebald to Marshall, 13 Aug 1948, *FRUS*, 1948, vi, pp.837–9; Marshall to Royall, 26 Aug 1948, ibid., pp.996–1000; Sebald to Marshall, 9 Dec 1948, ibid., pp.916–21; Schaller, *Occupation*, pp.129–32; and Lowe, *Containing*, pp.16–20.

87. 'Far Eastern Policy', Dening, minute, 24 Mar 1948, F8770/6139/23, FO 371/69927, TNA.

88. Bevin, minute, 25 Mar 1948, ibid.; Dening, minute, 1 Apr 1948, ibid.; Bevin, minute for Attlee, 3 Apr 1948, PREM 8/736, ibid. and Attlee, minute, 5 Apr 1948, ibid. See also C. Andrew, 'The Growth of the Australian Intelligence Community and the Anglo-American Connection', *Intelligence and National Security*, 4 (1989), pp.226–9.

89. Dening to Machtig, 7 May 1948, PREM 8/736, TNA and Dening to Machtig, 25 May 1948, ibid.

90. Shaw to Burton, 19 Mar 1948, *DAFP*, 1948–9, xiv, doc. 328; Dedman to Makin, 7 May 1948, ibid., doc. 340; and Saltzman to Makin, 8 Jul 1948, ibid., doc. 341. The Americans were forced to eventually send US troops to areas previously assigned to the BCOF in early 1949. See Saltzman to Makin, 7 Feb 1949, ibid.,

doc. 343. For Gascoigne's remarks on the council, see Gascoigne to MacDermot, 12 Feb 1948, F3453/45/23, FO 371/69828, TNA.

91. Washington tel. 2185, 10 May 1948, F6803/6139/23, FO 371/69926, ibid. and MacDermot, minute, 11 May 1948, ibid.
92. Washington tel. 2541, 29 May 1948, F7716/6139/23, ibid.
93. Washington tel.2546, 31 May 1948, F7845/6139/23, ibid. and FO tel. 5973, 2 Jun 1948, F7716/6139/23, ibid.
94. Memo. of conversation by Green, 28 May 1948, *FRUS*, 1948, vi, pp.788–94 and Washington tel. 218, 4 Jun 1948, F8097/6139/23, FO 371/69926, TNA. For the Chiefs of Staff's views, see Hollis to Alexander, 2 Jul 1948, DEFE 4/14, ibid.
95. McNeil, minute for Bevin, 3 Jun 1948, F8332/6139/23, FO 371/69927, ibid.
96. Washington tel. 3474, 15 Jul 1948, F9870/662/23, FO 371/69887, ibid.
97. Dening to Wright, 1 Jun 1948, F8091/6139/23, FO 371/69926, ibid. and memo. of conversation by Green, 28 May 1948, *FRUS*, 1948, vi, pp.788–94.
98. Attlee to Chifley, 21 Jul 1948, PREM 8/1169, TNA.
99. 'Political and Economic Future of Japan', FO brief, 8 Jul 1948, F9431/4/23, FO 371/69811, ibid.; Chifley to Attlee, 27 Jul 1948, F10555/4/23, FO 371/69813, ibid.; Australia (Govt.) tel. 197, 31 Jul 1948, ibid.; New Zealand (Govt.) tel. 147, 29 Jul 1948, ibid.; and King to Attlee, 26 Jul 1948, ibid. Evatt's remarks can be found in Pink to Bevin, 21 Jul 1948, F10731/662/23, FO 371/69887, ibid. and Gascoigne to MacDermot, 26 Apr 1948, F6724/6724/23, FO 371/69928, ibid.
100. Dower, 'Occupied Japan', pp.391–3.
101. 'Russian Interests, Intentions and Capabilities', JIC(48)9(0)Final, 23 Jul 1948, DEFE 4/15, TNA.
102. 'Discussion of Japanese Problems with the Commonwealth Prime Ministers', Bevin memo., n.d., F13872/662/23, FO 371/70196, ibid.
103. See 'Aide-Mémoire' handed by the State Department to British embassy, Washington, 18 Aug 1948, F11846/4/23, FO 371/69814, ibid.
104. 'Recommendations with Respect to United States Policy toward Japan', NSC 13/2, 7 Oct 1948, *FRUS*, 1948, vi, pp.858–62.
105. Schaller, *Altered*, p.17.
106. Tokyo tel. 1314, 11 Nov 1948, F15991/33/10, FO 371/69542, TNA.
107. Draper to Lovett, 14 Dec 1948, *FRUS*, 1948, vi, pp.1062–63.
108. Gascoigne to Bevin, 18 Dec 1948, F527/1015/23, FO 371/76178, TNA; Gascoigne to Bevin, 1 Jan 1949, F1336/1011/23, FO 371/76176, ibid.; and Evatt, minute, PMM(48)3, 12 Oct 1948, CAB 133/88, ibid.
109. Dening to Graves, 29 Dec 1948, F18545/33/10, FO 371/69550, ibid.

7 The Road to War

1. 'Red Sky in the East', *Sunday Observer*, 6 Feb 1949 and 'South-East Asia', *Manchester Guardian*, 5 May 1949.
2. Acheson memo. for Jessup, 18 Jul 1949, 890.00/7-1649, Roll 3, C0045, Central Files, The Far East, 1945–9, RG 59, NARA; Yost to Jessup, 18 Jul 1949, 890.00/7-1049, Roll 3, ibid.; and meeting in Kennan's room, 18 Aug 1949, 890.00/8-1849, Roll 3, ibid.
3. 'Eleventh Hour in China', *Economist*, 23 Apr 1949.
4. Dickover to Acheson, 12 Jul 1949, 890.00/7-1249, Roll 3, Central Files, The Far East, 1945–9, RG 59, NARA.

5. Acheson to Douglas, 20 Jul 1949, *FRUS*, 1949, ix, *The Far East: China* (Washington: United States Government Printing Office, 1974), p.50 and Douglas to Acheson, 22 Jul 1949, 890.00/7-2249, Roll 3, Central Files, The Far East, 1945–9, RG 59, NARA.
6. Bullock, *Bevin*, p.88.
7. Qing, *Allies*, p.101.
8. Tarling, *Britain*, p.271 and Bayley and Harper, *Forgotten Wars*, chp.11.
9. MacDonald to Killearn, 26 Feb 1949, 22/6/80, MacDonald papers, DUL and MacDonald to Bevin, 23 Mar 1949, F4545/1073/61, FO 371/76033, TNA.
10. Paskin to Dening, 22 Apr 1949, F8037/1072/61, FO 371/76031, ibid.
11. Graves to Scarlett, 18 Jan 1949, F1397/1015/10, FO 371/75738, ibid. and memo of conversation, 18 Jan 1949, 893.00/1-1849, Roll 13, LM 69, IAC 1945–9, RG 59, NARA; 'United States Policy Toward Southeast Asia', Policy Planning Staff paper, PPS 51, 29 Mar 1949, *FRUS*, 1949 vii, part 2, pp.1128–33; and Hayter to Jebb, 20 May 1949, W3062/2/500, FO 371/76383, TNA.
12. Wellington tel. 206, 20 May 1949, PREM 8/968, ibid. and Bevin to Makins, 24 May 1949, W3160/21/68, FO 371/76375, ibid.
13. Acheson to Douglas, 20 Jul 1949, *FRUS*, 1949, ix, pp.50–2; and Xiang, *Recasting*, pp.201–2.
14. Dening, minute for Strang, 29 March 1949, F2191/1072/61, FO 371/76031, TNA; Acheson to Douglas, 20 Jul 1949, *FRUS*, 1949, ix, pp.50–2; and Tarling, *Britain*, pp.329–40.
15. 'The United Kingdom in South-East Asia and the Far East', PUSC(32)Final, 30 Aug 1949, W5572/3/500, FO 371/76386, TNA and 'Regional Co-operation in Southeast Asia and the Far East', PUSC(53)Final, 30 Aug 1949, W4743/3/500, FO 371/76385, ibid.
16. R. Ovendale, 'Britain, the United States, and the Cold War in South-East Asia, 1949–1950', *International Affairs*, 58 (1982), pp.457–8.
17. Tedder, Attlee and Montgomery minutes in COS(48)136, 24 Sep 1948, DEFE 4/16, TNA.
18. Cabinet minutes in CM(49)6, 24 Jan 1949 and CM(49)11, 10 Feb 1949, CAB 128/15, ibid.; and 'Defence Estimates, 1949–50', Alexander memo., CP(49)16, 20 Jan 1949, CAB 129/32 Part I, ibid.
19. Montgomery, minute, confidential annex to COS(48)94, 7 Jul 1948, DEFE 4/14, ibid.; 'Defence Review', COS memo., DO(48)61, 14 Sep 1948, CAB 131/6, ibid.; 'Soviet Intentions and Capabilities 1949 and 1956/57', JIC(48)104(Final), 8 Nov 1948, CAB 158/4, ibid.; Ross, *War Plans*, p.151; and Leffler, *Preponderance*, pp.210 & 263.
20. 'Report of the Inter-Service Working Party on Shape and Size of the Armed Forces', COS(49)113, 30 Mar 1949, DEFE 5/13, TNA. See also Tedder, Slim and Fraser minutes, COS(49)48, 28–30 Mar 1949, DEFE 4/20, ibid.; 'Responsibility of Commonwealth Countries in the Far East', JP(49)36(0)(T of R), 7 Apr 1949, DEFE 6/8, ibid.; and 'Responsibility of Commonwealth Countries in the Far East', JP(49)36(0)(Final), 13 May 1949, ibid. For a fuller analysis of the Harwood report, see Barnett, *Lost Victory*, pp.88–97 and Murfett, *Jeopardy*, pp.86–90.
21. See Chifley to Attlee, 24 May 1948, *DAFP*, 1948–9, xiv, doc. 98; 'Australian Defence Co-operation', JP(48)81(Final), 11 Sep 1948, DEFE 4/16, ibid.; 'Anzam Area Boundaries', JP(49)102(Final), 8 Sep 1949, DEFE 4/24, ibid.; 'Allied High Command in War – Anzam Area', JP(49)160(Final), 22 Dec 1949, DEFE 4/28, ibid.; Attlee to Chifley, 29 Dec 1949, CAB 21/2537, ibid.; and Hack, 'South East

Asia', pp.315–17. American acceptance of the boundary can be found in COS minutes to Confidential Annex to COS(49)160, 28 Oct 1949, DEFE 4/25, TNA. See also W. D. McIntyre, *Background to the ANZUS Pact: Policy-Making, Strategy and Diplomacy, 1945–1955* (New York: St Martin's Press, 1995) and J. Williams, 'ANZUS: A Blow to Britain's Self Esteem', *Review of International Studies*, 13 (1987), pp.243–63.

22. Young, *Britain*, pp.148, 156; Kent, *Strategy*, pp.204–5; Bullock, *Bevin*, chps. 16–17; and Aldrich and Zametica, 'The Middle East', pp.259–64.
23. Tarling, *Britain*, pp.334–5 and 'The Colombo Conference', Bevin memo., CP(50)18, 22 Feb 1950, CAB 129/38, TNA.
24. 'The Position of the United States with Respect to Asia', NSC memo., NSC 48/1, 23 Dec 1949 in 'The Position of the United States with Respect to Asia', note by Secretaries to JCS, JCS 1992/6, 27 Dec 1949, RJCS: 1946–1953, MF 56, KCL. See also mem. of conversation by Butterworth, 12 Sep 1949, *FRUS, 1949, Vol.VII*, pp.1197–204. See also Schaller, *Altered States*, p.19.
25. See 'The Effect of Current Events on Proposed Wartime Strategy in South-East Asia', COS(50)89, 9 Mar 1950, DEFE 5/20, TNA and 'Strategy and Current Defence Policy in South-East Asia and the Far East', JP(50)47(Final), 6 Apr 1950, DEFE 4/30, ibid.
26. 'Defence Policy and Global Strategy', COS(50)139, 1 May 1950, DEFE 5/20, ibid.
27. Leffler, *Preponderance*, pp.298–9 and Lowe, 'Allied Occupation', pp.187–8. See also J. Dower, *Empire and Aftermath: Yoshida Shigeru and the Japanese Experience, 1878–1954* (Cambridge, MA: Harvard University Press, 1979).
28. 'Sir William Strang's Tour in South-East Asia and the Far East', Strang report for Bevin, 27 Feb 1949, F4447/1051/61, FO 371/76208, TNA.
29. Tokyo tel. 145, 10 Feb 1949, F2223/10345/23, FO 371/76215, ibid.; Tokyo tel. 172, 13 Feb 1949, F2328/10345/23, ibid.; Washington tel. 957, 16 Feb 1949, F2487/10345/23, ibid.; Tokyo tel. 172, 13 Feb 1949, F2328/10345/23, ibid.; memo. of conversation by Bishop, 16 Feb 1949, *FRUS*, 1949, vii, part 2, pp.655–8; and Schaller, *Occupation*, pp.164–5.
30. Dening to Graves, 14 Feb 1949, F2384/10345/23, FO 371/76215, TNA; Washington tel. 955, 16 Feb 1949, F2485/0345/23, ibid.; Dening, minute for Bevin, 23 Mar 1949, F4488/1023/61, FO 371/76023, ibid. and Pink to Scarlett, 25 Jun 1949, F9901/4/23, FO 371/76216, ibid.
31. Bishop to Butterworth, 18 Feb 1949, *FRUS*, 1949, vii, part 2, pp.659–62.
32. Schaller, *Altered*, pp.17–18.
33. 'Recommendations with Respect to United States Policy Toward Japan', Report by NSC, NSC 13/3, 6 May 1949 in 'Recommendations with Respect to United States Policy Toward Japan', Ives and Lalor note, JCS 1380/62, 9 May 1949, MF 47, RJCS 1946–53, KCL.
34. Acheson to certain Diplomatic Offices, 8 May 1949, ibid., pp.736–7; Dower, 'Occupied Japan', p.391; and Acheson, *Present*, passim.
35. Foster to Acheson, 13 May 1949, *FRUS*, 1949, vii, part 2, pp.744–6.
36. Franks to Bevin, 23 May 1949, F7919/10115/23, FO 371/76210, TNA. See also Hopkins, *Franks*, p.20.
37. Tomlinson, minute, 1 June 1949, F7919/10115/23, FO 371/76210, TNA.
38. 'Strategic Evaluation of United States Security Needs in Japan', JCS report, 9 June 1949, *FRUS*, 1949, vii, part 2, pp.774–7.

39. MacArthur's and the State Department's views are in Bishop memo. for Butterworth, 1 Apr 1949, ibid., pp.694–6.
40. 'Far East Strategy and Defence Policy', CIC(FE)(49)2(P), 12 Aug 1949, DEFE 5/15, TNA.
41. Brind's views are in Tokyo tel. 750, 13 Jul 1949, F10130/10115/23, FO 371/76210, ibid. See also Lowe, *Containing*, pp.19–21; idem, 'MacArthur', pp.56–8; and idem 'Allied Occupation', p.182.
42. Record of conversation between Kennan and Dening, 26 Jul 1949, W4528/2/500, FO 371/76383, TNA.
43. 'Japanese Participation in International Affairs', FO brief, 2 Sep 1949, F13321/1056/23, FO 371/76216, ibid.; 'Labour', FO brief, 2 Sep 1949, ibid.; and 'Reparations and Level of Industry', FO brief, 2 Sep 1949, ibid.
44. L. Xiang, 'The Recognition Controversy: Anglo-American Relations in China, 1949', *Journal of Contemporary History*, 27 (1992), p.319.
45. Nanking tel. 50, 13 Jan 1949, F671/1015/10, FO 371/75736, TNA; Coates, minute, 14 Jan 1949, ibid.; State Department tel. 43, 12 Jan 1949, 893.00/1-849, Roll 13, LM 69, IAC 1945–9, RG 59, NARA; memo. of conversation, 10 Jan 1949, ibid.; and Butterworth to Lovett, 10 Jan 1949, 893.00/1-1049, ibid. Bevin's views were handed to Butterworth by Graves on 11 Jan 1949, 893.00/1-1149, ibid. See also Nanking tel. 183, 12 Feb 1949, F2258/1015/10, ibid.; Coates, minute, 21 Feb 1949, F2631/1013/10, FO 371/75733; Nanking tel. 239, 2 Mar 1949, F3210/1015/10, FO 371/75743, ibid. and Stuart to Acheson, 28 Mar 1949, *FRUS*, viii, *The Far East: China, 1949* (Washington: United States Government Printing Office, 1978), pp.207–8.
46. Gaddis, *We Now Know*, p.65; Jian, *China's Road*, pp.68–70; idem, *Mao's China*, p.45; and Hunt, *Genesis*, pp.179–80.
47. 'Effects of Communist Successes in China', JIC(48)133(Revise), 6 Jan 1949, CAB 158/5, TNA. See also 'Communist Influence in the Far East', JIC(49)33(Final), 29 Apr 1949, CAB 158/6, ibid.
48. Addis to Heathcote-Smith, 11 Jan 1949, F1533/1019/10, FO 371/75785, ibid.; Coates, minute, 31 Jan 1949, ibid.; Beckett, minute, 1 Feb 1949; Dening, minute, 4 Feb 1949, ibid.; Scarlett, minute, 17 Feb 1949, F3305/1023/10, ibid.; Dening, minute, ibid.; and Sargent, minute, 18 Feb 1949, ibid. See also Jian, *Mao's China*, pp.39–40 and idem, 'The Ward Case and the Emergence of Sino-American Confrontation, 1948–1950', *The Australian Journal of Chinese Affairs*, 30 (1993), p.151–5.
49. Y. Kuisong, 'The Soviet Factor and the CCP's Policy Toward the United States in the 1940s', *Chinese Historians*, 1 (1992), pp.30–1; Nanking tel. 198, 17 Feb 1949, F2573/1015/10, FO 371/75741, TNA; Coates, minute, 21 Feb 1949, ibid.; and Scarlett, minute, 27 Feb 1949, ibid.
50. Coates, minute, 7 Mar 1949, F3255/1015/10, FO 371/75743, ibid. and Drumright to Acheson, 15 Feb 1949, 893.00/2-1549, Roll 14, IAC 1945–9, RG 59, NARA.
51. Hunt, *Genesis*, pp.173–4.
52. Cabinet minutes, CM(49)18, 8 Mar 1949, CAB 128/14, TNA.
53. Memo of conversation by Butterworth, 25 Feb 1948, 893.00/2-2549, Roll 14, IAC 1945–9, RG 59, NARA and Butterworth to Acheson, 17 Mar 1949, 893.00/3-1749, ibid.
54. J. Reston, 'U.S. will Now Follow Hands-off Policy in China', *New York Times*, 24 Apr 1949.

55. 'Prospects for Soviet Control of a Communist China', CIA report, ORE 29–49, 15 Apr 1949 obtained by the Foreign Office Far Eastern Department in F11453/10338/10, FO 371/75832, TNA. See also Burgess, minute, 22 Jun 1949, ibid., who thought this was a good report.
56. Shanghai tel. 516, 1 Jul 1949, F9684/1015/10, FO 371/75761, ibid.; Coates, minute, 6 Jul 1949, ibid.; and Scarlett, minute, 12 Jul 1949, ibid.
57. Scarlett to Coghill, 21 Jun 1949, F8354/1015/10, FO 371/75759, ibid.; Brimmell, minute, 5 Jul 1948, F9742/1015/10, FO 371/75761; and Coates, minute, 8 Jul 1948, ibid.
58. Jian, *Mao's China*, pp.44–8.
59. Dening, minute for Bevin, 16 Aug 1949, F12075/1015/10, FO 371/75766, TNA.
60. Franks to Bevin, 22 Mar 1949, F4595/1015/10, FO 371/75747, ibid. and Coates, minute, 2 Apr 1949, ibid.
61. 'Eleventh Hour in China', *Economist*, 23 Apr 1949.
62. Gaddis, *We Now Know*, pp.63–5; Goncharov, Lewis and Litai, *Uncertain*, pp.25–6 and C. Jian, 'The Sino-Soviet Alliance and China's Entry into the Korean War', *Cold War International Project: Woodrow Wilson International Center for Scholars* (1992), p.5.
63. 'Hong Kong', Creech Jones memo., CP(49)120, 23 May 1949, CAB 129/35, TNA.
64. FO tel. 4670, 29 Apr 1949, F5926/1015/10, FO 371/75750, ibid. The SIS report is in 'China: Shanghai/Nanking', MI2b report, 21 Apr 1949, WO 208/4575, ibid.
65. Memo of conversation, 29 Apr 1949, 893.00/4-2949, Roll 15, IAC 1945–9, RG 59, NARA.
66. Urquhart to Scarlett, 1 Dec 1948, F17436/33/10, F 371/69545, TNA
67. Shanghai tel. 349, 14 Dec 1948, F17634/33/10, FO 371/69546, ibid.; Nanking tel. 1160, 16 Dec 1948, F17842/33/10, FO 371/69547, ibid.; Coates, minute, 17 Dec 1948, ibid.; 'Shanghai', Scarlett note, 17 Dec 1948, F18147/33/10, FO 371/69549, ibid.; FO tel. 1043, 23 Dec 1948, ibid.; Shanghai tel. 388, 29 Dec 1948, F18434/33/10, FO 381/69550, ibid.; and minutes in COS(49)59, 25 Apr 1949, DEFE 4/21, ibid.
68. 'British Interests in China', memo. contained in Mitchell to Scarlett, 12 Jan 1949, F723/1153/10, FO 371/75864, ibid.
69. Cabot to Butterworth, 24 Mar 1949, 893.00/3-2449, Roll 14, IAC 1945–9, RG 59, NARA.
70. Cabot oral history, 18 Jul 1973, HSTL.
71. For the best account of this incident, see M. Murfett, *Hostage on the Yangtze: Britain, China, and the Amethyst Crisis of 1949* (Annapolis, MD: Naval Institute Press, 1991).
72. Shanghai tel. 315, 7 May 1949, F6541/1015/10, FO 371/75752, TNA; Coates, minute, 9 May 1949, ibid.; Butterworth memo. for Webb, 17 May 1949, *FRUS*, 1949, ix, pp.325–7; British Communities in China', FO memo., n.d., F10964/1611/10, FO 371/75942, TNA; and Shanghai tel. 526, 4 Jul 1949, F9793/1261/10, FO 371/75901, ibid.
73. Washington tel. 3288, 24 Jun 1949, F9263/261/10, FO 371/75900, ibid.; Scarlett, minute, 24 Jun 1949, F9198/261/10, ibid.; FO tel. 6508, 24 Jun 1949, ibid.; cabinet minutes, CM(49)42, 23 June 1949, CAB 128/15, ibid.; Nanking tel. 912, 25 Jun 1949, F9310/1261/10, FO 371/75900, ibid.; Shanghai tel. 294, 4 Jul 1949,

F9793/1261/10, FO 371/75901, ibid.; and Coates, minute, 14 Jul 1949, ibid. See also Butterworth to Acheson, 27 Jun 1949, 893.00/6-2749, Roll 16, IAC 1945–9, RG 59, NARA.

74. Shanghai tel. 294, 4 Jul 1949, F9793/1261/10, FO 371/75901, TNA.
75. C-in-C, Far Eastern Station Afloat, tel. 181244Z, 18 Jul 1949, F10769/1261/10, FO 371/75903, ibid. and Nanking tel. 1083, 21 Jul 1949, F10820/1261/10, ibid. Bevin's remarks were minuted down the margins of the telegram.
76. FO tel. 7303, 23 Jul 1949, F10861/1261/10, ibid. and FO tel. 7470, 29 Jul 1949, ibid.
77. Record of conversation between Kennan and Dening, 26 Jul 1949, W4528/2/500, FO 371/76383, ibid.
78. Washington tel. 3787, 1 Aug 1949, F11338/1261/10, FO 371/75904, ibid.; Tomlinson, minute, 3 Aug 1949, ibid.; Dening, minute, 4 Aug 1949, ibid.; and FO tel. 7581, 4 Aug 1949, ibid.
79. Canton to Far Eastern Department, 8 Aug 1949, F12201/1261/10, FO 371/75906, ibid.
80. Burgess, minute, 17 Aug 1949, ibid.; Tomlinson, minute, 18 Aug 1949, ibid., and Dening, minute, 25 Aug 1949, ibid.
81. 'Foreign Office Proposed Policy towards Communist China', MI2 memo. for DDMI, 25 Aug 1949, WO 208/4583, ibid.
82. Shanghai tel. 657, 6 Aug 1949, F11637/1015/10, FO 371/75765, ibid.
83. Cabinet minutes, CM(49)54, 29 Aug 1949, CAB 128/16, ibid.
84. Franklin, minute, 23 Nov 1949, F17349/1261/10, FO 371/75913, ibid.; Mitchell and Middleton to Strang, 12 Dec 1949, CHAS/C/3, China Association papers, SOAS; Scarlett to Graves, 21 Jan 1950, FC1261/24, FO 371/83424, TNA; Franklin, minute, FC1261/31, FO 371/83425, ibid. Franklin, minute, 14 Feb 1950, FC1261/34, ibid.; Graves to Scarlett, 4 Feb 1950, FC1261/31, ibid.; and 'Protection of British Interests in China against Nationalist Action', JP(50)19(Final), 1 Mar 1950, DEFE 6/12, ibid.
85. See 'The Position of the United States with Respect to Formosa', report by JSSC, JCS 1966/17, 9 Aug 1949, RJCS: 1946–1953, MF45, KCL; Tokyo tel. 1360, 15 Dec 1949, WO 208/4577, TNA, for the views of the US military and MacArthur. For State Department views, see Butterworth memo. for Acheson, 28 Dec 1949, *FRUS*, 1949, ix, pp.461–3; and memo. of conversation by Acheson, 29 Dec 1949, ibid., pp.463–7. On British views, see 'Implications of the Defection of the Nationalist Forces on the Security of Hong Kong', JIC(49)98(Final), 26 Oct 1949, CAB 158/8, TNA; 'Measures which might be Taken to Prevent Formosa and Its Military Assets Coming under Communist Control', JIC(49)99(Final), 27 Oct 1949, DEFE 4/26, ibid.; 'Security of Hong Kong – Effects of Possible Future Developments in Formosa', COS report, DO(49)73, 18 Nov 1949, DEFE 4/21, ibid.; and FO tel. 22, 8 Jan 1950, FC1022/30, FO 371/83279, ibid. See also N. B. Tucker, *Taiwan, Hong Kong, and the United States, 1945–1992: Uncertain Friendships* (New York: Twayne Publishers, 1994), pp.29–30.
86. 'Reinforcement of Hong Kong', Alexander memo., DO(49)32, 26 Apr 1949, CAB 131/6, TNA.
87. 'Hong Kong', Attlee memo., CP(49)119, 24 May 1949, CAB 129/35, ibid.; 'Defence of Hong Kong', Alexander memo., CP(49)118, 24 May 1949, CAB 128/35, ibid.; cabinet conclusions, CM(49)38, 26 May 1949, CAB 128/15, ibid.; and Ashton, Bennett and Hamilton (eds.), *DBPO, Series I*, viii, p.xxx.

88. MacDonald to Creech Jones, 30 Apr 1949, F6195/1061/10, FO 371/75839, TNA and Coates, minute, 3 May 1949, ibid.
89. MacDonald, minute, COS(49)73, 18 May 1949, DEFE 4/21, ibid.; Alexander, minute, COS(49)73, 18 May 1949, ibid.; Bevin, minute, SAC(49)5, 19 May 1949, CAB 134/669, ibid.; 'Hong Kong', Attlee memo., CP(49)119, 24 May 1949, CAB 129/35; and cabinet conclusions, CM(49)38, 26 May 1949, CAB 128/15, ibid.
90. Ottawa tel. 639, 28 May 1949, F7962/1192/10, FO 371/75873, ibid.; cabinet minutes, CM(49)42, 23 June 1949, CAB 128/15, ibid.; Colonial Office tel. 129, 6 Jul 1949, F10083/1192/10, FO 371/75877, ibid.; 'Current United Kingdom Policy in China and Hong Kong', JP(49)97(Final), 14 Sep 1949, DEFE 6/10, ibid.; and 'Implications of a Possible Chinese Communist Attack on Foreign Colonies in South China', COS, United States Army memo., 10 June 1949, JCS 1330/51, RJCS: 1946–1953, MF 56, KCL. See also J. Lombardo, 'A Mission of Espionage, Intelligence and Psychological Operations: The American Consulate in Hong Kong, 1949–64', in *Special Issue, Intelligence and National Security*, 14 (1999), pp.64–81.
91. 'Situation in South China as at 28th June 1949', JIC(49)44/10(Final), 24 Jun 1949, CAB 158/7, TNA; 'Recognition of Chinese Communist Government', JP(49)140(Final), 28 Nov 1949, DEFE 6/11, ibid.; 'A Review of the Threat to Hong Kong as at 4th October 1949', JIC(49)44/11(Final), 5 Oct 1949, CAB 158/7, ibid.; and 'Threat to Hong Kong', Price note, COS(50)143, 28 Apr 1950, DEFE 5/20, ibid.
92. Yost to Jessup, 18 Jul 1949, 890.00/7-1049, Roll 3, Central Files, The Far East, 1945–9, RG 59, NARA. See Xiang, 'Recognition Controversy', pp.321–9 for Anglo-American discussions on the economic embargo of a Communist China.
93. Douglas to Acheson, 29 Jul 1949, 890.00/7-2949, Roll 3, C0045, Central Files, The Far East, 1945–9, RG 59, NARA.
94. J. Chace, *Acheson: The Secretary of State Who Created the American World* (New York: Simon & Schuster, 1998), pp.219–20 and Leffler, *Preponderance*, pp.297–8.
95. 'China', Bevin memo., CP(49)180, 23 Aug 1949, CAB 129/36, TNA.
96. Muccio to Marshall, 12 Nov 1948, *FRUS*, 1948, vi, *The Far East and Australasia* (Washington: United States Government Printing Office, 1974), pp.1325–7; Saltzman to Wedemeyer, 9 Nov 1948, ibid., p.1324; Bishop to Butterworth, 17 Dec 1948, ibid., pp.1337–40; Leffler, *Preponderance*, p.253; and Matray, *Crusade*, pp.151–74.
97. 'Communist Influence in the Far East', JIC(48)113(Final), 17 Dec 1948, CAB 158/5, TNA; 'Effect of Communist Successes in China'. JIC(48)133(Revise), 6 Jan 1949, ibid.; and Scarlett to Holt, 28 Feb 1949, F3209/1015/81, FO 371/76258, ibid.
98. Tokyo tel. 516, 27 May 1948, F7609/1956/23, FO 371/69911, ibid.
99. Hoare, *Embassies*, pp.197–8.
100. Seoul tel. 83, 26 Oct 1948, F14961/511/81, FO 371/69947, TNA. See also Holt to Bevin, 19 Nov 1948, F17774/511/81, FO 371/69949, ibid. and Holt to Bevin, 6 Dec 1948, F18196/511/81, ibid.
101. Scott, minute, 27 Oct 1948, F14961/511/81, FO 371/69947, ibid.; Muccio to Marshall, 19 Nov 1948, *FRUS*, 1948, vi, pp.1331–2; and Farrar-Hockley, *Korean War*, i, p.26.
102. Toyko tel. no.1249, 29 Oct 1948, F15227/511/81, FO 371/69947, TNA and Tomlinson, minute, 2 Nov 1948, ibid.
103. Scarlett to Holt, 28 Feb 1949, F3209/1015/81, FO 371/76258, ibid.

104. See Stueck, *Korean War*, p.29; Cumings, *Origins*, ii, pp.325–76 and Weathersby, 'Soviet Aims', p.21.

105. J. Gaddis, *The Long Peace: Inquiries into the History of the Cold War* (Oxford: Oxford University Press, 1987), pp.95–6.

106. 'The Position of the United States with Respect to Korea', report by NSC, NSC 8/1, 16 Mar 1949 contained in JCS 1483/63, 18 Mar 1949, MF 51, KCL.

107. See draft memo. for Forrestal in 'The Position of the United States with Respect to Korea', JCS 1483/63, 18 Mar 1949, ibid.; and 'The Position of the United States with Respect to Korea', NSC 8/2, 22 Mar 1949, *FRUS*, 1949, vii, part 2, *The Far East and Australasia* (Washington: United States Government Printing Office, 1976), pp.969–78.

108. Drumright to Acheson, 28 Mar 1949, ibid., pp.979–80.

109. Editorial note in ibid., pp.1039–40; and Matray, *Crusade*, chp.8.

110. Holt to Scarlett, 27 Apr 1949, F7288/1015/81, FO 371/76258, TNA.

111. Tomlinson, minute, 23 May 1949, ibid.

112. See Rhee to Muccio, 14 Apr 1949, *FRUS*, 1949, vii, part 2, pp.990–1; Butterworth to Acheson, 18 Apr 1949, ibid., pp.992–3; and Muccio to Acheson, 6 May 1949, ibid., pp.1008–9.

113. Holt to Bevin, 30 Jan 1950, FK 1011/1, FO 371/84053, TNA; Farrar-Hockley, *Korean War*, i, p.30; Lowe, *Containing*, pp.179–80; and Stueck, *Korean War*, pp.27–8.

114. *The Times*, 6 Jul, 18 Aug & 5 Oct 1949.

115. Farrar-Hockley, *Korean War*, i, p.29.

116. *The Times*, 7 Sep 1949 and Bullock, *Bevin*, pp.716–20.

117. Memo of conversation, 9 Sep 1949, 711.00/9-749, Roll 10, C044, State Department Special Files: Northeast Asia, 1943–1956, RG 59, NARA.

118. Conversation between Dening and Butterworth at the State Department, 9 Sep 1949, F14256/1072/61, FO 371/76032, TNA and conversation between Dening, Butterworth and Livingston Merchant, 9 Sep 1949, F14193/1023/10, ibid.

119. Records mtgs. held at State Department, 13 Sep 1949, F14108–14109/1021/23, FO 371/76212, ibid. and record of mtg. at State Department, 17 Sep 1949, F14555/1021/23, ibid.

120. Dening to Strang, 15 Sep 1949, F14149/1024/6, FO 371/76024, ibid.; and Butterworth to Johnson, 2 Oct 1949, 740.00/9-749, Roll 10, C044, State Department Special Files: Northeast Asia, 1943–1956, RG 59, NARA.

121. Memo of conversation, 21 Sep 1949, 890.00/9-2149, Roll 3, C0045, Central Files, The Far East, 1945–9, ibid. and Attlee to Chifley, letter, 26 Sep 1949, PREM 8/966, TNA.

122. Nanking tel. 1391, 1 Sep 1949, F13102/1023/10, FO 371/75814, ibid.

123. See R. Ovendale, 'Britain, the United States, and the Recognition of Communist China', *Historical Journal*, 26 (1983), pp.139–58 and Xiang, 'Recognition Controversy', pp.319–43.

124. Porter, *Britain*, pp.38–9.

125. See minutes in JIC(50)50, 15 May 1950, CAB 159/7, TNA.

126. Lowe, *Containing*, pp.114–15; Goncharov, Lewis and Litai, *Uncertain Partners*, chp.3; and Jian, *Mao's China*, pp.52–3.

127. Leffler, *Preponderance*, p.337.

128. Franks to Bevin, 16 Jan 1950, F1022/5, FO 371/83013, TNA; and Franks to Bevin, 7 Feb 1949, FC1016/29, FO 371/83233, ibid.

129. Mitchell to FO, 1 Mar 1950, CHAS/C/4, China Association papers, SOAS; Shanghai tel. 248, 16 Mar 1950, FC1106/26, FO 371/83344, TNA; and record of Bevin's meeting with China Association, 16 Mar 1950, FC1106/30, ibid.
130. Lowe, *Containing*, pp.118–19 and Qing, *Allies*, p.107.
131. Gascoigne to Dening, 19 Sep 1949, F14735/1021/23, FO 371/76213, TNA.
132. Washington tel. 5740, 9 Dec 1949, F18486/1021/23, FO 371/76214, ibid.
133. Joint Chiefs of Staff memo. for Johnson, 22 Dec 1949, 740.0011/12-2349, Roll 10, C0044, US State Department Special Files: Northeast Asia, 1943–56, RG59, NARA and Johnson to Acheson, 23 Dec 1949, ibid.
134. Schaller, *Occupation*, pp.174–7.
135. Informal memo handed to Franks, 24 Dec 1949, 740.0011/12-2449, Roll 10, C0044, US State Department Special Files: Northeast Asia, 1943–56, RG59, NARA.
136. Lowe, *Containing*, p.22.
137. 'The Colombo Conference', Bevin memo., CP(50)18, 22 Feb 1950, CAB 129/38, TNA.
138. Douglas to Acheson, 17 Mar 1950, Folder 'Peace Treaty Developments since Sep 16, 1949', Roll 9, C0044, US State Department Special Files: Northeast Asia, 1943–56, RG59, NARA.
139. Discussion of Japanese Peace Treaty during London Visit, 5 May 1950, 694.00/5-556, Roll 10, C0044, US State Department Special Files: Northeast Asia, 1943–56, RG59, NARA and Lowe, *Containing*, p.23.
140. Jian, Mao's China, pp.54–5; K. Weathersby, 'Stalin', pp.275–6; and Lowe, *Containing*, p.182.
141. Ibid., p.181 and Cradock, *Knowing*, p.91.
142. Holt to Bevin, 5 Jan 1950, FK1011/1, FO 371/84053, TNA.
143. Dening, minute for Strang, 3 May 1950, F1022/15, FO 371/83013, ibid.
144. Gaddis, *Cold War*, pp.43, 164–5, Hopkins, *Franks*, p.159; and Franks oral history, 27 June 1964, HSTL.
145. Minutes in DO(50)11, 28 Jun 1950, H. J. Yasamee and K. A. Hamilton (eds.), *DBPO, Series II*, iv, *Korea, 1950–1951* (London: HMSO, 1991), doc. 4; minutes in CM(50)42, 4 Jul 1950, doc. 11; and Franks to Younger, 23 Jul 1950, doc. 25.
146. Lowe, *Containing*, p.194.

Conclusion

1. 'The Far East', *The Times*, 2 Jan 1950.
2. Hopkins, *Franks*, p.8.
3. M. Dockrill, 'The Foreign Office, Anglo-American Relations and the Korean War, June 1950–June 1951', *International Affairs*, 62 (1986), p.459.

Select Bibliography

Official papers

The National Archives, London
ADM   Admiralty records
AIR   Air Ministry records
BT   Board of Trade records
CAB   Cabinet Office records
DEFE   Ministry of Defence records
DO   Dominions Office records
FO   Foreign Office records
HW   Government Communications Headquarters records
PREM   Prime Minister's office records
WO   War Office records

National Archives and Records Administration, College Park, Maryland
RG 59   State Departments records
RG 165   War Department records
RG 218   Joint Chiefs of Staff records
RG 226   Office of Strategic Services (OSS) records
RG 353   Records of the Subcommittee for the Far East

National Archives of Australia, Canberra
A1838   Department of External Affairs: Central Office files
A2908   Department of External Affairs: Australian High Commission, London
A2937   Department of External Affairs: External Affairs Liaison Officer, London
A5954   Sir Frederick Shedden records

Liddell Hart Centre for Military Archives, King's College London
MF 44–57   Joint Chiefs of Staff records
MF 510–15   OSS/State Department Intelligence and Research Reports: Post-war Japan, Korea, and Southeast Asia

Private papers

British Library of Political and Economic Science, London School of Economics
Dalton papers
Meade papers
Webster papers

Churchill Archives Centre, Churchill College, Cambridge

Alexander papers
Cadogan papers
Churchill papers
Colville papers
Croft papers
Cunningham papers
Grigg papers
Jacob papers
Seymour papers
Strang papers

Durham University Library

MacDonald papers

Franklin D. Roosevelt Library, Hyde Park, New York

Roosevelt papers

Imperial War Museum

Montgomery papers
Field papers
Dening papers

Liddell Hart Centre for Military Archives, King's College London

Alanbrooke papers
Brind papers
Ismay papers
Mulleneux papers
Jacobs-Larkcom papers
Penney papers
Pyman papers

MacArthur Memorial Archives, Norfolk, Virginia

MacArthur papers

School of Oriental and African Studies Library, University of London

China Association papers
Ogden papers

Oral histories

Harry S. Truman Library, Independence, Missouri

Dean Acheson; Niles Bond; W. Walton Butterworth; John Cabot; Ashley Clarke; O. Edmund Clubb; William Draper; Oliver Franks; W. Averell Harriman; Robert

Lovett; Roger Makins; Livingston Merchant; Edmund Hall Patch; Edwin Pauley; Arthur Ringwalt; Charles Saltzman; and Philip Sprouse.

Official publications

(DBPO) Documents on British Policy Overseas, 1945–50, selected volumes (London).
(FRUS) Foreign Relations of the United States, 1944–1950, selected volumes (Washington).
(DAFP) Documents on Australian Foreign Policy, 1944–1950, selected volumes (Canberra).
(DCER) Documents on Canadian External Relations, 1948, selected volumes (Ottawa).
Cmd. 7709, *British Dependencies in the Far East 1945–1949* (London: HMSO, 1949).
The Earl Mountbatten of Burma, *Report to the Combined Chiefs of Staff by the Supreme Allied Commander South-East Asia 1943–1945* (London HMSO, 1951).

Newspapers

The Times, The Financial Times, Manchester Guardian, The Sunday Observer, The Scotsman, The New York Times, The Economist, Melbourne Herald, Sunday Pictorial, Madras Mail.

Memoirs, letters and diaries

Acheson, D., *Present at the Creation: My Years in the State Department* (London: W. W. Norton & Co., 1969).
Earl of Avon, *The Eden Memoirs: The Reckoning* (London: Cassell, 1965).
Blake, G., *No Other Choice: An Autobiography* (London: Jonathan Cape, 1990).
Borton, H., *Spanning Japan's Modern Century: The Memoirs of Hugh Borton* (Oxford: Lexington Books, 2002).
Byrnes, J., *Speaking Frankly* (New York: Harper and Bros., 1947).
Churchill, W., *The Second World War, v, Closing the Ring* (London: Cassell, 1952).
——— *The Second World War, vi, Triumph and Tragedy* (London: Cassell, 1954).
Dalton, H., *High Tide and After: Memoirs 1945–1960* (London: Frederick Muller, 1962).
Danchev, A. and Todman, D. (eds.), *War Diaries 1939–1945: Field Marshal Lord Alanbrooke* (London: Weidenfeld & Nicolson, 2001).
Dilks, D. (ed.), *The Diaries of Sir Alexander Cadogan, O.M. 1938–1945* (London: Cassell, 1971).
Dixon, P., *Double Diploma: The Life of Sir Pierson Dixon: Don and Diplomat* (London: Hutchinson, 1968).
Ferrell, F. (ed.), *Dear Bess: The Letters from Harry Truman to Bess Truman 1910–1959* (Columbia: University of Missouri Press, 1998).
——— (ed.), *Off the Record: The Private Papers of Harry S. Truman* (London: University of Missouri Press, 1997).
Harriman, W. A., and Abel, E., *Special Envoy to Churchill and Stalin 1941–1946* (London: Random House, 1976).
Kennan, G., *Memoirs: 1925–1950* (Boston: Little, Brown, 1967).
Leahy, W., *I Was There: The Personal Story of the Chief of Staff to Presidents Roosevelt and Truman Based on Notes and Diaries Made at the Time* (London: Gollancz, 1950).

Mare, A. de la, *Perverse and Foolish: A Jersey Farmer's Son in the British Diplomatic Service* (Jersey, La Haule, 1994).
Moran L., *Churchill at War 1940–45* (London: Robinson, 2002).
Munro, J., and Inglis, A. (eds.), *Mike: The Right Honourable Lester B. Pearson: Memoirs 1948–1957*, ii, *The International Years* (Toronto: University of Toronto Press, 1973).
Rix, A. (ed.), *Intermittent Diplomat: The Japan and Batavia Diaries of W. Macmahon Ball* (Melbourne: Melbourne University Press, 1988).
Sansom, K., *Sir George Sansom and Japan: A Memoir* (Tallahassee: The Diplomatic Press, 1972).
Sherwood, R., *The White House Papers of Harry L. Hopkins*, ii, *January 1942–July 1945* (London: Eyre & Spottiswoode, 1949).
Smith, W. B., *My Three Years in Moscow* (Philadelphia: J. B. Lippincott, 1950).
Truman, H., *Memoirs*, i, *Years of Decisions* (New York: Doubleday, 1955).
—— *Memoirs*, ii, *Years of Trial and Hope* (New York: Doubleday, 1956).
White, T. H. (ed.), *The Stilwell Papers* (New York: Sloane, 1949).

Secondary sources

Adamthwaite, A., 'Britain and the world, 1945–9: The View from the Foreign Office', *International Affairs*, 61 (1985).
Aldrich, R., *Intelligence and the War Against Japan: Britain, America and the Politics of Secret Service* (Cambridge: Cambridge University Press, 2000).
—— (ed.), *British Intelligence, Strategy and the Cold War, 1945–51* (London: Routledge, 1992).
—— and Hopkins, M. (eds.), *Intelligence, Defence and Diplomacy: British Policy in the Post-war World* (London: Frank Cass, 1994).
—— and M. Coleman, 'Britain and the Strategic Air Offensive Against the Soviet Union: The Question of South Asian Air Bases, 1945–9', *History*, 74 (1989).
—— Rawnsley, G., and Rawnsley, M-Y., 'Introduction: The Clandestine Cold War in East Asia, 1945–65' in Special Issue: The Clandestine Cold War in Asia, 1945–65: Western Intelligence, Propaganda and Special Operations, *Intelligence and National Security*, 14 (1999).
Allen, L., 'The Campaigns in Asia and the Pacific', *The Journal of Strategic Studies*, 13 (1990).
Andrew, C., 'The Growth of the Australian Intelligence Community and the Anglo-American Connection', *Intelligence and National Security*, 4 (1989).
Bates, P., *Japan and the British Commonwealth Occupation Force, 1946–52* (London: Brassey's, 1993).
Baxter, C., and Stewart, A. (eds.), *Diplomats at War: British and Commonwealth Diplomacy in Wartime* (Leiden: Martinus Nijhoff publishers, 2008).
Baxter, C., 'In Pursuit of a Pacific Strategy: British Planning for the Defeat of Japan, 1943–45,' *Diplomacy and Statecraft*, 15 (2004).
—— 'The Foreign Office and Post-war Planning for East Asia, 1944–45', *Contemporary British History*, 21 (2007).
Bayly, C., and Harper, T., *Forgotten Armies: The Fall of British Asia 1941–1945* (London: Allen Lane, 2004).
—— *Forgotten Wars: Freedom and Revolution in Southeast Asia* (Cambridge, MA: Harvard University Press, 2007).
Best, A., *Japan and Pearl Harbor: Avoiding War in East Asia, 1936–41* (London: Routledge, 1995).

Bischof, G., and Dupont, R. L. (eds.), *The Pacific War Revisited* (Baton Rouge: Louisiana State University Press, 1997).

Bix, H., *Hirohito and the Making of Modern Japan* (London: Duckworth, 2000).

Bond, B., and Tachikawa, K. (eds.), *British and Japanese Military Leadership in the Far Eastern War 1941–1945* (London: Routledge, 2004).

Boyle, P., 'The British Foreign Office View of Soviet-American Relations, 1945–46', *Diplomatic History*, 3 (1979).

Brower, C., 'Sophisticated Strategist: General George A Lincoln and the Defeat of Japan, 1944–45', *Diplomatic History*, 15 (1991).

Buckley, R., *Occupation Diplomacy: Britain, the United States and Japan 1945–1952* (Cambridge: Cambridge University Press, 1982).

Buhite, R. D., *Douglas MacArthur: Statecraft and Stagecraft in America's East Asian Policy* (Plymouth: Rowman & Littlefield Publishers, 2008).

—— ' "Major Interests": American Policy toward China, Taiwan, and Korea, 1945–1950', *Pacific Historical Review*, 47 (1978).

Bullock, A., *Ernest Bevin: Foreign Secretary, 1945–1951* (London: W. W. Norton, 1983).

Butler, J., *Grand Strategy, ii, September 1939–June 1941* (London: HMSO, 1957).

Chace, J., *Acheson: The Secretary of State Who Created the American World* (New York: Simon & Schuster, 1998).

Christensen, T. J., *Useful Adversaries: Grand Strategy, Domestic Mobilization, and Sino-American Conflict, 1947–1958* (Princeton, NJ: Princeton University Press, 1996).

Clemens, P., 'Operational "Cardinal": The OSS in Manchuria, August 1945', *Intelligence and National Security*, 13 (1998).

Coles, M., 'Ernest King and the British Pacific Fleet: The Conference at Quebec, 1944 ("Octagon")', *The Journal of Military History*, 65 (2001).

Cookridge, E. H., *George Blake: Double Agent* (London: Hodder, 1970).

Cortazzi. H. (ed.), *British Envoys in Japan, 1859–1972* (Folkestone: Global Oriental, 2004).

—— (ed.), *Japan Experiences: Fifty Years, One Hundred Views: Post-War Japan through British Eyes, 1945–2000* (Surrey: Japan Library, 2001).

Cradock, P., *Know Your Enemy: How the Joint Intelligence Committee Saw the World* (London: John Murray, 2002).

Cumings, B., *The Origins of the Korean War, i, Liberation and the Emergence of Separate Regimes 1945–1947* (Princeton, NJ: Princeton University Press, 1981).

—— *The Origins of the Korean War, ii, The Roaring of the Cataract, 1947–1950* (Princeton, NJ: Princeton University Press, 1990).

—— (ed.), *Child of Conflict: The Korean-American Relationship, 1943–1953* (London: University of Washington Press, 1983).

Day, D., *The Great Betrayal: Britain, Australia and the Onset of the Pacific War, 1939–42* (New York: Norton, 1988).

—— *Reluctant Nation: Australia and the Allied Defeat of Japan, 1942–45* (New York: Oxford University Press, 1992).

—— *John Curtin: A Life* (Sydney: Harper Collins, 1999).

—— *Chifley* (Sydney: Harper Collins, 2001).

Defty, A., *Britain, America and Anti-Communist Propaganda, 1945–53: The Information Research Department* (London: Routledge, 2004).

Deighton, A. (ed.), *Britain and the First Cold War* (London: St. Martin's Press, 1990).

Dennis, P., *Troubled Days of Peace: Mountbatten and South East Asia Command 1945–46* (Manchester: Manchester University Press, 1987).

Dockrill, M. and Hopkins, M. (eds.), *The Cold War* (Basingstoke: Palgrave, 2006).

Dockrill, M., 'The Foreign Office, Anglo-American Relations and the Korean war, June 1950–June 1951', *International Affairs*, 62 (1986).

Dockrill, S. (ed.), *From Pearl Harbor to Hiroshima: The Second World War in Asia and the Pacific, 1941–45* (London: St. Martin's Press, 1994).

Dower, J., *Empire and Aftermath: Yoshida Shigeru and the Japanese Experience, 1878–1954* (Cambridge, MA: Harvard University Press, 1979).

—— *Japan in War and Peace: Essays on History, Culture and Race* (London: Harper Collins, 1996).

—— *Embracing Defeat: Japan in the Aftermath of World War II* (London: Allen Lane, 1999).

Driberg, T., *Guy Burgess: A Portrait with Background* (London: Weidenfeld and Nicolson, 1956).

Edwards, J., *Curtin's Gift: Reinterpreting Australia's Greatest Prime Minister* (Sydney: Allen & Unwin, 2005).

Edwards, P., 'Curtin, Macarthur and the "surrender of sovereignty": A Historiographical Assessment', *Australian Journal of International Affairs*, 55 (2001).

Ehrman, J., *Grand Strategy*, v, *August 1943–September 1944* (London: HMSO, 1956).

—— *Grand Strategy*, vi, *October 1944–August 1945* (London: HMSO, 1956).

Embree, J., 'Military Occupation of Japan', *Far Eastern Survey*, 13 (1944).

Farrar-Hockley, A., *The British Part in the Korean War*, i, *A Distant Obligation* (London: HMSO, 1990).

Fenby, J., *Generalissimo: Chiang Kai-shek and the China He Lost* (London: Free Press, 2005).

Ford, D., 'Planning for an Unpredictable War: British Intelligence Assessments and the War Against Japan, 1937–45', *The Journal of Strategic Studies*, 27 (2004).

Frank, F., *Downfall: The End of the Imperial Japanese Empire* (New York: Random House, 1999).

Friedman, H., 'The "Bear" in the Pacific? US Intelligence Perceptions of Soviet Strategic Power Projection in the Pacific Basin and East Asia, 1945–1947', *Intelligence and National Security*, 12 (1997).

Gaddis, J., *The Long Peace: Inquiries into the History of the Cold War* (Oxford: Oxford University Press, 1987).

—— *We Now Know: Rethinking Cold War History* (Oxford: Clarendon, 1998).

—— *The Cold War* (London: Allen Lane, 2005).

Gallicchio, M., *The Cold War Begins in Asia: American East Asian Policy and the Fall of the Japanese Empire* (New York: Columbia University Press, 1988).

Goncharov, S., Lewis, J., and Litai, X., *Uncertain Partners: Stalin, Mao and the Korean War* (Stanford: Stanford University Press, 1993).

Hall, T., ' "Mere Drops in the Ocean": The Politics and Planning of the Contribution of the British Commonwealth to the Final Defeat of Japan, 1944–45', *Diplomacy and Statecraft*, 16 (2005).

Hasegawa, T., *Racing the Enemy: Stalin, Truman, and the Surrender of Japan* (London: Harvard University Press, 2005).

—— (ed.), *The End of the Pacific War: Reappraisals* (Stanford: Stanford University Press, 2007).

Hastings, M., *Nemesis: The Battle for Japan, 1944–45* (London: Harper Press, 2007).

Hattendorf, J., and Murfett, M. (eds.), *The Limitations of Power: Essays Presented to Professor Norman Gibbs on His Eightieth Birthday* (London: Macmillan, 1990).

Heinzig, D., *The Soviet Union and Communist China 1945–1950: The Arduous Road to the Alliance* (London: M. E. Sharpe, 2003).

Hoare, J., *Embassies in the East: The Story of the British Embassies in Japan, China and Korea from 1859 to the Present* (Surrey: Curzon Press, 1999).

Hopkins M., *Oliver Franks and the Truman Administration: Anglo-American Relations 1948–1952* (London: Routledge, 2003).

—— 'A British Cold War?', *Intelligence and National Security*, 7 (1992).

Horner, D., *High Command: Australia and Allied Strategy, 1939–1945* (Sydney: George Allen & Unwin, 1982).

—— *Inside the War Cabinet: Directing Australia's War Effort, 1939–45* (St. Leonards: Allen & Unwin, 1996).

Howard, M., *Grand Strategy*, iv, *August 1942–September 1943* (London: HMSO, 1972).

Hunt, M., *The Genesis of Chinese Communist Foreign Policy* (New York: Columbia University Press, 1996).

Jacobsen, M., 'Winston Churchill and the Third Front', *The Journal of Strategic Studies*, 14 (1991).

James, D. Clayton, *The Years of MacArthur*, ii, *1941–1945* (Boston: Houghton Mifflin, 1975).

—— *The Years of MacArthur*, ii, *Triumph and Disaster, 1945–1964* (Boston: Houghton Mifflin, 1985).

Janssens, R. V. A., *'What Future for Japan?' U.S. Wartime Planning for the Postwar Era, 1942–1945* (Amsterdam: Rodopi, 1995).

Jesperson, T. C., *American Images of China, 1931–1949* (Stanford: Stanford University Press, 1996).

Jian, C., *China's Road to the Korean War: The Making of the Sino-American Confrontation* (New York: Columbia University Press, 1994).

—— *Mao's China and the Cold War* (London: University of North Carolina Press, 2001).

Kahn, E. J., *The China Hands: America's Foreign Service Officers and What Befell Them* (New York: The Viking Press, 1975).

Kennan, G. (X), 'The Sources of Soviet Conduct', *Foreign Affairs*, 26 (1947).

Kent, J., *British Imperial Strategy and the Origins of the Cold War, 1944–49* (Leicester: Leicester University Press, 1993).

Kim, Y., 'The Origins of the Korean War: Civil War or Stalin's Rollback?', *Diplomacy & Statecraft*, 10 (1999).

Kimball, W., *Forged at War: Churchill, Roosevelt and the Second World War* (London: Harper Collins, 1997).

Kirby, S. W., *The War Against Japan*, iii, *The Decisive Battles* (London: HMSO, 1961).

—— *The War Against Japan*, iv, *The Reconquest of Burma* (London: HMSO, 1965).

—— *The War Against Japan*, v, *The Surrender of Japan* (London: HMSO, 1969).

Koshiro, Y., 'Eurasian Eclipse: Japan's End Game in World War II', *American Historical Review*, 109 (2004).

Kuisong, Y., 'The Soviet Factor and the CCP's Policy Toward the United States in the 1940s', *Chinese Historians*, 1 (1992).

Lacey, M. (ed.), *The Truman Presidency* (Cambridge: Cambridge University Press, 1989).

Leffler, M., *A Preponderance of Power: National Security, the Truman Administration, and the Cold War* (Stanford: Stanford University Press, 1992).

—— and Painter, D. (eds.), *Origins of the Cold War: An International History* (London: Routledge, 2005).

Levine, S., *Anvil of Victory: The Communist Revolution in Manchuria, 1945–1948* (New York: Columbia University Press, 1987).

—— 'A New Look at American Mediation in the Chinese Civil War: The Marshall Mission and Manchuria', *Diplomatic History*, 3 (1979).

Lewis, J., *Changing Direction: British Military Planning for Post-War Strategic Defence* (London: Frank Cass, 2003).

Liu, X., *A Partnership for Disorder: China, the United States, and Their Policies for the Post-war Disposition of the Japanese Empire, 1941–1945* (Cambridge: Cambridge University Press, 1996).

Louis, Wm. R., *Imperialism at Bay: The United States and the Decolonisation of the British Empire, 1941–1945* (Oxford: Clarendon Press, 1977).

—— *Ends of British Imperialism: The Scramble for Empire, Suez and Decolonization – Collected Essays* (London: I.B. Tauris, 2006).

Lowe, P., *Great Britain and the Origins of the Pacific War: A Study of British Policy in East Asia, 1937–1941* (Oxford: Clarendon Press, 1977).

—— *The Origins of the Korean War* (London: Longman, 1997).

—— *Containing the Cold War in EastAsia: British Policies towards Japan, China and Korea, 1948–1953* (Manchester: Manchester University Press, 1997).

McIntyre, W. D., *Background to the ANZUS Pact: Policy-Making, Strategy and Diplomacy, 1945–1955* (New York: St Martin's Press, 1995).

McKercher, B., *Transition of Power: Britain's Loss of Global Pre-eminence to the United States, 1930–1945* (Cambridge: Cambridge University Press, 1999).

Mastny, V., *The Cold War and Soviet Insecurity: The Stalin Years* (Oxford: Oxford University Press, 1996).

Matray, J., The Reluctant *Crusade: American Foreign Policy in Korea, 1941–1950* (Honolulu: University of Hawaii Press, 1985).

—— 'Captive of the Cold War: The Decision to Divide Korea at the 38th Parallel', *Pacific Historical Review*, 50 (1981).

May, G., *China Scapegoat: The Diplomatic Ordeal of John Carter Vincent* (Washington: New Republic Books, 1979).

Merrick, R., 'The Russia Committee of the British Foreign Office and the Cold War, 1946–47', *Journal of Contemporary History*, 20 (1985).

Messer, R. L., *The End of an Alliance: James F. Byrnes, Roosevelt, Truman, and the Origins of the Cold War* (Chapel Hill: University of North Carolina Press, 1982).

Miscamble, W., *From Roosevelt to Truman: Potsdam, Hiroshima, and the Cold War* (Cambridge: Cambridge University Press, 2007).

Murfett, M., *Hostage on the Yangtze: Britain, China, and the Amethyst Crisis of 1949* (Annapolis, MD: Naval Institute Press, 1991).

—— *In Jeopardy: The Royal Navy and British Far Eastern Defence Policy 1945–1951* (Oxford: Oxford University Press, 1995).

Nagai, Y., and Iriye, A. (eds.), *The Origins of the Cold War in Asia* (New York: Columbia University Press, 1977).

O'Neill, R., *Australia in the Korean War*, i, *Strategy and Diplomacy* (Canberra: Australian Government Publishing Service, 1981).

Osterhammel, J., 'Imperialism in Transition: British Business and the Chinese Authorities, 1931–37', *The China Quarterly*, 98 (1984).

Ovendale, R., *The English-Speaking Alliance: Britain, the United States, the Dominions and the Cold War, 1945–1951* (London: Allen & Unwin, 1985).

—— 'Britain, the United States, and the Cold War in South-East Asia, 1949–1950', *International Affairs*, 58 (1982).

—— 'Britain, the United States, and the Recognition of Communist China', *Historical Journal*, 26 (1983).

Pepper, S., *Civil War in China: The Political Struggle, 1945–1949* (Lanham, MD: Rowman & Littlefield, 1999).

Porter, B., *Britain and the Rise of Communist China: A Study of British Attitudes, 1945–1954* (London: Oxford University Press, 1967).

Purdy, A. and Sutherland, D., *Burgess and Maclean* (London: Secker & Warburg, 1963).

Qing, S., *From Allies to Enemies: Visions of Modernity, Identity, and U.S.-China Diplomacy, 1945–1960* (Cambridge, MA: Harvard University Press, 2007).

Ree, E. van, *Socialism in One Zone: Stalin's Policy in Korea, 1945–1947* (Oxford: Berg Publishers, 1989).

Remme, T., *Britain and Regional Co-operation in South-East Asia, 1945–49* (London: Routledge, 1995).

Reynolds, D., *Britannia Overruled: British Policy and World Power in the Twentieth Century* (Harlow: Pearson, 2000).

—— *Summits: Six Meetings That Shaped the Twentieth Century* (New York: Basic Books, 2007).

Roberts, A., *Eminent Churchillians* (London: Weidenfeld & Nicolson, 1994).

Robertson, K. G. (ed.), *War, Resistance and Intelligence: Essays in Honour of M. R. D. Foot* (Barnsley: Leo Cooper, 1999).

Robb-Webb, J., 'Anglo-American Naval Intelligence Co-operation in the Pacific, 1944–5', *Intelligence and National Security*, 22 (2007).

Sainsbury, K., *Churchill and Roosevelt at War: The War They Fought and the Peace They Hoped to Make* (London: Macmillan, 1994).

Sansom, G., *Postwar Relations with Japan* (New York: Institute of Pacific Relations, 1942).

—— *Japan* (London: H. Milford: Oxford University Press, 1944).

Sarantakes, N. E., 'The Royal Air Force on Okinawa: The Diplomacy of a Coalition on the Verge of Victory', *Diplomatic History*, 27 (2003).

—— 'One Last Crusade: The British Pacific Fleet and its Impact on the Anglo-American Alliance', *English Historical Review*, 121 (2006).

Schaller, M., *The American Occupation of Japan: The Origins of the Cold War in Asia* (Oxford: Oxford University Press, 1985).

—— *Altered States: The United States and Japan Since the Occupation* (Oxford: Oxford University Press, 1997).

Schonberger, H., *Aftermath of War: Americans and the Remaking of Japan, 1945–1952* (London: Kent State University Press, 1989).

—— 'The Japan Lobby in American Diplomacy, 1947–1952', *Pacific Historical Review*, 46 (1977).

Shai, A., *Britain and China, 1941–47: Imperial Momentum* (London: Macmillan, 1984).

Shaw, T., 'The British Popular Press and the Early Cold War', *History*, 83 (1998).

Sheng, M., 'America's Lost Chance in China? A Reappraisal of Chinese Communist Policy toward the United States before 1945', *The Australian Journal of Chinese Affairs*, 29 (1993).

Sherry, M., *Preparing for the Next War: American Plans for Postwar Defense, 1941–45* (London: Yale University Press, 1977).

Smith, B. F., *The War's Long Shadow: The Second World War and Its Aftermath: China, Russia, Britain, America* (New York: Simon and Schuster, 1986).

Spector, R. H., *Eagle Against the Sun: The American War with Japan* (London: Cassell, 2001).

—— *In the Ruins of Empire: The Japanese Surrender and the Battle for Postwar Asia* (New York: Random House, 2007).

Srinivasan, K., *The Rise, Decline and Future of the British Commonwealth* (Basingstoke: Palgrave, 2005).

Stewart, A., *Empire Lost: Britain, the Dominions and the Second World War* (London: Continuum, 2008).

Storry, R., *A History of Modern Japan* (London: Penguin, 1990).

Stueck, W., *The Road to Confrontation: American Policy toward China and Korea, 1947–1950* (Chapel Hill, NC: University of North Carolina Press, 1981).

——— *The Korean War: An International History* (Princeton, NJ: Princeton University Press, 1995).

——— (ed.), *The Korean War in World History* (Lexington: University Press of Kentucky, 2004).

Sugita, Y., *Pitfall or Panacea: The Irony of US Power in Occupied Japan 1945–1952* (London: Routledge, 2003).

Tarling, N., *Britain, Southeast Asia and the Onset of the Pacific War* (Cambridge: Cambridge University Press, 1996).

——— *Britain, Southeast Asia and the Onset of the Cold War, 1945–50* (Cambridge: Cambridge University Press, 1998).

Thorne, C., *Allies of a Kind: The United States, Britain, and the War Against Japan, 1941–1945* (Oxford: Oxford University Press, 1978).

——— *The Issue of War: States, Societies, and the Far Eastern Conflict of 1941–1945* (London: Hamish Hamilton, 1985).

——— 'MacArthur, Australia and the British, 1942–1943: The Secret Journal of MacArthur's Liaison Officer' (Parts I & II) in *Australian Outlook*, 29 (1975).

——— 'Chatham House, Whitehall and Far Eastern Issues, 1941–1945', *International Affairs*, 54 (1978).

Trotter, A., *Britain and East Asia, 1933–1937* (Cambridge: Cambridge University Press, 1975).

Tucker, N., *Patterns in the Dust: Chinese-American Relations and the Recognition Controversy 1949–1950* (New York: Columbia University Press, 1983).

——— *China Confidential: American Diplomats and Sino-American Relations, 1945–1996* (New York: Columbia University Press, 2001).

Ven, H. J. van de, *War and Nationalism in China, 1925–1945* (London: Routledge, 2003).

Wakeman, F., *Spymaster: Dai Li and the Chinese Secret Service* (London: University of California Press, 2003).

Wasserstein, B., *Secret War in Shanghai* (London: Profile Books, 1998).

Weathersby, K., 'Soviet Aims in Korea and the Origins of the Korean War, 1945–1950: New Perspectives from Russian Archives', *Cold War International History Project: Woodrow Wilson Center for Scholars* (1993).

Westad, O. A., *Cold War & Revolution: Soviet-American Rivalry and the Origins of the Chinese Civil War* (New York: Columbia University Press, 1992).

——— (ed.), *Brothers in Arms: The Rise and Fall of the Sino-Soviet Alliance, 1945–1963* (Stanford: Stanford University Press, 1998).

——— *Decisive Encounters: The Chinese Civil War, 1946–1950* (Stanford: Stanford University Press, 2003).

Williams, J., 'ANZUS: A Blow to Britain's Self Esteem', *Review of International Studies*, 13 (1987).

Willmott, H. P., *Grave of a Dozen Schemes: British Naval Planning and the War Against Japan* (London: Airlife, 1996).

——— *The Second World War in the Far East* (London: Cassell, 2000).

Xiang, L., *Recasting the Imperial Far East: Britain and America in China, 1945–1950* (London: M. E. Sharpe, 1995).

———— 'The Recognition Controversy: Anglo-American Relations in China, 1949', *Journal of Contemporary History*, 27 (1992).

Yahuda, M., *The International Politics of the Asia-Pacific, 1945–1995* (London: Routledge, 1998).

Yokoi, N., *Japan's Postwar Economic Recovery and Anglo-Japanese Relations, 1948–62* (London: Routledge, 2003).

Young, J., *Britain and the World in the Twentieth Century* (London: Arnold, 1997).

Zametica, J. (ed.), *British Officials and British Foreign Policy, 1945–50* (Leicester: Leicester University Press, 1990).

Ziegler, P., *Mountbatten: The Official Biography* (London: Phoenix Press, 2001).

Zubok, V. and Pleshakov, C., *Inside the Kremlin's Cold War: From Stalin to Khrushchev* (London: Harvard University Press, 1997).

Index